North Carolina beaches

Glenn Morris

A visit to

national seashores,

state parks, ferries,

public beaches,

wildlife refuges,

historic sites,

lighthouses,

boat ramps

and docks,

museums,

and more

REVISED AND UPDATED EDITION

North Carolina beaches

THE UNIVERSITY OF NORTH CAROLINA PRESS / CHAPEL HILL AND LONDON

Library of Congress
Cataloging-in-Publication Data
Morris, Glenn, 1950–
North Carolina beaches / Glenn
Morris. — Rev. and updated ed.
    p. cm.
Includes index.
ISBN 0-8078-4683-X (pbk.: alk. paper)
1. North Carolina — Guidebooks.
2. Atlantic Coast (N.C.) —
Guidebooks.   3. Coasts —
North Carolina — Guidebooks.
4. Beaches — North Carolina —
Guidebooks.   5. Recreation
areas — North Carolina —
Guidebooks.   I. Title.
F252.3.M658   1998
917.5604'43 — dc21   97-31528
                CIP

The paper in this book meets the
guidelines for permanence and
durability of the Committee on
Production Guidelines for Book
Longevity of the Council on
Library Resources.

05 04 03 02 01
6 5 4 3 2

Pages ii–iii: Public Access, Atlantic
Beach. (Courtesy of N.C. Coastal
Management Commission)

FOR KIPPIE MORRIS

Contents

FEATURE ARTICLES

Preface to the Revised Edition

North Carolina's marvelously complex coastline is neither easily traveled nor a simple, carefree place to call home. Life has a special flavor there, slightly briny with a bit of grit—it's never completely smooth. Things past, things present, things natural, and things manmade interweave, interlock, and sometimes collide in a startling study of harmony and conflict. North Carolina's barrier islands can be beautiful and serene, but they can be thunderously perilous as well. They follow an all-natural script: peace then conflict; swell then wave; calm then storm.

In this region the ocean can erase the land faster than a person can update a survey, map, or book. Landmarks of memory—houses, roads, or lines of dunes—can be swallowed up overnight, and within a year's time the oceanfront may change dramatically. This book is as "current" as the ocean permits it to be. Perhaps it will entice you to make a connection with a wonderful region where life *is* on the edge and nothing is permanent except change and the chance to grow with it.

Because the 1996 hurricane season wrought such dramatic changes to parts of the coast (and development affected others), revisiting these pages became necessary. Once again, every effort has been made to provide accurate and current information for this travelogue. Unfortunately, during the printed life of a book, some dates, hours of operation, admission fees, addresses, and phone numbers will undoubtedly change. At the coast, however, much more change can be involuntary and irrevocable. It is the double-edged easy-come, easy-go nature of the oceanfront that creates hardship for those who live there and inconvenience for those who seek one way or another to pin it down—either for a visit or for a guidebook.

Thanks to Roger Schecter, director of the North Carolina Division of Coastal Management, and the division's regional coordinators for their comments, corrections, and additions; to Rich Shaw, assistant director of the division, and John Taggart, Coastal Reserve coordinator, for answering many specific queries about programs and facilities within their areas of responsibility; to Warren and Linda Brandon for computer counseling; to my trial readers for their critiques and suggestions; to the University of North Carolina Press for its support and direction; to Paula Wald, copyeditor, for thoroughly combing these pages; to Pam Upton, assistant managing editor, for her patience; and to David Perry, acquisitions editor at the Press, coach, mentor, and friend.

Glenn Morris
August 1997

North Carolina beaches

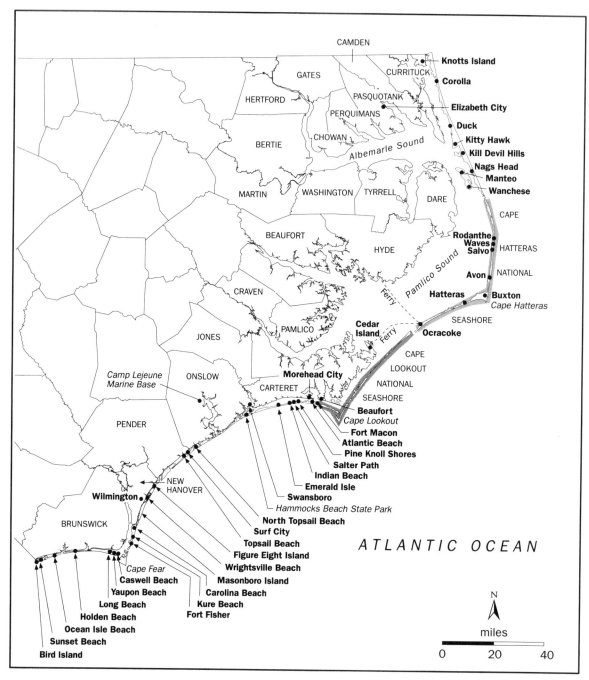

CAMDEN

GATES

HERTFORD

PASQUOTANK

PERQUIMANS

BERTIE

CHOWAN

Albemarle Sound

MARTIN

WASHINGTON

TYRRELL

DARE

BEAUFORT

HYDE

CAPE

Knotts Island

Corolla

Elizabeth City

Duck

Kitty Hawk

Kill Devil Hills

Nags Head

Manteo

Wanchese

Rodanthe
Waves
Salvo

HATTERAS

NATIONAL

Avon

Pamlico Sound

CRAVEN

PAMLICO

Ferry

Hatteras

Buxton
Cape Hatteras

SEASHORE

Cedar
Island

Ferry

Ocracoke

JONES

CAPE

LOOKOUT

NATIONAL

SEASHORE

Camp Lejeune
Marine Base

ONSLOW

CARTERET

Morehead City

Beaufort
Cape Lookout

Fort Macon

Atlantic Beach

Pine Knoll Shores

PENDER

Salter Path

Indian Beach

Emerald Isle

Swansboro

NEW
HANOVER

Hammocks Beach State Park

Wilmington

North Topsail Beach

Surf City

BRUNSWICK

Topsail Beach

Figure Eight Island

Wrightsville Beach

Masonboro Island

ATLANTIC OCEAN

Cape Fear

Caswell Beach

Carolina Beach

Yaupon Beach

Kure Beach

Long Beach

Fort Fisher

Holden Beach

Ocean Isle Beach

Sunset Beach

Bird Island

N

miles

0   20   40

Map I-1. Coastal North Carolina

Introduction

This book serves two purposes. First, it is a road map of the outer coast of North Carolina, providing information on public access to the ocean and sound waters; second, in a broader sense of the word *access*, it is a companion during a journey along the coast. In a geography of already broad horizons, *North Carolina Beaches* tries to stretch expectations to meet the possibilities that are out there, way out there, where earth, wind, and sky melt together.

Items covered in the guide include locations for parking (accessways), ferries, federal and state parks and preserves, private preserves open to the public, and other difficult-to-categorize locations that are worth a visit. Where it is available, I have included information about each listing, such as location, facilities, operating hours, and phone numbers.

Besides helping you save time planning a trip to the North Carolina coast, this guide will prompt you to sidetrack to some of the more unusual attractions en route. It's full of directions, suggestions, and reasons why you might want to linger longer during your stay.

During the journey, the guide will discuss certain natural features and phenomena regularly encountered at the coast, such as tides, waves, seashells, and bird life. Knowing a bit about the natural world of the ocean and sound waters is another way of "accessing" the coast and will enrich your visit.

In North Carolina, the coastline—where land meets sea—is complicated, and determining what constitutes "the coast" is difficult. If you want to go where waves continually break, your destination is the string of low sandy islands off of the mainland. It is the presence, shape, and location of these "barrier" islands (barriers to the open ocean) that make the North Carolina coast lengthy and complex. This book focuses on access along the barrier islands; some notable inner coast or soundside locations are included as well.

The state's mainland ends where the sounds begin. The combined sounds, Albemarle, Currituck, Core, Croatan, Pamlico, and Roanoke, comprise the second largest estuary in the nation, after the Chesapeake Bay. The barrier islands form the protective edge of the brackish sounds, and both islands and sounds vary substantially in size. In the northern half of the state, the penetration of the practically unbridgeable sound waters into the mainland still limits travel and commerce. In the southern portion of the coastal region, however, the sounds are not as wide and more easily bridged.

Ecological diversity thrives on the soundside. Land and water meet in an astonishing array of complex edge patterns: pine savannas, hardwood forests, sweeps of salt marsh, low and high swamps, even abrupt bluffs touch the wide brackish water of the sounds, bays, and estuaries. Everything else is sky and light.

The slightly more than 300 miles of "beachfront" comprise less than 10 percent of the total coastline

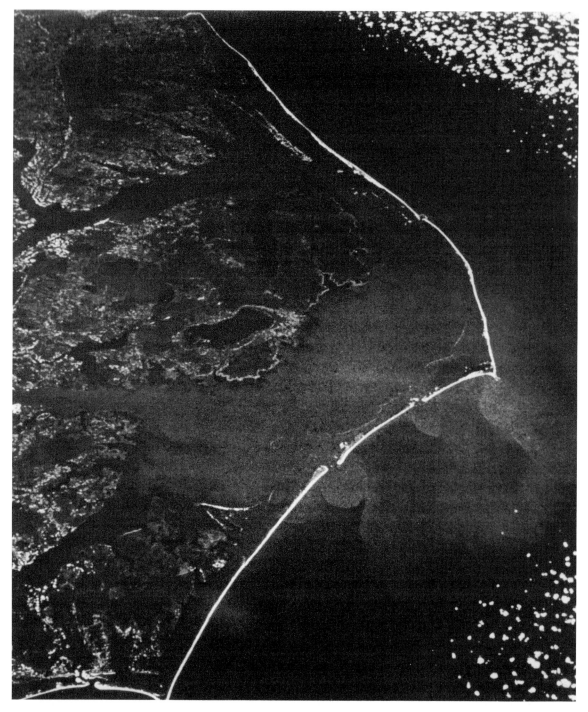

The Outer Banks as seen from an Apollo spacecraft. (Courtesy of N.C. Travel and Tourism Division and National Geographic*)*

mileage. With the sixth largest coastline in the nation, North Carolina has, by one measure, twenty-two "coastal counties," that is, counties that border on tidal waters.

Traveling along the North Carolina coast has never been simple or quick. A state map confirms that traversing the coastal region is convenient only for fish and birds, which can move about far more freely in this jigsawed area than people will ever be able to move. Even today you need a boat to reach some locations (and you still might need a car when you arrive).

The isolation has been both a blessing and a curse. It was a blessing because the few permanent inhabitants altered the islands very little, and lengthy stretches of beach and island remained open and windswept, "private" sandy paradises. However, this splendid naturalness brought the curse of discovery, and since the 1960s, more wood has been shipped to these islands as construction materials than probably ever grew in the original maritime forests that still struggle to survive along the coast.

Absolute isolation eroded in the 1930s when the state built bridges and scheduled ferries, making it possible for anyone to reach the beaches. Not surprisingly, many visitors decided to stay awhile. The resulting real estate boom on land that could be bought for as little as one dollar per acre began to alter the character that initially attracted people. Some older residents of the Outer Banks maintain that the traditional charm of islands such as Ocracoke began to decline with the arrival of paved roads in the 1950s. Others, including myself, find it amazing that so much fabulous oceanfront remains as wonderfully open as it is. There are very few locations with "urban" densities along the coast, and in many places you still have the luxury of feeling crowded if another person is *visible* on the beach.

In spite of the great demand for beachfront property, North Carolina offers some of the most varied coastal attractions between Atlantic City and Daytona. There are wild, untamed beaches, quaint fishing villages, family beaches, and "action" beaches that feature amusement rides and entertainment. You can visit remnants of the environmental systems discovered by the earliest European sea adventurers over 450 years ago and the restored fort they built for their protection. You can hang out in a high-rise time-share, too. The nice thing is, you can take your pick.

Geomorphology of the Coast

Nearly every visitor or resident of the Outer Banks thinks the islands are something special; every coastal geologist knows it. What sets the Outer Banks aside is the obvious—they are *way* out there. If they were closer to the mainland, like the islands south and west of Morehead City, their existence and configuration would be both more commonplace and more explainable geologically. The Outer Banks are a very unusual form of an otherwise predictable southeastern coastal feature—barrier islands.

Barrier islands exist worldwide where any gently sloping coastal plain borders the ocean. In the United States, every southeastern state has barrier islands in one form or another. In fact, the lack of them is exceptional in this part of the United States and is a feature that makes the Grand Strand of South Carolina so different.

Even within the expanse of a human lifetime, barrier islands move and change, responding to natural forces, primarily the sea and wind. While the Outer Banks march to many of these formative elements, their distance from the mainland generates speculation about their origin. Coastal geologists currently favor an explanation that links the establishment of the ancient Outer Banks and the observed landward migration of the islands with a gradually rising sea level.

Island building probably began after the last period of glaciation, the Wisconsin, ended approximately 12,000 years ago. Scientists are confident that at that time not only was sea level approximately 120 meters lower than it is today, but the Atlantic coast was 90 miles further to the east, at the approximate edge of the continental shelf. The melting polar ice caps began raising the level of sea, which continued for nearly 8,000 years, gradually halting within a few meters of the present level 4,000 to 5,000 years ago. As sea level climbed, the shoreline inched landward across the continental shelf moving vast quantities of sand before it in the form of beach deposits. River sediments from coastal plain deltas were pulled into the wave zone and also moved along the shore.

When sea level remained steady for a time during the period known as the Holocene, an age of comparative stability, wind and waves worked these large masses of sand and sediment into the precursors of our present barrier islands. Geological evidence seems to indicate that the complex set of forces affecting the formation of the islands—storm and wave energy, sea level, and sediment supply—reached an equilibrium at that pause, resulting in islands considerably wider than they are today. Behind the prehistoric beach was a gently sloping, forested coastal plain, carved by the Cape Fear, Neuse, Tar, Roanoke, and Chowan rivers and their principal tributaries.

Sea level began rising again, albeit at a much slower rate, 2,000 years ago. The ocean eventually breached the formative barrier islands, flooding the forested coast plain behind them. It also inundated the floodplains of the ancient coastal riverbeds, creating the sounds.

The islands "migrated" landward before the rising sea level in a sequence of steps that are repeated today. When the ocean breaches the islands, it fills in the shallow sound waters behind them with sand and sediment. This new fill, in the lee of dunes, supports pioneering vegetation and eventually becomes forested. Wind and wave action continues to push the dune line landward as the sea continues to rise. Dune sand blows past the now established forest, filling in the soundside marsh. Like a Slinky crawling over itself down a flight of stairs, the entire barrier island retreats landward before the rising sea.

This hypothesis, known as "barrier ridge drowning," seems to explain the geological idiosyncrasies of the Outer Banks. Fossil evidence of an extinct species of oyster normally inhabiting brackish waters discovered on the ocean side of the barrier islands strengthens the argument for this scenario by proving the migration of the island over once-inland oyster beds. Also, the mainland coast has the intricate patterning characteristic of flooded river valleys. But don't get too comfortable—the process is continuing.

The beachfront, particularly at inlets, is the least stable portion of a barrier island simply because it is the front line of the ocean assault. The shape of islands changes the most at these locations. We see island migration in the shearing of sand from a dune line, storm surge overwash on a road, or a sand-filled ground-level room of an oceanfront home. When the beach moves, an oceanfront home must move as well. Over decades the actual shape of the entire island changes. The ocean blusters and the islands don't argue; they respond passively.

Barrier islands offer some havens that are comparatively stable and protected and historically have been the places of the most permanent settlement. But for how long? The Cape Hatteras Lighthouse ruled ½ mile of beach 100 years ago; the beach extends merely fifty yards now. On the other hand, although most of the coastline retreats in a similar manner, many of the traditional village sites weather on.

The loveliness of the islands lured people and buildings to the barrier beaches. Ironically, if the beach were barren, wild, and natural, with no artificial structures as references on it, it would be difficult to see the natural movement. Without any fixed reference, the islands would appear stationary and unchanged. But our "permanent" additions—houses, docks, and roads—record changes in the islands like the numerals on a "sand" dial. The islands push against our permanence, showing our monuments and us to be renters, not owners. Perhaps this reminder drives us to cling defiantly to our castles built on these magnificent sands, and all we can really do is rail at the winds in protest.

Historical Perspective

By the time the first English-speaking peoples attempted settlement in the New World on Roanoke Island in 1585, Native Americans had fished, hunted, and farmed on nearly every island along the coast, in either permanent or seasonal villages. Because they had no written language, they left no written record of their culture. Present-day knowledge comes from firsthand accounts of explorers and reconstructions of villages by archaeologists and anthropologists.

John White, a member of the 1585 expedition whose drawings document the explorers' first glimpse of the New World, reported that there were twenty or more Native American villages in the vicinity of Roanoke Island, all probably allied with, if not related to, the Hatteras tribe, the first group to meet the European explorers and settlers. According to White, the Native Americans cleared villages out of the extensive maritime hardwood forests that covered the soundside of the islands, centering the village around a sweat lodge, which served as a common gathering place. Evidence favors the theory that the Native Americans were self-sufficient within their hunting and fishing regions and traded minimally. There is no indication that the vastness of the sounds and rivers restricted their mobility. In fact, at least one of the islands in Currituck Sound, Monkey Island, served as both a summer fishing village and a burial ground, as did Permuda Island in Stump Sound in Onslow County.

Spain gained, then lost, the early advantage in the settlement and exploration of North Carolina. In 1520, Pedro de Quexoiaan led an expedition from the West Indies to the Cape Fear region. One of the passengers, Lucas Vázquez de Ayllón, returned in 1526 with 500 men, women, and slaves and livestock to settle the "Rio Jordan," probably the Cape Fear River. The settlement soon withdrew, ravished by disease, to the South Carolina coast. Fever followed the relocation, eventually claiming Ayllón in October 1526. The 150 survivors abandoned the venture, boarded ships, and sailed to Santo Domingo.

In 1524 Florentine navigator Giovanni da Verrazano, sailing in the service of France, recorded the first exploration of the North Carolina coast. After landing in the Cape Fear region, he detailed observations of the coast as far north as Hatteras, incorporating them into a glowing report to Francis I. Englishman Richard Hakluyt published the account in 1582 under the title *Divers Voyages touching the Discoverie of America and Islands Adjacent*.

The Spanish then broadened their explorations along the coast. On August 24, 1566, an expedition led by Pedro de Coronas to find the Chesapeake Bay explored present-day Currituck County.

In England, Hakluyt's report engendered greater ambition for the profitable possibilities in the "New World." On March 25, 1584, Sir Walter Raleigh received a patent from Queen Elizabeth for the exclusive rights to and rewards of a New World colony. Raleigh secured investors and supplied a two-ship expedition commanded by Philip Amadas and Arthur Barlowe and piloted by the Portuguese navigator Simón Fernandez. The expedition entered Pamlico Sound through "Wococon" Inlet (present-day Ocracoke Inlet) on July 4, 1584.

Shortly thereafter, Barlowe and a few of his men sailed north in the sound to an island Native Americans called "Roanoke." There they had their first encounter with Native Americans, which went well. Eventually, the expedition returned to England with unusual passengers—Manteo and Wanchese, the first Native Americans to visit England.

Barlowe's subsequent report of the expedition increased the desire of Raleigh and the queen to attempt to colonize the New World, which was named "Virginia" in honor of the unwed Elizabeth. Raleigh once again rounded up investors, and on April 9, 1585, seven ships sailed from Plymouth carrying 108 men bound for the first colonization effort in "Virginia." The expedition was led by Sir Richard Grenville, Raleigh's cousin, with Ralph Lane along as "lieutenant gourvernour." The fleet reached Hatteras on July 22, 1585, and by August 17 had disembarked on Roanoke Island. After only ten months, failure to plant crops, lack of supplies, and deteriorating relations with the inhabitants forced the evacuation of the colony by Sir Francis Drake in 1586, leaving eighteen men to guard the fort that had been established there.

Intrigued by the reports supplied by Lane's group and undaunted by efforts to persuade him to abandon colonization attempts, Raleigh organized yet another expedition. The objective of this venture was to settle, farm, and establish a community in the deep-water region of the Chesapeake Bay. Women and children, livestock, and supplies were to be transported to the colony. Raleigh enlisted John White, the artist who had illustrated the explorations of the 1585 expedition, as "Governor" of the "Citie of Ralegh in Virginia." White's experience did little to prepare him for the events to come.

Raleigh's "second colonie" left England in the spring of 1587 led by the *Admirall*, piloted by Fernandez. White's difficulties began during the crossing, when he clashed with Fernandez over the continuation on to the Chesapeake region. Reaching Hatteras on July 22, 1587, they quickly proceeded to Roanoke Island to pick up Grenville's men, only to find the fort in ruins and the men missing. After Fernandez refused to sail north as planned, White ordered the colonists to disembark on Roanoke Island.

Here the colonists struggled to establish a community. On August 18, White's daughter Eleanor and her husband Ananias Dare gave birth to Virginia, the first child of English-speaking parents born in the New World. The colony quickly ran low on food and supplies. White reluctantly agreed to sail to England for provisions, leaving behind his daughter and granddaughter. The colonists promised to leave a sign if they abandoned Roanoke Island for the mainland.

The threat of European wars stranded White in England until 1590. When he returned to Roanoke Island, he found the colonists vanished, the settlement in shambles, and the letters "CRO" carved into a tree—believed to indicate Croatan, a nearby Indian village. The colonists were never found; the colony was lost. White returned to England, thus ending colonization attempts on the North Carolina coast. The efforts shifted north to the Chesapeake after Jamestown in 1607.

The first record of settlement in North Carolina was in 1653 when Nathaniel Batts purchased land from Native Americans in Perquimans County. Batts built a house around 1654 and was soon joined by others from Virginia. This southwestern migration from Virginia into the lands along the Albemarle Sound became the prevailing pattern. Settlement by other groups met with mixed success: dissident Puritans from New England moved to the Cape Fear region in a colonization effort that failed, and Swiss settlers founded New Bern in the early eighteenth century.

Compared to the Chesapeake Bay, coastal North Carolina's population grew slowly because of the treacherous ocean waters east of the Outer Banks, the shoaling inlets, and the lack of deep-water ports. Since the Cape Fear was the only major river along the North Carolina coast with direct outfall into the Atlantic Ocean, geography dictated settlement by "spillover" from Virginia, where deep-water supply was safely established.

Gradually communities grew along the sounds in the eighteenth century. The town of Bath incorporated in 1705, followed by New Bern and then Beaufort in 1723, each a port town but none with favorable access to the open ocean. Growth was slow. By 1729 the entire population of North Carolina was 30,000 whites and fewer than 6,000 blacks.

The mainland began to grow rapidly during the next decade, particularly along the deep water of the Cape Fear River. The populations of Brunswick, established in 1725, and Wilmington, approximately 1735, increased steadily; as early as 1732 the population of Brunswick was 1,200. Although the tidewaters that made navigation and north-south movement difficult relegated the early sound cities to secondary commercial importance, Wilmington continued to thrive as the sole deep-water port. Newcomers pushed inland, and trade routes linked ports with new inland cities.

The industrial revolution bypassed the coastal region. Agriculture, timber products, and fishing sustained the economy of eastern North Carolina, and the large older cities served as market centers. Elizabeth City, Hertford, Edenton, Williamston, Plymouth, Washington, New Bern, and Jacksonville

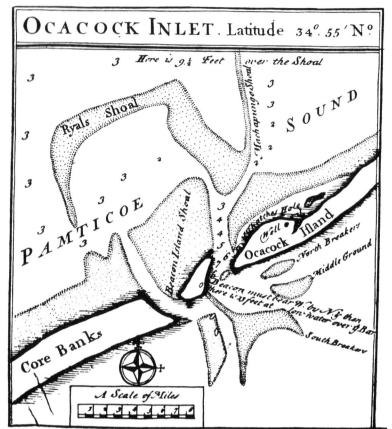

Edward Moseley's eighteenth-century map commemorates the legendary Blackbeard with the label "Thatches Hole." (Courtesy of East Carolina Manuscript Collection)

The destruction of Fort Ocracoke on 17 September 1861, drawing by Lieutenant LeRony. (Courtesy of Library of Congress)

served as seats of commerce and government. While the rest of North Carolina prospered and grew, the coastal region continued to grow and prosper, tied firmly to dependence on agriculture, large land-holding patterns, and slave labor.

By the time of the Civil War, North Carolina had two major ports, Wilmington and Morehead City, each linked to the Piedmont by railway. Fort Macon guarded the channel serving Morehead City and was quickly seized by the Confederacy. Confederate forces moved quickly to construct Fort Fisher to secure the more reliable deep-water port of the Cape Fear River.

Union ships blockaded the North Carolina coast beginning around 1862, but the erratic shoreline provided refuge for shallow-draft blockade-runners that smuggled arms and supplies across the sound waters, evading the larger, deeper-draft Union vessels. There were skirmishes at Hatteras Island and Roanoke Island during the war, and the Union ironclad ship *Monitor* swamped and sank offshore from Cape Hatteras while being towed from Hampton Roads, Virginia.

Although the war ended the antebellum social order, it did not change the character of the coastal economy. At the turn of the century, life in the coastal region of the state remained limited by its waters and enriched by its lands. This did not change until the middle of the twentieth century.

The barrier islands have been isolated and unpopulated for most of the state's history. A few traditional fishing communities, founded before the Civil War, persisted but did not thrive. Today Ocracoke is the only active community on the Outer Banks that originated in the early mercantile years of settlement. The village of Portsmouth also remains today, although it is uninhabited.

Beginning in the 1870s, the barrier islands came to the attention of two primarily very different groups of people: wealthy industrialists from northern states and mariners who regularly circumnavigated the treacherous waters. Both groups indelibly imprinted the islands. The industrialists discovered the isolation and the seasonal waterfowl populations wintering in the sounds. These men chartered hunting and fishing clubs, particularly in Currituck and Dare counties, and purchased thousands of acres for their private sport, in some cases protecting the land as private preserves for waterfowl until the present.

Meanwhile the loss of life due to shipwrecks off the islands called attention of another kind to the sandy shores. In response, the United States both improved the lighthouses along the coast and established U.S. Life-Saving Service outposts every seven miles along the Outer Banks. The life-saving stations, and the post offices that followed, put the barrier island hamlets on the official U.S. postal map, providing both identity and recognition. But for the headline-making rescues of the life-saving crews, in peace and war, little attention would be called to the Outer Banks until the 1940s. The exception, of course, was the arrival from Ohio in 1900 of two brothers named Wright, who began their quest for heavier-than-air flight at Kitty Hawk.

The most significant changes came to the Outer Banks beginning with World War II. The automobile and bridges, increased leisure time, inexpensive land, and a solidly growing economy all led to a building crush along the coast. However, today, after more than 400 years of visitation and habitation, it is still the remoteness and wild fragility of the islands that is the best-selling commodity in the region.

History on Parade

The opportunity to mix history with pleasure abounds both en route to the resort beach cities and when you arrive. It should be part of your "things to do at the coast" list. For example, the Fort Raleigh National Historic Site and the Wright Brothers National Memorial are two of the most important sites in the nation and are within 10 miles of each other.

One of the most important routes in the early settlement of North Carolina, US 17, travels through the eighteenth-century centers of commerce and government. This historic link between Williamsburg, Virginia, and Charleston, South Carolina, weaves inland from the coast. Nearly every community along its passage, including Edenton, Washington, New Bern, and Wilmington, made a mark on the early history of the state. Many are attractive small towns, rich in early architectural detail (see "US 17, the King's Highway").

These smaller towns wear their private and public restoration efforts like badges of honor. Bed and breakfast hostelries make the towns accessible, and open houses and seasonal gatherings allow these communities to show off their eighteenth-century charm. During the year, historical buildings in each are usually open for tours, offering a glimpse of earlier eras.

The Tryon Palace restoration in New Bern and the equally exquisite but more demure residential areas are an architectural treasure trove. The residential areas showcase more than two centuries of culture and artistry. Here you can sample the flavor of one of the most extensive "period" neighborhoods between Norfolk and Wilmington.

In contrast to Williamsburg, a faithfully and meticulously re-created living museum, most of North Carolina's coastal communities acknowledge their history without figuratively trapping it under glass. The homes and churches are still intact because of continual use. There is a charm and vibrancy to the towns tied to the rivers and sea because they are alive and well, restored and reused for living.

You can see a different type of evidence of history on the islands, revolving around the story of the seafaring life and the treachery of the coast. The legendary saga of the U.S. Life-Saving Service is re-enacted at Chicamacomico Life-Saving Station in Rodanthe and highlighted in exhibits at the Hatteras Island Visitors Center and at the North Carolina Maritime Museum in Beaufort, which also catalogs many facets of traditional coastal life, from decoy carving to boat building. You can't miss the lighthouses, but if you look carefully along the Outer Banks, you will see the recycled boathouses and crew quarters of the early life-saving stations (see "The Houses of Heroes"). Many of these buildings have a new commercial life as restaurants, motels, and real estate offices.

A detour here and there along the way will convince you that North Carolina's historical towns resonate with dignity and complement the vibrancy of the oceanfront with a more contemplative mood.

The Access Issue

Beach access has become a difficult issue in North Carolina. The development of the barrier beaches and the subdivision of lands encompassing traditional public-use locations (such as the headlands at inlets) legally restricted public access to the wet sand beach, that is, the beach covered between high and low tides. The proliferation of no-parking signs and "No Beach Access" signs closed off once-favorite sunning spots to all except those who could afford to own a house or to rent a cottage or motel room on the beach.

By the early 1980s, this reparceling of once-accessible oceanfront created a full-blown crisis, putting pressure on the few locations, such as the national seashores and state parks, where public access was permitted. North Carolina rated the lowest of sixteen coastal states on the access issue despite being blessed with around 300 miles of oceanfront and 4,200 miles of soundside shoreline.

In 1981, the North Carolina General Assembly, responding to public outcry over the findings of a legislative study documenting the lack of public access sites along the coast, established the Coastal Beach Access Program under the supervision of the Division of Coastal Management and provided a million dollars in funding for the first two years. The purpose of the program was to acquire, develop, and maintain public access to the wet sand beach. The legislature expanded the program in 1983 to include funding for estuarine sites, changing its name to the Coastal and Estuarine Water Beach Access Program. The General Assembly introduced a law codifying the common-law rights of public use of ocean and estuarine beaches in 1992. Building on the success, the appeal, and new access needs, the General Assembly amended and renamed the act in 1995 to the Public Beach and Coastal Waterfront Access Program, thereby giving it a broader directive.

The program quickly developed three types of access sites: regional, neighborhood, and local, which are described below in the section on "How to Use This Book." The guidelines for facilities are fluid since site conditions and funding determine the exact mix of improvements. Development of access-ways occurs as land and money become available.

Federal funds for the improvement of coastal access began to supplement the allocations of the General Assembly in 1985, and by 1988 the North Carolina coast boasted 138 public access facilities. The dramatic turnaround propelled the state to the national forefront in the number and quality of access areas. The demand has been acute from the beginning. In 1992, 24 local governments made applications to the Division of Coastal Management requesting more than $2 million in construction grants, for which only $350,000 had been appropriated.

It is a fact that some of the fastest-growing counties in the state are along the coast, and the growth only makes the need for access—and open space—more acute. In 1995, the General Assembly adopted a land-transfer tax and dedicated most of the funds for use by North Carolina's parks, with a fixed percentage in turn dedicated to the access program. The projected funds are significant and, most important, nondiscretionary, thus allowing the access program administrators the opportunity to plan for both maintenance of existing sites and future expansion.

Official sign denoting public beach access. (Courtesy of N.C. Coastal Management Commission)

The crux of the access crisis is parking. Most oceanfront communities provide adequate public access for pedestrians, but not everyone has a reasonable, safe walk. North Carolina law clearly establishes everyone's right to use the wet sand beach. However, without a place to park within a convenient distance of the beach and a clear passage over the dunes, this right is often more abstract than real.

Accordingly, the access program spends a sizable portion of its funding on finding suitable sites large enough to provide at least some parking. Each year, local governments in the 20 counties governed by the Coastal Area Management Act, which requires planning departments to address access, have an opportunity to submit requests for access project funds. Regional ocean access locations with large parking areas and restrooms are given priority in funding.

At present, municipal or county governments are responsible for initiating access project applications. Improved access benefits a community not only by bringing in tourism revenue but also by reducing conflicts between private landowners and the visiting public who usually simply want to get to the beach.

While the need for oceanfront access seems obvious, the need for soundside access locations may be even more pressing. Such access locations allow people to reach the waters that have been the traditional source of livelihood and recreation in coastal areas. Many lifetime residents of the barrier islands have found that they are cut off from traditional locations for clamming, fishing, or even such simple pleasures as crabbing or casting a net. The creation of parking and boat-launching facilities— sometimes developed with the assistance of federal monies in conjunction with other state agencies such as the Wildlife Resources Commission—increases the opportunity to pursue both old and new forms of water recreation. For example, the discovery of the North Carolina sound waters by wind-surfers has generated a powerful demand for soundside access sites.

Handicapped Access

The handicapped visitor to the coast will find access available in certain locations. Most regional access facilities and many of the larger neighborhood access areas constructed since 1990 are accessible to the handicapped.

Many access sites have dune crossovers with ramps that make them accessible to people in wheelchairs. However, not all of the dune crossovers have ramps that extend to the beach. Depending on the nature of the beach, the ramp may terminate at a gazebo overlook or a deck.

Most state parks and recreation areas are accessible to the handicapped; however, not all of these areas provide access to the beach front. All National Park Service properties are accessible, but while some trails in national wildlife refuges may be negotiable by wheelchair, many are not.

Enforcement of handicapped parking regulations varies among individual local governments. You must have a valid handicapped license plate to park in a designated space. In some locations, the fine for violating this regulation can be as much as $100.

The Division of Vocational Services of the North Carolina Department of Human Resources publishes a book entitled *Access North Carolina* that lists the handicapped facilities available at all public parks, recreation areas, and historic sites across the state. The book is available free of charge by contacting the Division of Travel and Tourism, North Carolina Department of Economic and Community Development, Raleigh, NC 27611, 1-800-VISITNC.

For more on handicapped access, see "How to Use This Book" below.

Beach Rights Issues

Although a landowner may legally deny access across his or her property to the beach, once you get to the beach, you have the right to be there. North Carolina case law has repeatedly upheld the right of the citizens of the state to use the "foreshore," that is, the wet sand beach, which is covered by the reach of high tide and exposed by the retreat of low tide. This portion of the oceanfront is reserved by the doctrine of public trust for the use of all. A 1983 ruling of the North Carolina Supreme Court reaffirmed this principle: "The long standing right of the public to pass over and along the strip of land lying between the high-water mark and low-water mark adjacent to respondents' property is established beyond the need of citation. In North Carolina private property fronting coastal water ends at the high-water mark and the property lying between the high-water mark and the low-water mark known as the 'foreshore' is the property of the state."

The legal principle supporting this right is the common law doctrine of public trust, a derivative of the English common law of sovereign rights, whereby the sovereign retains certain rights to be enjoyed by all citizens of the state. In the case of North Carolina, the state retains the rights to certain uses of land or waters that cannot be abrogated in any way by the state or any individual.

In 1991, the legal principle of prescriptive easement, which maintains that a privately owned road or path traditionally used as a public right-of-way must remain open to all even if the owner of the property objects, advanced efforts to gain public access in a case at Holden Beach. Since 1986, public access to the western end of the island and Shallotte Inlet had been closed off after the area was developed into a private community. The road to the inlet became a private road that only property owners and their guests could use. After a suit was filed claiming that the public had the right to use the road, the North Carolina Supreme Court reversed a lower court ruling denying access by claiming that since people had historically traveled along that route to reach the inlet, they had legally established a prescriptive easement to the road.

In 1992, legislation was introduced in the North Carolina General Assembly to codify the common-law right of the public to use ocean and estuarine beaches. The bill stated that public trust resources must be protected from "unlawful encroachments, usurpation, or interference with the customary free use and enjoyment of the ocean and estuarine beaches." It would have empowered the attorney general to bring civil action against any "person, State agency, or other legal entity" encroaching on the rights of the people to "freely use and enjoy the ocean and estuarine beaches." The bill also spelled out the conditions under which the court could order removal of a structure blocking access.

The legal battles ebb and flow as much as the tides, reflecting the complexity of public rights, private ownership, and the tenuousness of the beach itself. Two things seem certain: the public has the legal right to use the wet sand beach, and the state vigorously supports providing necessary public access.

Parks, Preserves, Reserves, and Refuges

Many governmental agencies and several private organizations hold title to lands along the coast that are open to the public. These are the large public places on the map—the seashores, parks, memorials, refuges, preserves, historic sites, and natural areas. Some have interpretive facilities and regular programming; others have few roads and no buildings and sometimes only restricted or difficult access, either by boat or off-road vehicle. These preserves, regardless of the managing agency, offer a different perspective on the coastal experience; they give access to wilder places and simpler times. The land comprising this complex "public domain" is notable because of its physical beauty as well as its natural, historical, and cultural importance.

Cape Hatteras and Cape Lookout national seashores are certainly the most visible and notable of all public lands in the region, securing more than one-half of the state's oceanfront mileage. In addition, the U.S. Fish and Wildlife Service manages seven wildlife refuges along the coast that are open to visitors.

The U.S. Department of Defense also controls large holdings along the coast as military bases, target ranges, and landing fields. The best known are Camp Lejeune at Jacksonville and Cherry Point Marine

Air Station at Havelock. The target range at Stumpy Point and the Naval Auxiliary Landing Field at Bogue can provide a high-energy punctuation to a generally low-key region. Visitation policies at the military sites vary, but generally the bases are open and the guards stationed at the entrance gates will direct you to the appropriate location for registration.

The U.S. Coast Guard maintains active bases serving the major inlets of the state and deeper waters with heavy boating traffic. The Coast Guard stations are generally open to the public, and the atmosphere is very friendly. The newest base at Oregon Inlet is worth visiting just for the historically respectful architecture of the main building. The Coast Guard also maintains the lights in the lighthouses, although other agencies may maintain the buildings.

The state of North Carolina manages five parks, four natural areas, three aquariums, three historic sites, and an underwater archaeological preserve. It also manages nine reserves under the supervision of the North Carolina Coastal Reserve system, a little-known but very successful state program established to protect the wild and natural coast. Parcel by parcel, as money and land become available, the program is obtaining some of the most important coastal ecological niches in order to secure them for research, education, and traditional use. In the words of one administrator, the reserve sites "are meant to be green space on the map." The more than 30,000 acres of lands and waters acquired so far encompass a diversity of habitats.

The reserve system originated in 1982 when the National Oceanic and Atmospheric Administration (NOAA) funded five years of acquisition for the National Estuarine Sanctuary Program. In North Carolina, four sites were accepted by the NOAA: Currituck Banks, Rachel Carson, Masonboro Island, and Zeke's Island. In 1988, this program became the National Estuarine Research Reserve, which managed the use of the lands for research, education, and compatible recreational activities. No additional funds were made available for acquisition, however.

In 1987, the state acquired fifty-acre Permuda Island in Onslow County from the Nature Conservancy, which had purchased the island to thwart destruction of its archaeological value. With the land in hand but no program to manage it, the General Assembly established the Coastal Reserve system, an administrative "umbrella" sheltering the previously protected estuaries and any other coastal properties that might subsequently come under state control. The result is a steadily growing collection of "coastal jewels" that includes not only Permuda Island but ecologically significant preserves in Kitty Hawk Woods, Buxton Woods, and upland acreage on Bald Head Island.

Your Child and the Coast

There are few fonder memories than being young and at the beach, but children's curiosity can place them in circumstances they may not be able to handle. Keep these precautions in mind when visiting the coast with your child.

- Keep your child in sight at all times. If you bring a book to the beach, bring a babysitter as well.
- Protect your child's skin from sunburn and eyes from glare and blowing sand.
- Protect your child's feet when crossing sand dunes, wading in shallow sound waters, or walking on piers or docks.
- Always be with your child when he or she is in the water, even in a tidal pool.
- If your child cannot swim, he or she should wear a life jacket.
- Be wary of rip currents that run parallel to the shore then suddenly out to sea. If your child is caught in one, help him or her to swim parallel to shore to break free.
- Do not let children swim near inlets.
- Never let a child wade in sound waters without a life jacket and sneakers.
- Jetties or rock groins can be slippery and dangerous. Do not let your child play on them.
- Keep your child away from jellyfish on the beach or in the water.
- Hold your child's hand when walking on a pier or dock.
- Teach your child never to walk up behind casting fishermen. Be particularly watchful on a pier.
- Place your fishing tackle out of reach of small children, or keep your tackle box securely fastened.
- Tar and oil may be removed from a child's skin with mineral oil instead of paint solvents.

Highways to the Coast

I-95 is the major north-south interstate in eastern North Carolina. This controlled-access roadway follows the western portion of the coastal plain. All of the major state roads and federal highways leading to the peninsulas of the coast intersect I-95. If you're traveling from the mid-Atlantic states along I-95, you can easily connect with the east-west routes that thread the major peninsulas.

I-40 has opened the doors to the beaches from Onslow to Brunswick County for Piedmont vacationers and I-95 travelers. Even though it is primarily an east-west interstate, it heads nearly due south from Raleigh. North Carolina highways 24, 41, 50, 55, 111, and 210 intersect I-40 and can be woven together to connect you to the coast. Before I-40, traffic corkscrewed steadily along US 421 south from Dunn, NC 87 from Fayetteville, or NC 211 from Lumberton. These routes still offer a local-color tour through rich agricultural lands and near several state historic sites and parks.

If you're traveling to North Carolina from the coastal counties of Virginia or South Carolina, US 17 is the primary route. From Virginia, US 17 goes south to Elizabeth City before following the northern edge of Albemarle Sound to New Bern. From South Carolina, it moves inland to Wilmington and then parallels the coast as far north as Jacksonville before heading further inland. US 17 threads through the historical heart of coastal North Carolina, though for most of its length it is far from the resort island towns. The appeal of history makes the route worthy of its own tour.

Map I-2. Routes to the North Carolina Coast

The Outer Banks of Currituck and northern Dare counties are served by two other major routes, US 158 and US 64. US 158 intersects I-95 at Roanoke Rapids and heads east across the Albemarle region to the Currituck mainland. It is a pleasant and scenic two-lane road, usually lightly traveled until Elizabeth City. The small towns passed along the way have many architecturally interesting structures, and the state has erected numerous markers commemorating the early history of the area. East of Elizabeth City, at Barco, US 158 merges with NC 168 from the tidewater region of Virginia, and traffic, particularly during summer weekends, becomes heavy. At this point, the road turns south. A high-rise bridge crosses the Intracoastal Waterway at Coinjock, where the traveling public of the eastern seaboard used to wait at an often-raised drawbridge as barges plied the waterway, and eventually the road crosses the Wright Memorial Bridge into Dare County.

US 64 intersects I-95 west of Rocky Mount, 136 miles from Manteo. This is the major east-west artery from the Piedmont, and therefore it is quite busy. It is a heavily used farm-to-market route, and many school buses and logging trucks travel it. The popularity of the Dare County Outer Banks for family camping brings additional slower-moving travelers to the roadway. Although the two-lane sections east of Tarboro can carry some frustratingly slow traffic, east of Williamston, US 64 is being widened to four lanes. The route passes through Williamston and Plymouth, two communities of historic interest, and there is a pleasant side trip to Pettigrew State Park and Somerset Place State Historic Site south of Creswell.

US 264 parallels US 64 as it sweeps along the mainland adjacent to Pamlico Sound. It is comparatively lightly traveled and offers an alternate route to Manteo from cities south of Washington and Greenville. It passes through several wildlife refuges and preserves and winds near Bath, a refreshing historical side trip. US 264 also passes by Swan Quarter, where there is a ferry depot to Ocracoke.

The major highway to Carteret County and Cape Lookout National Seashore is US 70, which links with I-95 20 miles west of Goldsboro. This is an excellent, well-traveled route, and from Kinston it is a four-lane divided highway to Morehead City and Beaufort. East of Beaufort, US 70 may be one of the most beautiful panoramic drives of the coast. It sweeps through the farms and woodlands of Carteret County, linking up with NC 12 for the trip to Cedar Island where you can reach another ferry to Ocracoke. This route traverses seemingly endless salt marshes, shimmering in the light and pungent with the briny, slightly fetid odor of the tidal creeks.

Travelers on US 70 heading to southern Carteret County or the Onslow or Pender County resorts should take US 258 from Kinston south to Jacksonville, where US 17 or NC 24 will take you to the resort city of choice. NC 58 is a "blue highway" alternate from Kinston to Swansboro and the southern Bogue Banks. Both US 258 and NC 58 pass through extensive forest and agricultural lands interrupted by small communities that serve the rural farming population. The drives are lightly traveled and a pleasant diversion from the major routes.

I-40 handles most of the Piedmont traffic to the Brunswick County beaches. Fayetteville and Charlotte residents should take NC 211, which crosses I-95 at Lumberton and shoots across the flat coastal plain counties.

Map I-3. Coastal Bicycling Routes

The Bicycle Option

The North Carolina coast is splendid country for cycling. My personal observation, however, is that it is not for solo riders or the fainthearted. Some roads, such as NC 12 along the Outer Banks, are too narrow and summer vacation traffic too heavy to make cycling a safe, enjoyable experience. Besides, if the automobiles don't drive you crazy, the mosquitoes may carry you away.

Spring and fall months offer the best mix of good weather and low traffic for trips along the Outer Banks roads. Also, drivers are less inclined to be impatient during these seasons.

The Bicycle Program of the North Carolina Department of Transportation provides maps of coastal bicycling routes upon request. The maps are detailed tour guides, useful for all-purpose travel but especially geared for bicyclists. Out of eleven designated bicycling trails across the state, five include major coastal highways, namely "Mountains to Sea," "Ports of Call," "Cape Fear Run," "Ocracoke Option," and "North Line Trace." The most extensive coastal bicycling route is the "Ports of Call" route, which covers portions of the historic colonial coastal trade routes from South Carolina to Virginia.

Other maps available from the Bicycle Program include "Around Pamlico Sound: Bicycling the Outer Banks," which provides an excellent starting point for planning and gives detailed information on loops and connectors. It also notes general information on places of interest along the way and campgrounds, but no addresses or phone numbers are included. More detail is available on the "Bicycling in Beaufort" map, which traces a 6-mile loop around this historic town.

For information, contact Bicycle Program, North Carolina Department of Transportation, P.O. Box 25201, Raleigh, NC 27611, 919-733-2804.

How to Use This Book

This book is organized by oceanfront county beginning with Currituck County in the north and concluding with Brunswick County in the south. Entries are listed in the same order that you would find them if you traveled along the beach from Virginia to South Carolina. The political geography of the Outer Banks forced some departures from the county divisions: Cape Hatteras National Seashore and Cape Lookout National Seashore are treated as separate units, even though they form parts of Dare, Hyde, and Carteret counties. The section on Carteret County, the parent county of Cape Lookout National Seashore, follows the Cape Lookout National Seashore section.

Each county and seashore division begins with a general introduction, which is followed by an "Access" section highlighting the most important access information, a general "Handicapped Access" section, and an "Information" section with addresses and phone numbers of sources for more detailed assistance. Specific attractions discussed within the major divisions are each followed by more specific "Access," "Handicapped Access," and "Information" sections. If there is no known access, handicapped access, or source for information, that section is not included.

The text tells you what you may expect to find at each location, providing verbal snapshots that animate the attraction and should make your visit richer. Each entry is a chatty assessment of the mood and character of its subject, sprinkled with anecdotal and historical information—figurative taffy to chew on.

"Access" sections give general information about access and the location of public beach and boating access sites, detailing some of the features you might expect to find. The highest priority has been given to locating as accurately as possible every public access site along the barrier islands. Since boaters, off-road-vehicle owners, and handicapped travelers have special access needs, an attempt has been made to specify locations that have facilities to serve them.

The "Handicapped Access" section qualifies the level of accessibility of a site for handicapped visitors, which for the purposes of this book means people who must use wheelchairs. Many dune crossovers along the coast are boardwalks that meet federal handicapped accessibility standards for the slope of ramped sections and the width of the walkway. It is not possible to include all of these locations in the "Handicapped Access" sections. Those locations listed as fully accessible to the handicapped have facilities such as restrooms, gazebos, or overlooks that are built to accommodate wheelchair travelers. Locations described as "negotiable" are possibly accessible to the handicapped; they are not barrier-free but are not totally inaccessible either. The accuracy of this assessment for any individual will, of course, vary, but it is an attempt to provide some information about a location's accessibility.

The following terms are frequently used throughout the book in descriptions of facilities at access sites.

Regional access sites are the largest access sites and offer the most facilities. They are the most reliable locations to plan to visit since they generally are designed for nearly all types of users, including those with special needs. Typically, a regional access site has from 40 to 200 parking spaces, restrooms, outside showers, water fountains, a gazebo or seating area overlooking the beach, and a dune crossover. Such sites may also have telephones, dressing rooms, picnic tables, refreshments, boardwalks, seasonal lifeguards (usually Memorial Day to Labor Day), and off-road-vehicle access to the beach. Additionally, almost all regional access sites are fully accessible to handicapped travelers.

Neighborhood access sites usually have between 10 and 50 parking spaces, a bike rack, a dune crossover, and trash receptacles. They may or may not have off-road-vehicle access and lifeguards. Typically, neighborhood access sites do not have restrooms, and handicapped accessibility varies considerably.

Local access sites generally have limited parking, which may or may not be paved, and a dune crossover.

A *dune crossover* is a controlled route through the dunes to the beach. Once you find an access site, the dune crossover is usually evident. Dune crossovers may be sand paths or wooden boardwalks, and they may have either steps or ramps for visitors in wheelchairs. Although every attempt has been made to provide up-to-date information, dune crossovers are regularly converted from sand paths to handicapped-accessible boardwalks. In some locations, dune crossovers may serve both off-road vehicles and pedestrians.

In the Cape Hatteras National Seashore section, the term *ramp* generally denotes an access location to the beach. Since much of the access in the seashore serves off-road vehicles, most ramps are reinforced for this purpose. Separate pedestrian dune crossovers may or may not be provided at any given location.

Unimproved access areas are usually unpaved, with room for one or two cars at best, and they have a signed dune crossover.

Maps and charts accompany the text. The maps correlate with the text, noting the major routes serving a location, regional access sites, and major landmarks. They should guide you directly to the main locations mentioned in the text. Fishing piers are shown on the maps to help orient you on the beach. The charts provide a graphic representation of the basic features at each main location discussed in the text and noted on the maps and the activities best suited to that location. They are meant to serve as an "at a glance" reference; specific information is found in the text.

Feature essays throughout the book discuss various coastal topics, differing in length according to the subject. They are offered as another form of access—as a means to let you sample the spiciness of the region. They also may help you satisfy a child's curiosity. At the very least, it is hoped these little diversions will enrich your visit by deciphering some of the natural world that you have chosen to visit.

Three appendixes follow the text. Appendix A is a categorical listing of types of destinations or agencies with their mailing addresses and phone numbers. Appendix B lists civic or cultural happenings along the coast, arranged by month, and a phone number is included for more information on each event. Appendix C compiles a monthly listing of fishing tournaments you may want to enter, including the location of each tournament and a phone number for further information.

Access Guide

Telephone Changes

Since this revised edition was first published in 1997, the area code for Currituck, Dare, Hyde, and Carteret Counties and for the Cape Hatteras and Cape Lookout National Seashores has been changed from 919 to 252. Also, travelers who need to make reservations on the North Carolina Ferry System may call toll free to their departing dock as follows: Cedar Island, 800-856-0343; Ocracoke, 800-345-1665; and Swan Quarter, 800-773-1094.

Currituck County

Area code 252

I remember fishing in Currituck Sound with my father and grandfather, catching incredible numbers of bass and bream, and spending two wonderful days somewhere that seemed to me to be an unendingly long ride away from my Piedmont home. I did not return until twenty years later when I lived in Virginia Beach and the Outer Banks was an easy 1½ hour drive by NC 168/US 158 through mainland Currituck County.

Currituck is more convenient to Virginia than North Carolina. For many northern vacationers, it's the route of passage to the Outer Banks. I became a regular on the two-lane roads and very fond of the county that felt snug and comfortable, fitting nicely into my memory of a place where the days on the water were long, the fishing endless, and the fish abundant.

So plentiful were the waterfowl wintering here once that the county name is a corruption of the Algonquian word *Coratank*, meaning wild geese. The Algonquians had both permanent and seasonal settlements in the county, some of which were on islands in the sound. Currituck has long been naturally bountiful, and the waterfowl population, along with farming, eventually became the basis of the rural economy following European settlement. During the later decades of the nineteenth century, residents made their living as market hunters, shooting thousands of waterfowl to ship them to the exclusive restaurants of the Northeast.

Today it is the traffic from the mid-Atlantic states south to the Outer Banks that swoops down through the rural small towns of Currituck County. Widening the old roads and bridges to accommodate the traffic disrupts the intimacy of a predominantly agricultural landscape, resonating with place names such as Marnie, Harbinger, Jarvisburg, Coinjock, Barco, Maple, and Sligo.

The countryside lazes away outside your automobile window as you pass field after field between the small communities and solitary farmhouses. It stretches east to the sound waters where residents fish and hunt and west to more fields and more farms. Summer brings some of the best truck farming you'll ever see. The roadside stands along NC 168 and US 158 bloom with produce well into fall.

The three separate land masses that comprise the county—the mainland, Knotts Island, and Currituck Banks—all touch the shallow freshwater basin of Currituck Sound. The peculiar county geography makes it impossible to travel from one land mass to either of the others without crossing the sound or the state line.

Except for the explosive development on the barrier beaches that includes an eighteen-hole golf course and multimillion-dollar houses, Currituck changes reluctantly. A ferry still carries children to school across the sound as it always has, but the wild ponies that once roamed freely at Corolla have been relocated to the extreme north beaches where there are, as yet, no paved roads and where the banks remain intact, one last wild place.

The fact that more of the county is water than land has everything to do with the current state of affairs. To the east of the mainland, protected from the open ocean by a barrier peninsula extending from Virginia, is Currituck Sound. These legendary, near-sacred waters among hunters and fishermen attracted many prominent northeastern industrialists to private hunting and fishing clubs during the 1920s.

In recent years, Currituck County has realized the advantages of promoting a type of tourism different from the traditional hunting and fishing retreats, namely oceanfront vacations. A building boom, which bottlenecked at the entrance to a private community north of Duck until 1984 when the state assumed responsibility for the road from Duck to Corolla, has now hammered to the very shadows of the Currituck Beach Lighthouse at Corolla.

While nearly all of Currituck south of Corolla creates new homes for visitors, state, federal, and private agencies have also secured new habitats for wildlife as well as field laboratories for research scientists studying barrier islands north of Corolla. All in all, the result seems to be about as "balanced" as development versus conservation will ever be.

When you cross Currituck Sound on the Wright Memorial Bridge, you arrive in Dare County on the east side of the bridge. The roadside stands here are selling lifestyles and getaways, not produce. Driving north on NC 12 past Duck, you cross back into a very different economic landscape to reach Currituck County again.

In Corolla, 24 miles north of the Wright Memorial Bridge, you are 55 miles by automobile from the Currituck County Courthouse. You are also years away from the mainland because the traditional landscape, and much of the tone of a way of life, is changing fastest on the Currituck Banks. From the turn of the century until the mid-1970s, things changed very little here. By the end of the 1980s, the original village of Corolla, which is a small, tree-covered settlement of solitude-loving souls centered around a small post office and several stores, found itself surrounded by self-contained resort developments. Corolla hasn't changed much, but the village atmosphere is mightily squeezed by the development around it.

The Currituck County coastline extends almost 27 miles south from the Virginia border, a windswept, low-profile barrier. While the glory days of Currituck hunting have passed, the legacy of the era exists as immense undeveloped acres of private land and wildlife sanctuaries. On these banks are

some of the highest and most active dunes remaining on the eastern seaboard, extensive maritime forests, and abundant marshes and shallow waters. Each year, approximately one-sixth of the Atlantic flyway migratory waterfowl population comes to Currituck. The banks north of Corolla are one of the most "natural" stretches of barrier island in the state and are likely to remain as such since several preserves, among them a component of the North Carolina National Estuarine Research Reserve system and the Currituck National Wildlife Refuge, prohibit passenger vehicle traffic through their property north of Corolla, except for vehicles that can drive on the wet sand beach.

Access to the Currituck Banks from the north is regulated in Virginia by Back Bay National Wildlife Refuge and False Cape State Park. Only residents of the North Bank communities of Swan Beach and Carova Beach who wish to drive to Virginia Beach along the beach may obtain a permit.

Access

Currituck County provides oceanfront access off NC 12 immediately north of the Pine Island subdivision. Additional access is in the Whalehead Beach subdivision. Ocean and soundside parking are available at the Currituck Beach Lighthouse in Corolla.

Access for the extreme North

	Fee	Parking	Restrooms	Lifeguard	Camping	Showers	Beach Access	Hiking	Trail	Handicapped	Boating	ORV Access	Fishing	Programs	Historic	Sand Beach	Dunes	Upland	Wetland
Knotts Island		•	•								•		•		•			•	•
Mackay Island National Wildlife Refuge		•	•					•	•		•		•					•	•

Bank settlements of North Swan Beach and Carova is by four-wheel-drive vehicle only. Ramp access to the North Banks for vehicles is provided at the north end of Corolla at the Tasman Drive access site.

In 1986 the county adopted a comprehensive ordinance restricting vehicular access to the beaches of Currituck. The main points of the ordinance are as follows:

— You cannot drive on the beach from May 1 to September 30 between the Dare County line and the Tasman Drive access ramp where a paved public road exists parallel to the beach.
— You can only drive on the foreshore or wet sand beach and no faster than 15 miles per hour when pedestrians are present.
— There are exceptions for commercial fishermen "engaged in the use of or setting seines" in the ocean.

There is a boat dock and pier into the sound at the Currituck Beach Lighthouse in Corolla. Public piers, boat tie-ups, and a boat ramp are also available at the former Whalehead Club, just south of the lighthouse. The North Carolina Wildlife Resources Commission maintains boating access sites into Currituck Sound at Poplar Branch at the end of NC 3, $7/10$ mile off of US 158 north of Grandy, and into the Intracoastal Waterway approximately one mile east of Coinjock on SR 1142.

Handicapped Access

Currituck County does not presently provide specific handicapped access facilities other than ramps. Corolla has private facilities that are handicapped accessible. The grounds of the Currituck Beach Lighthouse and the soundside boardwalk are manageable by wheelchair. Several of the dune crossovers in the Whalehead Beach subdivision meet federal handicapped standards.

Information

For information, contact Outer Banks Chamber of Commerce, P.O. Box 1757, Kill Devil Hills, NC 27948, 919-441-8144.

Knotts Island

The insular hamlet of Knotts Island is an island only in the strictest sense of the word. NC 615, the mainland tie to Virginia Beach, crosses a narrow tidal creek, Corey's Ditch, that links the North Landing River and Back Bay, the western and northern estuaries surrounding the high ground of Knotts Island. Knotts Island Channel completes the boundary, rippling between Currituck Banks and the east edge of Knotts Island.

Historically, Knotts Island is the driest ground between what were once some of the finest duck ponds and fishing waters in the country. Even today it is still a waterman's island: quaint, literally and figuratively insular, and charming for its out-of-the-mainstream perseverance in a simpler pace of life.

The approach to Knotts Island on NC 615 sets the stage for the quiet, low-key lifestyle at its destination. The roadway passes through the expansive marshlands of Mackay Island National Wildlife Refuge, surrounded by vast stretches of tawny marsh grass and, in winter, groups

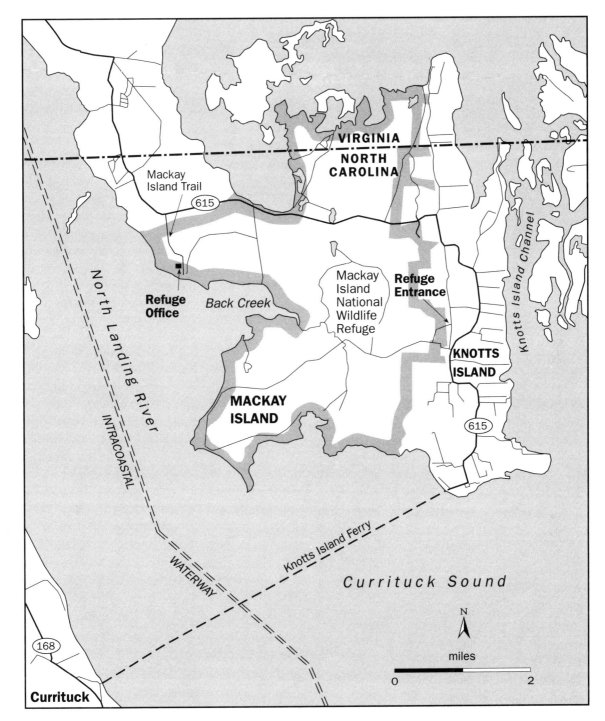

Map 1. Knotts Island

of dabbling ducks enjoying the safe haven. Knotts Island proper is little more than a post office, several small stores, an elementary school, a beautiful church, and scattered residences among farmed land. It is decidedly rural, with a greater concentration of homes near the water's edge than inland. All but a few of the homes are permanent residences, and those that are not are either private hunting club holdings or vacation homes.

This just-barely-an-island status has shaped the history and lifestyle of the residents. Until recent decades, most of the folks who lived there, like their families before them, somehow eked out a living on the waters of Back Bay and Currituck, usually by guiding hunters and fishermen. Today, more residents make their living off the island, commuting to better-paying jobs elsewhere.

There are several twists to life in Knotts Island that make modern-day living adventuresome. Local phone service goes to Virginia Beach; it is a long-distance call to the county courthouse in the village of Currituck across the sound. The post office is small-town personable and is one of the best places to get insider information. Young children attend school on the island, but high school children must cross the sound to go to school in Currituck. The free ferry to Currituck arrives and departs according to school hours.

When the ferry is scheduled for maintenance, usually in summer,

notices warning tourists of the interrupted service are posted within the city limits of Virginia Beach, along Princess Anne Road (NC 615) prior to the last detour to the mainland via Moyock.

Knotts Island is a tight-knit community (islanders who marry outside the community may even refer to their spouses as outsiders) but an easy place to visit. It is a fine place for a bicycle tour. There are a few private campgrounds as well as private homes that will host guests. However, unless you are making plans for an extended hunting or fishing trip, Knotts Island is best sampled as a day getaway or scenic detour from the more congested highways through mainland North Carolina and Virginia. It's one of the more curious corners of the state, still out of the way, which in and of itself is notable.

Access

Knotts Island is a community of private owners. There are no designated public access locations within the hamlet itself.

Information

For information, call the Knotts Island post office at 919-429-3252 or the Currituck Town Hall at 919-232-2075.

Mackay Island National Wildlife Refuge

In 1961, the U.S. Fish and Wildlife Service secured an adjacent complex of wetlands, ponds, and high ground known as Mackay Island, creating a national wildlife refuge for migratory waterfowl. Today, approximately 8,000 acres comprise the refuge: slightly more than 850 acres in Virginia and 7,150 in North Carolina.

Mackay Island proper is one of the largest of several patches of high ground within the refuge boundaries. The North Landing River and its tributary, Back Creek, separate Mackay as an island. It is not the island it used to be, however. The main refuge road once crossed a bridge over Back Creek and canoers and boaters could pass under the bridge and continue completely around the island, but since the bridge was replaced by a culvert crossing, boaters/canoers must portage the refuge road to make the loop.

Narrow, twisting tidal creeks thread the refuge. Most of them are subject to the characteristic wind tides that govern water levels in Back Bay, the North Landing River, and nearby Currituck Sound. Indian Creek once formed a free-flowing east boundary between the refuge and the homes and farms of Knotts Island, but it has silted and is slowly filling in as marsh.

Unless you have a boat, the practical northern limit of the refuge is the NC 615 causeway, the main road to Knotts Island. This causeway is one of the best locations for bird watching in the refuge during migratory periods in fall and spring. The Great Marsh Trail, located along the causeway, is a ⅓-mile loop for year-round hiking and bird watching.

More than 140 species of birds have been sighted at Mackay Island, including a spectacular wintering population of greater snow geese. The refuge is also home to deer, raccoon, nutria, and mink. The management team permits limited trapping and hunting within the refuge. These activities are regulated yearly, the numbers of hunters and days of hunting determined by the refuge mandate to provide waterfowl habitat.

Much of the land of Mackay Island came from the estate of Joseph Palmer Knapp, publisher and outdoor sportsman. Knapp constructed a mansion, since torn down, overlooking the North Landing River on Mackay Island and spent many winter hours hunting and fishing the waters of Currituck Sound. A great benefactor of the county, he was active in maintaining an environmental vigil over the ecology of the sensitive, shallow sound waters, and once donated $50,000 to control pollutants on the North Landing River that were threatening the waters of Currituck Sound and Back Bay. Committed to conservation and game management, he established the "More Game Birds in America

Foundation" in 1930, which later became Ducks Unlimited.

His role as benefactor extended to the people of Currituck as well. He was instrumental in providing the first free lunch program in a public school system in the state and built the Currituck School, now renamed as the Joseph P. Knapp Junior High School.

Access

The refuge office is located off of NC 615 and is open all year, 8 A.M. to 4:30 P.M. weekdays. Corey's Ditch, the Great Marsh Trail, and the canal adjacent the north bank of the causeway are open all year. You are permitted to drive the Mackay Island Road and walk or bicycle the Mackay Island Trail (4 miles) or the Live Oak Point Trail (6.5 miles) from March 15 to October 15 during daylight hours. Mackay Island Road is open for walking and cycling to the first gate from October 16 to March 14 during daylight hours. The trails and marshes are closed at this time for resting and feeding migratory wildfowl.

Visitors will find several access points along the causeway of NC 615 for boating or fishing in the surrounding waters. You may fish in all canals and bays only between March 15 and October 15. A valid North Carolina fishing license is required.

Information

For information, contact Mackay Island National Wildlife Refuge, P.O. Box 39, Knotts Island, NC 27950, 919-429-3100.

Knotts Island Ferry

The free ferry from Knotts Island to Currituck holds approximately 18 cars and takes about 50 minutes to cross the sound. During the summer (June 15–August 30), the ferry departs Knotts Island every 2 hours beginning at 7 A.M. and ending at 7 P.M.; Currituck departures begin at 6 A.M. and continue every 2 hours until 6 P.M. During the winter schedule, there are only five daily departures from the island beginning at 7:30 A.M. and ending at 5 P.M. and from the mainland beginning at 6:30 A.M. and ending at 3:45 P.M. The winter schedule serves schoolchildren who attend mainland schools from Knotts Island. Remember two things before heading to Knotts Island from Virginia Beach or the mainland. One, any repairs to the ferry are performed during the summer; if the ferry is out for maintenance, the closing of the route is well posted. Two, the ferry fills quickly during summer weekends; if you secure a place in line, stay there. It's a first-come, first-served system.

Information

To check the schedule, call the ferry dock at 919-232-2683.

Currituck Banks

Until the North Carolina Department of Transportation assumed control of the private subdivision road that etched along the soundside of the Currituck Banks north of what is now Sanderling to the village of Corolla in 1984, only residents of Corolla and Carova Beach and members of a few private hunt clubs had free and easy access to the Currituck portion of the Outer Banks. Others could reach the banks only by driving along the beach. The place was empty, if you can believe it today, even in summer. I know because I buried my car to the axles in soft sand next to the Currituck Beach Lighthouse and waited an hour before someone came along to help. There were probably less than 100 year-round residents living between me and Virginia at that time, perhaps as few as thirty. (One estimate for Corolla alone was eighteen, a number easily in the hundreds now.) Fortunately, the one resident who carried a chain in his truck came by. He hauled me out for the price of a laugh.

The road then was intermittently graveled and paved, taking a wandering course through the sparse, windswept peninsula. It split the island and was well back of the dunes for the most part, although it surged to the oceanfront to run along Lighthouse Drive in what is now called Whalehead Beach. At that time, there were a few second homes north of the Dare County line. Today NC 12 follows the same

alignment except for a soundside veer just past the Pine Island Tennis and Racquet Club.

The drive ended at Corolla, running out of pavement in the immediate vicinity of Winks Store, next door to the Corolla post office, which followed the lighthouse and the U.S. Life-Saving Service Station to Corolla in 1885. North of Corolla, to Virginia, stood several small settlements with permanent residences and second homes—wild, desolate places. The North Currituck Banks have long been used for cattle ranching, open grazing really. The practice continues to a limited extent today.

Long before the land rush to Corolla, speculators subdivided much of the North Banks into vacation lots. Would-be developers dredged finger canals into the island, a practice no longer permitted. The primary communities north of Corolla are Swan Beach and Carova Beach and are only accessible by four-wheel-drive vehicle. Very little has changed in these communities because access, from north and south, remains difficult.

Virginia Beach offers the most convenient services, but to reach Virginia Beach, residents must obtain permits to drive through False Cape State Park and the Back Bay National Wildlife Refuge. There is a lot of local color north of Corolla and many miles of beach. The individuals who own property there prefer isolation.

Nowhere else on the Outer Banks has a decade and a road made more

of a difference than it has in Currituck. Today it may be one of the most popular stretches of the Outer Banks. If you're walking around Corolla today, you might not be able to hear the ocean for the hammers. It seems that virtually every square foot of private land is under assault with a carpenter's level and skill saw. But for all the new construction, the Currituck Banks still retain a wild appeal. The natural appeal has become a selling point, forcing developers to be as environmentally sensitive as the state of the art permits them to be. A lot of people can visit now and enjoy a week's vacation, but there's not a lot of pavement. You share the maritime forest and interdune zone with the wild ponies of the North Banks.

Access
You can easily drive the family car to the Ocean Hill development north of Corolla, but you should stop there since the pavement ends. Access north of this point is by four-wheel-drive vehicle only at the designated ramp at Tasman Drive at the north end of the Ocean Hill development.

Currituck National Wildlife Refuge

In the late 1970s, the Nature Conservancy purchased approximately 1.7 miles of oceanfront and upland property from the Swan Island Club, a private waterfowl hunting club established nearly a century earlier. The property included about

800 acres of upland and a conservation easement on 1,400 acres of marsh, flats, and wetlands. The clubhouse and its outbuildings on Swan Island, southeast of Knotts Island in Currituck Sound, were not sold. The Conservancy transferred Swan Island and property it had purchased from the Monkey Island Club further south to the U.S. Fish and Wildlife Service as part of a new refuge for migratory waterfowl. Initially, the new refuge was to include the Conservancy property as well as additional purchases of nearly 15,000 acres of marsh, upland, and beachfront along the North Banks from Virginia to Dare County. However, the Department of the Interior nixed the proposal, and the Conservancy holdings became virtually the entire refuge.

The 1,787-acre Currituck National Wildlife Refuge is administered by the Mackay Island National Wildlife Refuge staff on Knotts Island, which is a 1½-hour drive away by the most direct route, along the peninsula beachfront. It is approximately 5 miles north of the town of Corolla and is divided into three separate tracts: the Mary Islands tract, north and west of Corolla in the sound; the Monkey Island tract; and the largest component, the Swan Island tract. Private property in Ocean Beach and Swan Beach separates the Monkey Island and Swan Island components.

Adjacent to the south boundary of the Monkey Island tract is a parcel still held by the Nature Conservancy that is used in research and wildlife management studies. It is sandwiched by the Currituck Banks component of the North Carolina Coastal Reserve system, a part of the National Estuarine Research Reserve system. The three agencies, the U.S. Fish and Wildlife Service, the Nature Conservancy, and the North Carolina Coastal Reserve, own the land from the marsh to the mean high-tide line. All three prohibit vehicular access on their property, and inland routes north from Corolla are plainly posted as off-limits. The multiple ownership will probably thwart any plans for a road north from Corolla, insuring the integrity of the tracts for research and wildlife habitat.

In any event, you can't reach the Currituck National Wildlife Refuge except by driving a four-wheel-drive vehicle on the beach or by boat. There is a boat landing in Waterlily, and if you head slightly northeast from there, you'll hit the Monkey Island portion of the refuge.

The refuge, particularly the Swan Island tract, has always been ideal habitat for wintering migratory waterfowl. The land is typical of the North Banks, a transitional area between northern and southern maritime vegetation. For example, both bayberry (*Myrica pensylvanica*) and its southern relative wax myrtle (*M. cerifera*) grow here. The higher elevations and forested portions of the site support deer, fox, raccoon, feral hogs, and horses. The marsh is habitat for muskrat, river otters, and mink and a portion of the Atlantic flyway waterfowl population that winters in Currituck. Refuge managers have confirmed nestings of the piping plover, an endangered species, in the dunes within the refuge, prompting them to closely monitor vehicular traffic there during the nesting season, June through July.

You may bird-watch, picnic, and walk in the refuge. Dogs must be on a leash. You can certainly fish and swim on the beach of the refuge, but your vehicle cannot drive further inland than the posted signs. Because the beach is narrow, the signs are posted about 50 feet within the refuge boundary to insure that vehicles will have a drivable route during high tides.

The refuge is so new that management officials are taking a wait-and-see attitude before further restricting refuge use. Because access is not easy, very few people other than the residents of adjoining Swan Beach and North Swan Beach mingle with the migratory residents.

One note of historical interest: in the Swan Island tract, the owner of a parcel of private property has relocated the old Wash Woods Life-Saving Station as a private residence.

Information

For information, contact Mackay Island National Wildlife Refuge, P.O. Box 39, Knotts Island, NC 27950, 919-429-3100.

	Fee	Parking	Restrooms	Lifeguard	Camping	Showers	Beach Access	Hiking	Trail	Handicapped	Boating	ORV Access	Fishing	Programs	Historic	Sand Beach	Dunes	Upland	Wetland
Currituck National Wildlife Refuge							•	•					•			•	•	•	•
Nature Conservancy Tract							•	•					•			•	•	•	•
Currituck Banks Research Reserve							•	•			•	•	•			•	•	•	•

Currituck Banks National Estuarine Research Reserve

In the summer of 1984, the Nature Conservancy gave the state approximately 960 acres of beachfront, dunes, maritime forest, marshes, flats, and islands, which became the third component to be acquired for the North Carolina National Estuarine Research Reserve system. The property, once owned by a private hunting association, the Monkey Island Club, extended from Monkey Island in the Currituck Sound eastward to include property on the North Banks.

The island itself, with its clubhouse and outbuildings, now belongs to Currituck County. It is presently not open to the public, but the lodge and outbuildings are serviceable and may in the future be used as a conference center. The northern portion of the island is one of the largest egret rookeries in the state, and part of the island was a summer fishing base and burial ground for Native Americans centuries prior to Currituck's settlement.

In the preserve holdings along the North Banks, the terrain has the typical mid-Atlantic vegetation pattern, with a dense shrub thicket and some maritime forest thriving behind the artificial dune line created by the Civilian Conservation Corps in the 1930s. Primary interest in the property by visitors is likely to be on the beachfront, however. Here the preserve offers a superb opportunity to see exactly what Currituck Banks looked like before the sand sprouted houses and condominiums. In fact, the juxtaposition of the preserve and Ocean Hill subdivision next door poses a timely contrast.

The proximity to Ocean Hill makes the preserve beachfront easily accessible by four-wheel-drive vehicle. While the primary research done in the preserve takes place within the 625-acre sound and marsh portion, 325 acres of dunes, shrub thicket, and maritime forest remain for other use. Although the preserve has definite boundaries, many visitors will perceive it, a tract owned by the Nature Conservancy, and the southern component of the Currituck National Wildlife Refuge as one unit of land. Indeed, the three agencies charged with managing these lands have signed agreements to allow the cooperative use of the lands for research projects.

During the warmer months, there's a lot of beach activity at the southern boundary of the preserve where it adjoins the private property of the Ocean Hill subdivision, and there are no plans to alter the traditional recreational use of the property. Plans call for establishing a small day-use area for beach recreation, funded by both county and state and with restrooms and perhaps a small parking area.

Access

Access is by four-wheel-drive vehicle, which by county regulation must stay seaward of the dune line. At high tide when the beachfront is impassable or during emergencies, vehicles may move inland to a sand-

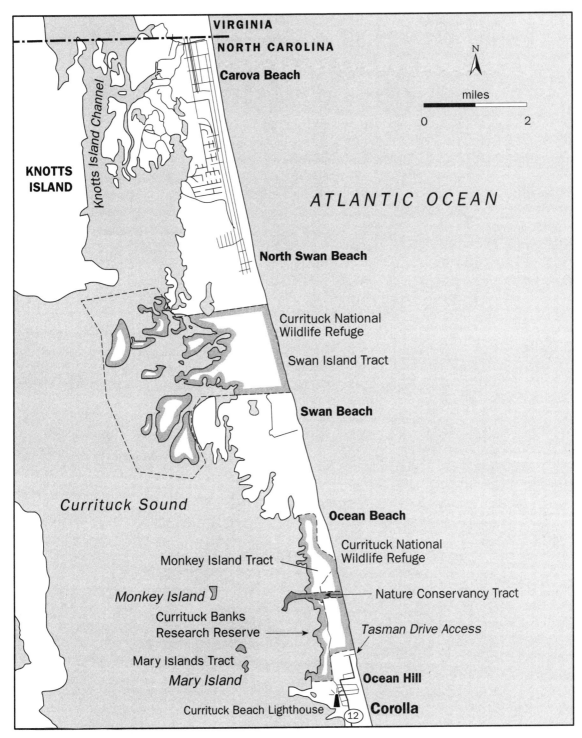

VIRGINIA
NORTH CAROLINA

Carova Beach

ATLANTIC OCEAN

miles
0   2

KNOTTS
ISLAND

Knotts Island Channel

North Swan Beach

Currituck National
Wildlife Refuge

Swan Island Tract

Swan Beach

Currituck Sound

Ocean Beach

Currituck National
Wildlife Refuge

Monkey Island Tract

Monkey Island

Nature Conservancy Tract

Currituck Banks
Research Reserve

Tasman Drive Access

Mary Islands Tract

Mary Island

Ocean Hill

Currituck Beach Lighthouse

12

Corolla

Map 2. Currituck Banks

track road. It is possible to walk the beach and stroll inland. Although insect repellent is advised, the seasonal deer flies and mosquitoes may carry you away no matter what you wear.

The U.S. Fish and Wildlife Service and the Currituck County sheriff patrol the preserve.

Information
For information, contact Northern Sites Manager, North Carolina Coastal Reserve, c/o Town of Kitty Hawk, P.O. Box 549, Kitty Hawk, NC 27949, 919-261-8891.

Corolla

Since the mid-1970s, old Corolla has been steadily surrounded by new houses and new permanent residents. The winter population, a measure of true change here, has soared. In the early 1980s Corolla was still an outpost where wild horses roamed free. Today it's a busy, end-of-the-road village.

If your last visit here was A.D. (antedevelopment), you will recognize the post office, the Corolla Chapel, and Winks Store, with the additional few shops side-by-side that made downtown Corolla. The Currituck Beach Lighthouse still towers over the community but with a wonderful new twist—it is the only major lighthouse on the coast consistently open to visitors.

The Corolla Light resort community spreads between NC 12 and the oceanfront. To the west of the now well-maintained roadway is the Whalehead development, drawing its name and inspiration from the county-owned Whalehead Club. Paved bicycle and stroller trails thread through the soundside live oak forest leading to roads that circle the yet undeveloped lots around the old Whalehead Club. The most startling visual contrast to the historical wildness of old Corolla is not the resort houses, however, but the bright green manicured turf of a pitch and putt course. It's too neat and green to fit in.

There's recently been a lot of new construction in Corolla, and the more or less original streets, Carotank, First, Second, Third, Coral Lane, and Bismark Drive, are overshadowed not by the lighthouse as before but by the larger, taller vacation homes in the new developments. There's a nice tip of the hat to the old ways in the naming of some of the streets on the soundside for the families of longtime residents.

The Corolla Light development built a commercial hub, Corolla Village Shoppes, north of the main entrance to the resort. Retailers cater to the summer visitors, but some items were obviously overlooked in the rush of newness—if you want to use a pay phone, you have to go to Winks Store. Corolla Village Shoppes does, however, provide restrooms in the northeastern-most building in the boardwalk-linked cluster.

One of the shops rents whatever you might want for beach recreation, from kites to surfboards to bicycles. There is adequate parking at the shops, but it's a long walk to the water. You might be able to slip in here and leave your car long enough to visit the Currituck Beach Lighthouse, but only if the parking spaces along Carotank Drive are full.

When you drive into the old village, look left under some fine loblolly pine trees. You'll see a noteworthy structure that houses a boutique, *Outer Banks Style*. It was the original Kill Devil Hills boathouse constructed in 1896. Not only did its crew witness the Wright brothers' first flight, but a member, John T. Daniels, snapped the photograph of the century—the picture of the first motorized airplane flight. Realtor Doug Twiddy purchased the building and moved it in 1984, preserving a valuable structure in life-saving station history. He restored the station to its original condition and used it as an office until moving next door. Inside, you'll see the original station sign and a Lyle gun. Other artifacts from the first flight and life-saving days are on display in the adjacent new offices.

Access
Development outpaced the county's ability to provide direct means to the oceanfront within the village. However, if you rent in the resort, you have full access to the beach east of the resort property. For visitors, about thirteen dune crossovers, marked by the familiar sunspots logo, serve the Currituck portion of the banks. The primary access for visitors to Corolla is in

Rods 'n' Reels 'n' Wheels

There are many lengths of coast where you may drive a car onto the beach. Some of the places with year-round access are the North Banks in Currituck County, Cape Hatteras and most of Cape Lookout national seashores (excluding Shackleford Banks), portions of Emerald Isle, the north end of Carolina Beach, and Fort Fisher State Recreation Area. In addition, many of the resort cities permit driving on the beach between Labor Day and Memorial Day, otherwise closing the beach to vehicles during the vacation season.

Because I am used to seeing vehicles on the beach, it seems normal to me. If you are new to the North Carolina coast, the practice may be shocking. However, it is an old custom; you can't fish in the surf along the national seashores, and much of the coast, without the shelter and mobility of a vehicle. Most drivers are well-intended fishermen, and their vehicle is their tackle shop/campsite on wheels.

In order to drive on the beach, you must abide by certain regulations. Your vehicle must be registered, currently licensed, and inspected. The driver must have a valid driver's li-cense or learning permit and must have minimum liability insurance. The vehicle and you are subject to all motor vehicle–operating laws of North Carolina (for example, no open alcoholic beverages in the vehicle, you must wear a seat belt, etc.) as well as the specific laws and regulations of the local government or managing agency, such as the National Park Service. Nearly every municipality that permits driving within its city limits requires that a special permit or license be promi-nently displayed. Permits can usually be acquired at the local city hall or police department.

You must use only the designated access ramps to reach the beach. Usually traffic must remain on the wet sand beach and the speed limit is 15 miles per hour when people are present. Certain portions of the national seashores may be closed to accommodate either people or the nesting of rare species of birds, such as the least tern, or pelagic turtles. The closed portions of the beach will be clearly marked. Obey those signs, or you will endanger the creatures and your wallet.

Certain municipalities prohibit ve-hicle access, and you cannot drive on the beach within the boundaries of Pea Island National Wildlife Refuge (extending approximately from the old Oregon Inlet Coast Guard Station to just north of Rodanthe). This refuge is administered by the U.S. Fish and Wildlife Service under a different mandate than that of the National Park Service and driving is prohibited within the refuge.

It is strongly recommended that you check with the local munici-pality or management agency about taking your vehicle on the beach. Accessibility by vehicles is subject to seasonal change and other local restrictions. You are responsible for being aware of those restrictions before taking your vehicle down to the water.

Most certainly, you can't drive on the beach with anything other than a car modified to permit extra-wide tires or a four-wheel-drive vehicle. Don't even think about going without a chain or rope and a shovel, and fol-low established roads or track other vehicles. While I've never seen reck-less driving, I've seen some stupid driving that left one car mired at an inlet with the tide on the rise.

	Fee	Parking	Restrooms	Lifeguard	Camping	Showers	Beach Access	Hiking	Trail	Handicapped	Boating	ORV Access	Fishing	Programs	Historic	Sand Beach	Dunes	Upland	Wetland
Tasman Drive ORV Access							•					•	•			•	•		
Currituck Beach Lighthouse	•	•	•				•	•	•	•	•		•	•	•	•	•	•	•
Whalehead Club		•						•			•		•		•				•
Whalehead Beach		•					•			•	•					•	•		
Pine Island Audubon Sanctuary								•								•	•	•	•

Whalehead Beach south of the village. Two well-marked turns take you to the access parking. From the south, turn east on Albacore Street (the Food Lion grocery store at the corner of NC 12 and Albacore is your landmark). There is a dune crossover and ramp for emergency vehicles only at the end of Albacore. From the north, turn east on Shad Street (the Corolla Light water tower at the corner of Shad and NC 12 marks the turn). There is a dune crossover at the end of Shad. Whalehead Beach subdivision consists of three streets parallel to the ocean: Lighthouse Drive, directly behind the dune line; Whalehead; and Corolla Drive, the westernmost street. East-west streets with fishy names cross these three. The dune crossovers are at the east end of the fish streets; public parking is not so obvious. The county has five very large paved parking lots along Whalehead Drive at the intersections with Shad, Sturgeon, Perch, Bonita, and Sailfish streets. The lots are not marked; just look for some-

thing paved large enough for a helicopter. There is also a commitment for a new parking area at Whalehead and Dolphin streets, near the fire department.

The sheriff's department seems fairly easygoing about parking as long as you do not violate a posted prohibition and your vehicle is completely off the road and not blocking a drive. In fact, one deputy provides hand-drawn maps showing the parking lot locations on the backs of the warning citations he issues.

Public parking is also available at the Currituck Beach Lighthouse on Corolla Village Road, a left turn off of NC 12 just south of the lighthouse property. If you turn right at the same intersection, you will find parking at the ocean terminus of Carotank Drive.

There are no public access points between the Whalehead Beach parking lots and the Dare County line, about 7 miles south. Ocean Sands is the largest private subdivision south of Whalehead Beach.

Adjacent to it is land owned by the Pine Island Club and then the Pine Island Audubon Sanctuary. None of these properties provide public access.

To drive north on the beach, the access area is at Tasman Drive, but you cannot drive south on the beach from there to the Dare County line between May 1 and September 30. However, if you are in pursuit of fish for commercial activities (setting seines), you can pretty much drive your vehicle anywhere. You had better be pursuing fish in a manner convincing to local law enforcement personnel or prepare to pay the $50 fine.

Handicapped Access
The county provides ramps that meet federal handicapped accessibility standards at the eastern ends of Tuna, Barracuda, Herring, and Coral streets in the Whalehead Beach subdivision.

The Corolla Village Shoppes has public restrooms that are handicapped accessible.

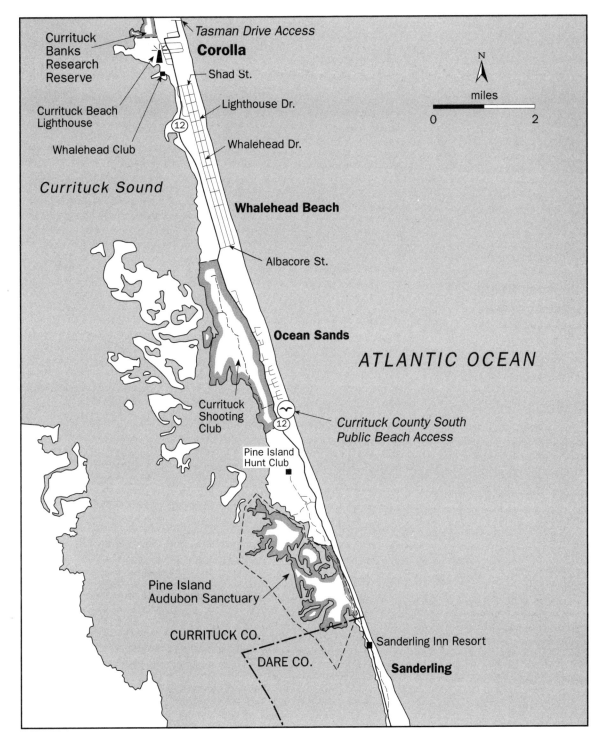

Map 3. Corolla to Sanderling

Rental cottages that have a boardwalk over the dunes may be considered handicapped accessible by real estate agents. However, check to make sure that the ramp doesn't extend from the second floor of a condominium.

Information

For information, contact Outer Banks Chamber of Commerce, P.O. Box 1757, Kill Devil Hills, NC 27948, 919-441-8144.

Currituck Beach Lighthouse and Lightkeeper's Quarters

When first lighted on December 1, 1875, the Currituck Beach light completed the network of major beacons on North Carolina's Outer Banks. The Currituck light filled the gap between Cape Henry at the entrance to Chesapeake Bay and Bodie Island at Oregon Inlet, giving mariners a series of lights to guide them along the coast from Cape Lookout north.

Since North Carolina's other major beacons were painted in the black-and-white patterns familiar today, the decision was made not to paint the Currituck light in order to distinguish it from the others. At the base of the 162-foot tall tower (measured to the very top), the walls are 5 feet 8 inches thick—all brick. The wall thickness tapers to a mere 3 feet at the top—still all brick.

The lighthouse is open from Easter until Thanksgiving. Inside are stairs, 214 to be exact if you count from ground level. For a $3 fee, you may climb to the 150-foot-high focal-plane gallery and enjoy the commanding view. The fee goes toward the renovation of the lightkeeper's quarters, a large Victorian duplex on the complex grounds.

The lightkeeper's house was originally precut, hauled across the Currituck Sound by barge, and assembled on site in 1876. Now it is a state property included on the National Register of Historic Places. In 1980 the state granted a fifty-year lease for the grounds and the lightkeeper's quarters to Outer Banks Conservationists, Inc. (OBC), a private, nonprofit organization that is turning the dollars contributed into the materials and effort needed to restore the unusual duplex. The U.S. Coast Guard granted the OBC a twenty-year lease for the lighthouse building but continues to maintain the lens area and the generators. The OBC is also working with the North Carolina Department of Cultural Resources to renovate a smaller residence that was moved here to accommodate another keeper.

As you step onto the grounds of the lighthouse, look carefully at all the trees. Then, when you go inside the building, look at the historical photographs of the lighthouse: there are few, if any, trees in photographs taken during the previous century or early in this one. The vegetation on the lighthouse grounds is a comparatively new feature of the site, perhaps not more than fifty to sixty years old. Up until the 1940s, Currituck Banks was open range for grazing cattle, and as many as 6,000 wild horses cropped the vegetation on the banks until the Great Depression. In the 1930s, Works Progress Administration and Civilian Conservation Corps teams were given the task of stabilizing the dunes of the Outer Banks. They bulldozed an artificial (and arbitrary) dune line, planted it with beach grass and sea oats, and planted pine trees inland. Once the pines survived the grazing and sheltered the landward side of the island, other plants could successfully germinate and grow. From the light, you are first startled by the amount of green below, the thickness of the soundside woods, and the composition of the island—dune to flats to shrub thicket to maritime forest to marsh.

At the west end of the parking area is a boardwalk that penetrates about 300 yards through the maritime forest, a freshwater cattail swamp, the adjoining marsh, and out into Currituck Sound. Although the walk can be buggy, it provides access not only to spectacular sunsets but also to the incredible evening song arising from the various habitats through which it passes. Note as you walk how the different habitats ease into one another— trees suddenly have sufficient dry ground to rise out of what seems to be hopelessly soggy footing. The grasses in late summer reach four feet, and the amphibian chorus an-

Currituck Beach Lighthouse, Corolla. The northernmost Outer Banks lighthouse, this fully automated, 160-foot, red brick structure dates from 1875. (Courtesy of N.C. Travel and Tourism Division)

nounces your stroll along the length of the boardwalk, alerting the world to your intrusion. The boardwalk is a great spot to take the kids crabbing, too.

Access

The lighthouse is open 10 A.M. to 6 P.M. daily except Sunday, but it closes if there is the least hint of lightning. There are more than 30 parking spaces along the south side of the property, and across NC 12, Coratank Drive leads to an ocean-front parking lot with 30 spaces. Both lots fill up quickly during the summer.

Handicapped Access

The grounds of the lighthouse are negotiable by wheelchair, but the lighthouse is not. The boardwalk meets handicapped standards. Two handicapped parking spaces are plainly signed.

Information

For information, contact Outer Banks Conservationists, Inc., P.O. Box 361, Corolla, NC 27927, 919-453-4939.

Whalehead Club

The Whalehead Club has remained the most lavish of the hunting clubs erected on Currituck Sound, even though for many years it was also the most forlorn. It still commands a peninsula overlooking Currituck Sound just southwest of the parking lot on Corolla Village Road that serves the Currituck Beach Lighthouse.

A new chapter is being written in the club's colorful history since the county of Currituck voted to buy the building in 1991 and renovate it for public use. The county agreed to purchase the building and surrounding 28 acres over a seven-year period for nearly $2.4 million, using funds from a county occupancy tax that must be used to promote tourism. Accordingly, the club will be renovated to become a wildlife museum and perhaps house several county offices. The building is also on the National Register of Historic Places.

The club was originally constructed during the 1920s by Edward C. Knight, Jr., a wealthy railroad baron from the Northeast attracted to the fine hunting and fishing in Currituck. One cannot help but imagine that Knight and Joseph Knapp, a publisher and the legendary benefactor of the county, were not in some way sharing the same sportsman's orbit of the super rich. Knight purchased the property, originally called the Lighthouse Club, after its all-male membership refused his young wife admission as a fellow hunter. He vowed to build a club worthy of emulation. The three-story, 20,000-square-foot house had 15 rooms, 12 bathrooms, a copper roof, and an electrical generator, a rare feature at the time. It was one of the few art nouveau houses on the East Coast, reportedly costing nearly $400,000. The inside matched the outside in grandeur, with Tiffany chandeliers, a custom-made baby grand piano, and walnut paneling.

The estate included an arched bridge over an artificial lagoon and a boathouse, both of which still stand. The bridge and boathouse design

are thought to be a reconstruction of structures noted by Knight's wife, Amanda Marie Louse LaBell, on a trip to Europe.

The building has been used as a boy's school, a Coast Guard research facility, and the focal point of a resort development. As late as the summer of 1991, the club was surrounded by the small humbling stakes left by surveyors, delineating the property lines of lots for waterside homes in a proposed development on the site. An osprey nested on one of the chimneys, scaffolding scaled the roofs, and the grassy expanse of the once-lavish grounds was favored by the wild ponies of Corolla. Still, the remnants of its finery commanded attention, much as an old and tarnished park gazebo—a remnant, but a fine one indeed.

Access

Following the recent purchase, you may now walk the grounds. The building is clearly visible from the lighthouse parking lot and the public boardwalk that extends into the sound from the lot.

There are 12 parking spaces, a boat ramp, and several boat tie-ups for use at the west end of the clubhouse.

Handicapped Access

The new museum is certain to be accessible for the handicapped. At present, it is possible to use a wheelchair on the roads around the club, but the grounds cannot be easily negotiated by wheelchair.

Information

For information, contact Town of Currituck, P.O. Box 39, Currituck, NC 27929, 919-232-2075.

Ocean Sands

The Ocean Sands subdivision, south of Whalehead Beach, covers about 3 miles of oceanfront property south of Crown Point Circle. Beach access is by rental from one of the many real estate agencies managing the private homes in the subdivision. Ocean Sands is a very quiet subdivision; there are no through streets and very little traffic except for residents and vacationers. For the entire 3-mile length from Crown Point in the north to Conch Terrace in the south, the land west of NC 12 is posted and wild. It is a mix of large, old vestigial sand dunes, live oak maritime forests, and the shrubby salt-tolerant vegetation characteristic of the North Banks. It is impossible not to wonder if the lengthy stretch of natural landscape will ever be developed. The posted property belongs to the Currituck Shooting Club, which previously owned the beachfront acreage that is now Ocean Sands.

Handicapped Access

Some cottages have boardwalks over the dunes that may be considered accessible by realtors.

Currituck Shooting Club

One of the newest additions to Currituck Banks, the Currituck Club golf course, has some of the oldest roots in the area. The Currituck Shooting Club was founded in 1857 and has long carried the reputation of being one of the oldest continually operating hunting clubs in the country. Its establishment even predates the heyday of waterfowl hunting in the legendary sound. In time, the club owned more than 2,000 acres of undeveloped land, from productive marsh to oceanfront property. The acreage has long been prized as marsh and shrub thicket that provides habitat for birds as well as animals. The original clubhouse building has been listed on the National Register of Historic Places.

With the glory days of hunting and isolation gone forever, the club turned over its extensive marsh to become part of the Currituck National Wildlife Refuge. The club began plans to develop the eighteen-hole golf course along NC 12, designed so that it is mostly secreted from view.

Access

Currituck County maintains an oceanfront regional access south of the entrance to the Currituck Club. There are 38 parking spaces, restrooms, showers, a boardwalk, and a ramped dune crossover.

Pine Island Club

The Pine Island Hunt Club property adjoins the land of the Currituck Club and once extended south to the Dare County line, a distance of 3½ miles. The club's ownership extended from sound to sea also. Needless to say the oceanfront property is more than prime: oceanfront house prices in what is known as Pine Island subdivision hover around (and soar above) a million dollars. One reason for the pricey values is the exclusivity of the house sites; another is that the land west of the highway will remain undeveloped as an expanded Audubon Society preserve. The lands are more or less closed to the public except for the Pine Island Tennis and Racquet Club, which has indoor courts for handball, squash, and tennis.

Access

Except for the racquet club, there is no public beach or sound access.

Pine Island Audubon Sanctuary

The National Audubon Society owns a strip of land nearly 3½ miles long, embracing 3,600 acres of marsh and wetland in Currituck Sound as a bird sanctuary. Two small wooden signs mark the limits of the preserve, which starts at the Dare/Currituck County line along the "S" curve adjacent to the health club at Sanderling and extends one mile north on NC 12. Originally the preserve was made up of nearly 2 miles of oceanfront set aside by the owner of the Pine Island Hunt Club in the early 1970s. Since that time, the preserve has increased the marsh and wetland acreage, which provides more favorable habitat to the migratory waterfowl. In return for the additional acreage, the Audubon Society released some of the original oceanfront and upland acreage to the benefactor, most likely for future development.

This area is one of the most stable portions of Currituck Banks and exemplifies the full range of barrier island ecosystems. Accordingly, it supports an outstanding cross section of both flora and fauna.

Access

Access is not very clear. The land is posted, but there are trails along the roadway that are frequently used. There is no parking along NC 12 as it passes through the refuge, and signs indicate that the preserve is off-limits. There is very little doubt that visitors to the Sanderling Inn and even the spa use the trail along the west side of NC 12 for hiking and bird-watching, in addition to jogging. There is no access to the beaches except by entry north and south of the refuge and walking to the preserve along the wet sand beach.

Information

Advance arrangements must be made for visiting by calling the refuge manager at 919-453-8430.

US 17, the King's Highway

US 17 is the historic route through the Albemarle region, the land along Albemarle Sound where the first permanent settlement in North Carolina flourished, arriving in these northeastern counties as "spillover" expansion from the successful settlement of Virginia's tidewater region. The route itself is not a direct line to the wet sand beach, paralleling the coast far inland from the beaches. It is, however, a historic side trip from the coast, and the small communities along the route are jewels of interest—well-kept, dignified towns. You can stop, look, and learn at each of them.

Much of US 17 today follows the original track that during the colonial period made it the royal post road, the major mail route from Williamsburg to Charleston. It became known as the King's Highway (a name persisting in South Carolina), connecting the principal ports and colonial settlements of Virginia, North Carolina, and South Carolina.

You can put together a very informal "Colonial Tour" by driving through the cities along the bays. In the Albemarle Sound area, you may enjoy all or a part of the Historic Albemarle Tour, which begins at Elizabeth City and threads around Albemarle Sound in a colonial loop filled with vintage buildings and fine interpretive displays.

Elizabeth City

Elizabeth City was a late bloomer by Albemarle settlement standards, authorized by the General Assembly in 1793, more than 100 years after the founding of Pasquotank County. First named Redding, the town was sited at the narrows of the Pasquotank River.

The community thrived after the completion of the Dismal Swamp canal in the early 1800s. Merchants capitalized on the engineering marvel that enabled goods-laden barges to reach deep-water ports in Virginia. Mercantile trading brought wealth to the town. Its location, however, brought the Union army in 1863, which destroyed much of the wealth by setting the town on fire.

Elizabeth City recovered from burning to regain prominence as a manufacturing and trading center by the early twentieth century. Today, nearly thirty blocks of the community comprise two historic districts. There are more than thirty buildings on the National Register of Historic Places, most private homes within walking distance of each other.

There's a finery here, much in Queen Anne style, that bespeaks a time of great wealth. See Elizabeth City on foot; a self-guided walking tour is available from the chamber of commerce. Make one sure stop, the Museum of the Albemarle, a division of the North Carolina Museum of History, which details the peoples and settlement of the Albemarle. The museum is located at 1116 US 17 South in Elizabeth City and is open 9 A.M.–5 P.M. Tuesday–Saturday, 2 P.M.–5 P.M. Sunday. For information, call 919-335-1453.

For information on attractions and accommodations, contact Elizabeth City Area Chamber of Commerce, 502 East Ehringhaus Street, P.O. Box 426, Elizabeth City, NC 27909.

Take a side trip south of the city off of NC 34 to the structures promoted as the "largest wooden buildings in the world." They are vintage, domed dirigible hangars dating from World War II, one of which still houses lighter-than-air craft.

Hertford

I like towns that snuggle up to rivers, where cypress trees stand like moss-draped pilings between the houses and a wind-chopped sheet of broad, dark water. Hertford is such a place, and has been since 1758. You can't sail further inland on the Perquimans River since it narrows, coils, and blocks passage past Hertford.

US 17 crosses these narrows in fine style over a swing bridge connecting a pair of arcs in the road to deposit you in downtown Hertford, on Church Street. Other town street names were borrowed from London 234 years ago; they still work, so they haven't been changed.

This may be Hertford in a phrase—it still works. Park your car behind the municipal building on Grubb Street and follow the twenty-five-site historic walking tour. You'll see at least that many places you'll want to buy. Hertford is meticulously, lovingly maintained and lived in; it's a small town where everybody knows everybody. Grab lunch at the Hertford Café or a snack from the Gingerbread Inn and Bakery, a turn-of-the-century bed, breakfast, and bakery.

Three miles south of town is a testimonial to the mason's art, the exquisite brick Newbold-White House. It is North Carolina's oldest home, built in 1685, and is open March 1 to December 22, 10 A.M.–4:30 P.M. Monday–Saturday. For information, call 919-426-7657.

Accommodations are limited. For information, contact Perquimans County Chamber of Commerce, P.O. Box 27, Hertford, NC 27944.

Edenton

There is very little doubt that the king's correspondence found its way to Edenton and that some irate messages went his way as well, most notably on October 25, 1774, the date of the Edenton "Tea Party." In-corporated as the provincial capital of North Carolina in 1722, Edenton became the center of settlement in the Albemarle region. The passing of time has burnished not blemished its early eminence.

The well-known photograph of Edenton—cannon in the foreground, house in the background—is a view of Edenton Bay and the Barker House, which is now the visitors center for Historic Edenton. A fifteen-minute film at the center introduces Edenton and its place in the history of the Albemarle region. Purchase the inexpensive walking-tour brochure at the Barker House, and stride out to see more than twenty structures worthy of notice, composed and settled in both place and time.

The architecture of five splendid structures—the Chowan County Courthouse, St. Paul's Episcopal Church, the James Iredell House, the Cupola House, and the Barker House—fixes Edenton in your memory. All of the buildings are more than 200 years old, and you will see echoes of Williamsburg in the courthouse's prominence over the Village Green.

The Barker House Visitors Center is open 9 A.M.–4:30 P.M. Monday–Saturday, April–October; 10 A.M.–4:30 P.M. November–May; 2 P.M.–5 P.M. Sunday. Tours are at 9:30 and 11 A.M., 1 and 2:30 P.M. April–October; 10:30 A.M. and 2 P.M.

November–March. For information, contact Site Manager, Historic Edenton, P.O. Box 474, Edenton, NC 27932, 919-482-2637 or 919-482-3663.

For information on accommodations, contact Edenton/Chowan Chamber of Commerce, Drawer F, Edenton, NC 27932, 919-482-3400.

Washington

Washington, North Carolina, is the first community in the United States named after George Washington. The town was originally named Forks of the Tar River by its founder, Revolutionary War veteran James Bonner, who renamed it to honor his commanding officer in 1776.

A magical transition happens directly beneath the bridge carrying US 17 south from Washington—the Tar River turns into the Pamlico River. The waterfront location of the town has not been kind. After Union troops torched abandoned naval stores here in 1864, the fire spread and burned many antebellum buildings. Some of the buildings listed on the self-guided walking tour survived this fire and another in 1900.

Washington blends its catastrophic survivors into a tight-knit, small community, easily walked and visited. Follow the walking-tour guide available from the Greater Washington Chamber of Commerce, which is on Stewart Parkway, the waterfront drive and promenade along the Pamlico River. The Old Beaufort County Courthouse at 158 North Market Street, now the public library, is the second oldest courthouse in the state. The Seaboard Coastline Railroad Depot serves as the Civic Center. Be sure to wander down East Main, past the National Register Bank of Washington building and into the residential district, to see how Washingtonians live.

Accommodations are limited. For information, contact the Greater Washington Chamber of Commerce, P.O. Box 665, Washington, NC 27889, 919-946-9168.

For a side trip, visit Historic Bath, the oldest incorporated town in North Carolina, which is 15 miles east. Stop at the visitors center for an orientation film before setting out on the easily walked tour of the tiny community. St. Thomas Church is the oldest existing church in North Carolina and is open for visitors. The notorious Blackbeard once called Bath home. Tickets for admission to historic homes may be obtained at the visitors center, which is generally open 10 A.M.–4 P.M. Tuesday–Saturday, 1 P.M.–4 P.M. Sunday. It is closed on Mondays beginning in November. For information, call (919) 923-3971.

New Bern

New Bern is the second oldest town in the state, settled in 1710 by Baron Christoph de Graffenreid with Swiss and Palatine immigrants. The town incorporated in 1723, and from 1746 until 1792, it was the colonial and state capital. The legislature met in several locations around the state, including New Bern, during this time, until moving permanently to Raleigh in 1792.

Tryon Palace, the restored colonial capitol, is a major attraction, which grandly builds on the historical self-consciousness of New Bern. The palace is faithfully restored to its period opulence and is surrounded by magnificent gardens. Historic tours are available. Visitors should not concentrate their entire time on Tryon Palace. Virtually the entire inner city is on the National Register of Historic Places. The town is a wealth of historical treasures, stately in its presentation and a pedestrian delight. The many architectural styles dotting the side streets provide a visually stimulating tour. Other major attractions include the Fireman's Museum and the Masonic Lodge, the oldest in the state.

For information, contact Craven County Convention and Visitors Bureau, P.O. Box 1413, New Bern, NC 28563, 919-637-9400 or 1-800-437-5767.

Many of these attractions, among others, are listed in the flyer, "Historic Albemarle," available by contacting Historic Albemarle Tour, Inc., P.O. Box 759, Edenton, NC 27932, 919-482-7325.

Dare County

Area code 252

What I like about Dare County is that when you drive there, you have no clue that you're going to the beach, unless you arrive by ferry from Ocracoke. Neither approach along US 158 from the north or US 64 and 264 from the south provides a hint of "beachiness." Instead, you zing through the endless coastal forests or farms, past a bit of roadside bustle at either Powells Point or Manns Harbor, behind another car full of inflatable water toys and fishing tackle.

Even after you bump-thump across Currituck or Croatan Sound and catch a glimpse of a lighthouse or the low line of the banks, you remain surrounded by trees. Suddenly, the road breaks out of the forests and you are looking at the sea oats beyond the flat roofs or beach grass and stilt-top houses. I remember childhood anticipation reaching a squealing fervor as we slow-laned through Manteo. I just wanted to see the waves—now!

Dare is the right place for that and more. Few counties in any state mix the energy of a free-wheeling, vigorous oceanfront with as many historically important and ecologically fascinating locations.

Topping the list are the more than 60 miles of some of the wildest and most accessible beachfront on the East Coast—the Dare County portion of the Cape Hatteras National Seashore. You can easily make more than one lengthy visit here and not exhaust the possibilities within its boundaries. There's so much beach that only the tide can cover it in a single summer.

This stretch of coast also includes the site of the first attempt by English-speaking people to settle the New World, the sands over which the first successful motor-powered flight soared, the highest sand dune on the East Coast, and the tallest brick lighthouse in the world. You can stand in the shade of one of the largest eastern maritime hardwood forests or enjoy the finest surf-fishing anywhere. Dare County wears many hats—from the unabashedly commercial to the modest, down-by-the-sea traditional—all in the face of a shaky coexistence with the sea. You'll see a little of both of these extremes and some of the gradations in between as you drive through the resort cities of Dare's lengthy barrier islands. It's a mix that's hard to match elsewhere.

Altogether, Dare encompasses 388 square miles of land and a lot more water—858 square miles to be exact. The county has three main segments: a mainland peninsula, Roanoke Island, and the barrier islands. The Dare County barrier islands, the state's easternmost outpost, comprise what is popularly referred to as the Outer Banks, from Duck in the north to Hatteras in the south. (The term should properly include Ocracoke and North and South Core Banks, Shackleford Banks, and Bogue Banks as well.)

Mainland Dare County is bounded by the Albemarle, Croatan, and Pamlico sounds and the Alligator River. Unpopulated is the rule—people are few and the communities are isolated amid vast acreages once owned by timber and farming corporations. In 1984, practically the entire mainland portion of Dare County was given to the U.S. Fish and Wildlife Service to establish the Alligator River Preserve, at the time the largest conservation gift ever made in the country. This refuge permanently protects one of the most pristine tracts of coastal forest and swamp remaining in the Southeast.

US 64 and 264 pass along the edges of the newly created refuge. Military jets pass over it en route to the multiservice target range west of Stumpy Point.

Few people visit this portion of Dare County. Except for two fishing hamlets, Manns Harbor and Stumpy Point, there are few facilities for travelers; most of the visitors to this section of the county come for the fishing and hunting. The riches of this majestic region are sequestered in the central and inaccessible portion of the peninsula.

Roanoke Island is the historical heart of the United States, the richly wooded isle where English-speaking people first attempted to establish a colony, an event commemorated at the Fort Raleigh National Historic Site. Bounded on the east by Roanoke Sound and the west by Croatan Sound, Roanoke has two main communities, Manteo and Wanchese. Still a local fishing village, Wanchese is the smaller of the two and slightly out of the way of the beach-bound traffic. Manteo, the county seat, bustles more. Traffic streams steadily along US 64/264, a few blocks west of this community's center. Development surged in the town in the early 1980s in advance of the four-hundredth anniversary celebration commemorating the first colony.

While the main landlord in Dare County is the U.S. Department of the Interior, the ocean is really in charge, particularly on the barrier islands. Historically (and presently), the ocean rearranges the beachfront with seeming arbitrariness, constantly redefining the county's boundaries. Bodie Island, Pea Island, and Hatteras Island are current names even though the inlets separating them have long closed. In October 1991, the sea tried to breach Pea Island again, swallowing fifty-year-old artificial dunes and nearly slicing through the NC 12 lifeline. That wasn't the first time and it certainly won't be the last. The ocean forces a dogged resignation among residents who cross their fingers during hurricane season and warily watch the dunes when "nor'easters" blow.

In August 1991, during the peak of the tourist season, Hurricane Bob tracked toward the Outer Banks with a projected landfall in Dare County. After local officials called for a voluntary evacuation, reporters asked why evacuation wasn't mandatory. The answer was simple and chilling: the bridges couldn't handle the traffic. Once you get there, you're there. Fortunately, the hurricane veered away from a direct hit.

The Outer Banks of Dare County are reasonably uniform in their physical characteristics and profile. A cross section of the islands would show them to be low in elevation, except for the artificially constructed dunes that the Civilian Conservation Corps built in the 1930s. The exceptions to this are the unusual stands of hardwood maritime forest in Nags Head and Buxton on older dune ridges and the massive dunes of Nags Head and Kill Devil Hills.

Typically, the beaches are wide and, due to the artificial dune line, slightly steeper than would occur naturally. Waves break with greater force in a shorter distance, carving an abrupt gradient; once, while body surfing, I rode a wave right into the beach, using my nose as a bumper.

The dune ridge is particularly evident in parts of the Pea Island National Wildlife Refuge south of Oregon Inlet where the dunes buttress the wet sand beach. However, a series of northeastern storms in the fall of 1991 chewed up the ridge, eating nearly to the road and leaving the roadway and the refuge ponds on the soundside unprotected. Before that storm, you almost fell to the beach from the dune crossovers because the dune ridge was so abrupt.

The beachfront changes compass alignment throughout the county. South of Rodanthe, the banks make a marked turn to the south. Above Rodanthe, then, the waves from "nor'easters" strike directly against the front of the beach; below Rodanthe, the storm action of the same "nor'easters" strikes the beach obliquely, paring away sand rather than pounding it free. Because of this, and the direction of prevailing winds as they tug at the sand, the profile of the dunes and oceanfront changes along the banks. The oblique wave action carves sharply into some stretches of the island. In the Ash Wednesday Storm of 1962, the ocean breached the dune line and severed NC 12 just north of Buxton.

People lived here long before tourism, and the commercial lifeblood of the oldest communities was the sea. Duck, Kitty Hawk, Manteo, Wanchese, Rodanthe, Waves, Salvo, Buxton, Frisco, and Hatteras were the original island villages. These communities grew with the establishment of the legendary life-saving stations of the late nineteenth century. Many homes, stores, and even station houses dating from this era are still standing. Here, older means wiser and closer to the soundside of the island.

A weathered serendipity cloaks the oldest parts of the villages, and it sometimes seems as though the tourism boom has visually overwhelmed these core areas, figuratively "outshouting" them for the attention of visitors. However, the villages survive on more than tourism. If you leave the beach and look around, you'll find the marinas, machine shops, and packing houses where the demanding life of commercial fishing survives. The Dare County banks are a hard place to be year-round. Being born to it helps.

Vacation construction started some years ago at Kitty Hawk and Nags Head, but it proceeded at a relatively slow pace even through the middle of this century. Great acreages on Bodie, Pea, and Hatteras islands remained undeveloped and were acquired for federal use for separate purposes in the 1930s and 1950s.

The boldest land acquisition program came in the 1950s for the Cape Hatteras National Seashore. The federal condemnation is still bitterly resented by some natives, but it established the basis of the booming tourism trade and protected the land from damaging development. However, it increased the value of the remaining private land, and it is on these holdings that resort building is thriving. Developers have already reached the limits and carrying capacity of the land in several of the historic communities.

From the Wright Memorial Bridge south to Whalebone Junction, Dare County is a vacation suburb. The three tourism-driven communities of Kitty Hawk, Kill Devil Hills, and Nags Head string continuously along the sands yet are distinguishable. Presently, most of the development is between the US 158 bypass and the ocean, but this is changing. The demand for second-home real estate is encroaching on the rich hardwood forests west of the bypass.

Visitors enjoy these three communities for what they are—jostling, energetic beach destinations—in addition to what is nearby—the Cape Hatteras National Seashore Recreation Area. The quieter hamlets of Rodanthe, Salvo, and Waves south of Oregon Inlet attract folks seeking fewer lights and less action.

The very northern Dare communities—Southern Shores, Duck, and Sanderling—are an easy drive from Roanoke Island. It's a whole new island world on the North Banks—still "beachy" but with a capital "B" for "Boutique."

Jockey's Ridge State Park is in the Nags Head town limits. The Wright Brothers National Memorial towers over Kill Devil Hills, and the Nags Head Woods Ecological Preserve protects a substantial acreage of the soundside maritime forest. Each is worth a stop.

The expanse of the unpopulated national seashore beach and the variety of recreational experiences make Dare County popular. You will queue up at some attractions, but along the national seashore, you can enjoy the luxury of having the beach much to yourself; everyone should try it at least once.

Access

The individual municipalities and management agencies in Dare County provide beach access locations. The towns of Kitty Hawk, Kill Devil Hills, and Nags Head funnel great numbers of residents and visitors to the beach easily with ample and convenient parking. The access locations are clearly signed along NC 12; regional access locations are posted along the US 158 bypass.

There seems to be little trouble finding an access location or parking space during the week, but weekends are crowded. Move out early.

Dare County provides numerous fishing and boating access locations, including boat-launching sites on the sounds. These locations are in addition to other facilities provided by the National Park Service, the U.S. Fish and Wildlife Service, and the North Carolina Wildlife Resources Commission, which are listed in the appropriate sections that follow.

In Duck, there is an unmarked basin and boat tie-up behind Wee Winks Square shopping center.

In Kitty Hawk, there is a boat ramp, docking space, and a large parking area at the end of Bob Perry Road.

On Roanoke Island, Dare County Airport Recreation Area next to the old Manns Harbor ferry dock has a boat ramp best suited for four-wheel-drive vehicles. There is a signed public boat-launching ramp just south of the Wanchese Fish Company building in Wanchese on Mill Creek. The Manteo Public Boat Landing, which includes a public boat ramp, dock, and parking area, is located at the east end of Ananias Dare Street in Manteo. The land south of the west end of the new Washington Baum Bridge is proposed as a boat-launching ramp and parking area. It is informally used as such at present.

In Avon, there is a harbor located at the west end of Avon Road.

In Buxton, the county owns the harbor just west of the village and east of Billy's Seafood Restaurant.

In Hatteras, the county has two parking spaces and a boat dock easement at the privately operated Hatteras Harbor Marina, where the public may use two boat ramps adjacent to the marina for a $4 fee.

There are also public boat-launching facilities on the mainland at Manns Harbor, Stumpy Point Basin, Lake Worth, Mashoes, and East Lake.

Handicapped Access

Most of the National Park Service facilities and all of the state parks and historic sites are handicapped accessible.

Handicapped accessibility to the beach varies with each municipality. All regional access locations and most neighborhood access locations are accessible to the handicapped. Site-specific information is listed in the specific discussions of individual municipalities that follow.

Information

For information, contact Dare County Tourist Bureau, P.O. Box 399, Manteo, NC 27954, 919-473-2138, or Outer Banks Chamber of Commerce, P.O. Box 1757, Kill Devil Hills, NC 27948, 919-441-8144 (North Beaches), 919-995-4213 (Hatteras Island and Ocracoke).

For information about Cape Hatteras National Seashore, Fort Raleigh National Historic Site, or the Wright Brothers National Memorial, contact Superintendent, Group Headquarters, Cape Hatteras National Seashore, Route 1 Box 675, Manteo, NC 27954, 919-473-2111.

The North Banks

Until 1984, there was a guardhouse on NC 12 at the northern border of Dare County north of the Sanderling Resort, restricting access further north to property owners and their guests. The solitude and isolated exclusivity of Currituck Banks left with the guardhouse that year. In many ways, so did old Duck, a charming fishing village in Dare County that became the epicenter of a real estate explosion that piled on the sands of all the available land north of Southern Shores.

If you drive from the northern end of Dare County to the US 158 bypass, you'll see about the best of the 1980s oceanfront development. It is private and it is exclusive by price alone—the Palmer Island Club property is at the northern limits of the county and many bank accounts.

Today, almost everything north of Southern Shores is new and experiencing a gush of celebrity as a trendy place to visit. In less than a decade, Sanderling and Duck became vacation destinations of a new order. Ten years ago, Sanderling was a back-dune shrub flat and Duck was a bend in the road with a fishing tackle shop, Wee Winks Grocery, a deli, a gallery, and the beginnings of second-home construction.

Sanderling sometimes causes confusion. It is posted as a village but it is a private resort beginning at the Dare County line and continuing south for a mile or two. It feels like a village though, and if you are renting a place there, you will be treated as a villager and have access to all the amenities packaged within the resort. Duck has a nice mix of wild and remote softened with specialty indulgences. There's no water slide, but there is sailboat and windsurfing rental. In fact, Duck mirrors the contradictions and conflicts of its mid-life visitors. It is the resort equivalent of the fat-free, all-natural, frozen yogurt hot fudge sundae.

Access

Day visitors will have a difficult time finding sufficient parking close to the ocean. There are no public access locations maintained by the county. Your best bet is to continue north to the access points at Whalehead Beach in Currituck County. The villages of Sanderling, Duck, and Southern Shores developed as a series of private subdivisions and

	Fee	Parking	Restrooms	Lifeguard	Camping	Showers	Beach Access	Hiking	Trail	Handicapped	Boating	ORV Access	Fishing	Programs	Historic	Sand Beach	Dunes	Upland	Wetland
U.S. Army Research Pier		•					•						•	•		•	•		
Duck		•											•	•		•	•	•	•
Public Boating Access: Duck Landing	•										•		•						•

have no formal public beach access. Beach access is by private rental.

From Currituck County south to Kitty Hawk, the only public access is at a U.S. Army Corps of Engineers research station, located just south of the Duck Volunteer Fire Department building. There are 20 parking spaces, and in spite of the ominous signs, folks are welcome to use them.

There is one unmarked boat basin and tie-up behind Wee Wink's Square shopping center in Duck.

Handicapped Access

The Sanderling Inn is accessible for the handicapped, and a boardwalk leads to a gazebo at the primary dunes.

Information

For information, contact Dare County Tourist Bureau, P.O. Box 399, Manteo, NC 27954, 919-473-2138, or Outer Banks Chamber of Commerce, P.O. Box 1757, Kill Devil Hills, NC 27948, 919-441-8144.

Sanderling

The symbolic heart of the Sanderling development is the Sanderling Restaurant and Bar, which is housed in the original Caffey's Inlet Life-Saving Station. The station was constructed in 1899, one of a series of outposts located every 7 miles along the coastline of Virginia and North Carolina. There were two stations at Corolla (including the lighthouse), one at nearby Ocean Sands, and so on down the Outer Banks. The station was named for Caffey's Inlet, which used to breach the banks just north of the Currituck County line before a storm closed it in 1828. The area remains one of the narrowest stretches of the North Banks.

In 1981, the building was placed on the National Register of Historic Places. In spite of its historic significance, the structure was severely deteriorated and only a thorough renovation for the Sanderling development saved it from collapse.

In 1985, Sanderling modified the old station to become a restaurant.

Personally, I think life-saving stations make very nice restaurants (at least the three I have visited). When you sit in the rich pine interior of the three-bay boathouse, you feel the echoes of security that the sturdily constructed building projects.

The original sign from the Caffey's Inlet Life-Saving Station is in the hands of the owners of Owens' Restaurant in Nags Head, which is housed in the old station house at Whalebone Junction.

Access

Beach access is by private rental.

Handicapped Access

The Sanderling Inn is accessible for handicapped individuals and a boardwalk leads to a gazebo at the primary dunes.

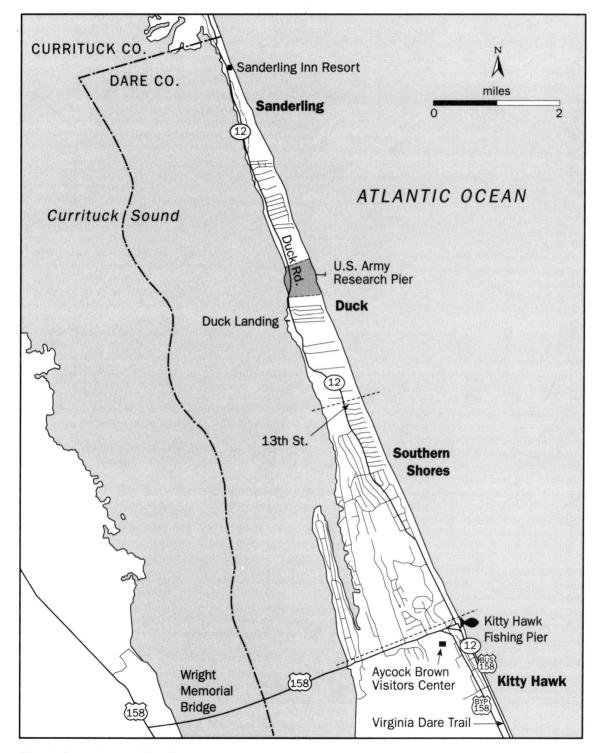

CURRITUCK CO.

DARE CO.

Sanderling Inn Resort

Sanderling

(12)

Currituck Sound

Duck Rd.

U.S. Army
Research Pier

Duck

Duck Landing

ATLANTIC OCEAN

N

miles

0   2

(12)

13th St.

**Southern
Shores**

Kitty Hawk
Fishing Pier

(12)

Wright
Memorial
Bridge

(158)

Aycock Brown
Visitors Center

BUS
158

Kitty Hawk

(158)

BYP
158

Virginia Dare Trail

Map 4. Sanderling to Kitty Hawk

Just What Is Level about the Sea?

It is a sound assumption that the rest of North Carolina is uphill from your beach perch. But how much so? Precise elevations of inland locations use the level of the sea as their base reference. But the ocean is not constant. Exactly where, then, is sea level?

Geologists wrangle with solving this "problem like Maria": "How do you trap a wave upon the sand," at least long enough to calibrate the heights of mountains and buildings and the depths of valleys worldwide? Sea level is surprisingly neither constant around the world, varying from shore to shore, nor static over time, having wildly fluctuated throughout prehistory. Evidence indicates that it is rising now.

The National Ocean Service uses a device known as a tide gauge to derive a base sea-level measure. A mechanical tide gauge is a simple device consisting of a float inside a perforated pipe. Wire links the float to a pulley, which in turn drives a screw-operated stylus that marks a clock-operated drum. The markings on the drum provide a time graph of the level of the sea. The perforations in the pipe are below tide level to minimize float movement from passing waves. To further reduce wave interference, geologists place tide gauges at the ends of piers extending several hundred feet from the shoreline. There are about 150 such locations throughout the United States, and one in Duck, the U.S. Army Research Pier, is occasionally open to the public for limited visitation.

Records reveal that tidal action varies within a month, between months, and from year to year. Because the longest cycle of tidal variation takes about 18.75 years, a continuous recording from a tidal gauge that is at least 19 years in duration qualifies to become a determinant of sea level at the station of record. Mean sea level, our base measuring reference for heights, is the average height from such a series of recordings.

Precise surveying can extend these levels across land to compare them with those obtained independently at other locations. The results are astonishing: sea level on the west coast of Florida is 7 inches higher than at east coast locations of the peninsula; the Pacific coast averages 20 inches higher than the Atlantic. You can claim to sail up-water if you pass through the Panama Canal into the Pacific, climbing nearly a foot.

These circumstances are unlevel-

U.S. Army Research Pier

The U.S. Army Corps of Engineers Coastal Engineering Research Center's Field Research Facility in Duck monitors physiographic changes along the coastline. The heart of this research station is its over 1,880-foot-long concrete pier, which was built to last and extends from the largest remaining tract of Duck beachfront that is not growing some type of house or condominium (176 acres). The site was acquired from the U.S. Navy in 1973, and the facility officially opened in 1980. Its purpose is to provide a study platform to collect long-term data on waves, currents, water levels, and bottom changes, particularly during storms. The station also serves as a location for numerous other experiments, including the testing of new instruments, as well as a place to study barrier island ecological trends.

It is one of a limited number of sites nationwide where scientists gather data to compute the long-term trends in sea-level fluctuation, making it an official tidal-monitoring station. There is a continually running tidal gauge at the end of the pier that hovers above the 25-foot water depth. The small outbuilding to say the least, and there is no completely satisfactory reason for the variation. Water temperature and barometric pressure have known effects that chip away at constancy— water expands when heated and rises in level when the atmospheric pressure is low. Prevailing winds, water density differences because of salinity, and the shape of the near-shore ocean bottom contribute to sea-level variation between locations. Even the rotation of the earth and its effect on major currents such as the Gulf Stream (which is lower on the east side than on the west) can rearrange sufficient water to alter sea level. Each of these factors differs between locations—they are local conditions—and can account for some of the intracontinental variations. So can the unsettling fact that some coastlines are sinking into the seas.

Historically, sea level changes at any given location as well. Data indicates that presently sea level is rising—or the land where any given tidal gauge is fixed is subsiding. A worldwide rise in sea level is called a eustatic change. Several factors or a combination of factors might be responsible for the observed increase: a change in the total amount of water held on land in the form of ice, snow, and bodies of water; a change in the capacity of the ocean basin through deformation, sedimentation, or volcanism; and changes in the total amount of water on the earth. Meteorologists and coastal geologists cite a climatic warming trend that is releasing water held in the form of ice and snow as the most likely cause of the recent rising level. If this is so, then we are faced with an inexorable, unstoppable, and unmanageable coastal alteration that could have catastrophic consequences.

Although such a transformation is a long-term change, telltale signs will be apparent. Once-safe cottages (and lighthouses) may soon topple into the surf, deprived of the protective sands of beaches that have been trifled away by the gradual rise in the ocean's surface.

Much as we might wish it so, the surface of the ocean is not steady. It is on the move—upward. Which brings to mind a disturbing question: How high is Mount Mitchell? Its elevation is 6,684 feet above sea level— for now.

ing at the end of the pier can be moved back into the protection of the main building on shore during severe storms—a necessary precaution since storm waves have actually slapped holes in this concrete pier.

A number of agencies including the National Ocean Survey and the National Weather Service use the site. Occasionally you may see the Coastal Research Amphibious Buggy (CRAB), a remarkable self-powered, three-legged tower that makes precise measurements of the sea floor just beyond the breaking waves.

Access

Don't let the fence intimidate you. These folks are nice and don't mind visitors. The facility is open 9 A.M. to 4:30 P.M. weekdays, and there is parking for about 20 cars. You may use the beach on either side of the pier. Do not walk through the service yard but follow the clearly worn paths that flank the buildings. Access may be restricted during ongoing experiments and certain times of the year.

Between June 15 and August 15, at 10 A.M. on weekdays, public tours provide an introduction to oceanography, showing the types of instruments used at the station and the ongoing experiments. Should you miss the tour, stop and read the gazebo displays in the parking lot. One fascinating map dates the known migrations of Oregon Inlet — it moves around a lot more than you would suspect.

Information

For information, contact the station at 919-261-3511.

Duck

Don't let the lack of public access to the beach keep you from going to Duck or you'll miss a major North Banks event. What fifteen years ago was a waddle in the sand between Southern Shores and Corolla is now the commercial and recreational center of the northern Outer Banks.

Duck boomed, and not from the sound of shotguns aiming at the namesake waterfowl but from the sound of hammers. Not-so-old-timers recall the Duck Deli, the Wee Winks Grocery, the Duck Blind Art Gallery, one tackle shop, and a United Methodist church as being Duck. A handful of residential structures and the "S" curve in the road that let you see Currituck Sound before swerving to avoid a splash completed Dare County's frontier outpost.

What's here today is the best of the get-away-from-it-all, but not *too* far, development of the last decade. There's still the air of solitude that has blessed these low barrier beaches for a long time, but the new

Duck hasn't weathered like the old Duck yet. It's still a little too new. The paint needs to peel. But what makes it work is the reasonably sensitive construction respecting the existing maritime forest. Unlike the more commercial locations further south, you don't see Duck all at once. The road snakes and winds, and the shopping clusters are just that — separate groupings along the road.

There has been an obvious attempt to inject an authentic flair into the architecture here. Scarborough Faire, a 1980s clustering of individual buildings linked with boardwalks, may be one of the most delightful shopping centers you will ever explore. The live oaks left behind by careful contractors make it a cool place to be. The Waterfront Shops, perched on the west side of the barrier, offer a fine view of the gorgeous sunsets over Currituck Sound. Other shopping clusters — Loblolly Pines, Wee Winks Square, and the Duck Soundside Shop — fill other seasonal retail demands for the many visitors.

Duck has been a destination for hunters since sometime in the nineteenth century — some speculate very early in the century. The namesake waterfowl populations are no longer evident. Instead of ducks in winter, visitors flock here nearly throughout the year. Possibly what brings them here is the fact that there are no motels or hotels but plenty of single-family homes available for vacation rentals instead. This emphasis on single-

family dwellings reduces required parking spaces and keeps development very close to the natural carrying capacity of the land. It may be a little glitzy for some, but it's a credible compromise between vacation dreams and natural realities.

Access

Beach access is by private rental.

Handicapped Access

Several of the commercial shopping areas such as Scarborough Faire and the Waterfront Shops are accessible for the handicapped.

Information

For information, contact Dare County Tourist Bureau, P.O. Box 399, Manteo, NC 27954, 919-473-2138, or Outer Banks Chamber of Commerce, P.O. Box 1757, Kill Devil Hills, NC 27948, 919-441-8144.

Southern Shores

Between Duck and US 158 is the almost completely residential community of Southern Shores, which incorporated in 1979, having steadily grown since the first houses were built there in the 1950s. The northern limit of the town is Thirteenth Street, just about 1.5 miles from downtown Duck.

One of the more compelling images of the Southern Shores oceanfront are some distinctive, flat-roofed concrete-block homes along NC 12, most of which are just north of US 158. Some are brightly painted and evoke thoughts of earlier Florida retirement homes. These modest, durable block houses now serve as a foil for the custom-home architecture that draws heavily upon the tradition distinguishing the U.S. Life-Saving Service stations of the nineteenth century.

Southern Shores' new town hall sits elegantly at the intersection of US 158 and NC 12. The recently completed building mimics the mass, detailing, and basic design of the life-saving stations that once stood along the banks.

Access

Southern Shores provides no public access to the beach but it does provide parking for members of the Southern Shores Civic Association. Only homeowners, tenants, and their guests may use the access areas. If you rent a cottage in Southern Shores, the realty agency will usually make the arrangements. To become a member, you must show proof of ownership or rental and pay a $2 fee.

Information

For information, contact Dare County Tourist Bureau, P.O. Box 399, Manteo, NC 27954, 919-473-2138, or Outer Banks Chamber of Commerce, P.O. Box 1757, Kill Devil Hills, NC 27948, 919-441-8144.

Aycock Brown Visitors Center

A stop at the new Aycock Brown Visitors Center at the junction of US 158 and NC 12, at the Kitty Hawk city limits, can save you time and update your tourism information. The visitors center has restrooms, picnic sites, pay phones, and easy access back onto the US 158 bypass heading south.

You can pick up various publications that highlight upcoming events and possible destinations, in addition to information on interpretive programs at the Cape Hatteras National Seashore and ferry schedules.

Locations are referenced in the publications to mileposts that are numbered 1 through 16 south from the Wright Memorial Bridge along NC 12 or Virginia Dare Trail, referred to locally as Beach Road. (NC 12 north from Whalebone Junction is signed as the Marc Basnight Highway.) There are milepost markers along the US 158 bypass as well. This is an excellent system for daytime navigation, but at night it is difficult to read the mileposts. I recommend that you ask for a landmark in addition to the milepost reference mark.

Be aware that it is more difficult to read the milepost markers on the widened bypass. You might have more success driving along Beach Road, but beware that traffic moves at a slower pace on this road, depending on the time of day and the day of the week.

One other practical tip is that left turns onto the bypass can be hazardous, particularly at night. If you can plan your route to avoid left turns onto the bypass from streets without traffic lights, you'll find errand running far less stressful.

Access

Aycock Brown Visitors Center is open year-round 9 A.M. to 5 P.M. daily.

Handicapped Access

The visitors center is fully accessible for the handicapped.

Information

For information, call the center at 919-261-4644 or 1-800-446-6262 on weekends.

Kitty Hawk

Kitty Hawk is the northernmost and smallest of the resort communities along the 16-mile playground between the Wright Memorial Bridge and the Washington Baum Bridge. The northern town limit is effectively US 158, which separates Kitty Hawk and Southern Shores. The popular notion is that Kitty Hawk is situated between NC 12 or Virginia Dare Trail (known as Beach Road) and the US 158 bypass, the five-lane expressway that serves as the commercial-services corridor for the community. This pairing of roads continues the full length of Kitty Hawk and Kill Devil Hills, ending at Whalebone Junction in Nags

	Fee	Parking	Restrooms	Lifeguard	Camping	Showers	Beach Access	Hiking	Trail	Handicapped	Boating	ORV Access	Fishing	Programs	Historic	Sand Beach	Dunes	Upland	Wetland
Aycock Brown Visitors Center		•	•							•				•					
Kitty Hawk	•	•											•		•	•	•	•	•
Public Boating Access: Bob Perry Rd.	•										•		•						•
Regional Access: Kitty Hawk	•	•	•		•	•				•			•			•	•		

Head. However, Kitty Hawk actually extends well into the great maritime forest west of US 158. Many of the approximately 1,500 permanent residents live in the Kitty Hawk woods, most residents being slightly closer to the sound than to the oceanfront. The Sea Scape golf community, carved out of the woods and dunes along the west side of the highway, is the most visible development. A new city hall building sits in a beautifully rich forest setting west of the bypass.

Kitty Hawk Road, SR 1206, leads inland through the original settlement of Kitty Hawk, perhaps settled in the late eighteenth century. The first inhabitants built within the shelter and safety of the extensive maritime forests covering the western portion of the barrier island. The houses of old Kitty Hawk, many of which are early twentieth century, are country farmhouses, not stylized vacation homes. Orville and Wilbur Wright stayed in such a farmhouse or "country house" when they first traveled to the desolate, windswept island. The architecture

reflects the need for durable year-round housing among the watermen and tradesmen who called Kitty Hawk home.

During the late nineteenth and early twentieth centuries, the only long-term occupants of the beach were members of the U.S. Life-Saving Service, which had a station at Kitty Hawk Road and Virginia Dare Trail.

Kitty Hawk has about 3.5 miles of oceanfront, between the Kitty Hawk Fishing Pier and the Kill Devil Hills city limits, just south of milepost 5; the Decharmarnel Campground on Virginia Dare Trail serves as an informal landmark of the city limits.

Kitty Hawk is growing, but not at the same rate occurring elsewhere in Dare County. The town is casual both in appearance and in attitude. The houses along the beachfront as well as the town there are simple and unadorned. Kitty Hawk doesn't resonate with the buzz of energy found in nearby Kill Devil Hills and Nags Head. Its mostly single-family residences and

businesses along Beach Road are small. There are a few sites for trailers and campers fairly close to the beach, and the town wears on you like a comfortable pair of cutoff jeans.

The beach at Kitty Hawk is generally steep and narrow. In past years, several cottages have fallen into the sea, and the sand in some locations rolls back over the road as well. Kitty Hawk has turned these sudden beachfront vacancies, not suitable for reconstruction and ineligible for beach replenishment, into access locations for visitors. A few houses along Virginia Dare Trail seemed poised for their last seasons.

Most of the land is privately held, but a few hotels or cottage rentals stand available within the city limits. There are some fine smaller places to rent, and even in peak season Kitty Hawk will be full and busy but not nearly as frantic as its neighbors.

Kitty Hawk Fishing Pier has a rough-hewn sturdiness appropriate to a long-standing, weatherbeaten platform. It's a good place to stop

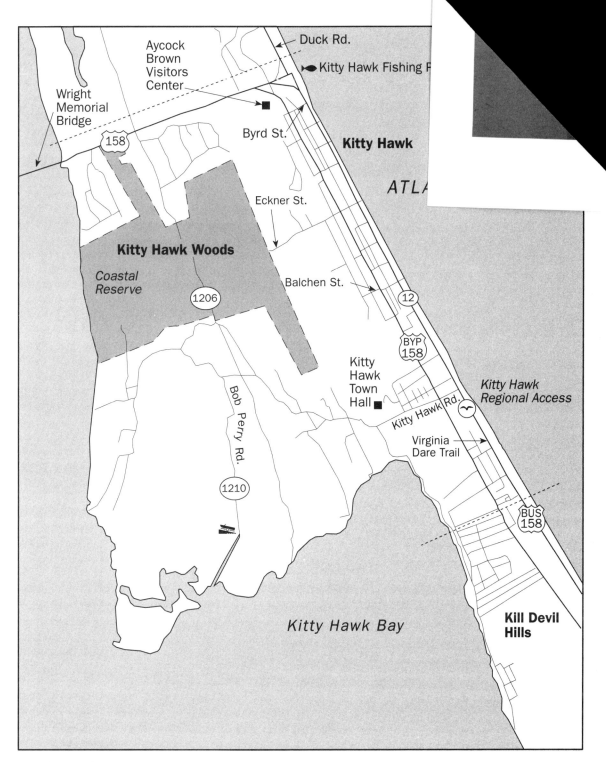

Map 5. Kitty Hawk

Beachgoers at Kitty Hawk. (Courtesy of N.C. Coastal Management Commission)

for a very large, very reasonable breakfast. Another attraction is the former Station Six Restaurant at Virginia Dare Trail and Kitty Hawk Road. The renovated Kitty Hawk Beach Life-Saving Station quarters, constructed in 1874, housed the restaurant. One of the original stations authorized for the Outer Banks by the U.S. Congress, it was part of Life-Saving District 6, along with six other stations along the North Carolina coast and three in Virginia Beach.

The architecture is stunning. The cypress was shipped by barge from the mainland, and the detailing in the carpentry is among the most intriguing and intricate of all the U.S. Life-Saving Service structures remaining today. The station was relocated from its earlier location on the beach in the 1970s. Its companion in lore and history, the old brown-shingled U.S. Coast Guard Station, once across Virginia Dare Trail from Station Six, has been relocated about one block south, saving it from undermining by the ocean. Its distinctive architecture and towering height make it easy to find. Just south of Station Six is the Kitty Hawk regional beach access site. The beach it serves took a lick-

ing during a storm in October 1991, and the ocean is growlingly close to the road.

Access

It's easy to find the access sites. Most of the major east-west streets have an access right-of-way at the beachfront. The town is planning to improve the access areas at the eastern end of Byrd and Balchen streets.

There is presently only one regional access site at Kitty Hawk, south of Kitty Hawk Road on Virginia Dare Trail about milepost 4.5. It has parking spaces for 50 vehicles and a bathhouse and restrooms, open 10 A.M. to 6 P.M. Lifeguards watch the beach during the summer season.

There is a boat ramp, docking space, and a large parking area at the end of Bob Perry Road. There is also an unimproved access site at the eastern terminus of US 158 (the road actually continues south at this point) near the Kitty Hawk Fishing Pier.

Handicapped Access

The regional access site south of Kitty Hawk Road is fully handicapped accessible.

Information

For information, contact Dare County Tourist Bureau, P.O. Box 399, Manteo, NC 27954, 919-473-2138, or Outer Banks Chamber of Commerce, P.O. Box 1757, Kill Devil Hills, NC 27948, 919-441-8144.

Kill Devil Hills

The tempo picks up considerably at Kill Devil Hills even though you ease into it from Kitty Hawk. The two communities share much historically. Before incorporating in 1953, Kill Devil Hills was a township within Kitty Hawk. But there seems to have been more room to grow and more willingness to do so in Kill Devil Hills, now the largest municipality in Dare County, with a year-round population of more than 4,000 and a seasonal population of 40,000. There are more seasonal businesses in Kill Devil Hills, and

the 4.7 miles of beach hop a little faster. There is more of a skyline and a little less space between buildings, too.

The origin of the name of Kill Devil Hills may have been a comment attributed to William Byrd dating from 1728. He reported that a New England rum favored by the inhabitants on these sandy and isolated shores of the Outer Banks was strong enough to "kill the devil." This remark, combined with the unusually large hills of sand dominating the barrier island, possibly led to the naming of the largest hill as "Kill Devil Hill" on an 1808 map.

Kill Devil Hills has always been dependably windy. Winds moved the sand around and kept Kill Devil Hills practically green-free from the maritime forest to the ocean. The large dunes migrated willy-nilly, back and forth, south to north with the annual cycle of steadily prevailing winds, and vegetation could not root in the moving sand. In the late nineteenth and early twentieth centuries, few obstructions such as beach grass, shrubs, or trees interrupted the breezes—it was a great place to fly a human-sized glider.

That's what two bicycle-building brothers from Ohio thought, anyway. After diligent research, they decided to bring their experiments to Kill Devil Hills, establishing a workshop at the foot of the 90-foot summit of Big Kill Devil Hill in 1900. Among the few witnesses to the repeated trials conducted over a three-year period were members of the crew that manned the Kitty Hawk Life-Saving Station who

assisted the brothers in their experiments. Memorabilia from those first flight attempts is visible at the Wright Brothers National Memorial, of course, but also at the offices of Twiddy and Company Real Estate in Corolla, where the Kitty Hawk Life-Saving Station was relocated and restored for private use.

It is difficult to envision Kill Devil Hills bare of trees or vegetation, but that was pretty much the case until the Great Depression. In 1928 the U.S. Army Corps of Engineers stabilized Big Kill Devil Hill by planting grass. When the sand from that dune and others nearby was anchored, the soundside vegetation had a chance to grow as well.

Kill Devil Hills has many private homes, but it also has many motels and locations that cater to the summer vacationers. Since the local economy hinges on tourism, the town actually markets its beach access program and provides clearly marked sites. During the summer season, finding a single room for one night during the weekend is difficult, but you will find access to the beach convenient.

Access

Kill Devil Hills provides 27 public beach access areas, 20 of which are improved and have parking spaces. Parking is on a first-come, first-served basis so arrive early. Do not block access to the beach for emergency vehicles. The access areas are clearly marked at many east-west streets crossing Virginia Dare Trail or NC 12 (Beach Road). The following neighborhood access loca-

	Fee	Parking	Restrooms	Lifeguard	Camping	Showers	Beach Access	Hiking	Trail	Handicapped	Boating	ORV Access	Fishing	Programs	Historic	Sand Beach	Dunes	Upland	Wetland
Kill Devil Hills		•	•	•	•		•						•		•	•	•	•	•
Regional Access: Ocean Bay Blvd.		•	•	•		•	•			•		•	•			•	•		
Public Boating Access: Kitty Hawk Bay		•									•								
Wright Brothers National Memorial	•	•	•					•		•				•	•				
Nags Head Woods		•	•					•	•	•			•					•	•

tions offer the most parking: Helga Street, Chowan Street, and Hayman Boulevard north of the Avalon Pier; and Fifth Street, Second Street, First Street, and Ashville Drive.

The nine streets south of Raleigh Avenue have beach access at their eastern terminus and intersect US 158 across from the Wright Brothers National Memorial. There is a regional access site with a bathhouse and restrooms on Ocean Bay Boulevard. To reach this site, turn east off of the US 158 bypass at the traffic light at Colington Road (Ocean Bay Boulevard), just past the Wright Brothers Memorial. South of the memorial are access locations at Clark, Calvin, Martin, and Atlantic streets.

Several ramps serve off-road vehicles. Between October 1 and April 30 you may drive on the beach.

The North Carolina Wildlife Resources Commission maintains a fishing and boating access area on Kitty Hawk Bay at Avalon Beach, ½ mile west of US 158 on Dock Street. Parking is available, and there is no launch fee. There is also a pedestrian access area to the sound at Hayman Street with parking and a pier for fishing or crabbing. It's a quiet spot with a guaranteed beautiful sunset. Take along some insect repellent if you're going to be there for any length of time.

Handicapped Access

The neighborhood access site at Second Street has a dune crossover and deck accessible for the handicapped.

The Ocean Bay Boulevard regional access site is completely handicapped accessible and has handicapped parking spaces.

Information

For information, contact Dare County Tourist Bureau, P.O. Box 399, Manteo, NC 27954, 919-473-2138, or Outer Banks Chamber of Commerce, P.O. Box 1757, Kill Devil Hills, NC 27948, 919-441-8144.

For a map of the town with a description of municipal services and important information for visitors, write Office of the Town Clerk, P.O. Box 1719, Kill Devil Hills, NC 27948.

Wright Brothers National Memorial

The pylon dedicated to the first motor-powered airplane flight dominates the west horizon of Kill Devil Hills. The other noticeable element in this historical composition is the nearly continual wind. If it hadn't been for this wind, the pylon might be in another state, perhaps Ohio.

With annual winds averaging 12 miles per hour and a soft, sandy beach for landing, Kill Devil Hills attracted inventors Wilbur and Orville Wright here between 1900 and 1903 for their flight experiments. You'll notice the "soft, sandy" landing spot is different today. The 90 feet of Big Kill Devil Hill, which supports the 60-foot pylon, was stabilized with grass in 1928.

The pylon was built with granite from Mount Airy, North Carolina, between 1928 and 1932 and was

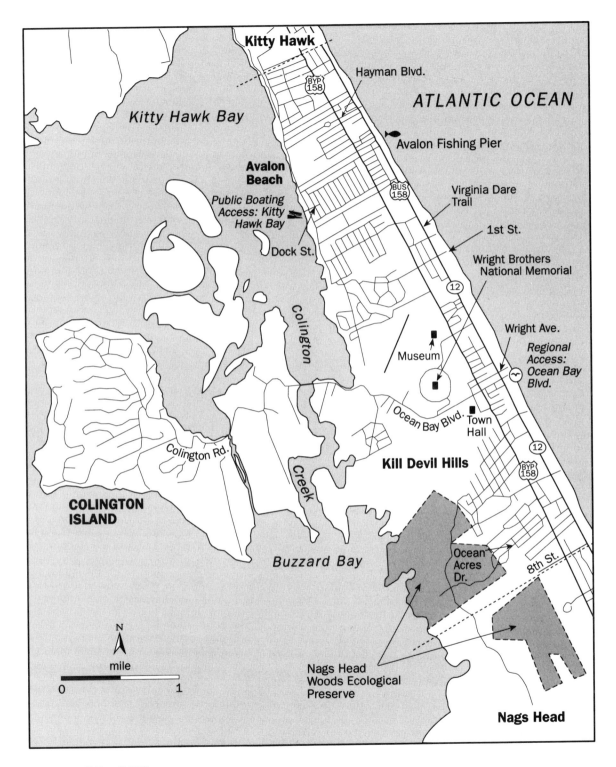

Map 6. Kill Devil Hills

The First Flight, 17 December 1903. (Courtesy of Library of Congress)

originally also to be a lighthouse. However, mariners used to the Currituck and Bodie Island lighthouses found this confusing, and the idea was abandoned. After its completion, builders imagined it would be a landmark for pilots during competitive cross-country flights. These races often used Kill Devil Hills as a terminus, demonstrating aviation's progress since December 17, 1903, the date of the first flight.

The pylon is stunning. At night the dramatic lighting makes it truly monumental. You can enter the monument and ascend 60 feet to an observation platform. Halfway up is a 1925 map of famous first flights to that date. The stairs are extremely narrow, and access is limited to summer months and special events.

A visitors center documenting the Wright brothers' achievements is open year-round and has replicas of the 1902 glider and the 1903 heavier-than-air craft. Outside the visitors center, the humble distances of humankind's first four powered flights are measured on the ground. As you walk them, overhead you are likely to see the jet contrails far above a sky of freely gliding gulls and terns. These exhibits represent the bridge between the two.

Interpretive talks bring life to the memorial, personifying the historical moment with anecdotal embellishment about the Wright brothers' trial-and-error effort. They are regularly scheduled and shouldn't be missed.

One tip: Shoes are a must if you walk to the monument. Kill Devil Hill and the field of the memorial grounds are covered with prickly pear cactus.

Access

The Wright Brothers National Memorial is open 9 A.M. to 5 P.M. (7 P.M. in summer), and there is an admission charge of $4 per car or $2 per person, which is good for seven days. You may visit the interior of the monument from June 16 to Labor Day, 3 P.M. to 4:30 P.M., if weather permits.

Handicapped Access

The visitors center is handicapped accessible although some assistance may be needed on the back patio. Wheelchairs are available in the center.

Information

For information, contact Wright Brothers National Memorial, c/o Superintendent, Cape Hatteras Group, Route 1 Box 675, Manteo, NC 27954, 919-441-7430.

Nags Head Woods Ecological Preserve

One of the finest remaining examples of a once-prevalent maritime ecosystem of the mid-Atlantic coast lies within the town limits of Kill Devil Hills and Nags Head—Nags Head Woods. The Nature Conservancy manages more than 1,100 acres of forest that matured in the sheltered lee side of the massive sand dunes. This unique preserve is open for limited visitation.

The Nature Conservancy purchased an initial 420-acre tract of land in 1978, most of which is in Kill Devil Hills. In 1984, the town of Nags Head bought 300 acres of similar woods within the town limits immediately south of the original Nature Conservancy land and agreed to let the conservancy manage the parcel. In October 1991, the town of Nags Head and the Nature Conservancy jointly purchased an additional 389-acre tract, immediately south of the 1984 Nags Head tract. In keeping with precedent, the conservancy manages this addition as well. Trails through the woods originate from a visitors center on the Nature Conservancy land. The center has parking and provides

interpretive material that helps explain the significance of Nags Head Woods.

The preserve is a very complex piece of the Outer Banks. Within its boundaries are 300–500-year-old trees (southern red oaks), freshwater ponds with rare aquatic plants, nesting sites of several threatened and endangered birds, among them the osprey and pileated woodpecker, and plants that are at the extremes of their geographic range, such as woolly beach heather, a tough, diminutive, dune-field plant that has not been found further south than Nags Head Woods. The woods are sheltered by two great sand dunes, Run Hill and Jockey's Ridge, that deflect salty winds, allowing the forest to perpetuate and survive. The mix of plants may seem ordinary to visitors from Piedmont locations since similar plant associations are found far to the west and at considerably higher elevations. However, this is one of a very few places where you will find such associations on the Outer Banks.

Perhaps the greatest pleasure in Nags Head Woods is the hush of the isolated forest cove, only a very big dune away from the sights and sounds of a resort beach. Two trails penetrate the woods, one ¼ mile long and the other 2¼ miles. Interpretive guides to the loop walks are available at the visitors center.

Special programs such as guided canoe tours of the sound adjacent to the woods are offered occasionally during the summer. Naturalists

conduct the tours, and a small fee is charged for the outing.

There is a sign directing you to the visitors center from the US 158 bypass at Ocean Acres Drive, just before milepost 10. Turn west at McDonald's Restaurant onto Ocean Acres Drive and continue toward the sound. The road in the preserve is not paved.

Access

The center is open to Nature Conservancy members Monday–Friday during daylight hours and on Saturdays between Memorial Day and Labor Day. Nonmembers may visit Tuesdays, Thursdays, and Saturdays, 10 A.M. to 3 P.M. You must register in the center before hiking the trails.

Handicapped Access

At present, the trails are not wheelchair accessible, but there is a ramp to the observation deck of the visitors center and there are accessible restrooms in the center.

Information

For information, contact Nags Head Woods Ecological Preserve, Visitors Center, 701 West Ocean Acres Drive, Nags Head, NC 27948, 919-441-2525.

Nags Head

Nags Head is the weathered, historic heart of the summer resorts on the Outer Banks, popular as a

Roll Tide Roll

Do you feel drawn to an ocean moonrise? Physically pulled? The moon moves oceans—why not people? It commits gravity on the high seas, and we call this influence the tides. Molecule by molecule, the sea answers to the gravitational draw of the moon and sun. Each molecule moves on cue, and the sea crawls up and back on the sands to a metronome that beats from the heavens. What draws the sea most is not the sun's infinitely larger mass but the smaller moon's proximity.

The more you visit the coast, the more the tidal pattern becomes apparent to you. Inasmuch as the moon rises later each day by an average of 50 minutes, the high tide also occurs later on subsequent days. In fact, the full tidal cycle is 24 hours and 50.4 minutes. You may also notice that as the moon passes through its phases, waning from full to new then waxing to full again, the height of the tidal rise corresponds. When the moon, earth, and sun are aligned during the full and new moons, the highest or spring tides swell landward. The combined gravitational pull of the sun and moon summons the ocean waters to their greatest flood, about 20 percent greater than normal. In addition, the moon's elliptical orbit carries it closer to the earth once every revolution. If this minimal orbital distance coincides with the new or full moon, perigean spring tides result—the highest of the cyclical tidal flows. During quarter phases of the moon, when the direction of the gravitational pull of the moon and sun are perpendicular to each other, the lowest, or neap, tides occur. The period between spring tides and neap tides is fourteen days, corresponding to the time lapse between full and new moons and the lapse between the moon's quarter phases.

So much for the astral mechanism behind the tides—if only tidal variation were so straightforward. As with almost everything about the ocean, the tidal picture is far more complicated, particularly along a shoreline as geographically jigsawed as North Carolina's. Local tidal variations are something you have surely noted, even if only in glances at the tidal tables published daily in coastal

retreat since the 1830s. Its resort value began similarly to other sea island getaways—as a refuge from the heat, humidity, and mosquitoes of mainland plantations. The history of its development parallels the stories of Kitty Hawk and Kill Devil Hills. There are local spins to each, but there are more similarities than differences.

The center for this early escapism was Old Nags Head, on the sound. A road south of Jockey's Ridge State Park angles back to the vicinity of the old village center. A few of the older homes can be seen, but it is otherwise an unremarkable side trip.

A bustling hotel on pilings, literally over the water, stood near here in the 1850s, with a dock for a shallow-draft paddle-wheel steamer that brought visitors from Roanoke Island and mainland towns such as Elizabeth City (the point of departure for the Wright brothers). This original hotel burned during the Civil War, but another followed in its place in the 1870s. Sometime in the late Victorian era, a mule-powered railway began carrying visitors across the island to the ocean.

The present oceanfront community began when some of the residents sold "worthless" lots on the ocean to wealthy coastal plain residents who eventually built summer cottages on their beachfront lots large enough to accommodate the entire family plus servants. These rustic cottages, several of which remain, became the nucleus of the early resort development.

Nags Head stayed "exclusive" and

newspapers. Why doesn't high tide occur everywhere at once? Because the great rolling wave of high tide set in motion by the varying cosmic alignments is modified by the topography of the local shoreline.

When it is "hoigh toid" on the "soundsoid"—as Ocracoke natives would say—it is not high tide across the sound at Swan Quarter. Similarly, the shifting inlets of the Outer Banks have different occurrences of highs and lows. The slope of the ocean or sound basin, the width of an inlet, and the depth of a channel leading from ocean to sound all affect the timing of tidal highs and lows. Simply put, the water cannot move through the inlets easily, and so high tide comes later—on average—the greater the distance from open ocean water.

Armed with the detailed knowledge of such local conditions, the U.S. Coast and Geodetic Survey can predict the time and approximate height of the tide at any given location. The knowledge of the tidal cycles is tremendously important for commercial and sportfishermen who must navigate inlets and pursue fish that feed on the flooding or rising tide.

North Carolina's semidiurnal or twice-daily tidal rhythm—two high tides and two low tides each day—is normal for the Atlantic coast. The highs and lows that occur are very similar, covering or failing to cover approximately the same amount of beach as the previous pair in the tidal cycle. Yet this pattern is not the norm for the Pacific coast, where a high high tide then a low low tide are followed by a lower high tide and a higher low tide. Along the Gulf coast, tidal change is minimal during a given day—one swelling for a high and one exhalation for a low. Since the different tidal patterns can't be attributed to changes in the moon and sun, other factors must govern this rhythm—factors that are tremendously complex.

Tidal knowledge is useful: low tides are for clamming and shelling, high tides are for fishing and safer navigation. While the particulars of tidal flux along the coast vary, they are as predictable as the phases of the moon, for good reason.

virtually inaccessible until the construction of the Wright Memorial Bridge carrying US 158 to the island in the early 1930s. The completion of the bridges from Manns Harbor to Roanoke Island and from there to the Outer Banks in the early 1950s launched a resort-building bonanza. The development that began at Nags Head spread rapidly to the north but much more slowly to the south.

There are approximately 11 miles of beachfront in this very narrow community, slightly more than a mile wide at the north boundary. South of Whalebone Junction, where US 64 ends (or begins) and where Virginia Dare Trail or NC 12 changes its name to Old Oregon Inlet Road, Nags Head backs up to the inland maritime shrub and marsh habitat of the Cape Hatteras National Seashore.

Most of Nags Head's hotels and motels, including some of the old classics of the beachfront like the First Colony Inn, are north of Whalebone Junction. South of Whalebone Junction, the community is primarily residential—nearly 5 miles of beachfront homes.

Along Virginia Dare Trail stand approximately thirty houses that comprise an informal "Nags Head Cottage Historic Area," although there is no official zoning designation setting the area aside for preservation purposes. The cottages were placed on the National Register of Historic Places in 1977 for their architectural distinctiveness. Even without a guide, you should be able to identify most of the historic buildings. These vacation

Nags Head Woods. (Courtesy of N.C. Travel and Tourism Division)

homes, much weathered, have endured since the turn of the century. Perhaps the greatest testament to their appeal is that they have established an architectural form that is mimicked by the builders of an era almost a century later.

Mixed with such salt-bleached charm are the seasonal businesses and enterprises that thrive between Memorial Day and Labor Day. There are some classic and enduring locations along Virginia Dare Trail that seem to have been there forever, such as Owens' Restaurant slightly north of the old Whalebone Junction site. The main commercial district is located along the US 158 bypass.

On November 24, 1991, the 114th anniversary of the shipwreck of the USS *Huron*, citizens of Nags Head and state officials gathered to mark the establishment of the first North Carolina Historic Shipwreck Preserve. The wreck is in 20 feet of water near milepost 11.5, approximately even with the end of the Nags Head Pier. A display in a gazebo detailing the wreck is located at the beach access parking area at the ocean end of Bladen Street.

Access

There are currently 33 signed access sites of various sizes within the town limits and nearly 500 parking spaces in 23 improved sites. There is a regional facility with 60 parking spaces, restrooms, showers, and summer lifeguards at the Old Nags Header site at Bonnett Street

along Virginia Dare Trail (Beach Road) between mileposts 11 and 12. Another similarly sized regional access site known as Epstein South is off of Virginia Dare Trail at about milepost 15.25, just north of the tennis courts at the Village Beach and Tennis Club. This site also has restrooms, showers, and a dune crossover ramp.

All access areas are signed from Virginia Dare Trail. If you're in a hurry, remember that many east-west streets terminate in public access locations. Along the nearly 10 miles of shoreline, there are access sites about every ½ mile, even closer near the northern city limits.

Nags Head once applied an ingenious method for naming its east-west streets, whereby street names at particular milepost markers begin with the same letter, following alphabetical order from north to south. For example, at the northern city limits at milepost 10, the east-west street names once all began with the letter A—Abalone, Albatross, etc. Over time, however, the scheme has not been consistently followed, but it is useful to remember that Whalebone Junction (and Jennette's Fishing Pier) is at Gulfstream Lane—in the G's; if you are looking for a street address further down in the alphabet, you would head south of Whalebone Junction.

Other major neighborhood sites with improved spaces are provided at the eastern terminus of each of the following streets: Abalone, Bainbridge, Barnes, Bittern, Blackman, Bladen, Conch, Enterprise, Epstein

Midway, Epstein North, Forrest, Glidden (with off-road-vehicle access), Governor, Gulfstream, Gull, Hargrove, Holden, Hollowell, Huron, Juncos, and Town Hall.

Handicapped Access

The two regional access sites are fully handicapped accessible.

There are also handicapped facilities at the sites at Enterprise Street, Epstein Midway, and Gulfstream Street.

Information

For information, contact Dare County Tourist Bureau, P.O. Box 399, Manteo, NC 27954, 919-473-2138, or Outer Banks Chamber of Commerce, P.O. Box 1757, Kill Devil Hills, NC 27948, 919-441-8144.

Jockey's Ridge State Park

It's sand-in-your-shoes time. The immense sand dune inland from the US 158 bypass is Jockey's Ridge, the tallest sand dune on the East Coast. Jockey's Ridge State Park covers 414 acres and is the result of another provident rescue by the Nature Conservancy, which saved the dune from bulldozers in 1975. (Yes, someone was actually going to try to remove Jockey's Ridge.) The state now insures the continuation of what is essentially a rite of passage on the Outer Banks: climbing Jockey's Ridge. What else do you do with a sand dune 10 stories tall?

	Fee	Parking	Restrooms	Lifeguard	Camping	Showers	Beach Access	Hiking	Trail	Handicapped	Boating	ORV Access	Fishing	Programs	Historic	Sand Beach	Dunes	Upland	Wetland
Nags Head	•	•					•			•			•		•	•	•	•	•
Regional Access: Old Nags Header	•	•	•		•	•				•			•			•	•		
Regional Access: Epstein South	•	•					•			•			•			•	•		
Jockey's Ridge State Park	•	•						•						•	•		•	•	•

The height of Jockey's Ridge varies from 110 to 140 feet above sea level. It is one of a series of historic dunes throughout the Outer Banks that includes Run Hill, Engagement Hill, Pin Hill, and Seven Sisters. Although its geological origin is disputed, its historical presence is not; early explorers noticed it and mapped it as early as 1775. Despite its "mobility," the dune has changed very little in size or configuration since 1949, as revealed by aerial photographs of that time.

There are few finer laboratories for witnessing the tug of war between wind and sand than Jockey's Ridge. The prevailing wind moves it slightly southwest, but each year other winds push it back northeast. Seasonal changes in breezes roll the sand from one side to the other, and although thousands of visitors climb it each year, their tracks are simply erased. From the top of the dune you can see how mobile the surface is. For many years, an adjoining novelty-golf concession would have

to dig out of winter's loess to open the summer season.

You can climb the dune and fly a kite or run down its side or slide down its side or roll down its side, then splash in the rainwater trapped in the hollows. It's certainly one place where your children can run free—and barely get out of eyesight.

The view from Jockey's Ridge is magnificent, especially for sunsets. The dune is more comfortably climbed in the early or later hours of the day. On hot days, shoes are a must, particularly for children. On very windy days, sunglasses or other eye protection is recommended. Leave the dune if a thunderstorm is imminent; it is the highest location around and a frequent target of lightning strikes.

Hang-glider enthusiasts trudge their wings to the top for a flight with a sure soft landing, in compliance with park restrictions. Watch for low-flying people.

For alternative recreation, pick

up the park flyer, "Tracks in the Sand." It's the guide to a 1.5-mile nature walk along the backside of the dune with keyed drawings of the tracks of animals that live on the dune or in the nearby maritime forest. It takes about 1½ hours to complete the walk.

Access

A new, expanded visitors center, parking, and restroom facilities are located off of the US 158 bypass. The park is officially open only during daylight hours (but how do you close a dune?).

Handicapped Access

The ranger's headquarters, restrooms, and some of the picnic shelters and pathways near the restrooms are accessible to the handicapped.

Information

For information, contact Jockey's Ridge State Park, P.O. Box 592, Nags Head, NC 27959, 919-441-7132.

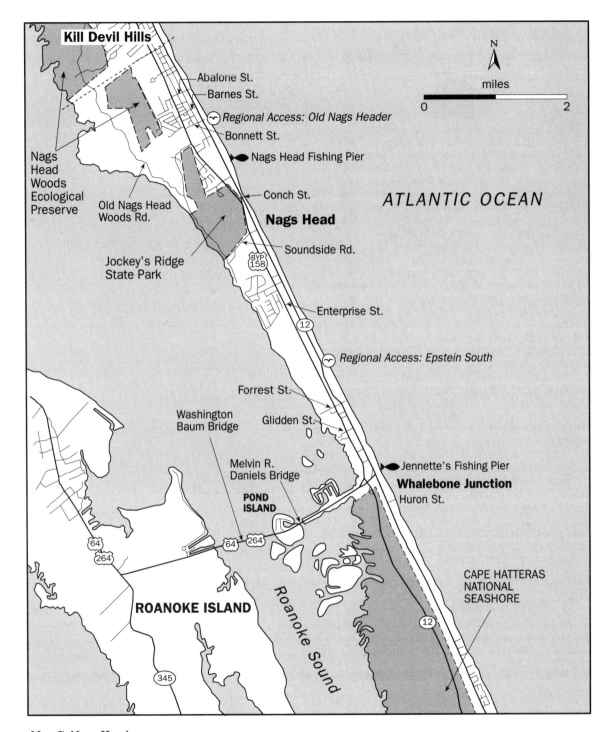

Kill Devil Hills

Abalone St.
Barnes St.
Regional Access: Old Nags Header
Bonnett St.
Nags Head Fishing Pier

Nags
Head
Woods
Ecological
Preserve

Old Nags Head
Woods Rd.

Conch St.

Nags Head

Jockey's Ridge
State Park

Soundside Rd.

BYP
158

Enterprise St.

12

Regional Access: Epstein South

Forrest St.

Washington
Baum Bridge

Glidden St.

Melvin R.
Daniels Bridge

Jennette's Fishing Pier

Whalebone Junction

Huron St.

**POND
ISLAND**

64   264

ROANOKE ISLAND

64

264

345

Roanoke Sound

CAPE HATTERAS
NATIONAL
SEASHORE

12

ATLANTIC OCEAN

N

miles

0   2

Map 7. Nags Head

NORTH CAROLINA SEA BATHING.
Nag's Head Hotel.

THIS extensive establishment, recently improved, will be opened for the reception of Visitors, superintended by the Junior Partner, A. J. BATEMAN, on the 1st day of July. The Hotel situated in view of the Ocean, presents a magnificent prospect. The great benefits resulting from Sea Bathing and the sea breeze, are becoming more known and appreciated daily. No place can be more healthy or possess a finer climate than Nag's Head. The Bathing is unsurpassed in the United States. We have engaged a good Band of Music, our Ball Room is very spacious and will be opened every evening. Active and efficient assistants have been engaged, and no exertions will be spared to render it in all respects an agreeable and interesting resort. A Rail Road will be completed early in July from the Hotel to the Ocean, that persons preferring a ride to walking may be accommodated.

The steamer Schultz will make a trip every Saturday from Franklin Depot, Va., to Nags' Head, commencing July 12th, immediately after the arrival of the Cars from Norfolk, and returning leave Nags' Head Sunday evening, at 5 o'clock. Passage from Franklin $3, Riddick's Wharf, Winton, &c., $2 50, Edenton to Nags' Head $2. Meals extra. The Schultz will make several Excursions to Nags' Head through the season, due notice of which will be given. The Packet schr. Sarah Porter, Capt. Walker, will make two trips from Edenton, (N. C.,) to Nag's Head each week through the season, leaving Edenton Tuesday and Friday, at 8 o'clock, A M. The Packet schr. A. Riddick, Capt. Dunbar, will make three trips each week through the season. from Elizabeth City, (N. C.,) to Nag's Head, leaving Elizabeth City immediately after the arrival of the Stage Coach from Norfolk, Va. Passage on each Packet $1. meals extra. Board per day at the Hotel $1 50. By the week at the rate of $1 25. By the two weeks at the rate of $1. By the month at the rate of 75 cents per day. Children and Servants half price. The patronage of the public is very respectfully solicited.

RIDDICK & BATEMAN.

June 11, 1851 38-2m.

An advertisement in an 1851 issue of the North State Whig describes the facilities of the Nags Head Hotel, Outer Banks. (Courtesy of N.C. Department of Archives and History)

The area above Whalebone Junction during the Ash Wednesday Storm that hit Nags Head in March 1962. (Courtesy of Outer Banks History Center)

Hang gliding along the dunes at Jockey's Ridge State Park. (Courtesy of N.C. Travel and Tourism Division)

Whalebone Junction

The intersection of US 158, US 64/264, and NC 12 bears one of the most curious nicknames of any intersection in North Carolina—Whalebone Junction. The origin of the name goes back to the 1930s when the all-sand roads that served the Outer Banks came together here. A service station at the intersection, which closed around the time the US 158 bypass was built, displayed whale bones from a beached leviathan.

There is a wonderful interpretive access area, on the south side of the causeway and east of the Melvin Daniels Bridge, that has a gazebo and boardwalk extending into the salt marsh. Displays illustrate and explain the natural history of the salt marsh.

There is a 50-space parking lot, west of the bridge on the south side of the causeway, that provides bridge access for fishing.

Washington Baum Bridge

A causeway leads west from Whalebone Junction, connecting Pond Island and Cedar Island on the way to Roanoke Island. Until 1990 and the opening of the high-rise Washington Baum Bridge, a swing bridge in service since the mid-1930s governed boat traffic in the sounds and automobile traffic on the causeway. Besides making travel across

the sounds easier, the Washington Baum Bridge offers a terrific view of the barrier skyline as it vaults you onto the Outer Banks.

The causeway is more than a passage, it's a nautical hello to the Outer Banks. Marinas and boat ramps extend from the road into the estuary. Crabbing and fishing are permitted in traffic-safe locations along the route, including on the Melvin R. Daniels Bridge, east of the Washington Baum Bridge.

Access

South of the Washington Baum Bridge on Roanoke Island is a brand-new access area with a boat-launching ramp and a paved and lighted parking lot providing access to sound waters. Local fishermen began coming to the site almost immediately after the opening of the bridge because of the elbow room. They also like the quietness caused by the fact that the bridge elevates the highway sounds. It makes good shade, too.

Besides the unofficial fishing locations, Pirate's Cove Marina, in the Pirate's Cove development on the north side of the Washington Baum Bridge on Roanoke Island, offers charter and head-boat fishing trips offshore.

Roanoke Island

Roanoke Island is the site of the first attempt by English-speaking people to establish a permanent colony in the New World. Its two

primary communities, Manteo and Wanchese, are named for the Native Americans who traveled to England with the returning members of the original 1584 expedition.

One of the few corners of the Outer Banks that is not completely dependent on tourism dollars, Roanoke Island is solidly anchored in a maritime way of life. This wooded, 11-by-2.5-mile island includes the Dare County seat at Manteo and the headquarters of the Cape Hatteras National Seashore. After you drive through the slightly urban pinch of Manteo, you will find Roanoke Island to be mostly rural and residential.

The island has much to offer that many people miss because it is "on the way" to the beachfront communities. Among the attractions you should plan to visit are the *Elizabeth II* State Historic Site; the North Carolina Aquarium; and the Fort Raleigh National Historic Site, nestled on the north end of the island along with the Lindsay Warren Visitors Center and the adjacent Elizabethan Gardens. During the summer, these attractions stay extremely busy, particularly the aquarium, so arrive early.

If Roanoke Island is your first introduction to the Outer Banks, stop at the state rest area off of US 64/264 at the north end of the island. The Dare County Tourist Bureau staffs a kiosk with workers who will help you find your destination and advise you of any pertinent travel information. They will know about special events, festivals, and other timely happenings. Pick up a welcome packet, which includes an Outer Banks Vacation Guide, providing an excellent listing of places and services. There are picnic tables, restrooms, and telephones for your use as well. The kiosk is staffed from 10 A.M. to 6 P.M. daily, usually from March 1 through November.

Access

Dare County maintains a boating access location on Roanoke Island and within the town limits of Manteo and Wanchese. There is a boat ramp at Dare County Airport Recreation Area, south of the North Carolina Aquarium at the end of Airport Road.

There are plans for a boat ramp, basin, and public parking south of the Emergency Medical Service Center west of US 64 on Bowsertown Road.

Handicapped Access

The individual federal, state, and municipal attractions have accommodations for handicapped travelers.

Information

For information, contact Dare County Tourist Bureau, P.O. Box 399, Manteo, NC 27954, 919-473-2138, or Outer Banks Chamber of Commerce, P.O. Box 1757, Kill Devil Hills, NC 27948, 919-441-8144.

Manteo

The Dare County seat and the commercial center of Roanoke Island, Manteo is a delightful community that is too often overlooked by travelers in their headlong charge to the Outer Banks. The name honors the Native American chief who sailed to England with Amadas and Barlowe on their return voyage in 1584. The town significantly renovated its waterfront prior to the July 1984 four-hundredth anniversary celebration of the first attempt by English-speaking peoples to establish a colony in the New World at Roanoke Island. The charming retail district that was created along the waterfront captures the flavor of the region without overpowering the modest scale of the town. As Manteo attracts more visitors each year, the word spreads that its waterfront is a fine destination.

Manteo has put a fine foot forward to make you welcome. Parking is ample and plainly signed, and many restaurants and shops serve your needs. The pedestrian is welcome downtown; you can walk about freely while the traffic crawls by.

If you approach Manteo from the west during the summer, you will see the city's crepe-myrtle greeting. The small trees line US 64/264 from Old Airport Road for approximately ½ mile in a florific pink welcome, which further along turns to white. At the intersection of US 64/264 and Budleigh Street at the central light of the small community, you

will see the Dare County Tourist Information office on the northeast corner of the junction. Budleigh Street leads to the waterfront at a sign that directs you to the "Business District." You may also turn at SR 400, at a sign announcing the "Historic Waterfront."

Turn east on Budleigh and you will feel the hurry being let out of your trip; the streets narrow and the pace slows. Where Budleigh Street ends downtown, turn left to find a metered municipal parking lot with a 3-hour limit between the Tranquil House Inn, a waterfront hostelry with a spirited revival of vernacular architecture, and the new three-story waterfront development that features condominium space above the restaurants, apparel shops, and antique stores that are the commercial anchor of the waterfront.

A municipal boardwalk along the waterfront winds past the many private boats moored there to the Washington Creef Memorial Park, the construction site of the *Elizabeth II*, a full-scale reconstruction of a sixteenth-century sailing vessel, named for one of the ships that brought the first colonists. The ship is plainly visible across the basin when in port.

The red-brick county courthouse is at Queen Elizabeth Avenue and Walter Raleigh Street. If you continue your explorations west and south, following SR 400 or Fernando Street, you will wind your way to the very dignified, low-key Roanoke Inn. An easy walk east from downtown on Ananias Dare Street will

	Fee	Parking	Restrooms	Lifeguard	Camping	Showers	Beach Access	Hiking	Trail	Handicapped	Boating	ORV Access	Fishing	Programs	Historic	Sand Beach	Dunes	Upland	Wetland
Washington Baum Bridge (proposed access)		•						•			•		•						•
Roanoke Island		•	•	•				•		•	•		•	•	•			•	•
The *Elizabeth II*	•	•	•					•		•				•	•				
Public Boating Access: Manteo		•									•							•	•
Fort Raleigh National Historic Site		•	•					•	•	•				•	•			•	
North Carolina Aquarium, Roanoke Island		•	•							•				•	•				
Dare Co. Airport Recreation Area		•									•		•						•
Public Boating Access: Wanchese		•									•		•						•

take you over the waterfront basin to the site of the *Elizabeth II*. It's also refreshing to wander north to John Borden Street or Devon Street, through residential areas of the town and past a small cemetery, and then head north on Winginia Street. Along the way you will enjoy some of the largest, loveliest loblolly pines you are ever likely to see. It is difficult to imagine that these serene woods could be any lovelier, even to the first colonist who found them as virgin forest to their European eyes.

Access

Manteo provides a public dock along Fernando Street with several parking places. Also, the Manteo Public Boat Landing is at the east end of Ananias Dare Street, adjacent to the bridge that leads to the *Elizabeth II*.

Handicapped Access

Handicapped parking spaces are provided in the off-street parking lot next to the Tranquil House Inn on the waterfront.

The municipal boardwalk and public dock are handicapped accessible from a small parking area on Fernando Street, across from the Roanoke Inn.

Information

For information, contact Dare County Tourist Bureau, P.O. Box 399, Manteo, NC 27954, 919-473-2138, or Outer Banks Chamber of Commerce, P.O. Box 1757, Kill Devil Hills, NC 27948, 919-441-8144.

Roanoke Island Festival Park

Cross the bridge at the end of Ananias Dare Street and you step into living history at Roanoke Island Festival Park. Visit a recreated 1580s New World settlement, chat with interpreters in period dress, enjoy the docudrama, "The Legend of Two Path," and tour the remarkable *Elizabeth II*, a full-scale reconstruction of a sixteenth-century sailing vessel. The ship is named for one of the vessels on Raleigh's 1585 expedition to Roanoke Island. Nearly 70 feet long and 17 feet wide, the *Elizabeth II* is genuinely seaworthy, part of the marvelous authenticity of her construction. The ship is open for guided tours when in port. Although the sailing schedule is not too heavy, the ship makes occasional commemorative

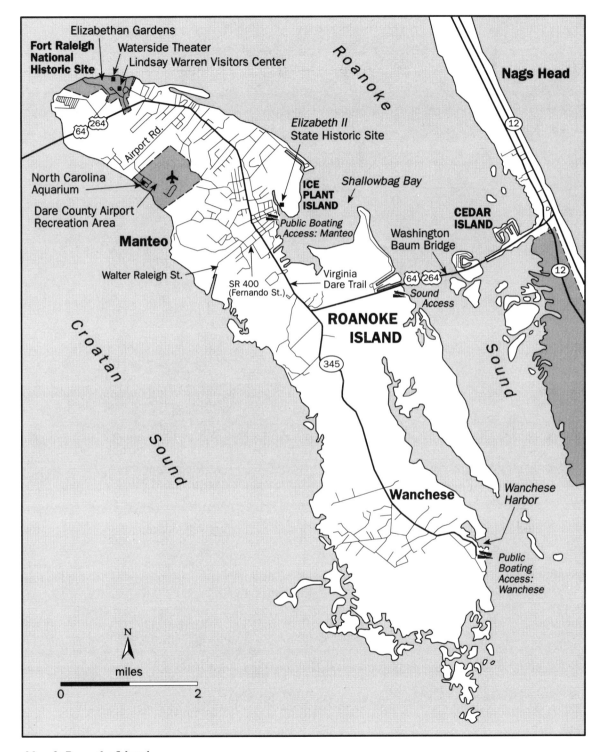

Map 8. Roanoke Island

The Elizabeth II, *a reconstruction of the ships used during the era of Sir Walter Raleigh's Roanoke voyages four hundred years ago, berthed at the Manteo waterfront. (Courtesy of N.C. Travel and Tourism Division)*

voyages. As you walk the decks, you develop a healthy respect for the travelers who placed their fate in the care of a captain and such a small ship.

The ship was officially dedicated on July 13, 1984, as a part of the four-hundredth anniversary celebration of the first colonization attempt in the New World at Roanoke Island. As the *Elizabeth II* neared completion, it became apparent that it was landlocked since the design of the vessel made it unable to sail out of its construction berth. A channel was dredged to enable the ship to reach open water.

A much expanded Outer Banks History Center opened here in 1997. It includes a large theater and space for detailed exhibits documenting early life on the Outer Banks. The center has restrooms and a picnic area.

Access

There is an admission charge with discounts for children and senior citizens. The center is open April–October, 10 A.M. to 6 P.M. daily, last tour at 5 P.M., and November–March, 10 A.M. to 4 P.M. Tuesday–Sunday, last tour at 3 P.M.

Handicapped Access

The *Elizabeth II* Visitors Center, restrooms, and picnic area are fully accessible for the handicapped. The ship is not easily accessible for the handicapped.

Information

For information, contact *Elizabeth II* State Historic Site, P.O. Box 155, Manteo, NC 27954, 919-473-1144.

North Carolina Aquarium, Roanoke Island

One excellent reason to stop at the North Carolina Aquarium on Roanoke Island is to find out what shares the water with you. The newly expanded facility provides an eyeball-to-eyeball introduction to the ecology of the high-energy beaches of the Outer Banks and offers the chance to peer deep under the waves to see creatures of the depths in their home environment as well.

Two touch-and-feel tanks provide hands-on handshakes to indigenous Outer Banks creatures. An atrium display provides a home for river otters, too. The big show, however, is the silent swirl of sea creatures in the two-story 285,000 gallon exhibit which has a one-third scale replica of the USS *Monitor* as a feature.

It is not possible to detail here the variety of programs and special events the staff hosts during the summer months. The place fairly jumps with ecological educational opportunities, and every visi-

tor leaves a little richer in his or her knowledge of the Outer Banks.

Be warned that if you wait to visit the aquarium on a rainy day, you will meet the entire summer population of the area there. Make it one of your first stops instead.

Access

The aquarium is open 9 A.M. to 5 P.M. daily during the summer; hours are shortened in the off-season. There is an admission fee.

Dare County maintains a boat-launching ramp next to the aquarium.

The North Carolina Wildlife Resources Commission maintains a fishing and boating access area on East Lake at Mashoes, 3 miles north of Manns Harbor off of SR 1113. Parking is available, and there is no launch fee.

Handicapped Access

The aquarium and restroom facilities are accessible to handicapped travelers.

Information

For a recorded listing of programs at the aquarium, call 919-473-3493. To schedule group visits, call 919-473-3494.

Fort Raleigh National Historic Site

The Fort Raleigh National Historic Site is north of Manteo. It is the location of the Lindsay Warren Visitors Center, which provides inter-

pretive programs for Fort Raleigh. The grounds of *The Lost Colony* summer drama, the headquarters of the Cape Hatteras National Seashore, and the privately maintained Elizabethan Gardens are adjacent. You can easily spend several hours exploring these attractions.

The heart of the complex is the restored earthwork moat and fort originally constructed here to protect the members of the Ralph Lane colony in 1585. The earthworks you see today were reconstructed in 1950 by the National Park Service based on the remains of original fortifications uncovered during archaeological investigations from 1936 to 1948. The site represents the birthplace of English-speaking settlement in North America.

The Lindsay Warren Visitors Center at the fort introduces you to the colonial history of the Outer Banks. A film narrates the history of colonization efforts during the sixteenth century. An Elizabethan-era reading room has been re-created as an example of the quarters of the aristocracy who bankrolled Sir Walter Raleigh's voyages. Displays show original artifacts, such as a wrought-iron sickle, that were uncovered here and compare the cultures that ultimately collided in the early years.

Between the visitors center and the fort is a monument commemorating the christening of Virginia Dare, the first child born to English-speaking people in the New World. Beyond the fort is the Thomas Hariot Nature Trail, named after

Good Wood

Put yourself in a waterman's boots eighty years ago—fishing, a little farming, and maybe guiding for sportsmen. You're tied to the water like a boat to a dock. Wood means a lot to you. It's your boats, docks, and decoys; your siding, shingles, fences, and posts; your whittling, if you have time.

There's no building supply store; there are no wood preservatives. So pick a tree, waterman, you've got repairs to make. Which wood is good wood?

It must be durable and last through winter ice and torpid summer heat. It must not rot or at least it must rot slowly enough to be worth spending valuable time felling, hauling, barking, splitting, and shaping. Once fashioned, it will be in contact with water and air and the fungi that bring deterioration. It will be tested.

It must be buoyant, lightweight, smooth-grained, and splinter-free; sandable, workable, and easily shaped and turned with the boat-builder's tools and the carver's knife. If it were also aromatic, the shavings might sweeten the air.

It must be nearby, it must be plentiful, and it must be free or close to it.

There was such a tree once: Atlantic white cedar, known botanically as *Chamaecyparis thyoides*. Watermen called it juniper, a misnomer derived from its resemblance to eastern red cedar, a *Juniperus* species. It is a wetland species with a native range extending between Maine and Florida. The Great Dismal Swamp and the peninsula between Albemarle and Pamlico sounds once sheltered some of the largest stands of this soggy-ground evergreen within its range.

It became the waterman's tree and subsequently one of the most valuable commercial species in the East. Beginning in the late nineteenth century, railroads and drainage ditches siphoned away the swamp's protective bogginess. The pure stands of juniper were open for harvest, and by the time of the Great Depression, most of the virgin stands were gone. How much timber was cut? At one time juniper stands may have covered some 62,000 to 112,000 acres within the Great Dismal Swamp alone. Today, between 6,000 and 7,000 acres of juniper remain.

In fact, some estimates place the current Atlantic white cedar acreage at only 10 percent of its original size

the scientist who wrote reports describing the explorations of the Lane colonists in the New World. Hariot's words provide the narration on this self-guided tour that winds you through both time and the natural woodlands.

The Waterside Theater, the location for the summer drama *The Lost Colony* by Pulitzer Prize–winning author Paul Green, is just north of the fort. The site of the first outdoor drama in the United States, the theater is open during park hours, but the Roanoke Island Historical Association sets up the schedule for the summer drama.

The entrance to the Elizabethan Gardens is visible from the visitors center. This 10-acre formal garden is maintained through the cooperative effort of the Garden Clubs of North Carolina and the state. The gardens rival any formal gardens in the state for their design authenticity and the extensive collection of plant materials. The plant selection obviously cannot duplicate sixteenth-century English gardening because of the coastal climate, but it is faithful to the styles of the Elizabethan era. True to form, it functions as a controlled retreat for strolling in the heart of the wilderness, a theme appropriate to the settlement of the New World. It is designed to have year-round appeal as well as seasonal highlighting. It is exquisite in any season but especially in summer, when annual plantings come to the fore. Antique statuary are also prominently featured as a part in North Carolina. The reduction in acreage is probably a direct result of land management practices in the timbered regions. The timber was harvested and the land was drained and put to other uses. Much of the timber considered old-growth today is second-growth timber from natural reforestation occurring after the initial logging onslaught of the turn of the century.

Commercial harvesting of this secondary growth boomed again starting in the mid-1970s, and the logging techniques employed may have far more severe consequences than the lumberjack methods of the past. The ditch digging and road building are altering the groundwater characteristics of the stands of juniper, which love wet feet. The question yet un-answered is, will juniper reseed and return?

The few remaining old-growth stands will soon go to the sawmill, and unlike other trees commercially lumbered, there is no large-scale replanting. Atlantic white cedar stands need assistance to recover from cutting; seedlings must have direct sunlight. It is thought that firing the clear-cut area to remove growth and debris may help—after all, the stands recovered somewhat from the initial harvest of nearly 100 years ago. However, in those early days, the swamp remained a swamp even after the timber was felled, whereas today the swamps are being drained.

The tree is not in danger of extinction, but the reduction in range and the loss of Atlantic white cedar habitat does mean the loss of the other components of this unique environmental niche. An important component of maritime heritage is also threatened. Juniper skiffs, boats, and decoys *are* the waterman's story—as traditional to the region as hunting and fishing.

Some juniper stands remain in the Alligator River National Wildlife Refuge, and reforestation efforts are under way in the Great Dismal Swamp. You will see an occasional planting of ornamental use in a home garden around older properties. The *Elizabeth II* in Manteo harbor is planked with juniper. It's good wood—everything a waterman could ask for, including the smell of the shavings.

of this well-executed formal garden complex.

Access

Fort Raleigh National Historic Site is open 9 A.M. to 8 P.M., 9 A.M. to 6 P.M. Sunday, during the summer drama season; 9 A.M. to 5 P.M. during the rest of the year. The Lindsay Warren Visitors Center is open 9 A.M. to 5 P.M. Performances of *The Lost Colony* are usually staged from mid-June through August and begin at 8:30 P.M., Monday–Saturday; ad-mission is $10 for adults, $5 for children under 12. The Elizabethan Gardens are open all year from 9 A.M. to 5 P.M. (8 P.M. in summer), except Saturdays and Sundays during January and February. Admission is $2.50 for adults; children under 12 are admitted free.

Handicapped Access

Most of the facilities at the fort are handicapped accessible or negotiable for wheelchair travelers with minimal assistance. Access to the auditorium in the visitors center is restricted because of a narrow doorway and steep slope. New restrooms are planned to provide accessible facilities.

The Waterside Theater is accessible. Wheelchairs are available at the theater, and wheelchair spaces are provided. Restrooms are accessible with some assistance.

The Elizabethan Gardens are negotiable by wheelchair with assistance.

Elizabethan Gardens, Roanoke Island. (Courtesy of N.C. Travel and Tourism Division)

Information

For information about Fort Raleigh National Historic Site, call 919-473-5772. For information about performances of *The Lost Colony*, call 919-473-3414. For information about the Elizabethan Gardens, call 919-473-3234.

For further information, contact Dare County Tourist Bureau, P.O. Box 399, Manteo, NC 27954, 919-473-2138, or Outer Banks Chamber of Commerce, P.O. Box 1757, Kill Devil Hills, NC 27948, 919-441-8144.

Wanchese

Wanchese is a hard-working fishing and boat-building village at the south end of Roanoke Island. The village is named after the Native American who accompanied his chief Manteo to England on the 1584 return voyage of colonists Amadas and Barlowe.

In spite of the shoaling of Oregon Inlet, which threatens commercial fishing out of this port, the boats bring in steady catches. Seafood vendors at Wanchese usually have low prices on fresh seafood, certainly worth the side trip to fill

up a cooler before returning inland. If you don't have a cooler or ice, they sell those, too. A restaurant overlooks the water, naturally, and the air is scented by the pungent breezes you would expect from fishermen's wharfs.

Wanchese stands in sleepy contrast to the comparative "bustle" of Manteo because the fishing boats leave before sunrise. The village keeps older, more traditional rhythms of work and life than the nearby county seat. In many respects, the few miles between them could be years.

As you approach Wanchese, the

first inkling of a community is the glistening white siding of Bethany Methodist Church at a fork on Old Wharf Road, which winds around and connects with other streets, eventually looping back to the main road. You can go either way at the fork, but if you go left, you'll reach the seafood packers quicker.

Residents offer crafts, services, and bed-and-breakfasts out of their homes. Folks are friendly and easy-going, so drive friendly. Watch out for horses and children in the streets—this is a village not used to through traffic.

Access

Dare County maintains a public boat ramp and dock on Mill Creek in Wanchese, just south of the Wanchese Fish Company building.

Information

For information, contact Dare County Tourist Bureau, P.O. Box 399, Manteo, NC 27954, 919-473-2138, or Outer Banks Chamber of Commerce, P.O. Box 1757, Kill Devil Hills, NC 27948, 919-441-8144.

West by Southwest: US 264 from Manteo

The following are some of the places you might see if you headed southwest on US 264 from Manns Harbor instead of making a beeline due west on US 64.

Immediately after the junction with US 64 just west of Manns Harbor, US 264 enters the nation's newest and largest wildlife refuge, the Alligator River preserve. In 1984, the Nature Conservancy assisted in the transfer of more than 120,000 acres of land from the Prudential Insurance Corporation and an agricultural subsidiary, Prudlo Farms, to the Department of the Interior. The gift was the largest single private land donation ever recorded, and it became the core of the nearly 150,000-acre refuge.

Although primarily a pine pocosin (an elevated swamp), the preserve contains extensive virgin stands of Atlantic white cedar—once the waterman's choice for boatbuilding and decoy carving. Several streams are pure enough to support spawning of the American sturgeon, and the surrounding waters of Pamlico and Croatan sounds and the Alligator River have an immeasurable value as an estuarine environment.

One of the fringe benefits of traveling this road in either spring or midsummer is the fragrance. Sweetbay magnolia, which blooms in spring, and loblolly bay, a late-summer flowering tree, line the roads. Both have very conspicuous white flowers, and each provides a sweet fragrance that is a delight.

The preserve supports a substantial number of wintering waterfowl, deer, and black bear and is now the site of one of the most radical (and, so far, successful) wildlife repopulation programs—the reintroduction of the red wolf, once native to the coast. A nocturnal hunter, the extremely shy red wolf likes the marshy upland and thick forest habitat of Alligator River. There is every indication that the reintroduction has resulted in mating pairs that have had success with new broods.

Several have been killed by automobiles, and refuge officials ask that you drive carefully if you travel through the refuge at night. If you spot a red wolf or a seemingly large dog, please report the sighting by calling the headquarters at 919-473-1131.

Stumpy Point

Stumpy Point is a commercial fishing community on Stumpy Point Bay. Turn east on SR 1100, which skirts the bay and eventually follows a small tidal creek that serves as a commercial boat basin. This end of the community is known as Drain Point. At the end of the spit, the North Carolina Wildlife Resources Commission maintains a fishing and boating access area with parking. The view to the east is across Pamlico Sound to the Pea Island National Wildlife Refuge.

The vastness and low relief of the landscape features are nearly overwhelming here. On calm days, the slack, glassy waters of Stumpy Point Bay are serene, excellent waters for blue crabs. Most of the fishing boats working out of the boat basin are crabbers.

As you drive this route, you will likely hear the shriek of military aircraft. Inland from Stumpy Point is a joint military command bombing range that is not included in the Alligator River preserve and is off-limits to unauthorized personnel.

Engelhard

Engelhard is a wonderfully compact, rural community, where you can buy hand-scooped ice cream cones at a service station on the outskirts. There's also a Department of Transportation roadside park, which is an attractive minigarden where visitors can get information about Hyde County attractions. The town itself marks a transition from coastal forest and timber management to an agricultural landscape. It comes as a nice relief to the previous miles through the coastal plain forests.

You can't tell it from town, but Engelhard is on Far Creek, which feeds into Pamlico Sound. The North Carolina Wildlife Resources Commission maintains a fishing and boating access area just east of US 264 at the northern town limits.

Lake Landing Historic District

US 264 comes to Farrow's Fork, an intersection with SR 1114, just north of the community of Amity, one of the older settlements in the county. This is also the entry to one of the state's most unusual historic areas, the 13,400-acre Lake Landing Historic District, which is on the National Register of Historic Places.

This purely agricultural historic district features twenty-five houses and structures on an approximately 15-mile loop tour through the region. The tour route loops south on SR 1114 to the community of Middletown. From there it continues on SR 1108 to White Plains, intersecting with SR 1110 to reach the town of Nebraska. From Nebraska the loop returns via SR 1116 to US 264 at Lake Landing, just south of Lake Mattamuskeet. Six homes along US 264 west of Lake Landing are also on the tour.

Even if you were unaware of being on a tour, you would recognize the historical integrity of the structures you pass, including the incredible Octagon House that dates from 1857 and is fully restored and open for visitation. What you see is exquisite planter architecture—Greek Revival, Federal, Georgian, Queen Anne—a multiplicity of fine homes and outbuildings, each unit gloriously intact and still actively farming, so it seems.

Each of these houses, particularly most of the ones along the south side of US 264, are sited about the same distance off of the highway, and their backyards are about ¼–½-mile long—beautiful fields that reach to the woods of the Gum Swamp.

All of the lands in this district were originally a part of the early eighteenth-century Mattamuskeet Indian Reservation. By the late 1720s, Europeans had bought the land from the Native Americans or had otherwise secured patents and began farming. What you see today represents more than two centuries of agricultural tradition.

There is a historic pamphlet available to guide your tour. Copies are usually available at the roadside park in Engelhard or in the Hyde County Courthouse in Swan Quarter or you can send for one by writing the Hyde County Historical Society, P.O. Box 159, Engelhard, NC 27824.

Lake Mattamuskeet National Wildlife Refuge

Even if it didn't include almost 50,000 acres of preserve, Lake Mattamuskeet would be an enticing natural feature. The circumstances of its origin are disputed to this day. Almost 3 feet below sea level, the lake has an average depth of only 3 feet. North Carolina's largest natural lake, it is more than 18 miles long and 6 miles wide. Since 1934, the 40,000 acres of lake surface plus 6,500 acres of adjoining marshland, 3,000 acres of pine and hardwood forest, and nearly 300 acres of cropland have constituted a magnificent refuge for migratory waterfowl, principally whistling swans, Canada geese, and dabbling ducks such as pintail, black ducks, and mallards. Many more species have been sighted, and the refuge publishes a listing of avian visitors.

The big story at Mattamuskeet began at the turn of the century when the lake was purchased by investors and an attempt was made to drain the lake permanently and farm the bottomland. The world's largest pumping station, now known as Mattamuskeet Lodge near New Holland, was built, and the lake was drained into what is known as Grand Canal. The lake was indeed farmed, but nature soon made it a lake again. The refuge soon followed.

NC 94 bisects the lake, and US 264 swings along its southern borders. A network of county roads circumvents the east, north, and west boundaries of the refuge.

There is an excellent observation tower at the refuge headquarters at New Holland and ample bird-watching at any point around the lake. Fishing and hunting are permitted in accordance with refuge regulations. Hunting visits are limited to assigned blinds, determined by lottery, overlooking the water at the south edge of the property.

For information, contact Lake Mattamuskeet National Wildlife Refuge, Route 1 Box N-2, Swan Quarter, NC 27855, 919-926-4021.

Swan Quarter National Wildlife Refuge

The ferry from Ocracoke passes through Swan Quarter National Wildlife Refuge just offshore from the village of Swan Quarter. The refuge comprises 15,500 acres of marshland bordering Pamlico Sound and is a migratory waterfowl refuge. An additional 24,450 acres of the sound adjacent to the refuge have been closed to hunting by presidential proclamation.

For information, contact Swan Quarter National Wildlife Refuge, Route 1 Box N-2, Swan Quarter, NC 27855, 919-926-4021.

Gull Rock Game Land

The North Carolina Wildlife Resources Commission manages an 18,856-acre game land between the Mattamuskeet and Swan Quar-

ter refuges. These lands are open to hunting subject to federal regulations. Unpaved SR 1164 leads 7 miles south from New Holland to a boat ramp at East Bluff Bay. The ramp is open year-round.

Swan Quarter

US 264 does not go directly through Swan Quarter, but you can easily detour through the community, a very brief but worthwhile interlude on your return, if for no other reason than to see Providence United Methodist Church, the church "moved by the hand of God."

Belhaven

This small harbor town on the Pungo River is reached by detouring onto NC 92 off of US 264. This is possibly one of the most peaceful detours you will ever take, so take it.

The River Forest Manor, a country inn in an old plantation house, is set up to serve the traffic on the Intra-coastal Waterway. There is also the Belhaven Memorial Museum upstairs in town hall, an eclectic complication of the late Eva Blount Way.

Bath

This historic town was the first colo-nial port of entry. Founded in 1705, Bath is the oldest town in the state. Bath perches on a bluff overlooking the Pamlico River, and as the evolving colony became more commercially inclined, the safe harbor played an increasingly important role in trade and mercantile development.

Named for the Earl of Bath, one of the original eight Lords Proprietors of the English colony that became North Carolina, the small commu-nity, while becoming tremendously important, never became more sub-stantial than it is. The town's size has changed little in its almost 300 years of existence.

It is a jewel of a city and has bene-fited handsomely from restoration and conservation efforts. The state has sought to insure that visitors understand the importance of this small community by staffing a full-time visitors center at the Historic Bath State Historic Site. The center is open 9 A.M.–5 P.M. Tuesday–Saturday; 1 P.M.–5 P.M. Sunday. A 35-minute film depicts the history of the state's oldest city.

Several restored buildings may be toured for a nominal fee. One notable attraction is St. Thomas Episcopal Church, erected in 1734, the oldest church in continuous use in North Carolina.

For information, contact Historic Bath State Historic Site, P.O. Box 148, Bath, NC 27808, 919-923-3971.

Goose Creek State Park

Goose Creek State Park is a 1,200-acre park located 7 miles east of Bath and south of NC 92 and US 264 on SR 1334. The park includes sandy beaches along the Pamlico River and has a boat ramp for fishing access to the waters of Pamlico Sound. River swimming is also permitted as well as primitive camping.

Pamlico River Free Ferry

East of Bayview, NC 306 leads to a free ferry crossing over the Pamlico River. There are ten departures daily north and south. This is very out of the way and will carry you past the fossil-rich Texas Gulf Phosphate mine and to the town of Aurora, once the potato capital of North Carolina, now home of the Aurora Fossil Museum, an astonishingly rich collection of the fossil finds of the mines.

Cape Hatteras National Seashore   Area code 252

One of the longest and most attractive—if most tenuous—stretches of beach on the East Coast begins at Whalebone Junction, where NC 12 departs the bustle of the summer resort cities of northern Dare County to begin its sinuous route through Cape Hatteras National Seashore. One bridge, one wildlife refuge, one ferry ride, two counties, and eight villages later, NC 12 ends at the Ocracoke Island Visitors Center. On this journey, the passage is as much a destination as the final black-top loop on Ocracoke. For many, Cape Hatteras National Seashore is synonymous with the best of the Outer Banks. It is the nation's first national seashore, dating from the first acquisitions in 1935 and continuing through the 1950s, when the boundaries were completed. It was officially authorized as a national seashore in 1953.

Sand, sea, vegetation, and people struggle in a shaky war of attrition along the 75-mile-long, 30,000-acre recreation area. People live here much as they always have, cheerfully but nervously. The ocean laps at their feet and can move the islands around like dust on a shelf. The three islands of the seashore—the nearly 9 miles of Bodie Island, the crooked arm of Hatteras, and the exclamation point of Ocracoke—have been breached by the ocean numerous times in recorded history.

No two visits to the seashore are ever the same since the beach is never the same. Still, some places seemingly never change. You begin to expect certain constants—the lighthouses, the villages, the infinity of telephone poles marching to the horizons. Even the artificial dune line constructed by the Civilian Conservation Corps in the 1930s (which was whacked badly during a storm in October 1991) is an expected feature. Over time, these constants become benchmarks for measuring change along the length of the seashore.

Names linger on here even after the geography changes—Bodie Island and Pea Island are islands no more. The folks who live here have long memories, and they know who's in charge. The names honor periods of mappable stability, hoping perhaps to evoke more of it.

Traveling south from Whalebone Junction, you pass through the maritime shrub thicket and brackish marsh west of south Nags Head. The road is winding and lovely here, framed by wax myrtle shrubs on either side. To the east are the rooftops of the private beach cottages. To the south is Bodie Island Lighthouse, with a planting of southern yellow pine trees along its entry drive.

Crossing the Herbert C. Bonner Bridge over Oregon Inlet brings you down the narrow spine of the banks, which turns south at Rodanthe, continuing to Buxton. At Buxton, the seashore encompasses massive natural dunes along with the stable pine and hardwood forest known as Buxton Woods. After Frisco, the seashore narrows before flaring wide at the safe harbor of Hatteras Village.

A ferry ride takes you to Ocracoke—long, flat, and sparsely vegetated—the most isolated island in an otherwise very accessible length of seashore. Ocracoke Island is the charm on the sand bracelet, either the beginning or the end of your Outer Banks exploration. If you arrive from the mainland—from Cedar Island or Swan Quarter—you start with the quietest place along the seashore. If it's quiet you want, don't leave; Ocracoke has more of it than any other location on the Outer Banks. If you arrive at Ocracoke from Hatteras, it is an unpretentious climax. Either way, it still epitomizes the independent, yet nature-dependent, character of the Outer Banks.

Now a vacationer's paradise, the seashore once was a mariner's nightmare, better known for disaster than for pleasure. Hundreds of oceangoing vessels have run aground on the ever-varying shoals. Less than a hundred years ago, twelve stations of the U.S. Life-Saving Service, the forerunner of the U.S. Coast Guard, and three lighthouses watched over the "Graveyard of the Atlantic," where more than 400 ships have met their final port.

Legend and lore have literally washed ashore here, and the ocean will sometimes pull back the shrouding sands to reveal a piece of long-lost vessel. Landward, the vestiges of that time are preserved in special places such as the Little Kinnakeet and Chicamacomico U.S. Life-Saving Service stations on Hatteras Island, the lightkeeper's quarters and lighthouses of Bodie Island and Cape Hatteras, and, on Ocracoke, the oldest continually operating lighthouse in the state.

The pace of life and tourism at the seashore picked up considerably in 1964, when the high-rise Herbert C. Bonner Bridge opened, linking Bodie and Hatteras islands. Before then, ferries served the few residents of the islands' small villages. Still, the seashore retains a disconnected, slightly isolated air. You may easily reach all locations along NC 12, but life here continues on an independent, relaxed schedule.

The following are suggestions that will make your visit smoother and more rewarding during the busy summer season:

— Pick up a copy of "In the Park," which is available at all park service visitors centers as well as other Outer Banks visitors centers. It lists the schedule of interpretive programs and other important information about the seashore.

— Confirm a room reservation before you go during summer weekends and fall fishing weekends.

— Confirm ferry reservations needed to leave Ocracoke Island by calling the Ocracoke reservation line, 800-345-1665.

— Note the park service campground vacancy listings posted at the Whalebone Junction Information Center.

— If you are going to drive on the beach, take a shovel and a tow rope or chain.

Access

Cape Hatteras National Seashore and its southern sibling, Cape Lookout National Seashore, exist to protect and "to conserve the natural and historic objects and the wildlife therein and to provide for the enjoyment of the same in such manner and by such means as will leave them unimpaired for the enjoyment of future generations," according to the National Park Service Organic Act of August 25, 1916. The intent is translated into miles of ocean and sound access. As the issue of beach access becomes more complicated, additional pressure is placed on national resources like these seashores to provide access. Access is controlled, however, in order to protect the fragile seashore ecosystem.

The practical result of this is that virtually the entire 75-mile length of the national seashore is accessible. You must park only at the numerous designated parking areas, and you will want to since they are safer and since NC 12 is narrow and the shoulders are soft sand.

If you're looking for a stretch of beach all to yourself, count the number of cars at the parking pullovers. It is unlikely that any will be vacant during the summer, but once you are on the beach, your privacy is limited only by how far you want to walk. A cooler with something to drink and eat is all you need to be self-sufficient and solitary within the boundaries of the seashore.

Dune crossover ramps are numbered, and there is parking at most crossover locations. The number-ing is a useful reference for surf fishermen and law enforcement personnel, but the numbering doesn't mean that the ramps are spaced at regular intervals. Basically, you drive until you see one you like.

The park service also maintains several major access facilities in addition to the numerous pullovers and ramps. These are described below in the discussions of specific locations within the seashore.

Certain portions of the seashore may be closed to protect the nesting areas of rare species of birds or animals, such as the least tern or pelagic turtles. The closed portions of the beach will be clearly marked. In addition, you cannot drive on the beach within the boundaries of Pea Island National Wildlife Refuge (extending approximately from the old Oregon Inlet Coast Guard Station to just north of Rodanthe) since it is administered by the U.S. Fish and Wildlife Service, which prohibits off-road driving here.

Camping is permitted on a first-come, first-served basis at the campgrounds at Oregon Inlet, Cape Point, and Frisco. You may make reservations for the Ocracoke Campground. The campgrounds are open mid-spring to mid-fall, generally. Frisco closes in early September; Oregon Inlet, Cape Point, and Ocracoke close at the end of October. There is usually a staff person on duty by 7 A.M., and you may arrive as late as 11:30 P.M. and self-register if staff are unavailable.

The park service does not take telephone inquiries directly at the campgrounds. Reservations for the Ocracoke Campground may be secured in person at the campground, by mail at the national seashore headquarters, or through DESTI-NET by calling 1-800-365-2267 (with a major credit card). There is a $10 fee ($12 for Ocracoke) per night per campsite. Each campsite has cold showers, restrooms, drinking water, picnic tables, and outdoor grills. There are no utility hookups. The park service provides garbage-dumping stations near the Oregon Inlet, Cape Point, and Ocracoke campgrounds. One practical tip: if you are camping in a tent, use long stakes; it's windy out there and the sand does not provide much purchase.

Bicycle trips here are best taken in fall or spring. During the summer months when traffic is heavy, NC 12 is dangerous and there is not enough road to compensate for any error. The road seems big enough on paper, but a slow-moving camper behind a bicycle makes traffic back up and drivers can do crazy things.

Winters on the seashore can vary from bluebird days to bone-chilling cold. Wave energy increases, tourists decrease, and seashelling is wonderful. Winter visits give you a chance to come face-to-face with the residents and the isolation. If you ever want to feel as though you own an island, visit the seashore in late February.

Handicapped Access

Generally speaking, most of the structures and all of the visitors centers in the national seashore that are managed by the National Park Service are accessible to the handicapped. This includes restrooms, such as those at the Whalebone Junction Information Center, the Bodie Island Visitors Center, the Hatteras Island Visitors Center, and the Ocracoke Island Visitors Center.

Cape Point and Oregon Inlet campgrounds each have at least one bathhouse that accommodates handicapped travelers. Although reservations are only accepted at the Ocracoke Campground, the park service attempts to assign handicapped travelers a campsite close to an adapted bathhouse.

Dune crossover ramps or decks accessible to the handicapped are available at Sandy Bay Oceanside Access (south of Frisco), ramp 55 near the Hatteras ferry docks, and ramp 70 at Ocracoke Beach.

Handicapped parking spaces are provided at the visitors centers and the lighthouses.

Information

For information, contact Superintendent, Cape Hatteras National Seashore, Route 1 Box 675, Manteo, NC 27954, 919-473-2111.

For campsite availability, call the Bodie Island Visitors Center at 919-441-5711.

Emergency numbers: in case of life-threatening emergencies, call 911; for other types of emergencies, call 441-4134 (north of Oregon Inlet), 986-2144 (south of Oregon Inlet), 928-4831 (fires or medical emergencies in Ocracoke), or 928-7301 (Ocracoke sheriff's office).

The park service must adjust its schedule of services, hours of operation, and interpretive programming to funding levels. Reduced operating hours and closings (even campgrounds) are possible. Call before you go.

Whalebone Junction Information Center

The Whalebone Junction Information Center is the first pullover in the Cape Hatteras National Seashore. It is a useful stop since it is staffed by Dare County Tourism Bureau personnel. These folks can help you gauge campsite availability farther south as well as offer information on private accommodations. Campground information is posted here but may not be precisely current. Nevertheless, you can estimate your odds at securing a vacant space in the first-come, first-served system, and you can also double-check the ferry schedule to Ocracoke. In a perfect world with light traffic, you are slightly more than one hour away from the Ocracoke ferry. There are also restrooms here.

Park personnel are available at the Bodie Island Visitors Center farther south.

Handicapped Access

The restrooms are handicapped accessible.

Bodie Island

As you drive south from the Whalebone Junction Information Center, you are on Bodie (pronounced "Body") Island. Don't look for an inlet at the northern end of the "island," it's gone—New Inlet shoaled-in near present-day Kitty Hawk. At the southern end is Oregon Inlet, opened in 1846. The name Bodie Island generally refers to the peninsula south of Whalebone Junction.

Bodie Island provides a serene introduction to the Cape Hatteras National Seashore. The first 5 miles is a causeway that winds through wax myrtle thickets, by freshwater ponds, and beside the grassy meadows of the low-profile island. The drive is a study in summer greens, created by the jungle-dense vegetation that crowds the road. In fall, the wild grape vines turn yellow, threading through the durable olive of the wax myrtle, and sumac plumes reach red for the sky.

The road winds in such a curious fashion that it plays tricks on your mind. The only landmark plainly visible, the Bodie Island Lighthouse, seems to move around, changing from one side of the road to the other. You may stop at several small, two-car capacity pullovers with elevated observation platforms placed advantageously for bird-watching,

	Fee	Parking	Restrooms	Lifeguard	Camping	Showers	Beach Access	Hiking	Trail	Handicapped	Boating	ORV Access	Fishing	Programs	Historic	Sand Beach	Dunes	Upland	Wetland
Whalebone Junction Information Center		•	•																
Coquina Beach		•	•	•		•	•							•	•	•	•		
Bodie Island Lighthouse and Visitors Center		•	•					•	•	•				•	•			•	•
Oregon Inlet Campground	•	•	•		•	•	•						•			•	•		
Oregon Inlet ORV Access		•									•	•				•	•		
Oregon Inlet Fishing Center		•	•								•		•						
Herbert C. Bonner Bridge		•						•	•				•			•	•		•

usually best in winter. Eventually, the horizon widens as the maritime shrub thicket pulls back from the road and the lighthouse stays put on the west side of NC 12. At sunset, the lighthouse provides a beautiful setting for a photograph.

Coquina Beach

Coquina Beach is the first public beach access site you come to traveling from the north on NC 12 through the Cape Hatteras National Seashore. It's on the east side of the road, about 5.5 miles south of Whalebone Junction.

Coquina Beach is one of the widest, nicest beaches along the entire seashore. The width of the beach above the high-water mark varies between 75 to 100 yards of sand, wide indeed by Outer Banks standards. This stretch of sand has been damaged extensively in the past, however. In 1973, the ocean breached the dunes here completely, destroying the original shelter, located where the picnic shelters are now.

The name of the beach honors the brightly colored bivalve creature—the coquina clam—that digs into the sand with each return of the swash. Tidal pools, great for children, occur regularly here, particularly during the early summer, and the shelling is moderately good, although the high wave energy of nearby Oregon Inlet damages them quickly. Fishing is usually good, especially to the south of the parking area toward the inlet.

As recently as the summer of 1992, the main parking area was characterized by a tall dune line that protected it from the sea. One of the most notable features of this recreational turn-off and a user area were the several unusual picnic shelters covered from the sun by louvers aligned to cast shade during summer. They floated above the tables like abstractions of hovering gulls and the shadow patterns were as fascinating as the shade was welcome.

In the winter of 1992–93, storms knifed into this beach, shaved the sand away, and wrecked the picnic shelters and the parking area. The park service had to retreat. A much-improved, fully accessible bathhouse and boardwalk is the result.

The dune crossover leads to the hull and keel of the *Laura A. Barnes*, now partially covered by migrating dunes—a reminder of the relocation of the visitor facility, where the ship's bones were once in the middle of the parking lot. Sand seems to slowly cover her, much as she had been after wrecking off the

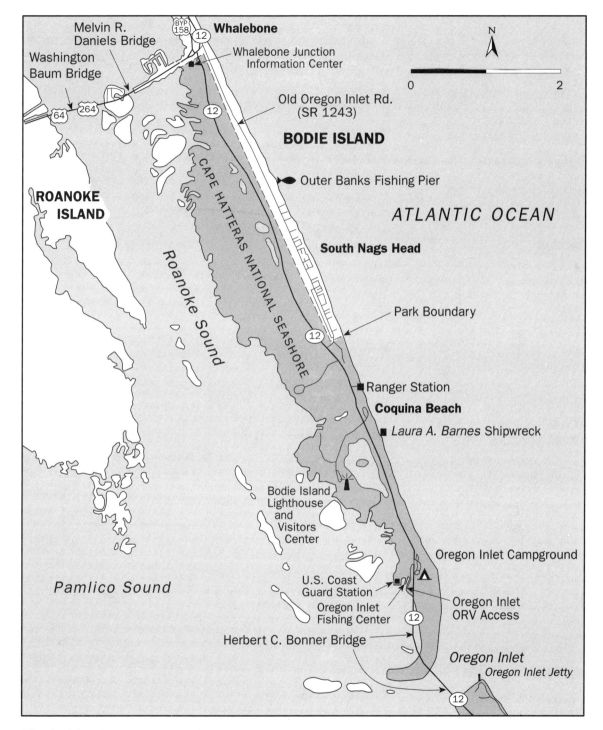

Map 9. Whalebone Junction to Oregon Inlet

coast on June 1, 1921, in a sudden squall.

The park service holds a regular schedule of historical and ecological programs here during the summer. Check the schedules at the Whalebone Junction Information Center or consult a copy of "In the Park," a publication available at visitors centers throughout the seashore that provides information on special programs.

Access

The area is open during daylight hours only.

Off-road-vehicle access is periodically restricted depending on the width of the beach.

Handicapped Access

The restrooms are accessible.

Bodie Island Lighthouse and Visitors Center

The horizontally striped Bodie Island Lighthouse has served mariners and Oregon Inlet since 1872. The present structure is the third attempt to establish a lighthouse along this stretch of coastline—the first lighthouse was destroyed because of improper construction, and the second by the retreating Confederate army. Although its location in the woods may seem surprising, it can be explained by the fact that it was once closer to the inlet, but the inlet moved.

This functioning lighthouse is maintained by the U.S. Coast Guard, which does not allow visitors into the structure. The top of the focal plane of the lens is 156 feet high, and the light is visible 19 miles out to sea. The light blinks in a repeating sequence of 2 seconds on, 2 seconds off, 2 seconds on, and 22 seconds off.

In May 1992, the lightkeeper's quarters were opened as the Bodie Island Visitors Center after a $430,000 restoration. Future interpretive displays at the center will concentrate on the topic of lighthouses.

The center provides information on the availability of campsites in the Cape Hatteras National Seashore, and park rangers are available to answer questions. Be sure to ask for the publication, "In the Park," which details the summer schedule of interpretive programs for all age groups along the entire length of the seashore and also includes newsy items about the status of restoration efforts at other park properties. There are also restrooms at the center.

A nature trail on the west side of the parking lot leads to the sound. During the summer, the park service schedules programs on the natural history of Bodie Island along the trail.

Access

The center is open during daylight hours, 9 A.M. to 6 P.M., during summer months, with reduced hours in spring and fall. If you plan to take the soundside trail after hours bring plenty of insect repellent.

Handicapped Access

There is a paved path to the visitors center and a sandy walkway leading to the soundside trail.

The restrooms at the visitors center are handicapped accessible.

Information

For information, call the Bodie Island Visitors Center at 919-441-5711.

Oregon Inlet Campground

The oceanside Oregon Inlet Campground is one of the most popular of five campgrounds operated by the National Park Service in the Cape Hatteras National Seashore. It is usually open from mid-April to mid-October. Campsites are available on a first-come, first-served basis, and the campground usually rents close to its capacity. The fee for a campsite is $10 per night, with 120 spaces to choose from. Because of the annual fall surf-fishing runs in the waters adjacent to the campground, weekend space through the October closing is difficult to get. There are no utility hookups, but there are restrooms, cold showers, drinking water, picnic tables, and outdoor grills. Because of the sandy location, the park service recommends longer and wider tent stakes and mosquito repellent and netting during the warmer times of year.

Access

The campground opens at 7 A.M. and you may arrive as late as 11:30 P.M. to set up.

Handicapped Access

There are presently no handicapped facilities, but there are plans to upgrade the site. Contact the National Park Service for specific information.

Information

For information, stop by the Bodie Island Visitors Center or call 919-441-5711.

Oregon Inlet Off-Road-Vehicle Access

An unpaved off-road-vehicle access ramp on the east side of NC 12 just before the Herbert C. Bonner Bridge serves the north shore of Oregon Inlet. Only four-wheel-drive vehicles or vehicles modified to drive on soft sand should attempt to drive along the shore to Oregon Inlet. The park service may restrict travel north of the inlet depending on the width of the beach, the number of visitors in the Cape Hatteras National Seashore, or wildlife nesting seasons.

Access

Access is year-round unless restrictions are posted.

Information

For information, call the Bodie Island Visitors Center at 919-441-5711.

Oregon Inlet Fishing Center

A large marina and convenience store, known as the Oregon Inlet Fishing Center, are privately operated concessions licensed by the National Park Service. With the food-rich waters of the Gulf Stream a mere 35 miles to the east, the center does a bustling charter-fishing business. All necessary fishing gear, baits, and food supplies are available at the store, which also has a small eating area and grill, especially popular around breakfast time with the fishermen. Dioramas of mounted game fish of the type frequently caught in the local waters fill several display cabinets.

Fishermen and cars swarm across the pavement like crabs on the beach. By mid-June it's easy to tell who is crew and who is visitor by the tan lines.

You may also launch your own craft at a public boat ramp. There is ample parking for vehicles with trailers.

The U.S. Coast Guard completed a new multimission station on land adjacent to the marina in 1991. The station was established to replace the smaller building on the north end of Pea Island that was no longer serviceable due to shoaling of the boat slip used by the Coast Guard rescue vessels. The new building is not only large but exceptionally handsome, drawing from the architectural heritage of the life-saving and U.S. Coast Guard stations of the Outer Banks.

Access

The center is on the west side of NC 12 immediately before the Herbert C. Bonner Bridge as you head south. The store and marina open very early, usually closing around dusk. Hours vary with the season—and with the fishing.

Handicapped Access

Ramps serve the store and restaurant and there are restrooms that accommodate handicapped travelers.

Information

For information on charter fishing, contact Oregon Inlet Fishing Center, P.O. Box 533, Manteo, NC 27954, 919-441-6301.

The Oregon Inlet Coast Guard Station may be called at 919-987-2311.

Herbert C. Bonner Bridge

The Herbert C. Bonner Bridge is the link to the remainder of the Cape Hatteras National Seashore Recreation Area, spanning the shifting waters of Oregon Inlet. The bridge is named in honor of North Carolina congressman Herbert C. Bonner, who worked ambitiously

Where Does the Sand Go?

One gusty April day several years ago, my two-year-old daughter and I were fishing at the north end of Pea Island National Wildlife Refuge, on the south shore of Oregon Inlet. The tide was receding through the inlet, the wind driving from the northwest, slapping the water against our sandy beach. The current in the channel was strong enough to dance eight ounces of lead directly out to sea, and fishing was frustrating.

My daughter wandered near the edge of the inlet and I grabbed her arm just as a foot of beach crumbled from beneath her feet and disappeared. That same wind-driven, strengthened, and directed tidal current sliced sand off Pea Island just as a woodworker would plane a plank. We watched the north end of Pea Island shorten 10 feet in about 2 hours. The Great Sand Cruncher was at work.

Nature incessantly rearranges the beaches of the barrier islands, stealing from one area and depositing elsewhere. The water that plays out on the sandy apron must recede, and as it furrows seaward it carries particles of beach with it. Wave action in the surf zone suspends the sand in the churning froth. Most of this sand moves parallel to the beach in a littoral current, a process known as longshore transport of sand. Along North Carolina's barrier beaches, most longshore transport runs in a north-to-south course.

Confirmation of the magnitude of longshore transport and the subsequent depositing of the once-suspended sand is most readily observed at Oregon Inlet at the south end of Bodie Island and Cape Point at the easternmost extreme of Hatteras Island. As you cross the Herbert C. Bonner Bridge over the Oregon Inlet, notice the wide expanse of sandy beach curling under the bridge and fanning out into the inlet. Most of this expanse did not exist when the bridge opened in 1964. Indeed much of the bridge spans what appears to be perfectly stable land, which also arrived via longshore transport from beaches to the north.

for the construction of the bridge and died in 1965, a year after the bridge opened. Besides providing transportation across the inlet, the bridge is used by fishermen who bottom-fish the inlet waters from a short catwalk on the east side of the south end of the bridge.

A storm originally blasted the passageway through Oregon Inlet in 1846, and until the bridge was constructed in 1962–64, crossing was by boat or ferry only. Since the construction of the bridge, the inlet has been migrating steadily southward at the rate of 75–125 feet per year. As Oregon Inlet moves south, sand deposits beneath the northern end of the bridge while the ocean gnaws at the north end of Pea Island. Now nearly the first mile of the bridge is over the sandy beach of Bodie Island. At present, the inlet gives every indication of trying to close, which would likely force the opening of another inlet elsewhere to allow the natural movement of tides.

On October 6, 1990, a "nor'easter" tore a dredge, the *Northerly Isle*, free of its moorings in the inlet and slammed it into the bridge, sending 370 feet of the roadway into the channel. Suddenly it was the "good old days" and Hatteras was again an island—no access, interrupted utilities, and no steady stream of truck-delivered supplies. The state got a "crash" course in how to operate a ferry system across the inlet and another postcrash course in bridge repair. Panic spread among the 3,110 vehicle owners who were visiting on Hatteras Island. It took five days to clear them from the

For all the deposition on the south end of Bodie Island, there is severe, corresponding erosion on the north end of Pea Island, the headland on the other side of Oregon Inlet. The old roadbed that ends abruptly here once looped around the headland, and cross shoaling and erosion have closed the U.S. Coast Guard Station at the inlet.

Littoral currents move the sands that are carved away from the headland parallel to the Outer Banks and deposit them further south at Cape Point and at the treacherous fan of submerged sand known as Diamond Shoals, east of the Cape Hatteras Lighthouse.

The direction of wave and storm attack work hardest on the beaches from Virginia south to Cape Hatteras. The waves strike strongly and the sand is eroded and transported southward, perhaps permanently. The same forces cannot take as strong a bite out of the beaches between Cape Hatteras and Cape Lookout, and accordingly they have a lower erosion rate and in some instances are actually gaining sand. Further south at Sunset Beach, deposition from longshore transport has added nearly ¼ mile of sand in front of once right-on-the-beach vacation houses.

In the tangled dynamics of barrier islands, longshore transport is a part of the natural equilibrium of the island. The sand must and will move. The same system that carries sand away from any given beach is likely to be bringing sand to the same location, provided there is an available source of sand. Deposition occurs where currents spread out or otherwise lose velocity and the particles drop to the bottom, at inlets and flattened bottom profiles like Cape Point.

Watch the sand in the surf someday when an offshore wind is brisk and waves are rolling and see if it doesn't slide sideways on return. It is tired of one location and searching for a beachfront elsewhere, pausing now and again in its longshore journey.

islands via the southern ferries.

Meanwhile, daily commuters to Nags Head from Rodanthe had to start their days much earlier to compensate for the time delay caused by the accident. Finally, electrical power was restored on November 2, and by early December, ferry service across the inlet moved into full swing. By February 1991, workers repaired and reopened the bridge, a job initially estimated to take six months.

The temporary loss of the bridge reaffirmed the dependency of the Outer Banks economy on year-round tourism and on the bridge as well. Memories had shortened considerably, it turned out, and the good old days weren't quite so good.

Caution: Currents are very strong in Oregon Inlet when the tide is running; extreme care should be exercised when boating or fishing in the inlet. Swimming in or near the inlet is not advisable under any circumstances.

A parking area to the left of the bridge's south end allows access to the point and also to the catwalk on the bridge. There are no restrictions on access, and if you can park, you can fish here.

Oregon Inlet Jetty

Oregon Inlet is one of the most fickle of the sound-to-sea passageways on the Outer Banks. It is constantly shoaling, and the passage through it is so precarious that only shallow-draft vessels and good skippers try it. This unpredictability has nearly strangled commercial fish-

	Fee	Parking	Restrooms	Lifeguard	Camping	Showers	Beach Access	Hiking	Trail	Handicapped	Boating	ORV Access	Fishing	Programs	Historic	Sand Beach	Dunes	Upland	Wetland
Pea Island, North End	•	•					•						•			•	•		
Old Coast Guard Station	•	•					•						•		•	•	•		
Pea Island National Wildlife Refuge	•	•					•	•	•	•	•		•			•	•	•	•
Pea Island N.W.R. Canoe Launch	•	•									•		•						•
Rodanthe	•	•										•			•	•	•	•	•
Chicamacomico Life-Saving Station		•												•	•				

ing in Wanchese and has caused the loss of several very expensive fishing trawlers. In response to the crisis, a controversial proposal was made to construct jetties to secure the inlet.

The debate over the proposal was furious. Proponents of the plan argued that it would protect the bridge from erosion as well as secure the channel for commercial fishermen; opponents countered that the jetties would only secure the inlet at the expense of down-current locations, which would very likely suffer erosion. The compromise is the $13.5 million, 244,000-ton, 9-foot-tall, ½-mile-long curving granite "terminal wall" on the north end of Pea Island, the south side of the inlet.

Almost immediately after the North Carolina Department of Transportation completed construction of the jetty in January 1991, sand began to accumulate on the landward side, part of its original purpose. It seemed to be working— so far. It also provided a fine fishing spot to landlocked anglers, who parked at the old Coast Guard Station nearby to lug fishing gear nearly a half a mile across soft sand to reach the jetty.

The Department of Transportation subsequently posted "No Trespassing" signs along the sandy approach to the jetty, warning that the area was dangerous since the rocks are slippery when wet. So far, however, the state doesn't seem inclined to enforce the measure. In fact, the Department of Transportation doesn't have enforcement staff, so a cold war of turned heads is the order of the day.

Access

As there is no public access to the jetty, the people you see fishing there must be a mirage.

Oregon Inlet Coast Guard Station (Retired)

The original 1923 U.S. Coast Guard Station on the north end of Pea Island is still maintained by the Coast Guard, even though its major functions have been transferred to a new multimission station across the inlet. The original location had to be abandoned when erosion of the inlet shoaled the channel to the boat slip used by the service's rescue vessel. Visible from the road and bridge, the building is on the National Register of Historic Places.

Access

After crossing the Herbert C. Bonner Bridge, take the first left-hand turn into the parking area at the foot of the bridge. This is the primary access to the inlet. There are portable toilets and litter receptacles at the site.

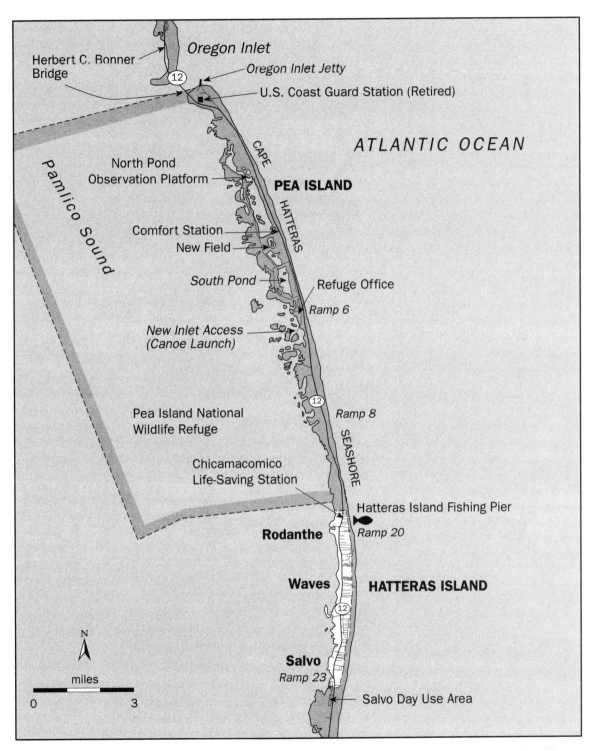

Herbert C. Bonner Bridge

Oregon Inlet

Oregon Inlet Jetty

U.S. Coast Guard Station (Retired)

ATLANTIC OCEAN

CAPE HATTERAS

PEA ISLAND

North Pond Observation Platform

Pamlico Sound

Comfort Station

New Field

South Pond

Refuge Office

Ramp 6

New Inlet Access (Canoe Launch)

Ramp 8

Pea Island National Wildlife Refuge

SEASHORE

Chicamacomico Life-Saving Station

Hatteras Island Fishing Pier

Ramp 20

Rodanthe

Waves

HATTERAS ISLAND

Salvo

Ramp 23

Salvo Day Use Area

N

miles

0   3

Map 10. Oregon Inlet to Salvo

Information

For information, call the Oregon Inlet Coast Guard Station at 919-987-2311.

Pea Island, North End

At the north end of Pea Island, there is an informal access site with parking and portable toilets for day visitors. The road serving this area is the old road to the original U.S. Coast Guard Station, now operating out of a new facility across Oregon Inlet.

The remnants of several paved roads fan eastward from the parking area, all that remain of more extensive recreational facilities destroyed by past storms. At one time, there was a loop drive and restrooms approximately ½ mile east of the road. The hike to the beach is considerably shorter now but rewarded by the quiet waters beyond the pull of the inlet currents and in the lee of the jetty.

This area has a narrow sand beach, open for sunbathing and fishing. Tidal currents are extremely strong close to the inlet, and fishermen may find it difficult to keep weighted lines in place. The lee of the jetty provides quieter water.

Swimming is not advised, except far to the east of the parking area, away from the Oregon Inlet channel. Shelling is only fair, partly because of the turbulence of the inlet waters. The beach widens and the dune line created by the Civilian Conservation Corps in the 1930s be-

comes more stable as the shore arcs south.

Before the jetty was completed, northwest winds and outgoing tides sometimes combined to shave as much as 10 feet of shoreline per hour from the north end of Pea Island. Parts of the island literally disappeared, and under such conditions small children could not be left alone at the water's edge, since it could crumble beneath their feet.

Access

Take the second left-hand turn after crossing the Herbert C. Bonner Bridge and park on the old road. There are portable toilets and litter receptacles.

Information

For information, contact Refuge Manager, Pea Island National Wildlife Refuge, P.O. Box 1969, Manteo, NC 27954, or P.O. Box 150, Rodanthe, NC 27968, 919-987-2394.

Pea Island National Wildlife Refuge

In 1938, 5,915 acres of barrier sand dunes, ocean beaches, salt marshes, and tidal creeks were set aside as the Pea Island National Wildlife Refuge. A system of dikes and freshwater ponds were constructed to provide habitat and to enable refuge personnel to grow certain types of grasses and other food plants for the migratory waterfowl. The refuge occupies the northern 13 miles of the island south of Oregon

Inlet and is managed to benefit wildlife, although it welcomes people as guests.

In addition to the major portion of property actually on the island, there are 25,700 acres of "proclamation" waters—added by presidential proclamation—in adjacent Pamlico Sound that provide forage and habitat. The principal recipient of this protection is the greater snow goose, whose numbers were severely depleted at the time the refuge was established but have now significantly recovered from that ebb.

The most popular time for waterfowl watching is during the fall and winter months when Canada geese and snow geese join approximately twenty-five species of ducks here. Several trails and dikes crossing the freshwater ponds provide locations for stealthily viewing the inhabitants. Peregrine falcons have also been spotted during this season.

Approximately 4.5 miles south of Oregon Inlet is the North Pond Trail parking area and comfort station. The loop trail is about 4 miles long and passes around the North Pond. Should you go for a hike around the North Pond, wear a long-sleeved shirt and long pants and carry plenty of insect repellent. The refuge teems with deer flies, or green flies, persistent and vicious pests. An observation platform on the east side of NC 12 is not too far from the partially submerged boiler of the Federal steamer *Oriental*, wrecked in the ocean during the Civil War.

Pea Island National Wildlife Refuge, Cape Hatteras National Seashore. (Courtesy of N.C. Travel and Tourism Division)

One memorable feature of the refuge is the steep barrier dune bull-dozed into place and planted by the Civilian Conservation Corps during the 1930s. Repeated storms in the mid-1990s leveled the dune line in some locations, propelling the surf to within 20 feet of NC 12. The absence of additional sand has forced the relocation of the highway inland from the visitors center to a point just south of the old headquarters at New Inlet. This buys time for NC 12 and makes viewing the New Field and South Ponds from the road easier.

The beaches of Pea Island are open for swimming and fishing year-round. It's a good bet you will find a serene beach, but you will have to do without restrooms or conveniences. If you don't see another car at a turnout, you are not likely to see anyone else on the beach.

The refuge closes some access areas during the nesting of certain shorebirds to prevent visitors from disturbing the birds. For this reason there are no trails around the New Field and the South Pond. The North Pond trails, however, are always open.

The visitors center is on the west side of NC 12, approximately 3 miles from Oregon Inlet. During the summer months, bird-watching walks and children's discovery programs are hosted by refuge staff. From October through Thanksgiving, Saturday bird-watching walks are scheduled.

The refuge is gradually upgrading visitor facilities. Trail improvements are financed by donations, so the progress is slow. The improvements will include two new observation platforms with viewing telescopes at each.

Camping, campfires, hunting, guns, driving on the beach, and unleashed dogs are prohibited. Dogs are not allowed on the pond sides of NC 12, and you cannot fish in the ponds.

Access

Volunteers staff the refuge office between April and October, 8 A.M. to 4 P.M. weekdays.

There are eight parking areas serving the refuge, all plainly visible from NC 12. There is a soundside parking area and canoe launch just south of the refuge office at New Inlet, an excellent location for crabbing and fishing. Restrooms are also provided there.

Handicapped Access

The comfort station at North Pond is accessible. The trail over the dike and between the ponds and the restrooms at the parking area, part of the North Pond Trail, is negotiable by wheelchair. Renovations to the refuge may improve facilities for handicapped travelers.

Information

For information, contact Refuge Manager, Pea Island National Wildlife Refuge, P.O. Box 1969, Manteo, NC 27954, or P.O. Box 150, Rodanthe, NC 27968, 919-987-2394.

Rodanthe

Rodanthe is the first of the "private" communities surrounded by the Cape Hatteras National Seashore, often referred to as part of a trilogy: Rodanthe, Waves, and Salvo. Pronounced "Ro-dan'-theh," the name is somewhat easier to pronounce than the original community name, Chicamacomico Banks. The name change came in 1874 with the U.S. Post Office. The new name originates from an obscure flower that doesn't grow anywhere near the Outer Banks.

The first thing you see when you enter Rodanthe from the north is the Mirlo Beach development, bearing a name riveted in local history. This new development—four-story fantasies in cedar shakes—appropriates one of Rodanthe's most evocative proper names and puts it right at the town limits. The *Mirlo* was a British vessel destroyed by either a German mine or torpedo in 1918. The crew of the Chicamacomico Life-Saving Station rescued most of the stricken sailors from the flaming vessel offshore from Rodanthe. The development's styling is fanciful, and in my opinion, lacks the solid, salt-of-the-earth, indeed, heroic characteristics that come to mind when murmuring the name, Mirlo. It is an astonishing gateway to Rodanthe, evidence of the new real estate boom that is finding these once-isolated sands.

As you weave through the settlement, you are unaware that the Outer Banks make a geological shift

The Plight of the Piping Plover

A small shorebird, nearly invisible against the dry sand of the dunes, currently buys time against extinction on the not-nearly-lonely-enough segments of the barrier beaches. The piping plover is one of several species that nest at the base of the dunes above the normal high-tide line, in the same sands that people like to walk and build on. The loss of nesting habitat due to increased foot traffic and construction is one of the reasons biologists cite for placing the piping plover, named for its "piping" song, on the federal endangered species list as of January 10, 1986. Fortunately, this small shorebird is finding refuge in the existing preserves along the Outer Banks. But people must help the piping plover and other sand-nesting species survive—it's as easy as sticking to the trails and minding the signs.

April and May are the critical times to mind your dune-climbing manners on the isolated beaches of Cape Hatteras and Cape Lookout national seashores. These are the months when the nesting season begins for the piping plover and other birds that leave their eggs in simple depressions in the warm sands. Joining the piping plover in nesting habits are, among others, the least tern, the gull-billed tern, the common tern, and skimmers.

Adult piping plovers will feign an injured wing to draw you away from an unseen nest. This behavior may be the only clue you will receive that you are near a nest. Unlike the plovers, common terns, which nest in colonies, will attack and aggressively defend their nests.

The plover and the least tern are the two species of most concern. By some counts the petite plover's numbers are down to around 700 pairs along the eastern seaboard, along which it migrates. The beaches of such places as Pea Island, Cape Hatteras Bight, Ocracoke Island, and much of Cape Lookout are prime nesting habitat. When they were unpopulated, the plovers and other birds could leave their camouflaged eggs in the open to hatch, threatened only by the pillaging of either raccoons or larger birds that steal chicks. Today, what threatens the population is a decreasing amount of suitable coastal habitat for breeding, human disturbance that prevents successful nesting, pets that disturb or destroy nests, and developments that create trash, which attracts wild predators such as skunks, raccoons, and foxes.

Stay out of the portions of the seashores that are restricted. The eggs are extraordinarily difficult to see and you might step on a nest, crushing the eggs—probably the only way you'll know that you've found a nest. If you find a nest of chicks (most likely in midsummer) in an unprotected area, notify the appropriate personnel so that confirmation of the sighting can be made. The U.S. Fish and Wildlife Service is in charge of the protection program for the piping plover, but other National Park Service and State Parks personnel will relay the information to them.

---

to head due south just past Rodanthe. Rodanthe is actually the end of a prehistoric island that extended into the sea beyond the present-day community following the same compass alignment as Pea Island. In 1611 the remnants of the island were charted as Cape Kendrick, east of present-day Salvo. Cape Kendrick disappeared sometime in the seventeenth or eighteenth century, and the remnants of the submerged spit are now known as Wimble Shoals.

The crook in the banks and the shoals off-shore brought U.S. Life-Saving Station Number 179 to the village of Chicamacomico in 1874.

As the station grew, so did the community.

Rodanthe today still has the salt-scoured veneer of a self-contained village. There is a basin still used by commercial fishermen as a public harbor, even though the land around the basin is privately owned. There is a lot to learn about the town, but it is reserved for those who commit to joining Rodanthe. Life on this narrow shelf of sand is difficult, and the challenge of living here breeds fellowship.

Some residents of Rodanthe still celebrate "Old Christmas" on January 6, a vestige of the Julian calendar, replaced by the Gregorian calendar in the mid-eighteenth century. The information about the updated calendar took a long time to reach these isolated residents, and when it did, they saw little reason to change.

While Rodanthe is a slow place in the vacation-charged traffic stream streaking along NC 12, tourism is beginning to drum up changes. Several developers have found that the community (along with Waves and Salvo) has a rustic appeal that makes it a desirable stop.

Rodanthe offers numerous places for overnight and lengthier stays, from cottages to motel rooms. With its sister communities, it has become a camping center of sorts. The three towns offer more than 500 campsites with utility hookups. One of the striking images in Rodanthe is the open land and well-groomed look of the large campgrounds on the ocean and sound, even when chock-full.

The Hatteras Island Fishing Pier, at Atlantic Drive and Ocean Drive, is the center of oceanfront activity. You can bet either the fishing or the waves will be up, and both bring visitors to the beach.

Access

There are no designated public beach access sites in Rodanthe. There is public parking at one large lot near the Hatteras Island Fishing Pier, provided through the courtesy of the adjacent Hatteras Island Resort. The pier charges a fee, both for fishing and sightseeing. There is off-road-vehicle access at the pier parking lot, but it is closed between May 15 and Labor Day.

Handicapped Access

There are no public handicapped facilities here. Some of the private resorts and campgrounds may have accommodations for handicapped travelers.

Information

For information, contact Dare County Tourist Bureau, P.O. Box 399, Manteo, NC 27954, 919-473-2138, or Outer Banks Chamber of Commerce, P.O. Box 1757, Kill Devil Hills, NC 27948, 919-441-8144.

Chicamacomico Life-Saving Station

The Chicamacomico Life-Saving Station first came into service in 1874 and maintained an active vigil over the nearby coast until the U.S. Coast Guard closed it in 1953. Since the station housed heroes, it's fitting that it should now be the subject of heroism of a different kind. In the early 1980s, the Chicamacomico Historical Association, a private, nonprofit group, took over the maintenance of the complex, which was in disrepair, and is saving it from disintegration.

The station is a classic example of the indigenous institutional architecture that the U.S. Life-Saving Service and its successor, the U.S. Coast Guard, adopted for their Outer Banks stations. The cottage-like complex was both office and home for the station keeper and crew. The buildings were all constructed for one purpose—saving the lives of the shipwrecked.

During the heyday of the station's activity—from its inception through World War II—life was spartan and demanding for the crew members. The crew stood ready, particularly during the winter months, to be heroic on demand. While this is true of every station and its crew along the Outer Banks, the valor shown at Chicamacomico is legendary in the history of the service.

From these sheds in August 1918, crew members launched the boats

Beach apparatus drill reenactment, Chicamacomico Life-Saving Station near Rodanthe. (Courtesy of N.C. Travel and Tourism Division)

that ferried the survivors of the British tanker *Mirlo*, which was ripped apart by either a German mine or torpedo in the shipping lanes off the Outer Banks. The ship and waters were aflame, the British crew scattered around the burning vessel. Most of the vessel's crew were saved. While the rescue brought medals from the British

government, it was just another day on the job for the crew of Chicamacomico. The rescue had been accomplished under the determined direction of J. A. Midgett, one of the many members of the local Midgett family who served in the Life-Saving Service. In 1930, the Coast Guard recognized the heroism of the *Mirlo* rescue, awarding each of the six-

man crew the Grand Cross of the American Cross of Honor; five of those brave crew members were Midgetts.

The restored quarters are open to the public and showcase exhibits highlighting historic moments and rescues. During the summer, the park service holds mock life-saving drills to demonstrate the rescue techniques that were standard among all the crews from Virginia Beach to Ocracoke. During the demonstrations, the station comes to life as in days of old. Once you see the effort needed to merely stage a rescue for an audience on a sunny day, you can let your imagination picture a rescue on a stormy, moonless night.

Access

The station is generally open during the summer during daylight hours. There are no restrictions on parking and walking the grounds when the station is closed. The National Park Service posts the schedule of the life-saving drills; in past seasons they have been held on Thursdays at 2 P.M.

Information

For information on how to participate in the restoration effort, contact Chicamacomico Historical Association, Inc., P.O. Box 140, Rodanthe, NC 27968.

Waves and Salvo

Waves and Salvo are next on the southward journey. Both are small; Waves, in particular, seems gone before you get there. It catches the eye, mostly because of the large cedar trees and the nestled-in look. Some of the homes and churches along the highway peek out from behind a treescape, unusual on the seashore to this point.

NC 12 scoots through Waves and then curves back toward the center of the island, entering Salvo.

The border between the two is not distinct, and the communities blend into one another. As one resident noted, "There's supposed to be a boundary here somewhere but folks don't seem too sure about it."

Salvo is growing at a quickened pace, sprawling across the low grassy flats to the east of the highway but far behind the dune line, which is protected by restrictions of the Cape Hatteras National Seashore. The sky seems bigger, the horizon spread out, as though you've passed through a gate. A few trees grow along the soundside, but you feel as though you're in a meadow. As you approach the National Park Service day use area south of Salvo, there is an undeniable serenity in the passage.

Likewise, the southern approach to Salvo is one of the most gentle visual transitions along the entire Outer Banks. First there are the grassy flats, then some maritime shrubs, and slowly the punctuation of houses, churches, and trees appears and you have slipped right into a community. Your speed slows to the pace of local drivers. The highway hugs the soundside of the island, and the houses and stores are clustered along its route.

The name Salvo apparently originates from an incident during the Civil War. After a Union naval officer commanded his sailors to "give it a salvo" or broadside of cannon fire, the name "Salvo" was entered

into the records and superseded the original name of Clarksville.

Access

Beach access is primarily by rental of a private cottage or a campsite at one of the many large private campgrounds.

The National Park Service maintains a soundside day use area just south of Salvo. This is one of the prime locations for windsurfing and there is ample parking at what used to be campsites. It is a short walk from the former campground to the sound. There are also dumping stations. During the summer, the park service staffs a lifeguarded swimming area across NC 12 from the day use parking.

Handicapped Access

The park service area has a bathhouse that is accessible for handicapped travelers. There are no other public handicapped facilities in Waves or Salvo, but some of the private resorts and campgrounds may have accommodations for handicapped travelers.

Information

For information, contact Dare County Tourist Bureau, P.O. Box 399, Manteo, NC 27954, 919-473-2138, or Outer Banks Chamber of Commerce, P.O. Box 1757, Kill Devil Hills, NC 27948, 919-441-8144.

Salvo to Avon

If you want to be alone with your thoughts, the length of NC 12 between Salvo and Avon is the ribbon of roadway for mind and solace. The scenery is wondrously constant: a sinuous dune line, mounding masses of evergreen foliage, the slate-green of the sound waters beyond the thickets of shrubbery, the hypnotic march of the utility poles, the cinema of the sky. This is one of the most magical lengths of roadway left along any coast. Don't wonder about what's on the other side of the dunes, park the car and look. Here is the place where your mind may drift freely and imagine what the Outer Banks were like more than 100 years ago.

Ten miles south of Salvo, the Little Kinnakeet Life-Saving Station stands in isolation. The life-saving crews lived here, in the middle of nowhere—waiting for disaster, paid to risk their lives, walking the winter beaches, rowing into the teeth of storms. There are plans to restore the station and use it as a visitors center as soon as funds become available.

Access

The National Park Service maintains several parking turnouts and off-road-vehicle access ramps between Salvo and Avon. The ramps are numbered, and ramps 23, 28, and 30 have large parking lots. Beach driving is recommended only for four-wheel-drive vehicles or vehicles modified to negotiate the soft sands between the parking area and the packed wet sand beach.

At least six soundside off-road-vehicle trails give fishermen and others access to the sound waters between Salvo and Avon.

Avon

Avon was once a small village served by a small basin for fishing boats. It is still home to a number of fishermen, but since the 1980s it has reached a density of development surpassing any village this side of Oregon Inlet. The houses are thick on the sands and becoming thicker. Avon is picking up a resort rhythm and look, which is a broadside shift in character from its beginnings.

At Avon, you have passed into the realm of the surf fishermen. You can tell because tires become larger and vehicles ride higher above the ground. Many local enterprises and anglers are in constant radio contact with others on the Outer Banks, particularly during the fishing runs of spring and fall. Stay on the wire and you can pick up immediate information on what is biting where, a little gamesmanship notwithstanding. Surf-fishing locals will drop everything and head to the beach if the radio chatter says the bluefish have come in.

You'll find a private fishing pier, open to the public for a fee, with parking for the pier. This pier is renowned in the surf-fishing subculture for record catches of red drum, also known as channel bass. Red drum is diehard fishermen's fishing, sometimes in the worst of weather because of their "shoulder season" migrations, and it was from this pier that a world-record 90-pound red drum was caught.

Access

Avon has no designated public access locations to the beach, but it's easy to find a parking spot for either sunbathing, fishing, or swimming. A harbor at the west end of Avon Road gives access to the sound. Once you leave town, you are back on the Cape Hatteras National Seashore and the access ramps are spaced about every 3 miles.

Ramp 34, south of Avon, is a traditional fishing hot spot for bluefish or for red drum during their spring and fall runs. Ramp 38 provides access to the ocean and the sound. Ramp 41 provides beach access just north of the Buxton village limits.

Information

For information, contact Dare County Tourist Bureau, P.O. Box 399, Manteo, NC 27954, 919-473-2138, or Outer Banks Chamber of Commerce, P.O. Box 1757, Kill Devil Hills, NC 27948, 919-441-8144.

Canadian Hole

If you are windsurfer, Canadian Hole is holy water—a place to set sail and go—farther, faster. These sound waters, ½ mile north of the Buxton village limits, bear the name Canadian Hole because so many

	Fee	Parking	Restrooms	Lifeguard	Camping	Showers	Beach Access	Hiking	Trail	Handicapped	Boating	ORV Access	Fishing	Programs	Historic	Sand Beach	Dunes	Upland	Wetland
Salvo Day Use Area	•	•				•	•	•		•			•			•	•		•
Canadian Hole	•	•									•	•	•			•	•		•
Public Boating Access: Avon		•									•		•						•

Canadians come here to windsurf. It has been called one of the finest windsurfing locations in the nation, and in fall and winter, by Canadian standards, the water is warm.

You can't miss the soundside access location since you will see fender-to-fender minibuses in the parking lot and windsurfers flying across the water. Enjoy reading the license plates, but brush up on your French before asking any questions. The National Park Service built a parking lot here in 1988 and it filled up; they enlarged it in 1990 and it stays full. Plan to arrive early if you want a parking place. Folks that windsurf are passionate about it and easily spend the entire day on the water.

There are surf shops in Buxton and Avon that have windsurfing equipment for sale or rent. The village of Avon is steadily becoming an international resort, and the new guests add a wonderful patois to the music of traditional speech. The sport and the Canadians are here to stay. C'est bon!

Access

The parking is on a first-come, first-served basis. There are portable restrooms. Overnight stays are not permitted, so don't plan to camp in your car.

Information

The park service occasionally schedules interpretive programs at the site. Inquire at the Hatteras Island Visitors Center, beside the lighthouse, for specific times and programs, or call 919-995-4474.

Buxton

As you approach Buxton and see the Cape Hatteras Lighthouse directly ahead on NC 12, you know that you've arrived at the figurative heart of the Outer Banks. The first glimpse of the barber-pole-striped light is one of the most exhilarating sights along the entire island chain. What framing for a lighthouse: grassy flats and dunes to the east, the grass feathering west to maritime shrubs, black needle-rush in the marshy flats, and the great gray-blue pond of Pamlico Sound. If possible, arrive at Buxton at dusk as the light begins its nightly work. It is an assuring, transfixing spectacle, and nearly every car that comes to town makes the turn to the lighthouse before checking in at a motel or continuing on its journey.

Although the village of Hatteras is actually southwest, Buxton is the town that means "Hatteras" to many visitors. The confusion lingers because of Buxton's proximity to Cape Hatteras, the tip of which is Cape Point, the sandy spit of land southeast of the Cape Hatteras Lighthouse that is the visible portion of the "corner" of shoals and shallows that all north-south ocean travelers, fish or vessel, must negotiate. This is where the action is: waves, wind, water, and winding reels. When people say, "Going to Hatteras, fishing," they mean they are going to the point, give or take a mile or five, where there will be a jam of anglers crowded together hoping for the Big One.

The southwest bend in the island occurring at the Cape Point elbow changes the effect of prevailing winds and waves on the land. Large sand dune ridges have formed, and

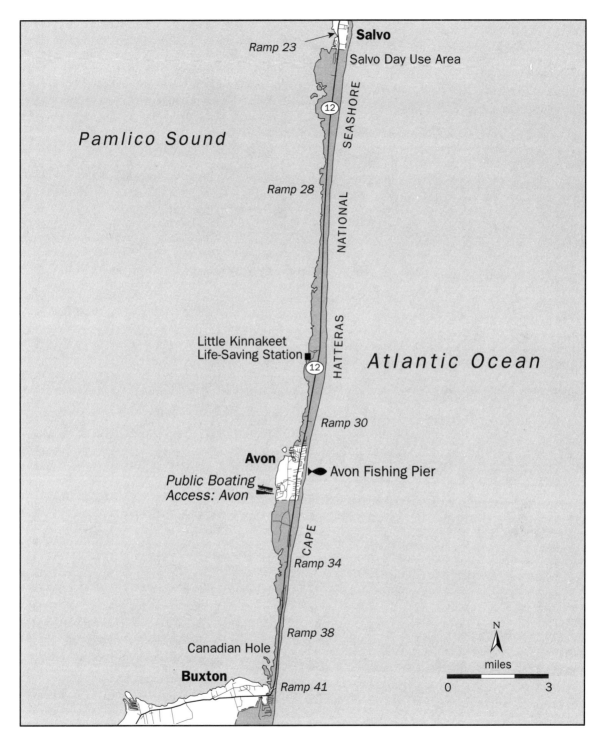

Salvo

Ramp 23

Salvo Day Use Area

Pamlico Sound

12

Ramp 28

SEASHORE

NATIONAL

HATTERAS

Little Kinnakeet
Life-Saving Station

12

Atlantic Ocean

Ramp 30

Avon

Avon Fishing Pier

Public Boating
Access: Avon

CAPE

Ramp 34

Ramp 38

Canadian Hole

Buxton

Ramp 41

N

miles

0   3

Map 11. Salvo to Buxton

Surf fishing on the Outer Banks. (Courtesy of N.C. Travel and Tourism Division)

Wild Rides on the Soundside

There is a new use for the Wrights' stuff on the Outer Banks. The brothers brought their timely invention and lofty dreams here because of the constant, steady winds. Today, this same resource drives more down-to-earth dreams, skimming them across the frothing waters of Pamlico Sound. Windsurfers are cutting a wake in one of the breeziest water sports around.

Dolphin-quick and butterfly-bright, these sailing surfers may have found their Mecca on Hatteras Island, actually just west of land. While the ocean here has long been a surfer's haven because of wind-ginned waves, the slacker soundside waters held no promise for wave riders. Harnessing the perennial breezes has changed the appeal of Pamlico Sound. Now the waters between Buxton and Avon are coming into their own as *the* place not to be bored with a board—provided you have a sail.

So dependable is the wind and so appealing the location that one particular patch of wind and water has developed an international reputation. Welcome to Canadian Hole, so named because of the multicolored migration of sails and sailboards from our neighbor to the north. Check out the other license plates as well; from Avon south to Buxton, there is a definite continental flair. Canadian Hole is considered by those in the know to be one of the best rides in the nation. The interest runs high enough to support at least one surf shop at Buxton. Entry-level equipment can cost nearly $1,000 and individual lessons as much as $30 or more. But what a ride!

The principle behind windsurfing is not complicated—far easier to master than surfing, but far more expensive as well. Unlike a surfer who is dependent on waves, a windsurfer is restricted only by the complete absence of wind. Soundside or surfside, windsurfers ride as long as the wind blows, or until their arms tire. Riders balance their body weight against the force of the wind on the sail; the more forceful the wind, the more the rider must lean over into it to compensate. Steady, unvarying winds that bully the sand about make for ideal long runs. As you might imagine, gusty winds present problems, as does a sudden becalming on the run out from shore.

Canadian Hole has no lock on ideal conditions. In fact, the prevalence of sound waters all along the North Carolina coast insures that any location which is a haven for sailing will soon be a hotspot for windsurfing. Free from surfers' restriction to breaking waves, the sport of windsurfing is probably one of the fastest-growing water sports. The steady winds that once pushed catboats across the sound on fishing and oyster runs will now push windsurfers all along the coast.

Windsurfers are not passengers; they join with board and sail, fused by the dream of flight before the wind and above the water—just as free from the wind-driven sand as the Wright brothers ever were. Advocates call it the ride of a lifetime; watching their brilliant-hued, buoyant-hulled fins flitter across the sound, you understand why.

---

you can see a sample of these as you drive south along NC 12 through the village. These dune ridges shelter inland interdune spaces from salt spray. In the lee of those breezes grows an extensive maritime forest.

The combination of island width, wooded protection, and high ground has sheltered a community here since the earliest days of European settlement. Prior to that, Buxton was the site of a Native American village, a story told at the small Native American Museum in neighboring Frisco.

Although it is the most bustling community adjacent to the national seashore, Buxton is still heavily

	Fee	Parking	Restrooms	Lifeguard	Camping	Showers	Beach Access	Hiking	Trail	Handicapped	Boating	ORV Access	Fishing	Programs	Historic	Sand Beach	Dunes	Upland	Wetland
Buxton		•	•		•		•	•	•	•		•	•		•	•	•	•	•
Cape Hatteras Lighthouse		•	•				•	•	•	•				•	•	•	•		
Buxton Woods Nature Trail		•						•	•					•				•	
Buxton Woods Coastal Reserve								•										•	•
Cape Point Campground	•	•	•		•	•	•			•		•	•			•	•		
Cape Point Beach		•	•	•			•					•	•		•	•	•		
Frisco Campground	•	•	•		•	•	•	•				•	•			•	•	•	
Frisco Day Use Area		•	•			•	•			•			•			•	•		
Sandy Bay Access		•				•	•			•			•			•	•		•
Hatteras Island Access (Ramp 55)		•					•			•		•	•				•	•	
Hatteras Ferry	•	•	•																

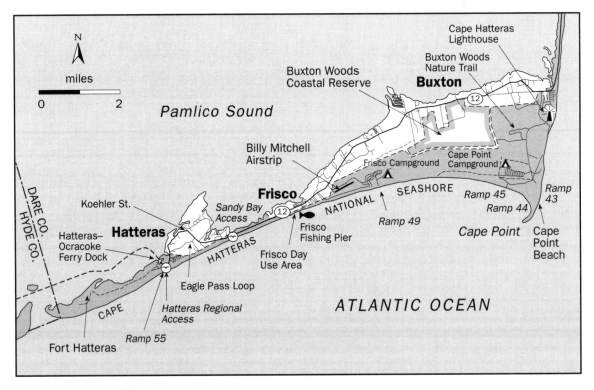

Map 12. Buxton to Hatteras Inlet

Women and boys weave fishing nets on the Outer Banks around 1899. (Courtesy of North Carolina Collection, University of North Carolina Library)

wooded. It looks noticeably different from communities north of it — there are lots of trees, for one thing, and you enter the village at the closest point in the entire community to the ocean. From about the softball field south, you drive into what was once a hilly, forested fishing village. Although much woods remains, what stands out on the drive are the skeletons of pine trees, killed by the salt spray of a mid-1990s hurricane.

Buxton appears slightly unorganized. Individual enterprises stand side-by-side with older houses. Shopping is not yet a Buxton attraction, so there is an inherent utilitarianism about most of the stores, which remain open all year. Some of the restaurants could but don't. Buxton doesn't have to entice visitors; they come anyway, and when they do, they're welcomed but not catered to.

The village is easy to become comfortable in as long as you are aware this is not a resort. There is just as much civilization as you could want, including very early breakfasts and baked goods. A short ride or bike trip away is all the wild water you can use in one visit. As you can imagine, this is not the kind of place that can easily be kept secret. The greatest evidence of Buxton's popularity is the stream of summer vehicles moving through the village to go to the Cape Hatteras National Seashore facilities that are southeast of the commercial and residential parts of the community.

Cape Point has made Buxton the mecca of surf fishing, particularly in fall and spring. Fishing season brings an older and friskier group of children to Buxton, as friendly a group as will ever tow you out of deep sand. When the fish are running, it's a grand time to visit. Buxton hosts the exclusive Outer Banks Invitational Fishing Tournament. The organizers have limited the numbers of teams because it's such a popular event. Finding a place to stay during the tournament may be far more difficult than catching a fish.

With this as background, you can understand why the phrase "going to Hatteras" is less an exact direction than it is a shift in consciousness, usually accompanied by a dreamy, faraway look.

Access

The motels and cottages you see as you enter the community are the closest accommodations to the water. Unless you stay in one of these, plan to commute by car or bicycle to the waterfront. If you have a bicycle with you, then you will find it much easier to gain access to the beach.

The park service controls beach access and provides designated parking areas and off-road-vehicle ramps. To reach the access sites, turn south at the sign for the Cape

Hatteras Lighthouse and Hatteras Island Visitors Center. Follow the wooded drive until the left turn leading to the lighthouse, where there is limited parking. You may also turn right and follow the signs to the campground and a larger parking area further south at Cape Point Beach. You may park on the shoulder of the road unless otherwise posted.

Don't make the mistake of turning on Old Lighthouse Road, which dead-ends at an old naval facility. It has been turned over to the Coast Guard and is used by retired military personnel, active personnel, and dependents. Until the spring of 1992, when the practice was discontinued by the secretary of the interior, V.I.P. quarters were available to high-ranking government officials for nominal rates.

Dare County owns the harbor just south of the village.

Handicapped Access

The best access location for handicapped travelers is at the Cape Hatteras Lighthouse and the lightkeeper's quarters, where all buildings are accessible. There is a path to the beach from the parking lot that has a firm surface. Arrive early to secure a parking place.

Information

For information about accommodations, contact Dare County Tourist Bureau, P.O. Box 399, Manteo, NC 27954, 919-473-2138, or Outer Banks Chamber of Commerce, P.O. Box 1757, Kill Devil Hills, NC 27948, 919-441-8144.

For information about campsite availability at the nearby Cape Hatteras and Frisco campgrounds, inquire at the Hatteras Island Visitors Center, beside the lighthouse, or call 919-995-4474.

Cape Hatteras Lighthouse and Hatteras Island Visitors Center

The Cape Hatteras Lighthouse is the world's tallest brick lighthouse and one of the most recognizable maritime symbols in the world. The 208-foot-tall light casts a revolving beam visible 20 miles out at sea, warning mariners of the treacherous waters of Diamond Shoals, which reach to the east-southeast and have claimed many a ship. Each of the two beacons makes one full rotation every 15 seconds, visible as a flash every 7.5 seconds. The National Park Service is responsible for maintaining the barber-pole-striped light tower, while the U.S. Coast Guard operates the actual light.

In 1999, the lighthouse was one of the most endangered structures along the coast. When its lamps were first lit in 1871, the edge of the sea was more 1,500 feet away, but by February 1999, the ocean had gnawed to within 150 feet of its base. Choices were stark: move it or lose it.

The National Park Service decided to move both the tower and the double lightkeeper's quarters adjoining it. In February contractors literally tunneled under the lighthouse, separated it from its foundation, placed a platform with rollers beneath it, jacked it up, and put it on tracks leading to a new foundation 2,899.57 feet to the southwest, 1,600 feet away from the ocean. On July 9, 1999, 23 days after actual moving began, the journey was over. By November 13, 1999, the light was relit in its new location.

The old double lightkeeper's quarters serves as both a museum and the Hatteras Island Visitors Center. Exhibits detail the history of the lighthouse as well as the exploits of the Life-Saving Service, which operated along the length of the Outer Banks from the 1870s through World War II. Interpretive programs are regularly scheduled here. One of the chief interpreters, Ranger Rany Jennette, is the son of one of the last lightkeepers of Cape Hatteras and lived part of his childhood in the principal lightkeeper's quarters. There are also a gift shop and restrooms at the center.

Access

There is parking for the visitors center, sunbathers, swimmers, and fishermen on the lighthouse grounds, but you must arrive before 10 A.M., particularly during summer, to find a space. Between 10 A.M. and 2 P.M., spaces are particularly hard to come by. You may also park along the shoulder of the entrance road. Follow designated footpaths to reach the beach. There are restrooms at the parking area.

The park is officially closed at dusk, but the hours don't seem to be strictly enforced.

Handicapped Access

The Hatteras Island Visitors Center is accessible. A path to the beach has a firm surface leading to the dune line.

Information

For information, call the Cape Hatteras Lighthouse and Hatteras Island Visitors Center at 919-995-4474.

Buxton Woods Nature Trail

The Buxton Woods Nature Trail is maintained by the National Park Service in the only mixed pine and hardwood forest remaining in the Cape Hatteras National Seashore. Nearly one-third of this ecosystem is within the boundaries of the park. The short loop trail departs from a picnic area that is off the road to the Cape Point Campground. The compacted sand trails wind through the dense and varied canopy of a thriving forest that exists because it occurs on sequential ridges of sand parallel to the ocean. This ridge-and-swale pattern protects the forest canopy from the "shearing effects" of salt-laden wind.

The self-guided trail has interpretive markers that detail the natural history of the woods and the curiosities the trail passes. The woods are dominated by large pines, with dogwoods, oaks, and blue beech trees in the interior. Although the woods themselves are not aesthetically memorable, the forest is significant because, with the freshwater ponds and specialized herbaceous plants, it occurs on the Holocene dunes of a sandy island. The many familiar species of plants here may not seem particularly extraordinary either, but again context is everything. One marker along the trail calls attention to a large flowering dogwood, quite remarkable on the barrier islands. You may also see the sharp, spreading fronds of the dwarf palmetto, a species common in South Carolina but at its extreme northern range in Buxton Woods.

The trails also lead to several freshwater ponds where freshwater bass and bream are successfully living on the Outer Banks. The presence of the water underscores the perhaps little-understood role that the woods play in the maintenance of groundwater replenishment for the aquifer that is the sole source of drinking water in Buxton. Elsewhere in Buxton, unprotected portions of the woods are being subdivided into lots for permanent and second homes. Though the long-term effect of developing the woods is unknown, the potential threat to the groundwater from the additional septic systems and wells and the elimination of the filtering and percolation provided by the woods could be irreversible.

These issues are a part of the story of the fragile and interlocking nature of life on Hatteras Island. It's difficult to think of Buxton Woods as anything other than a rumply jungle, tangled with vines and sometimes visited by snakes. However, just being "the woods" may be the highest and best use of the land.

Access

Instead of turning left off the entrance drive as you would to go to the lighthouse, turn right to reach the Buxton Woods Nature Trail. Parking is available at the site. Take plenty of insect repellent. The first 50 yards of trail, as you move out of the cedar thicket and into the shelter of the first dune line, is a seasonal deer fly paradise. After your walk, check carefully for ticks.

Handicapped Access

Although the trail is compacted, it is probably not sufficiently compacted for someone in a wheelchair to make the complete loop without assistance.

Information

For information, stop at the Hatteras Island Visitors Center, beside the lighthouse, or call 919-995-4474.

Cape Point Campground and Cape Point Beach

The Cape Point Campground is at the southern end of the main road serving the Cape Hatteras Lighthouse and Hatteras Island Visitors Center. The campground is open from mid-April through mid-October, which coincides with the best times for fishing. Restrooms, cold showers, and a fish-cleaning station are provided at the campground. Campsites are available on a first-come, first-served basis. Although it is possible to walk to Cape Point from the campground, it is heavy slogging in soft sand. It is better to drive to the parking lot at Cape Point Beach, and bring a cooler so that once you get to the beach you can stay there.

Access

Turn right off the entrance drive (away from the lighthouse) to reach the campground. Continue on the main drive just past the turnoff to the campground, and you will see the ramp leading to Cape Point Beach, a large fish-cleaning station with running water, and trash cans. To your left or the north past this station is a large parking lot serving the curving spit of sand closest to Cape Point. You should arrive by 10 A.M. during the summer or on weekends to make sure to find a parking place.

The campground is open from mid-April to the end of October. A ranger is usually there by 7 A.M. You may self-register if space is available and staff are not. Ramp 45 provides beach access from the campground.

Handicapped Access

There is one campsite reserved for the handicapped, which includes a cutout picnic table. The bathhouse at the campground includes a handicapped accessible shower with a ramp but no fold-down seat.

There is a boardwalk over the dunes from the parking area at Cape Point Beach, but there are no handicapped accessible restrooms.

Information

For information, stop by the Hatteras Island Visitors Center, beside the lighthouse, or call 919-995-4474.

Cape Point

Cape Point is the altar of the surf-fishing temple that is the Outer Banks—a narrow salient of sand heading almost due east from the Hatteras Island elbow. The point moves like a skate tail, whipping through the compass points, varying widely in geographic orientation, as the waves and currents that swirl offshore roll into the land. A storm in October 1991 sliced it cleanly away, but in some form or another, the waves are building it again.

Charged waves, steered by currents from north and south, meet at Cape Point. As you stand at the point, you can see waves breaking from two directions simultaneously. It's an explosive display, giving credence to oceanographers' claims that the beach energy at Cape Hatteras is the highest on the East Coast.

The collision occurs because waves, driven by winds from out in the ocean moving toward land, refract or bend, trying, as all waves do, to break nearly parallel to the shore. At Cape Point, a wave starts to "bend around" the submerged extension of the point beyond the visible beach. By the time it reaches breaking depth, it has nearly folded in half.

Cape Point has always been southeast of the Cape Hatteras Lighthouse, but the ocean decides exactly how far southeast. Wave action reshapes the point almost daily and repeated visits over several seasons reinforce the fact that, relative to the Cape Hatteras Lighthouse, Cape Point moves around substantially.

At Cape Point, the axis of the Outer Banks makes a pronounced shift from a slightly west of south to a decidedly south of west direction. Instead of the almost frontal assault that the ocean makes on beaches north of Cape Point, waves driven by northeast winds slice obliquely at the sands (and islands) south of the point. The waves slide sand sideways along the beach, and the barrier islands south of Cape Point have a characteristically long, low profile instead of the abrupt dunes and shore of the human-altered beach to the north.

Aerial view of Cape Point at Cape Hatteras. (Courtesy of N.C. Travel and Tourism Division)

The place where the islands shift direction makes an ideal fishing location since any northern or southern migration of fish following the Outer Banks must "turn the corner" at Cape Point. Red drum (or channel bass) and bluefish are two popular game species that circumnavigate Cape Point during their spring and fall migrations, moving through the breaking waves. Fishermen are also predominately seasonal creatures and populate the point in the greatest numbers when the fish are passing on their semi-annual journeys, but some are there at any time of day, any day of the year.

When the fish come to the point, so do the people. A bluefish blitz in Buxton is a four-alarm event. If you've been there at such a time, you know how nearly comic it is when hundreds of people are standing shoulder to shoulder trying to fish in the same spot. Even if you don't fish, go to the point to watch, and try to figure out why, all other things being equal, one person is catching fish but no one else is.

Access

Beach closings are clearly posted. Cape Point can be reached by foot from the parking lot at Cape Point Beach, but the lengthy walk through soft sand and sometimes water-covered flats is difficult. Instead, if you have a four-wheel-drive vehicle, drive to ramps 43 and 44 where you can cross over the dunes to reach Cape Point. Follow the numerous vehicle tracks that indicate crossable sand leading to the point. Even four-wheel-drives can become mired in the sand, but rarely is anybody stranded; the location is too popular for someone not to pass by in a short period of time to help first then laugh afterward. If you don't have a four-wheel-drive vehicle, stick out your thumb and somebody will pick you up.

Information

For information, stop by the Cape Hatteras Visitors Center, beside the lighthouse, or call 919-995-4474.

Buxton Woods Coastal Reserve

North Carolina owns slightly more than 800 acres of Buxton Woods as a part of the North Carolina Coastal Reserve. The state-owned land is located approximately halfway between Buxton and Frisco and joins wooded land in Cape Hatteras National Seashore. The only road into the preserve is a dirt road that slips into the woods off of NC 12, the traditional access into the woods and the only means of seeing more than the acreage along the highway.

Currently, the state intends to maintain the woods as a research preserve, which will remain undeveloped to provide a habitat for island wildlife and a big green place on the island. There are no plans at present to open the property for additional access or to build interpretive facilities. The Division of Coastal Management is negotiating to purchase additional property to increase the size and integrity of this unusual maritime forest.

Information

For information, contact Reserve Manager, 5001 Masonboro Loop Rd., 1 Marvin Moss Ln., Wilmington, NC 28409, 910-962-2470.

Frisco

Frisco straddles the winding course of NC 12 from Buxton south and west nearly to Hatteras. It encompasses a post office and a small village, but the buildings don't cluster at the center of the community. Frisco is a collection of independent businesses and residents that line the roadway beneath the shade of the pines and hardwoods near the waters of Pamlico Sound. Some homes hug the highway, and in a few places houses are burrowed into the island's interior or perch above Pamlico Sound, barricaded from traffic by the maritime forest.

Explore Frisco, by car or bicycle. It's linear and level. In contrast to Buxton, Frisco is sleepy. The relative jump of commercial activity and traffic in nearby Buxton levels off here. If you get the feeling that life, like NC 12, is winding down from a hard straight run, you're right. Want not, worry not in Frisco.

Frisco is a soundside traditional village. Several marinas and private boat slips along NC 12 have restaurants, seafood retailers, and exquisite long, quiet creeks leading to open water. The oceanfront is miles away by car but just over the sand dunes and through the woods by crow. At the west end of town, you sense the oceanfront again as you reenter the Cape Hatteras National Seashore on the way to Hatteras. Only when you reach the extreme southwest corner of the community does the road curl out of the forest with a view of the primary dunes.

Frisco is also the location of the 3,000-foot Billy Mitchell Airstrip and airport, approximately one mile west of Frisco center. From this field, General Mitchell of the U.S. Army Air Corps took off on the historic bombing demonstration directly offshore from Frisco that would eventually result in the complete rethinking of naval battle tactics and strategic planning. In 1921, he and his squadron sank a captured battleship with bombs dropped from the planes. Surprisingly, even after this demonstration, the military establishment remained reluctant to accept the capabilities of air power in naval warfare for years afterward.

The road that leads to the airport winds past some monumental dunes ending at the National Park Service campground. Even if you aren't interested in camping, this campground is worth walking through to see the commanding view of the undulating grass-covered dune field as well as experience the delightful breezes. It is one of the most beautiful spots on the seashore, with a dramatic view of the ocean from the upper campsites. The beach here lies in the curve of the Cape Hatteras Bight, the protected bay south of Cape Point, and frequently has calmer water than the beachfront north of Cape Point. Parking is adequate, and the walk from the campground to the beach is no more than ¼ mile.

At the southwest limit of the town is the Cape Hatteras Pier, or Frisco Pier as it is locally known, which extends some 600 feet into the ocean. The pier is open 24 hours a day between April 1 and November 30. There is parking at the base of the pier, and the pier charges admission for sightseers as well as fishermen.

South of the pier stretch several miles of comparatively unvisited beach with a steep, narrow profile. Driving is prohibited here. Also, several private campgrounds on the western edge of Frisco offer sites. Most are close to the pier, with reasonable ocean access.

Access

The park service provides several access ramps, public parking areas, and the campground. The campground is a short ride east from NC 12 at Frisco. It is open from mid-June to early September, and spaces are first-come, first-served. It is sequestered between parallel dune lines and adjacent to an extensive high-dune maritime forest. Cold showers and restrooms are provided. A splendid and isolated stretch of beach with lifeguards during the summer is available for campground users. Ramp 49 is near the campground; from

there, a wonderful wandering trail leads across the interdune flats and then over the primary dunes to the beach. Shoes are recommended for this hike. Driving on the beach southwest of the campground is restricted due to the nesting of loggerhead turtles and the narrow beachfront. Cape Hatteras air strip is adjacent to the campground entry drive.

South of Frisco is the Sandy Bay Oceanside Access. Here the parking is very close to the primary dune line because the island narrows. The beach here has lifeguards during the summer. On the north side of NC 12 is the Sandy Bay Sound Access.

The last ramp, number 55, is near the ferry docks at the village of Hatteras.

Handicapped Access

Frisco Campground is not accessible.

Both the Sandy Bay Oceanside and Sound Access sites have handicapped restrooms. The Sandy Bay Oceanside Access also has outside showers. Sandy Bay Oceanside Access and ramp 55 have ramps and boardwalks that are handicapped accessible leading to an observation deck overlooking the dunes.

Individual businesses and campgrounds may have facilities for handicapped travelers.

Information

For information, contact Dare County Tourist Bureau, P.O. Box 399, Manteo, NC 27954, 919-473-

2138, or Outer Banks Chamber of Commerce, P.O. Box 1757, Kill Devil Hills, NC 27948, 919-441-8144.

Frisco Day Use Area

On the oceanside just south of the fishing pier in Frisco is the Frisco Day Use Area. This site is plainly visible just after the road curves back behind the primary dunes along one of the most narrow lengths of Hatteras Island. As the name implies, the access site is reserved for daytime use and provides a means to reach the sheltered waters of the Cape Hatteras Bight.

Approximately one mile south on the north side of NC 12 is the Sandy Bay Soundside Access, and across NC 12, closer to Hatteras, is the Sandy Bay Oceanside Access.

Access

The Frisco Day Use Area has paved parking places, full restrooms, cold showers, and a dune crossover ramp. There is parking and a dune crossover ramp at Sandy Bay Oceanside.

Handicapped Access

Frisco Day use is fully handicapped accessible.

Sandy Bay Soundside has a handicapped accessible ramp leading to a soundside overlook.

Diamond Shoals

You're not likely to visit the exact location, but southeast of Cape Hatteras is a place that has shaped the history of the islands you visit today. The waters of Diamond Shoals have made Cape Hatteras a mariner's nightmare.

Extending from Cape Point, the shoals are covered by shallow waters of varying depth—the essential terror of the place. The warm waters of the Gulf Stream collide with the cooler, slow-moving, closer-to-land flowing remnants of the Labrador Current, creating turbulence and danger. It is also the kind of ocean mixing bowl that creates a rich feeding ground for fish at all levels of the ocean food chain.

There are three separate shoals, the innermost being Hatteras Shoals, then Inner Diamond Shoals, followed by Outer Diamond Shoals. Channels pass between the three— Hatteras Slough separating Hatteras and Inner Diamond shoals and Diamond Slough between Inner and Outer Diamond shoals—but they are ever-changing and unreliable. Navigation charts of the shoals are covered with disclaimers and danger signs. Besides the Cape Hatteras light, a Diamond Shoals light tower stands at the extreme eastern edge of the hazard. When the tower was erected in 1967, it replaced a lightship that had been on duty for more than fifty years.

This extensive, shifting, and shoaling navigation hazard has claimed countless commercial and pleasure craft. Indeed, so numerous are the recorded shipwrecks around the waters of Cape Point, that they have earned the nickname of the "Graveyard of the Atlantic."

According to one estimate, 1,500 vessels have been lost in the passage from Cape Henry, Virginia, to Cape Fear. Diamond Shoals in particular tempted mariners in the days of sail. To avoid extensive delays, north- or southbound maritime traffic would try to skirt these waters as closely as possible. However, cutting this corner is dangerous, and some have paid dearly for attempting it.

Hatteras

The village of Hatteras is at the southwest end of the island, a few miles south of Frisco. The road squeezes between marsh and dunes along this narrow pinch of the island, part of the Cape Hatteras National Seashore. As you approach, the roofs, steeple, and trees of the village to the west of the road are alluring, like an Emerald City at the end of the long road. By the time you've zoomed this far along the banks, you anticipate reaching Hatteras. It's the last easily accessible outpost on the barrier islands—figuratively and somewhat literally, the end of the road at the edge of the water.

Before you reach the village, you pass one of the newer access locations, with parking and a boardwalk dune crossover. The National Park Service bans vehicles from driving on this excellent people-free length of beach during the summer months. It is a frequent nesting site for pelagic turtles and a favorite sunning site for visitors, since the beach faces southeast. Next you

will pass a bit of history—Durant Station, a motel named for the renovated Durant Life-Saving Station that stands on the site. You can sleep in a bit of history here.

Most visitors to Hatteras are passing through on the way to or from Ocracoke. NC 12 traffic pulses with the gorging and disgorging of the Ocracoke ferryboats. If you are in a hurry to reach the ferry, turn left on Eagle Pass Loop, which winds through a residential section of the village and delivers you to the ferry dock slightly quicker than the main route. But if you have more time, park your car and walk through the village. You'll learn a lot about the fabric of existence on the Outer Banks.

Hatteras living is simple and for the most part unadorned, at least it seems so from outward appearances. Somehow, though, there always seems to be time for flowers, particularly in front of the small houses along Koehler Street, SR 1237, which meets NC 12 beside the Burrus Red and White Grocery, a local institution. Downtown Hatteras begins informally at "The Slash," the small creek you cross as you drive south on NC 12. Next there is a municipal building, a church, a bank, a few offices across the street from the grocery, and, before you know it, you're passing houses, hotels, and marinas.

Land use in the village overlaps in a manner that would cause a city planner to cringe—houses stand next to offices that are next to marinas, cemeteries separate houses—portraying life as it evolved at the time. Because of the unpredictability of the village, there are more things to be discovered—a private fishing club, a pony pen, an old homestead site overlooking the marsh, even abandoned earthworks. The sense of discovery can extend right down to the architecture. There are bungalows, traditional frame farmhouses, colonnaded facades, and chimney-buttressed houses that radiate durability. There are satellite dish antennas, too.

Hatteras, along with Wanchese, is one of two major fishing centers on the Outer Banks. Commercial fishing sustains the island throughout much of the year, long after the head-boat and charter-boat captains have finished their sportfishing days in the sun. However, tourism and second-home construction are filling in parcels of land as well as some of the voids that come with the insular nature of living here and the reality of fishing as a source of income. Merchandise and food-stuffs that do not fit within the stereotypes of a commercial fishing village are beginning to appear on grocery store shelves. The newcomers who stay through the summer are bringing new tastes and investment dollars to the community, and Hatteras is slowly responding. For example, Hatteras now has a doughnut shop that caters to the early-morning fishing traffic. But in the quiet along Koehler Street, a sense of community and neighborliness remains. You can tell by the flowers.

Since the access through Hat-

teras Inlet to the Atlantic has been far more stable than the passage through Oregon Inlet to the north, charter fishing is a thriving business in Hatteras. All types of sound, open water, and half- and full-day fishing trips are available. If surf fishing is your pleasure, you might note that many of the local fishermen take the ferry to Ocracoke to surf fish— a clue visitors should keep in mind.

Access

The park service maintains two beach access locations with parking and dune crossovers. The first is the Sandy Bay Oceanside Access, just north of the town limits. The Sandy Bay Sound Access is on the north side of NC 12. The second is a large access area with parking for about 25 cars at the Ocracoke ferry dock. A wooden ramp slightly more than 100 yards long leads over the primary dune line to the wide beach. The road to the access area also leads to the Hatteras Coast Guard Station and a ramp that provides four-wheel-drive access to the South Beach area, the point of land to the north side of Hatteras Inlet that is gradually curling southwest into the inlet. The point is easily 2 miles from the ramp. If you can reach it, there's a lot of very nice beach and good surf fishing as well.

Dare County maintains one boat slip and two parking spaces for unloading at the Harbor Seafood Marina on the west side of NC 12. There is a 4-hour limit on the use of the slip. The public slip is available at the private marina because the U.S. Army Corps of Engineers

maintains the channel between the sound and the basin.

Handicapped Access

Sandy Bay Oceanside has an accessible observation deck overlooking the dunes.

The access area at the ferry dock, Ramp 55, is accessible to handicapped travelers and a boardwalk extends to a deck at the crest of the primary dunes.

The ferry landing has restrooms accessible to handicapped travelers.

Information

For information, contact Dare County Tourist Bureau, P.O. Box 399, Manteo, NC 27954, 919-473-2138, or Outer Banks Chamber of Commerce, P.O. Box 1757, Kill Devil Hills, NC 27948, 919-441-8144.

Graveyard of the Atlantic Museum

Adjacent to the beach access site at the Ocracoke ferry dock is the site of the proposed Graveyard of the Atlantic Museum, which will interpret both the natural and the navigational history of the Outer Banks. Planning for the museum is completed; fund-raising is the focus of the current effort.

Particular features of the museum will include exhibits on the Union ironclad *Monitor*, sunk nearly due east from this point in a storm in 1862 while being towed following its historic sea battle with the CSS *Merrimac* at Hampton Roads, Virginia, earlier.

Fort Hatteras

At the very south end of Hatteras Island, approximately 2 miles south from the Ocracoke ferry dock, are the earthwork remains of a Confederate fort constructed to facilitate raiding on the Union traffic through the inlets. The Confederate soldiers were driven out of their positions in 1861 as the Union secured the sea lanes and inlets of the Outer Banks to prevent the Southerners from receiving supplies by sea. Access to the fort is by foot or off-road vehicle from the National Park Service ramp.

Hatteras Ferry

The free ferry from Hatteras Island to Ocracoke is a ride worth waiting for—how long you wait depends on both the time of day and time of year. At times it may seem as though you are leaving the mainland connection alongside everybody else. The traffic is especially intense during holiday weekends and the summer. But if you have to wait in line, waiting to go to Ocracoke is about as nice as a wait can be. You may be able to strike up a friendship with a fellow traveler while waiting for your ship to come in. Play the waiting game: walk to the dock, look for the ferry, walk back, throw a frisbee, play some cards.

The ferry service schedules departures every 30 minutes during daylight hours from April 15 to October 15, and during winter, every hour on the hour, 5 A.M. to 5 P.M., as well as at 7, 9, and 11 P.M. Throughout the summer season, as many as six vessels may be in service to handle the large numbers of visitors continuing their trip to Ocracoke. Placement on the ferries is on a first-come, first-served basis, and the personnel who direct traffic onto the ferries are very astute at delaying those who they think have jumped in line.

It can be a wonderful passage for children and big kids, too. Gulls and terns follow the ferry looking for an easy feed. Take some crackers or bread and toss caution and the crumbs to the wind—both will probably never hit water. Some of the gulls are tame and adept enough to maneuver with the ferry and take food from your fingertips.

The ferry route skirts close to the island at first before heading west into the sound and curling back east to the sheltered ferry dock on Ocracoke Island. You may move about freely after the vessel is under way, and there are restrooms on the ferry. When you step off of the ferry, you'll be in Hyde County.

Information

For information, call the North Carolina Ferry Division at 919-726-6446, or the Hatteras ferry dock at 919-928-3841.

Hatteras Inlet

Hatteras Inlet has been a primary passage between Pamlico Sound and the Atlantic Ocean since a hurricane split the barrier island in 1846, also opening Oregon Inlet. Maps prior to 1760–70 show an inlet closer to Ocracoke Village, which would have isolated the higher, more stable portions of the island where the village was established.

The inlet for the most part has been fairly stable as a navigable channel. The reliability of Hatteras Inlet presents an alternate outlet to commercial fishermen of Wanchese who must fight the constant shoaling of Oregon Inlet. However, a glance at a map will show that churning to Hatteras Inlet from Wanchese is not cost efficient since it adds to the fuel consumption as well as the time that a vessel is not fishing. Trawlers are not geared for speed or cruising, but the long ride is better than running aground.

For all its relative stability, however, Hatteras is an inlet on the move. In 1955, erosion took away an abandoned U.S. Coast Guard Station at the north end of Ocracoke in the inlet.

The Houses of Heroes

The decorative architecture of more recent Outer Banks vacation homes, characterized by wide dormers, hip roof towers, shingled siding with carpenter Gothic ornamentation and lighter painted trim, draws from the buildings of one of the legendary institutions along the North Carolina coast, the U.S. Life-Saving Service, forerunner of the U.S. Coast Guard. Twenty-four life-saving stations once were sentinels along the Outer Banks, roughly every 7 miles from Virginia Beach south to Ocracoke. The Chicamacomico station at Rodanthe is probably one of the best known, but many more are visible and adapted to different uses.

The stations, first authorized by Congress in 1874 with initial funding for twelve, were built to last and housed heroes—there's no other word for the crews and station keepers. The job description was simple, the demands incredible: walk the beach every night for eight months a year, and if a ship is sinking, rescue whomever you can.

The treacherous waters nicknamed "Graveyard of the Atlantic" brought the stations. The stations in turn each provided steady employment for six crew members at $120 a year and $200 a year for the station keeper. While their rescues became legendary and are well chronicled at visitors centers on the Outer Banks, the buildings became community landmarks, often the only building visible along the lonely, empty, sand-swept shoreline.

They were buildings of distinction, pure and simple. Essentially there were two components to a station, the quarters and the boathouse. Sometimes other buildings supported the needs of these two. The boathouse was a single large room like a garage, usually with three bays for the high prow surf boats. The quarters were sometimes over the boathouse. Some stations had distinctive watchtowers capping the main building.

The stations were wood, and some, such as the Currituck lightkeeper's quarters, were prefabricated and shipped to their locations. The wood was often Atlantic white cedar, locally known as juniper, cut on the mainland. The siding and roof were cedar shakes. An extensive guttering system carried rainwater to a cistern for storage. The stations were constructed with a Victorian carpenter Gothic flair, and it is their decorative brackets adorning end gables and paneling used as trim that have been creatively adapted for use in new houses.

In 1915 the U.S. Life-Saving Service became the U.S. Coast Guard, a change that meant little in the day-to-day operation of the lonely Outer Banks stations. But by the 1930s, the need for the stations declined, and the Coast Guard began to decommission them, only to reactivate them during World War II. Following the war, the stations were decommissioned and sold. Only one, at Ocracoke, remains in active use today.

The remainder are not all gone, nor are they forgotten. They just wear different hats, as restaurants, motels, offices, or visitors centers, such as Chicamacomico. The following are a few to watch for as you drive the Outer Banks.

One is a private residence within the boundaries of the Currituck National Wildlife Refuge north of Corolla.

Twiddy and Company Real Estate maintain offices in two former stations, the Wash Woods station in Carova and the Kill Devil Hills station, which Twiddy moved to Corolla.

The Sanderling Restaurant and Bar in Sanderling is the former Caffey's Inlet Life-Saving Station, which is on the National Register of Historic Places. The original sign is at Owens' Restaurant at Whalebone Junction in Nags Head, along with other service artifacts.

Station Number 6 at milepost 4.5 on Virginia Dare Trail in Kitty Hawk survives from 1874, but it has been moved back from the oceanfront. This is one of the more ornate Gothic structures and is now a restaurant. South along Virginia Dare Trail is the old Kitty Hawk Coast Guard Station, now privately owned.

While Owens' Restaurant is not a renovated station, its evocative architecture painstakingly creates a widespread assumption of authenticity that is reinforced by the decor, including one of the finest collections of genuine service artifacts and memorabilia in the state.

South at Pea Island is a newly abandoned Coast Guard Station; a new multimission station has been constructed next to the Oregon Inlet Fishing Center.

At the Pea Island National Wildlife Refuge headquarters are the foundations of the old Pea Island station, the only all-black life-saving station in the history of the service.

Chicamacomico at Rodanthe is on the National Register of Historic Places and is currently operated by the private Chicamacomico Historical Association. This is the station made famous by the Midgett family, six of whom lived and served here. Seven Midgetts have won the Coast Guard Gold Medal and three the silver, a family accomplishment unmatched.

South of Avon is Little Kinnakeet station, one of the original life-saving stations constructed along the Outer Banks. Its isolated location best captures the severity of being in the service. The National Park Service began restoration work in the summer of 1991.

At Hatteras Village, there is the Durant Station, open as a motel.

Even in their new uses, the buildings have a distinctive look that used to be hard to miss. Now, with nods to vernacular influence in architecture catching hold, they are being discreetly surrounded by look-alikes.

Hyde County

At some point just before it docks on Ocracoke Island, the ferry from Hatteras enters Hyde County, most of which is on the mainland, 2½ hours west by another ferry. Ocracoke Island and the remainder of Hyde County are separated by more than miles, however.

Mainland Hyde County is comparatively untraveled except by those who love to bird-watch or hunt waterfowl. The majority of the county was once high swamp or pocosin, drained to create farmable, habitable land. A necklace of fishing villages laces the Pamlico Sound waters, but all in all, the mainland is not on the tourist loop. This works in its behalf, however, for the town life and lifestyles that dominate in the county represent a very honest and unchanging profile of a rural, agricultural lifestyle vanishing rapidly elsewhere in the state.

The primary commerce of mainland Hyde County is agriculture in a big, big way. The farms are vast. For example, some of the homes along US 264 south of Lake Mattamuskeet have backyard gardens that are ½-mile long. Also, the Lake Landing National Register Historic District, so designated for its archetypical settlement patterns of family farms, churches, and commercial buildings, comprises 13,400 acres—with only twenty-five buildings.

There are 634 square miles of land in Hyde County—and Ocracoke may have around 10 square miles at a guess. As you can see, this outer bank is outnumbered, too.

Commercial fishing is also a big industry in the county; in Ocracoke it's obvious, but the crab fishery at the mainland village of Swan Quarter is also a major center. Much of the mainland is managed timberland. These private holdings by timber and paper companies are tremendous in number and in size. In addition, a significant portion of the county is managed as two national wildlife refuges: Swan Quarter and Lake Mattamuskeet.

Lake Mattamuskeet is the largest naturally occurring lake in the state. A shallow basin, barely 6 feet deep at some points, Lake Mattamuskeet is prime waterfowl refuge. The lake is spanned by NC 94, and improved roads circumnavigate the lake, affording access to boat docks and the permitted hunting blinds. Hunting in the refuge is very limited and heavily controlled.

The Intracoastal Waterway skews across the county from a neck of the Alligator River in a southwest line north of Lake Mattamuskeet until it reaches the waters of the Pungo River. The passage is 20 miles long, the longest inland traverse of the waterway.

Tourism in the form of hunting and fishing also is extremely important to the economy of the mainland county, which doesn't have any population center larger than a village. In fact, Ocracoke Village is one of the largest permanent communities in the county and brings in a significant part of its tourism and tax revenues.

Ocracoke is a natural and cultural extension of the barrier island chain, not a colony of the mainland. The differences between island and mainland life are beginning to heat up more than just a little. Ocracoke wants to leave Hyde County to join Dare County, which is closer and marches to the same tourism drumbeat. It makes a lot of sense, and it sure would simplify the coast.

Information

For information, contact Hyde County Chamber of Commerce, P.O. Box 178, Swan Quarter, NC 27855, 919-925-5201.

Ocracoke Island

As recently as twenty-five years ago, at least one resident of Ocracoke had never been off the island. When pressed by the reporter to explain why, the independent-minded soul (an elderly woman by my recollection) replied, "I never saw any need to."

For me, it is the unspoken communication of that story that made such a lasting impression about this particular woman and Ocracoke. She found her place in this life and on this earth—the tiny island at the end of NC 12—and it was satisfying. It must be wonderful to feel that way about a place.

Ocracoke is an island that could stir such sentiments. Life on the island is real but narrowly focused, unpretentious, and straightforward.

In spite of large numbers of visitors, the island still turns inward and is nearly, in some ways, anachronistic. It is a beautifully worn pocket watch in the digital era. It lingers in another time, much as South Carolina's Daufuskie Island and some corners of the Eastern Shore of Maryland and Virginia. The shared experience of living on Ocracoke infuses residents with powerful loyalty. I have not sensed the same balance of communal devotion, acceptance, and friendliness anywhere else on the coast.

The residents are loyal not just to the place but to the combination of place and how it shapes a way of life. A minister who once pastored the Methodist church there summed it up nicely when he said, "Here, you're born a member of everything whether you join it or not."

Ocracoke is an appealing counterpoint to the more cosmopolitan Outer Banks to the north (believe it or not, Hatteras is worldly by comparison). Naturally, the numbers of people going to this 16-mile-long spit of sand and wooded village create a dilemma. More than a few travelers begin any discussion about Ocracoke with "When I first went there . . ." There are those who visited when the only way to travel to the island was by mail boat, shortly after electricity and a good number of years before community water came to the village. They lament the inevitable alteration in the Ocracoke of their memory because of improved access, discovery, and tourism. There are specific complaints about newer buildings that are nontraditional in design, commercial enterprises that cater to tourism, and traffic. In general, the complaints reveal an edginess about the homogenization of Ocracoke Island, the sanding of its distinguishing elements—primarily remoteness—to make it smooth and more convenient. Ocracoke has changed, is changing, and will change further, but it will always be Ocracoke.

The island includes 775 acres of private land surrounded by the Cape Hatteras National Seashore.

	Fee	Parking	Restrooms	Lifeguard	Camping	Showers	Beach Access	Hiking	Trail	Handicapped	Boating	ORV Access	Fishing	Programs	Historic	Sand Beach	Dunes	Upland	Wetland
Ocracoke Island		•	•	•	•	•	•	•	•	•	•	•	•	•	•	•	•	•	•
Ocracoke North End		•					•									•			
Ocracoke Pony Pen		•								•				•	•			•	•
Ocracoke Campground	•	•	•		•	•	•	•	•			•	•			•	•		
Ramp 70 (Ocracoke Beach)		•		•			•			•		•	•			•	•		
Southpoint Rd.												•	•			•	•		

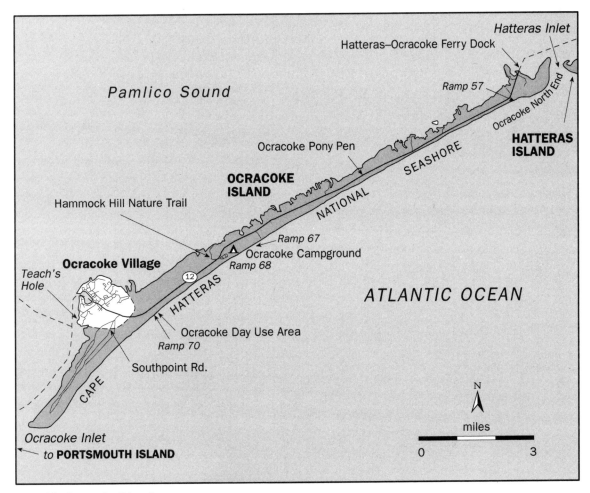

Map 13. Ocracoke Island

Although the residents will probably always resent the method of condemnation of the island for its purchase as seashore holdings, they recognize that if it had not been for the seashore protection, Ocracoke would now be like Nags Head. Because there is little private land, the island is exclusive; because the island's ability to provide fresh water and dispose of waste is limited, it is likely to remain small and charming. Ocracoke will always be a distinctive village. More shops and hotels will probably come, the population will steadily grow, and some of the wonderful insular traditional ways of life may be tempered by the next generations, but the changes will occur on island time.

If this is your first visit, I suggest you arrive without any preconceived notions or schedules. Let the island unfold to you as you drive south, looking over your shoulder at the sea as it gnaws at the north end of the island threatening the road. Let antsy drivers pass you, and look at what they miss. Cruise between the grassy flats and the low overwash dune field, marking your passage by utility poles and occasional osprey nests.

Stop at the pony pen, cross the small creek at Six-Mile Hammock (6 miles from the village), and then drive slowly into town. Make your first visit a time to walk around to talk with residents. Talk about the weather, ask which fish are running and the best bait to buy, and listen to the wonderful islander pronunciation. You'll pick up the richness quickly.

The beach to the east of the village is not exceptional, but the spell of the entire island makes it seem so. The island encompasses a wide prairielike grassland where the famed ponies once ran freely, gnarly live oak trees, and Teach's Hole, where Blackbeard died. There's the Ocracoke Lighthouse, the Coast Guard Station, the British Sailors' Cemetery, the new Ocracoke trolley, and the old, reliable Community Store. There's the post office, the wonderful, rambling Island Inn, the magic woods of Springers Point, and a few patches where the old cement-and-shell road buckles. There are Scotch bonnets on the north end and mullet in the sound. There is first and foremost Howard Street, a place to walk along the sand lane of bygone days.

No one can paint you a picture of what to expect at Ocracoke, for there is really nothing like it elsewhere. Visit the post office or the Community Store, walk past the wonderfully tended family cemeteries that snuggle in the middle of residential streets. When you step onto the island, you step into a community; you can experience it or you can look at the postcard views and read the guidebooks as you drive through.

Ocracoke is probably one of the most written-about locations in the state, beginning with Carl Goersch's *Ocracoke*, published in 1956, a descriptive and delightfully anecdotal book considered to be one of the classic works about the island at the beginning of the present era. *Ocracokers*, by Alton Ballance, unintentionally reads as a follow-up volume, bringing the story left dated in Goersch into contemporary times. Between the two, you can develop a rich feel for the island and the intimacy between the residents and the place.

It is not wise to visit Ocracoke in the summer without a ferry or room reservation. If you are day-tripping from Hatteras, note the ferry schedules and allow yourself plenty of time to line up for your turn at crossing. The ferry dock is not a nice place to sleep, but you wouldn't be the first.

Access

The National Park Service maintains several beach access locations on Ocracoke. Ramps 59, 67, 68, 70, and 72 may be used by vehicles to reach the wet sand beach. There is a parking area at the ferry dock serving the north end and additional parking at ramp 68 at the Ocracoke Campground. About 3 miles south is ramp 70 at the Ocracoke airstrip (you'll know it by the wind sock). The beach between Ramp 67 and the day use parking area is closed to vehicles seasonally. Lifeguards are at the day use area and ¼ mile north of Ramp 70. From this ramp, it is about a 4.5-mile walk to the south end of the island and Ocracoke Inlet. The entire seashore is open to the public, but you are strongly advised to park only at designated parking spots or on a paved or hardened surface.

Handicapped Access

The Ocracoke Pony Pen has a parking turnout that's accessible to handicapped travelers.

The Ocracoke Island Visitors Center is accessible for handicapped travelers. The Ocracoke day use area, ramp 70, has a boardwalk leading over the primary dunes to an observation deck. Various private facilities have handicapped accommodations.

Information

For information about accommodations, contact Hyde County Chamber of Commerce, P.O. Box 178, Swan Quarter, NC 27855, 919-925-5201; Ocracoke Civic Club, Box 456, Ocracoke, NC 27960, 919-928-6711; Dare County Tourist Bureau, P.O. Box 399, Manteo, NC 27954, 919-473-2138; or Outer Banks Chamber of Commerce, P.O. Box 1757, Kill Devil Hills, NC 27948, 919-441-8144.

For additional information, call the Ocracoke Island Visitors Center at 919-928-4531 or contact Superintendent, Cape Hatteras National Seashore, Route 1 Box 675, Manteo, NC 27954, 919-473-2111.

Emergency numbers on Ocracoke Island: 928-4831 (fires and medical emergencies), 928-7301 (sheriff's office).

Ocracoke North End

After you drive off the ferry from Hatteras, park your car to explore the north end of Ocracoke Island, a shelling hot spot. The fishing at the mouth of the inlet is not too bad either. Because this end of the island stays wide, low, and flat, in stormy weather, the waves surge over the sandy spit and deposit shells from offshore and the intertidal zone. In these sands, you are likely to find different species of mollusks than those living in the waters off of Hatteras Island. Angel wings, turkey wings, razor clams, and even some helmet-shell species turn up more frequently here. The state shell, the Scotch bonnet, begins to appear in profusion along the strand of Ocracoke.

The island's latitude, orientation, and proximity to the Gulf Stream account for the shift to warmer-water molluscan species. The low-energy nature of the ocean, a generally gentle wave action, doesn't grind the shells up as severely as the ocean does north of Cape Hatteras. Early risers following storms get the best pick of shells, and you will certainly have much better luck in the winter months when there are fewer visitors competing for the same treasures.

Access

Parking is available at the ferry docks, or you may park along the side of the road about 200 yards south of the ferry dock—the place is obvious.

Ocracoke Pony Pen

Unlike their cousins at Corolla, the Ocracoke ponies live in a 170-acre fenced pasture, which prevents them from wandering across the highway. The National Park Service feeds them daily and sees that a veterinarian is called when needed, something that was impossible when the animals roamed wild in the late 1950s and early 1960s.

The ponies are direct descendants of Spanish mustangs and are anatomically distinct—having a different number of vertebrae—from horses that come from English-speaking countries. Given the turbulent nature of the Outer Banks ocean passage, it seems likely that a shipwreck brought the first ponies to the island, but it is not known when this occurred. The ponies thrived. At one time, there were several hundred roaming free on the island, and each year there was a pony penning and auction.

Islanders have long used the ponies. The U.S. Life-Saving Service trained them to haul boats on the beach, and some were harnessed to buggies. In the 1950s there was even a mounted boy scout troop on the island that lassoed, trained, and cared for their own horses.

Small, lithe, and durable, the ponies roam free within the confines of their enclosure, which secures several miles of rich grassland and freshwater sources. A marker at the pen, which is located on the west side of NC 12, details what is known about their origin and remarkable physiology. You also may see a ranger on mounted patrol, riding a horse native to the park.

Seashell Serendipity

Shelling has nothing to do with looking and everything to do with just being there, pretending you're not looking, strolling the beach, casual-like. You successfully stalk the perfect sand dollar (or keyhole urchin) or the pristine Scotch bonnet not when you're looking for one but when it's your turn to find one. Shelling is a sport out of your control; all you can do is go to the court and hope someone shows up with the ball.

It is serendipity; it is half-buried treasure. This is why we all do it, this and the fact that it is without a doubt one of the few glorious, free, money-back-guaranteed things left to do.

There are few places better for shelling than the Outer Banks between Cape Hatteras and Cape Lookout. Here nature has set in motion a process that brings an unusually large number of different shell species together—shells whose organisms normally do not inhabit the same waters.

The cold waters of the Labrador current slink down the eastern seaboard, bringing with them a drift of cold-water species such as the surf clam, the quahog, and the knobbed whelk, its left-handed look-alike, the lightning whelk, and their smooth cousin, the channel whelk. These shells are commonly discovered between the Virginia border and Cape Hatteras.

Hop the ferry to Ocracoke and sample the southern fauna such as the angel wings, the giant murex, the heavily armored helmet shell, the giant tun, and of course, the Scotch bonnet, the official seashell of North Carolina. These shells, among others, are rarely found further north.

What happens off of the North Carolina coast is that colliding currents from different environments bring some of their resident seafloor life with them. Semitropical-water shells commute north with the Gulf Stream, and the Labrador currents bring seafloor "snowbirds" south. The salient of Cape Hatteras is a difficult corner for ships; you can imagine the challenge it is for these creatures to "turn," and so it becomes the turning point for shelling fortunes.

Nearly 1,300 species of mollusk have left their calling cards along the Outer Banks, so you are likely to discover a personal-first find on almost any trip—unless you have been shelling for a very long time. The species-distribution records are updated annually to accommodate the "strays" that beach far afield from their normal waters. Almost any foray on the beach, particularly in winter, is going to bring an unusual discovery.

Access

There is parking at the pen. The horses are fed daily at approximately 8:30 A.M. and 6 P.M., which you are invited to watch.

Handicapped Access

The parking area at the pen accommodates handicapped travelers.

Information

For information, call the Ocracoke Island Visitors Center at 919-928-4531 or contact Superintendent, Cape Hatteras National Seashore, Route 1 Box 675, Manteo, NC 27954, 919-473-2111.

Ocracoke Campground

Ocracoke Campground is on the east side of NC 12, 3 miles north of the village of Ocracoke. It is the only National Park Service campground that will take reservations. There is a $12 fee per night per campsite, and the campgrounds are open mid-spring to mid-fall. There are 130 tent and trailer spaces but

Why winter? Mainly because the typically stormy seas during that season deposit more shells where you may find them. Also, fewer people visit the beach this time of year to pick over the shells. Pick an isolated stretch of beach following a February storm, and not only is it all yours, but the shelling can be phenomenal.

Summer tactics have to be different, except for the timing—after a storm is still best. The best place is where there are the least people or where there is no easy access. The north end of Ocracoke is probably the most easily accessible bountiful location, year in and year out, for the mix of shells from north and south. If the surf's edge fails to yield a prize, glean the sand-blown overwash flats landward of the surf zone. The more adventuresome you are, the richer the reward. Hire a boat in Ocracoke to guide you to Portsmouth Island, just across Ocracoke Inlet. This scarcely visited part of Cape Lookout National Seashore is one of the undersearched areas for shelling or other flotsam. Farther south, Core and Shackleford Banks, also part of Cape Lookout, offer the greatest likelihood of successful shelling because of fewer visitors. But shelling following a storm has one disadvantage—wave damage. The systems that beach so many shells in these locations beat them up pretty badly as well. You'll find a shelling bounty on Core Banks, but you'll turn over many a shattered part looking for the select whole shell.

Other locations that merit searching are the still lightly traveled beaches of Currituck County and special spots such as Hammocks Beach State Park and Masonboro Island much farther south. As you move closer to Cape Fear along the barrier islands, the possibility of finding the delicate sand dollars, sea biscuits, and keyhole urchins increases, primarily due to the comparatively gentle slope of the beach and the generally lower wave energy, which allows these shells to wash up intact.

The North Carolina Aquariums at Roanoke Island, Pine Knoll Shores, and Fort Fisher have representative shells (both occupied and empty) on display. *Sea Shells Common to North Carolina*, a guidebook, is available from the University of North Carolina Sea Grant Program, 105 1911 Building, North Carolina State University, Raleigh, NC 27650. The booklet may also be obtained from the North Carolina Maritime Museum in Beaufort.

no utility hookups. The campground has a bathhouse with cold showers, restrooms, drinking water, and a dumping station. The campsites are windy and bare, and there is no shade. Long tent stakes are advised, since Ocracoke can be the windiest of the campgrounds.

The campground offers ample access to the wide sandy beaches of the island. In the past, the beach had a lifeguard, but now lifeguards are on duty during the summer only at the beach at ramp 70 further south. Ramp 68 provides access to the beach here, but the beach south from this ramp is closed to vehicular traffic from Memorial Day to Labor Day. There is also a self-guided nature trail that leads through an ecological cross section of the island.

Access

Check-in time is noon. If you reserve a campsite, the park service will hold it until 8 A.M. the next day. Better call if you will miss the 8 A.M. deadline.

This is a good place to hit the beach, but the park service would prefer you to swim at the day use area.

Information

To make reservations, call Mistix at 1-800-365-CAMP, which takes most major credit cards, or stop by the campground in person to secure a site or a reservation for a future date.

Ramp 70 Access Area

Slightly north of Ocracoke Village, you will find ramp 70, also known as the airport ramp since the Ocracoke airstrip is nearby. The parking lot is in a low area known as the plains. It is open year-round and is the only convenient crossing if you want to spend the day at Ocracoke Inlet. The inlet is approximately 5 miles south of the ramp, accessible by foot or four-wheel-drive vehicle.

The National Park Service provides lifeguards at the beach here during the summer. The beachfront to the south is relatively isolated, and bathers or shellers seldom visit. In the past, the isolation of the south beaches generated a notoriety for nude sunbathing. The park service looked the other way, in a manner of speaking, but enforcement priorities have changed and skinny-dippers or nude sunbathers may be fined.

The south beaches are sometimes the location for nesting sites of pelagic turtles as well as certain bird species that lay their eggs in shallow depressions in the sand, such as the piping plover or the least tern. During such times, the beach is posted, and you must con-fine your vehicle to the wet sand beach. There is often excellent fishing on the spit of sand that curls into Ocracoke Inlet at the south end.

Access

Parking is first-come, first-served.

Handicapped Access

This parking turnout allows you to drive as close to the water as any location on Ocracoke. There is a boardwalk leading over the primary dunes to an observation deck.

Information

For information, call the Ocracoke Island Visitors Center at 919-928-4531 or contact Superintendent, Cape Hatteras National Seashore, Route 1 Box 675, Manteo, NC 27954, 919-473-2111.

Southpoint Road

South of the turn for the Ocracoke airstrip and nearly opposite the Café Atlantic Restaurant and Bar is Southpoint Road, the sand road leading to the southern point of the island. This 3-mile route is suitable for four-wheel-drive vehicles only.

The southern point at Ocracoke Inlet is a terrific location for shelling and fishing, and there are usually fewer people there. Pack a cooler and picnic lunch and go explore wildest, remotest Ocracoke.

Ocracoke Village

Ocracoke Village is on the sound-side, at the highest location on the island above sea level, rimming the basin known to locals as "the Creek" and to others as Silver Lake. The highway swings around the north side of the lake, a winding path past the commercial heart of the island. A mixture of cedars, live oaks, yaupon, and the grape-tangled growth in young pines marches up close to the road, sheltering the houses behind. The salt spray shears the tops from the few large trees on the island, and the gnarled and wild limbs seem to press the houses down into the soft gray sand with an effect both mysterious and enchanting.

Settlers first arrived at Ocracoke in the early eighteenth century. The inlet to the south has been continuously open since recorded history, the longest of any in the state. The town's early commerce swelled with the maritime, mercantile economy that passed through the inlet to mainland ports, the oceangoing vessels pausing to unload their cargo to shallow-draft ships that then crossed the sound. In the nineteenth century, when Ocracoke received designation as a port with a permanent crew of pilots, the village began its steady growth.

The inlet, by the way, is dependable but not deep, certainly not deep enough to hide a submarine as Tom Clancy suggests in *The Hunt for Red October*.

	Fee	Parking	Restrooms	Lifeguard	Camping	Showers	Beach Access	Hiking	Trail	Handicapped	Boating	ORV Access	Fishing	Programs	Historic	Sand Beach	Dunes	Upland	Wetland
Ocracoke Village		•	•					•		•	•		•		•			•	•
Ocracoke Lighthouse		•								•				•	•			•	
British Sailors' Cemetery		•													•				
Ocracoke Island Visitors Center		•	•							•	•			•	•				
Ocracoke Ferry		•	•																

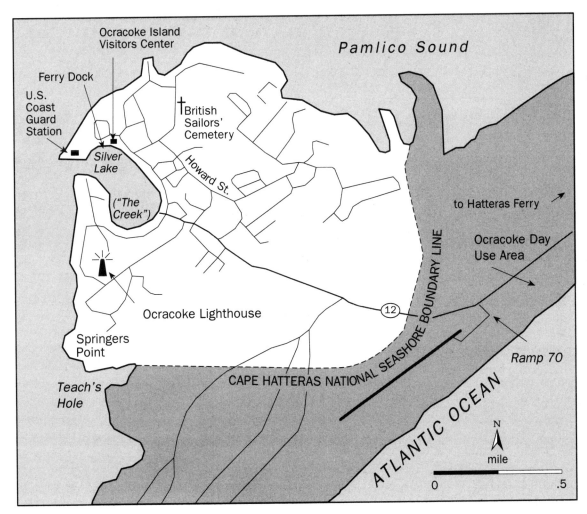

Map 14. Ocracoke Village

Ocracoke Village. (Courtesy of N.C. Travel and Tourism Division)

The Ocracoke Lighthouse is the most visible reminder of the early mercantile era, having been in continuous use longer than any other on the coast. Other major players in the village history were the U.S. Life-Saving Service in the late nineteenth century followed by the U.S. Coast Guard. In fact, in one way or another, government has always been prominent here. During World War II, the navy created the ferry dock and transportation system, and following the military's departure, the park service became the largest landholder on the island in the 1950s.

Today, tourism and fishing are the major contributors to the local economy. Tourism is not new, but the volume of traffic is. It's always been a tight little island; now it's much tighter in summer. To accommodate the tourists and the growing number of permanent residents, there is now a water tower to serve the approximately 250 available rooms and the permanent population of about 700.

Ocracoke Village is bicycle size. NC 12 curves around the north side of Silver Lake and loops to a halt at the ferry dock, where ferries serve Swan Quarter and Cedar Island. Adjacent to the ferry are the National Park Service Office and Interpretive Center for the Cape Hatteras National Seashore and the U.S. Coast Guard Station, constructed in 1934. On your way to the loop, you will pass the Community Store, the bread-and-butter stop of the island for years, the Ocracoke post office, and O'Neal's Dockside, the fishing and charter center for the island. There are several specialty shops, among them, the Gathering Place, a restored home relocated to prevent its demolition and now filled with works by local craftspeople.

If you don't have a bike, then walk through the village. Mosquitoes might keep you company at night, but they're not unbearable. Bring some insect repellent and strike out at dusk. Your wanderings through the side streets will show you a lively community. Be sure to visit the British Sailors' Cemetery, the lighthouse, and the sandy, bowered walk of Howard Street.

Once you arrive in the village, there's very little reason to start your car unless you are driving to the oceanfront access locations.

Access

The closest beach access is at Ramp 70.

You may park at the lot next to the Ocracoke Island Visitors Center, and there is limited pullover parking on the island, which you may use as long as you don't block travel lanes or access to boat slips or launches.

The park service maintains Silver Lake Marina, 400 feet of dock space at the park service headquarters. There is no dockage fee. If you find a place open simply tie up. There is a 14-day limit during the summer months.

Handicapped Access

The Boyette House and the Silver Lake Motel are the only accommodations that advertise handicapped facilities. Some of the rental cottages accommodate handicapped travelers.

Information

For information about accommodations, contact Hyde County Chamber of Commerce, P.O. Box 178, Swan Quarter, NC 27855, 919-925-5201; Ocracoke Civic Club, Box 456, Ocracoke, NC 27960, 919-928-6711; Dare County Tourist Bureau, P.O. Box 399, Manteo, NC 27954, 919-473-2138; or Outer Banks Chamber of Commerce, P.O. Box 1757, Kill Devil Hills, NC 27948, 919-441-8144. The Ocracoke Civic Club publishes a directory and map with excellent listings of accommodations and features; the club also maintains an answering machine to take incoming calls.

For information about park programs, call the Ocracoke Island Visitors Center at 919-928-4531 or contact Superintendent, Cape Hatteras National Seashore, Route 1 Box 675, Manteo, NC 27954, 919-473-2111.

Ocracoke Lighthouse

The Ocracoke Lighthouse has been in operation since 1823, making it the oldest continually operating lighthouse in North Carolina and, after the Sandy Hook Lighthouse in New Jersey, the second oldest in the United States. To reach the Ocracoke Lighthouse, turn off of NC 12 onto the road that passes in front of the Island Inn. A little over ¼ mile down the road, you'll come to the lighthouse, surrounded by a picket fence nearly as famous as the lighthouse itself.

The squat white tower is modest by the standards of the other lighthouses on the Outer Banks. A mere 75 feet tall, with 5-foot-thick walls, the focal plane of the light is at 65 feet. Its steady white beacon is visible 14 miles at sea, signaling safe harbor. It was one of four authorized by Congress in the late eighteenth century, along with Cape Hatteras, Cape Lookout, and the Baldhead light at the mouth of the Cape Fear River. The purchase for the original one-acre lot was voided because the construction didn't begin before 1801, as specified in the contract of sale. The existing two-acre site was purchased for $50 from Jacob Gaskill, a member of a family still prominent on the island today, and this time construction proceeded quickly.

At the time of construction, the light guided mariners to the entrance to the only reliable inlet north of Cape Lookout. The reach of Diamond Shoals at Hatteras made the Ocracoke light doubly important. A ship sailing north around the Outer Banks that could see the light at Ocracoke would know it was on a collision course with the shoals. It could then tack to the east, riding the Gulf Stream current north as it makes its natural curl around Cape Hatteras.

The lightkeeper's quarters, constructed at the same time as the light, is currently in use as the residence of a National Park Service ranger.

Access

The lighthouse is presently undergoing renovation and is not open to the public, but the grounds are. The restoration is expected to take several years.

Handicapped Access

The lighthouse grounds are negotiable by handicapped travelers.

Information

For information, call the Ocracoke Island Visitors Center at 919-928-4531 or contact Superintendent, Cape Hatteras National Seashore, Route 1 Box 675, Manteo, NC 27954, 919-473-2111.

Silver Lake

One of the most scenic basins you are likely to see as you travel this coast or any other, Silver Lake is the tidal basin and harbor of Ocracoke, the central body of water that serves the town. Natives refer to it as "the Creek." If you arrive by ferry, you power past the U.S. Coast Guard Station on the north side of the entrance, a shrubby spoils area, and some private residences on the south. Before you, nearly dead center at the east end of the basin, is the shingled roof of the Island Inn, one block away. The Ocracoke Lighthouse peaks above the trees to the southeast.

Arriving by car from Hatteras, you first see Silver Lake through a framing of small dock houses, trees, and private homes on the southwest horizon. It is an approach that is best timed for sunset.

The dredged and bulwarked entrance to the basin, the only way in and out, is deep enough to serve the ferries and Coast Guard vessels. Before World War II, the Creek was a very shallow tidal basin, according to some accounts about the same size but not more than 4–5 feet deep. The navy, which had an extensive base on the island to monitor German submarine activity in nearby "Torpedo Junction," dredged the basin during World War II. The bulwarks were added because the larger vessels that use the Creek create a wake that causes erosion.

If you awaken early, before the sun rises high, and stroll around the basin, or do the same at sunset, you will see gulls on pilings, mullet and menhaden skipping over the water, and the low-gunnel, high-prow wooden fishing boats designed to ride the sound waters safely while their captains work—photographs waiting to be taken against the backdrop of waterside buildings.

Nobody will tell you not to wade in Silver Lake, and nobody will mind you taking your children crabbing or fishing here either.

There are several marinas here; private docks are plainly marked.

British Sailors' Cemetery

One part of Ocracoke Island, the British Sailors' Cemetery, is not privately held nor does it belong to the Cape Hatteras National Seashore. It belongs to the United Kingdom, a legacy of the war that shattered these peaceful shores during the 1940s.

In 1942, German submarines operated practically unchecked off of the Outer Banks, and by the end of April 1942, they had sent sixty-six vessels rounding the point at Cape Hatteras to the bottom. The region became known as Torpedo Junction. Unprepared for submarine warfare, the United States suffered tremendous losses as the U-boats operated with impunity.

The United Kingdom responded by sending experienced crews and antisubmarine vessels to the Outer Banks. One of the ships was the HMS *Bedfordshire*, a 170-foot-long converted commercial fishing vessel. The *Bedfordshire* reported at Ocracoke with four officers and thirty-three crew members and began patrolling east of the island.

On May 11, 1942, in the ship's second full month of patrol, the *Bedfordshire* was torpedoed and all crew members were lost. Within three days, two bodies washed ashore and were identified by islanders as British sailors Thomas Cunningham and Stanly Craig. The Williams family donated the land adjacent to their family cemetery as a burial site for the two men. A week later, two more bodies, dressed in similar clothes but not identifiable, came ashore and were placed in the same cemetery.

The small cemetery is along a side street a block beyond the west end of Howard Street, and you may visit any time. It is maintained for the British government by the U.S. Coast Guard. Above the graves flies the Union Jack, the flag of the United Kingdom. Each year, on or about May 11, the British consulate in Washington sends a staff member to Ocracoke for a private memorial service.

A plaque on the cemetery fence quotes Rupert Brooke's poem, "The Soldier": "If I should die, think only this of me: / That there's some corner of a foreign field / That is forever England."

Teach's Hole

The dense maritime forest on Ocracoke Island's west side, Springers Point, faces a shallow indentation and navigable channel known as Teach's Hole, the snug harbor of the infamous Edward Teach, or Black-beard, during the early eighteenth century.

Virginia's Royal Governor Alexander Spotswood, perceiving Blackbeard and his fellow pirates as a threat, sent Lt. Robert Maynard and two sloops south to trap Teach in his current port of call, Ocracoke. They found Teach in this very haven, and Teach was beheaded during hand-to-hand combat by Maynard's boarding party. Several of Maynard's men were killed in the costly fight, but all of the pirate's band were killed or captured and hung later. Legend has it that Teach's body circled his grounded ship seven times before it sank. Teach's head made one last sailing trip, mounted on the bowsprit of Maynard's sloop as it returned to the mainland as confirmation of his death. Apparently the secret of the location of the hiding place of Teach's buried plunder died with him. It is allegedly still on the island.

You can reach Teach's Hole by boat or by a long walk along the sound beach from the south jetty of the cut. You have to cross private property to reach the wooded portion of the island overlooking Teach's Hole. Request permission before you do.

Ocracoke Island Visitors Center

The Ocracoke Island Visitors Center is opposite the toll ferry dock and provides information about the Cape Hatteras National Seashore and the village of Ocracoke. During the summer season, the center bustles with activity. If you disembark the ferry with little or no idea what to do, then go to the center. The helpful staff will give you information about attractions and locations on the island or elsewhere in the seashore.

Most importantly, the visitors center and its amphitheater are the hub for many of the interpretive programs about Ocracoke. A full schedule of events is posted for these activities, which usually begin in mid-June and continue until Labor Day. Programs target various ages, and children usually find most of them enjoyable. In past years, the programs have included morning bird walks, cast net fishing demonstrations, exhibitions on pirates, and historical presentations on Ocracoke. Participants in certain limited programs such as soundside snorkeling are chosen by drawing names out of a hat.

The center also provides maps and various materials on both Cape Hatteras and Cape Lookout National Seashore. Information on the availability of campsites is also provided upon request. There are also restrooms at the center.

Access
The center is open during the summer from 9 A.M. to 6 P.M. daily. After Labor Day, the schedule varies. There is parking at the center.

Handicapped Access

The center is accessible to handicapped travelers.

Information

For information, call the visitors center at 919-928-4531 or the ranger station at 928-5111.

Ocracoke to Portsmouth Island

Across Ocracoke Inlet lies Portsmouth Island, part of North Core Banks, which is in the Cape Lookout National Seashore. Ocracoke is the place closest to the island and the deserted village of Portsmouth there. The National Park Service licenses Ocracoke residents to operate ferry services to the island. The Ocracoke Island Visitors Center will have information on the options for making the trip to Portsmouth.

One local option offers a slice of Outer Banks life. For many years, the Austin family has ferried visitors to Portsmouth in their sturdy boats, dropped them off for several hours of exploration, and returned them across the inlet. The Austins charge $40 round-trip for two or less and $15 each for three or more. The family enterprise is authorized by the park service in accordance with U.S. Coast Guard regulations, continuing a service they provided to previous generations of island residents. The park service also lists Dave McLawhorn as providing the same service for the same rates.

Be sure to take insect repellent, sunscreen, and something to drink with you. If you're going fishing, take plenty of everything, including comfortable shoes. You will walk a fair distance when you reach Portsmouth.

For more information, see the section on Portsmouth in the chapter on the Cape Lookout National Seashore.

Information

For information on local ferry services, stop by the Ocracoke Island Visitors Center or call the center at 919-928-4531. The Austins may be reached at 919-928-4361 or 919-928-4281. Also contact Portsmouth Island ATV Excursions at 919-928-4484.

Ocracoke Toll Ferry

The North Carolina Department of Transportation operates two ferry routes connecting Ocracoke Island to the mainland. One route crosses northwest across Pamlico Sound to the village of Swan Quarter, the county seat of Hyde County, Ocracoke's parent county. The other route crosses southwest to Cedar Island in Carteret County; various connections then lead to the beaches of Cape Lookout National Seashore as well as Carteret County's resort beaches. Both rides will transport you to new and different types of explorations of North Carolina's coast.

Disembarking from the Cedar Island ferry is the beginning of the Outer Banks travel experience for many travelers (which means you'll have to read this book backward); others arrive at the ferry at Ocracoke as the southern terminus of their vacation.

Since the ferry from Ocracoke to Swan Quarter primarily serves traffic to the seat of county government, its schedule varies less with the season. There are two departures daily, at 6:30 A.M. and 12:30 P.M. Departures from Swan Quarter to Ocracoke are at 9:30 A.M. and 4 P.M. The ride takes approximately 2½ hours. Reservations are urged.

The Cedar Island ferry operates a seasonal schedule. There are four departures daily from 7 A.M. until 4 P.M., in either direction, from April 15 through May 31 and from September 16 through October 31; five departures daily from 7 A.M. until 4:20 P.M. from June 1 through September 15; and two departures daily from November 1 through April 14, departing Ocracoke at 10 A.M. and 4 P.M. and Cedar Island at 7 A.M. and 1 P.M. The ride takes 2¼ hours.

The name of the driver and the license plate number of the vehicle making the crossing must be given when making reservations. Reservations must be claimed at least 30 minutes prior to departure and are not transferable. It is strongly advised to be on time for all departures. The cost is $10 for a passenger car under 20 feet long, $20 for larger vehicles or combinations, $1 for bicyclists, and $.50 for pedestrians.

Information

Reservations are strongly recommended and may be made up to thirty days in advance by calling the Ocracoke reservation desk, 800-345-1665.

Swan Quarter

A ferry from Ocracoke transports you to Swan Quarter, the historic seat of Hyde County. A commercial fishing village conveniently near the Lake Mattamuskeet and Swan Quarter wildlife refuges, Swan Quarter is one of the finest stops you can make with an empty cooler and a taste for fresh seafood. Follow the signs from the ferry past the soybean fields and forests into downtown. Turn south and the road will take you to where the shrimping and crabbing fleets dock, where you can stock up on fresh seafood to take home.

Approaching Swan Quarter from the ferry, you slip into the town sideways. The town is small and dignified. At the corner of NC 45 and SR 1129, the main street of the small town, stands the Hyde County Courthouse, listed in the National Register of Historic Places. Handsome, modest homes line the streets of this residential community. One of the most striking features are the massive loblolly pines on the north side of the community, along SR 1129, which leads northeast to US 264.

Several churches front SR 1129, including Providence United Methodist Church, located at the corner of Main and Church streets. Known locally as the "church moved by the hand of God," this church is the subject of one of the more intriguing legends of the area. The story has it that after the congregation's offer to purchase a building site was refused by a landowner, they built a wood frame church on brick piers elsewhere. On the day of the building's dedication, a terrible flood struck Swan Quarter (which is only 10 feet above sea level), and lifted the church from its piers, floated it down the street and around a corner, and dropped it smack in the middle of the lot originally selected. The previously reluctant owner took the hint and deeded the land to the congregation. A church history is available that tells a detailed version of the story.

Swan Quarter was first settled in early 1836 when it became the county seat. It is believed that the town is named for Samuel Swann and was originally called Swann's Quarter, where "quarter" referred to a division of land. It was incorporated in 1903 but repealed the charter in 1929.

For information on the surrounding area, see "South by Southwest: US 264 from Manteo."

Information

For information, contact Greater Hyde County Chamber of Commerce, P.O. Box 178, Swan Quarter, NC 27885, 919-925-5201.

A Slice of Island Life

There are multiple habitats and multiple dwellers in those habitats on the barrier islands of North Carolina. Not all habitats are developed equally on all islands; the shape and extent of habitats vary according to external factors such as the prevailing winds and physical factors such as the width of the island. Nevertheless, there is a predictable sequence of barrier island habitats. If you were to go for a sea-to-sound walk on a "typical" barrier island, the following are the places you would find and some of what you would find in those places.

Beach

There are two parts to a beach, the foreshore, which is the beach covered by the tides, and the backshore, that part of the beach beyond the reach of the tides but not part of the dunes. You spread your towel on the backshore, splash in the foreshore.

Wave action shapes the foreshore. It is a high-energy environment (for animals and children) where footprints are erased each evening by the tides. The constant wave action makes life here challenging, and only a few creatures call it home. Two of the most abundant and amusing are the brightly colored coquina clam and the mole crab. The co-

quina buries rapidly into the sand as waves recede. Occurring in vast colonies, each clam has bright individual markings. Mole crabs tunnel backward into the sand as waves recede, filtering food with their antennae.

The backshore is an extremely hot environment, with very little growing there or choosing it as a permanent niche. This is the home of one of my favorite creatures—the nighttime sideways-stalking ghost crab. These swift-moving creatures tunnel deeply into the sands to remain cool, scooting out to feed and wet their gills in order to breathe in the evening. Their antics are wonderful, and they are quick! Try to catch one—they can move 2 yards in a heartbeat.

The most spectacular users of this habitat are the pelagic turtles, which crawl to the backshore to excavate their nests and lay eggs in early summer.

Dunes

Dunes occur where wind can pile sand into mounds and vegetation has an opportunity to stabilize it. The dunes closest to the ocean are known as frontal or primary dunes and take the full force of wind-driven salt spray and the storm surge of an unruly ocean. If the dunes go, the habitats (and houses) behind them go also. It is a severe environment.

One of the most important functions of an intact dune system is to deflect salt spray–laden wind upward, buffering the island from the killing effects of sea water. Only salt-tolerant plants can live on a dune and, in so doing, anchor it. Perhaps the most elegant of all beach plants, sea oats thrive on the dunes, easily recognized by their tall "flags" of seeds.

Frequently there are parallel lines of dunes with a trough between the two. Usually on the back or secondary dunes, sheltered from the salt spray, you can begin to see the development of woody shrubs, tolerant of the heat and the arid conditions but still sculpted—sheared just above the height of the primary dunes.

Few things live in the dunes, but several species of shorebirds, the endangered least tern and piping plover, along with royal terns, nest in shallow depressions or flats at the base of the dune zone. Walking on the dunes can jeopardize their habitat.

Medanos

If you let the wind pile sand high enough and keep it free of vegetation, you have a medano, a sand dune on the move. Such dunes are active and naturally move, sometimes suffocating adjacent maritime thickets and forests. The most well known medano is at Jockey's Ridge State Park, but there are others as well, including the now-stabilized Kill Devil Hill.

Barrier Flats

Some locations have flat, grass-covered plains behind the primary dune lines, a place where water may stand after a hard rain. Usually such areas are behind a relatively low dune line, and the plants that thrive here are able to withstand the periodic inundation.

Here you will meet two of the barrier islands' most notorious inhabitants, the mosquito and the deer fly.

Thickets

What you will try to push through next is the maritime shrub thicket that develops naturally where the land is sheltered from oceanic influence by distance and dune height. The woody plants of this pioneering zone, southern wax myrtle, yaupon, bayberry, and red cedar, are sturdy, but they huddle before the salt spray, sometimes forming glorious sculptural mounds, lumps of green in the forbidding hot sands behind the dunes.

Thickets are a sign of stability, har-

boring many creatures you would see in thickets inland—rabbits, raccoons, oppossums, mice, and sometimes snakes.

Maritime Forest

The thicket is the leading edge of a forest, which will survive only if protected from salt spray either by distance from the ocean or by natural dunes. It can be a full-fledged forest as in Kitty Hawk, Nags Head, and Buxton Woods, virtually indistinguishable from inland forests. Historically, these areas are the highest and safest on the islands and provide the most diverse growing conditions for plants and food and shelter for animals. The dominant hardwood tree in the maritime forest is the live oak, which, at the limit of its range on the northern islands, is gnarled and weathered, never reaching the overpowering and elegant proportions it can attain in more southern latitudes. Inevitably there are pioneering pines growing in the maritime woods, as well as American holly and yaupon holly. In some locations, such as Nags Head Woods Ecological Preserve, the woods look like ordinary woods, but they are uncommon for where they are—on a barrier island. The maritime forests that remain offer one of the few glimpses of a coastal habitat that

lingers nearly intact from the time of the first European contact.

Salt Marsh

Invariably you step out of the forest and into the muck, sinking, at some points ankle-deep, into the salt marsh, the soggy, grassy habitat influenced by tidal waters on the soundside of the island. The forest and thicket shrubbery, hard-pressed to withstand a salty environment, fade, and black needle rush occupies the highest marshy ground, terrain that is intermittently flooded and characteristically above the normal tide line.

The more pervasive the tidal influence, the more abundant salt marsh cordgrass or spartina. Spartina forms the shimmering expanses of marsh that sweep across the horizon, growing in soil that is inundated daily. Without a doubt, this is the most productive habitat of the many that you can find along the coast. It is the nursery for many species of animals that inhabit the waters adjacent to the barrier islands, and the decaying spartina becomes the food at the base of the food web that ultimately can sustain all creatures that inhabit the coast, including humans.

Cape Lookout
National Seashore

Area code 252

On the south side of Ocracoke Inlet is Portsmouth Island, the northern portion of the lengthy Core Banks and the first link in the 55-mile-long chain that is the Cape Lookout National Seashore. Authorized in 1966, Cape Lookout is the younger, wilder sibling of the Cape Hatteras National Seashore. The major difference between the two is evident immediately: there are no bridges to Cape Lookout National Seashore.

You will find Cape Lookout as peaceful as Hatteras is energizing, as solitary as the other is social, and powerfully, desolately beautiful. Cape Lookout National Seashore is "the edge of the sea," in the words of one of the most insightful observers of this coastline, Rachel Carson.

The two seashores are paired opposites. Cape Hatteras National Seashore, wonderfully storied and saturated with significant historical interest, is intensively developed, has easy access for visitation, and accommodates many visitors. In contrast, Cape Lookout figures more prominently in local and regional history, existing in a quiet calm of appreciation, preserved in an undeveloped and comparatively pristine state. Cape Lookout National Seashore is no less rich but certainly less well known and talked about than Cape Hatteras.

In many respects, Cape Lookout is a living laboratory, protected and preserved so that barrier islands in their natural state may be studied and enjoyed. It is one of 260 Biosphere Reserves worldwide, an outgrowth of the Biosphere Program established by the United Nations in 1971. In its capacity as Cape Lookout National Seashore South Atlantic Biosphere Reserve, the seashore serves as a research "constant," managed for conservation purposes. The islands, offshore locations, and the water above them are all included in the reserve. The participation of the seashore in the Biosphere Program strongly influences the management plans of the National Park Service and decreases the likelihood of human encroachment. There is not a paved road or readily available source of water on the Cape Lookout barrier islands. Except for park service volunteers, there are no residents. What the seashore does have are miles of beach and marsh, singularly outstanding fishing, terrific bird-watching, and some of the finest shelling in North Carolina.

There are several component islands to Cape Lookout. Core Banks is the single name given to the longest barrier complex in the seashore. The artificial opening of a new Drum Inlet south of where sand had filled in an old inlet long ago, thwarting a natural process creating a single barrier island, divides the complex into North and South Core Banks. These two stretch their sandy lengths northeast to southwest, shielding the coast and creating Core Sound. The barriers are aligned with the prevailing winds of the region, which has resulted in a low, almost flat island profile, void of any significant dunes. Core Banks is for the most part a narrow, thinly vegetated barrier, little more than a spit of sand. If you have visited the north end of Ocracoke or the narrow beach between Avon and Buxton without its artificial dunes, then you have an image of Core Banks. The wind won't let the sand lie, streaming it along the beachfront in stinging ankle-high sheets. There's hardly a dune for shelter of any kind for any creature, and the shrubby growth of the mid-island flats with its few brushy tangles and nearly indistinguishable hummocks of beach grass thwarts any desire to pause. Extensive marshes fringe the backside of the banks like the lacing of a doily, creating the rich productive fisheries that support commercial crabbing and clamming and offer fine flounder fishing.

The abandoned but preserved village of Portsmouth is on North Core Banks. In the 1770s, this was the largest community on the Outer Banks. Except for resident volunteer park staff, it has been vacant since the last resident left in 1971. On South Core Banks is the wonderful diamond-patterned Cape Lookout Lighthouse, first illuminated on November 1, 1859, and the only major lighthouse that operates during the day. The Coast Guard maintains the fully automated light, which serves as a major navigational aid for mariners circumventing the treacherous Frying Pan Shoals southeast of the lighthouse. It is also a prime guide to the entrance of Beaufort Inlet to the west. One of the four great lighthouses on the Outer Banks, Cape Lookout Lighthouse has two rotating airport beacons that make a complete revolution every 30 seconds, appearing as a flashing beacon every 15 seconds, with a focal height of 150 feet, visible more than 12 miles out at sea. The curiously painted lighthouse invokes a diamond shape, hence seemingly more appropriate for Diamond Shoals further north. But when the Light House Board authorized the painting of the four towers for daytime identification on April 17, 1873, it decreed that "Cape Lookout Tower will be checkered, the checkers being painted alternately black and white."

The old lightkeeper's quarters are used by the park service as a residence for a volunteer ranger who lives on the island. The U.S. Coast Guard once maintained a station on Cape Lookout south of the lightkeeper's quarters, which are now used by the North Carolina Maritime Museum in Beaufort for programs.

The Cape Lookout Hook is the sandy promontory to the southwest of the lighthouse that curls north. Cape Lookout and the sandy ocean beaches offer some of the finest shelling and fishing within the seashore. The water is shallow here and currents are mild.

At Cape Lookout, the coast makes another severe shift in direction and the barrier islands after Core Banks align fully east and west. One such island, the next in the chain, is the last component of the seashore and the wildest of the islands, Shackleford Banks. On Shackleford Banks, the shift in orientation allows the prevailing winds to pile sand in immense dunes that spill into the only maritime forest of any significance in the seashore. Shackleford Banks once supported several small villages, and the largest village, Diamond City, was the whaling center of the North Carolina coast during the eighteenth and nineteenth centuries. Today, the island is closed to motorized traffic and is proposed as a wilderness.

The seashore came about in an unusual manner. The state of North Carolina condemned and then purchased Core Banks, north and south, and deeded it to the federal government for use as a national seashore, and Shackleford was condemned by the federal government. Property owners from that period still hold leases on the islands, and some hunting clubs retained twenty-five-year leases. Through the mid-1970s, there were fishing shacks clustered in various locations along Core Banks, used as overnight shelters. Such areas were called "shacktowns" by leaseholders, and the owners of the shacks were officially squatters, with no title to the property. The area has since been razed and returned to nature. Over many years, island users moved nearly junkable vehicles to the island and drove them across the sand until they sank or died, abandoning them where they stopped. The park service had the vehicles removed, a process that took several years.

Historically, the villages notwithstanding, the islands of the seashore have served as seasonal outposts for hunting and fishing, activities still allowed within the boundaries when conducted according to state laws. Ring-necked pheasant, an oriental bird, were introduced to Core Banks by hunters and have flourished. In addition, there are substantial populations of bob-white quail. Dogs may be used to hunt but must be restrained when not actually hunting.

Humans have little altered the natural state of the islands. Park service personnel note only three significant intrusions: the artificial opening of Drum Inlet, the jetty at the Cape Lookout Hook, and the state-mandated opening of Barden Inlet between Cape Lookout and the east end of Shackleford. None of the buildings within the seashore interfere with the natural processes of the island.

In October 1991, a "nor'easter" parked off the coast and spent days building seas and sending them crashing into and over the Outer Banks. There was statewide anxiety about the damage inflicted on Cape Hatteras and the beach communities of Dare County, but there was little concern over Cape Lookout. Everything happened as nature intended: the waves washed over the islands, rushing to the sound, dissipating their energy and rolling the islands imperceptibly toward the mainland. Portsmouth Village flooded as it always has, and the combination of waves and water performed some badly needed weeding on the low islands of the seashore, clearing vegetation to improve the habitat for some species of birds. What happened is what should happen—the island adjusted to meet the demands of the storm. Following the storm, the island began to rebuild—as did cottage owners in Dare County who had enough land left to build on.

Cape Lookout beckons with the allure of unreachable, untamed islands, no matter whether your vantage point is Ocracoke, Cedar Island, or one of the "downeast" villages of Carteret County, the parent county of the seashore. Part of the appeal is the remoteness and inconvenience. It is a special place and not for everybody. To reach the islands you must buy passage on one of the many private ferries or cross in your own boat. When you reach the seashore, you must carry whatever you bring along and walk to your destination. The only thing provided is 55 miles of beach, enough room for all comers. One ranger reported that one July 4 he counted only twelve visitors in 25 miles of beach. In fact, the busiest season is between Labor Day and mid-December, when the fish are moving.

Some rental cabins are available for overnight stays on North and South Core Banks, the only improved facilities open to the public on the islands. Essentially, though, the Cape Lookout experience is a wild one, for the hardy beachgoer and nature lover who revels in solitude and the sound of the sea.

The Cape Lookout National Seashore Visitors Center is in newly renovated quarters at Shell Point on Harkers Island, which is in sound waters north of the bend of Cape Lookout. It is a gorgeous, windswept site, at the end of the main road of the island. The islands of the seashore are on the horizon to the east and south, appearing as a continuous thread of land from this distance. The lighthouse and the tree line of Shackleford Banks stand above anything else that you can see from the visitors center parking lot.

Access

Access to locations within the seashore is by boat only. The usual routes are across Ocracoke Inlet from Ocracoke, across Core Sound from the mainland villages of Atlantic and Davis, or across Back Sound from Harkers Island or Beaufort. If you have your own boat, there are no restrictions on landings.

There are numerous marinas and boat-launching ramps that serve the seashore, many of which are detailed below and in the chapter on Carteret County.

If you do not have a boat, the park service authorizes individuals who meet certain stringent requirements to operate ferry services. Amazingly, a round-trip lift to one of the islands is still priced as low as $12 per person. However, it is a complicated business, and operators change frequently.

Ferry operators at Davis and Atlantic can transport vehicles. All vehicles must have a valid Cape Lookout vehicle permit (available from ferry operators or at Park Headquarters). Vehicles must meet all state license, safety, and inspection requirements; drivers must have a valid driving license. You can drive only on officially marked roads or on the beach if it is not marked as closed. No vehicles are permitted on Shackleford Banks.

You should plan to be completely self-sufficient during your visit, whether you're camping or day-tripping, since there are virtually no facilities for visitors. Cape Lookout Lighthouse has a restroom, and park service volunteers live in the lighthouse keeper's quarters and at Portsmouth Village. Here's a minimum checklist of items to take: food, drinking water (at least 2 quarts per person per day), protective clothing from sun and rain, a hat, sunglasses, sunscreen lotion, insect repellent, and shoes suitable for walking in hot sand. If you are going fishing at Cape Lookout, you can take a cooler since a shuttle will take you round-trip from the ferry dock at the lighthouse to the point for $8. Fortunately, a boardwalk extends from the lighthouse to the beach, eliminating a 1.5-mile walk through soft sand to reach the surf.

Camping is primitive since there are no developed campsites. Insect repellent and long tent stakes are advised. Mosquito netting helps tremendously for a good night's sleep. Bring plenty of water for cooking and drinking, and the rangers suggest that you bring lots of food. You will eat more here than you usually do.

Pets are prohibited throughout the National Seashore because of continuing violations of pet restraint regulations.

The local regulations of the North Carolina Marine Fisheries apply to size limitations on some saltwater species and on any shellfishing for clams, crabs, or oysters in the sound waters. As long as you are not in closed waters, regulations allow recreational clamming (up to 100 per day for personal use) and crabbing, by drop line.

Hunters must meet all state and federal game standards and licensing requirements.

Information

For information, call the Cape Lookout National Seashore Visitors Center at 919-728-2250, 8 A.M. to 4:30

Cape Lookout Lighthouse. (Courtesy of N.C. Travel and Tourism Division)

P.M. daily, or contact Superintendent, Cape Lookout National Seashore, 131 Charles Street, Harkers Island, NC 28531, 919-728-2250.

Cape Lookout National Seashore Concession Ferries and Cabins

The following ferry operators meet National Park Service and U.S. Coast Guard regulations and have been listed as providers of transportation to Cape Lookout National Seashore. You must make your reservations directly with them and verify the rates as well as the schedules. Some operators also have rental cabins or beach transportation within the seashore.

Portsmouth Village: Trips to Portsmouth Village depart from Ocracoke. Typical charges are around $40 for two or fewer or $15 each for three or more for a round-trip passage. You may call the Austin family at 919-928-4361 or 919-928-4281, or Portsmouth Island ATV Excursions at 919-928-4484. Call the Ocracoke Island Visitors Center at 919-928-4531 for additional approved operators.

North Core Banks: Morris Marina, Kabin Kamps, and Ferry Service operates a ferry that leaves from a dock north of Atlantic, which is on US 70 at the northeastern tip of Carteret County, and docks about 7 miles north of Drum Inlet and 16 miles south of Portsmouth Village. The ferry ride is $13 per person round-trip. The four-car ferry will take your vehicle over for $65–$85 round-trip. The Morris family also rents 20 cabins in the Long Point Cabin Area between April and November for $31–$132 a night, depending on the season and the size. The smallest sleeps four, the largest twelve. Cabins have safe water for drinking, showers, and restrooms but no electricity. Contact Morris Marina, Kabin Kamps, and Ferry Service, 1000 Morris Marina Road, Atlantic, NC 28511, 919-225-4261.

South Core Banks: Alger Willis Fishing Camps operates a ferry service to the Great Island Cabin Area, 7 miles south of Drum Inlet and approximately 14 miles north of Cape Point. The ferry departs from the community of Davis, on US 70, and can transport vehicles. The fee is approximately $13 per person round-trip and $60–$85 round-trip for a vehicle. There are approximately 20 cabins available from April to November for $22–$132 a night. Contact Alger Willis Fishing Camps, Inc. P.O. Box 234, Davis, NC 28524, 919-729-2791.

Beaufort to Cape Lookout/ Shackleford Banks: Outer Banks Ferry Service, Barrier Island Adventures, 328 Front Street, Beaufort, NC 28516, 919-728-4129; Island Ferry and Tour Service, 300 Front Street, 919-728-6888 or 919-728-5247; Lookout Cruises, Beaufort Docks, 919-504-SAIL; Good Fortune Sail Charters, 919-247-3860; Mystery Tours, 919-726-6783 or 919-728-7827 (boat).

Camping in the Cape Lookout National Seashore. (Courtesy of N.C. Travel and Tourism Division)

Harkers Island to Cape Lookout/Shackleford Banks: Barrier Island Transportation Co., Inc., Harkers Island Fishing Center, Harkers Island, NC 28531, 919-728-3907, 919-728-3908, or 1-800-423-8739 (North Carolina only); Cape Lookout Ferry Service, Calico Jack's Inn & Marina, 919-728-3575; Sand Dollar Transportation, Barbour's Harbour Marina, 1390 Island Road, 919-728-6181, 919-504-3939, or 1-800-281-3978.

Morehead City to Shackleford Banks: Anderson/Muns Maritime, Inc., 6th and Evans Street, Morehead City, NC 28557, 919-728-3988 or 919-240-2177.

Information

Call 919-728-2250 for a touch-tone listing of ferry services. For additional information write Superintendent, Cape Lookout National Seashore, 131 Charles Street, Harkers Island, NC 28531.

Portsmouth Island

Portsmouth Island is the name given to the northeast end of the low barrier island known as North Core Banks, the northernmost section of the 55-mile-long Cape Lookout National Seashore. Swash Inlet, an intermittently flooding breach in the barrier where wind tides flood the tidal flats behind the dune line, separates Portsmouth Island from the remainder of North Core Banks. The island is one of the few locations on this barrier to have sufficient elevation above sea level to permit settlement. The now-deserted village of Portsmouth, established by an act of the North Carolina General Assembly in 1753, occupies the highest and most habitable acreage of these limited sites.

During its heyday in the eighteenth century, Portsmouth was a major port of call for all shipping into North Carolina, eventually becoming the state's busiest seaport. Oceangoing vessels would put in at Portsmouth to transfer their cargo to smaller craft for the continuation of the journey across shallow Pamlico Sound to Bath or Washington, a practice known as "lightering." Portsmouth was sufficiently important to North Carolina's economy that British troops seized and occupied the port along with the port of Ocracoke during the War of 1812. Portsmouth thrived until a storm carved Hatteras and Oregon inlets in 1846, after which Ocracoke Inlet soon shoaled, and Portsmouth's commercial days were over.

In 1971, the last two residents moved to the mainland, ending the continuous occupancy of the village since the early 1700s. The twenty-one surviving structures of the village, including a church, a life-saving station, and the island's schoolhouse, still stand proudly on the high ground, a haven from the sea but not from time. The freshly painted yellow houses and the blue and white Methodist church are the centerpieces in a 250-acre historic district that is on the National Register of Historic Places. The Dixon/Salter House serves as a visitors center, and the church is also open to the public.

There are several private holdings on Portsmouth Island, some leases authorized by the park service, as well as cemeteries still visited and tended by descendants. The park service requests that visitors to the island respect private property.

Although the National Park Service maintains a ranger station in the village, the island has no facilities or concessions of any kind. You should take everything you'll need during your visit. Overnight stays are permitted, but make sure to bring supplies, especially water and insect repellent.

The flats of the island are substantial—wide areas of sand, sometimes dry and sometimes covered with nearly 2 feet of water. Winds from the north can pile the water onto the island and build a moat between you and the beach. If you are hiking to the beach from the village, be prepared for a walk of about a mile, not all of it easy, not always dry, and none of it insect-free.

For day-trippers, Portsmouth is one of the shelling hot spots on the Outer Banks. Storms frequently scatter thousands of shells on the wide flat beach, and the competition for shells is limited. If you go in late winter or early spring, you have your pick of the flotsam and jetsam and most likely an almost guaranteed shelling success. Fishing is also unsurpassed on Portsmouth. For both, however, you have

	Fee	Parking	Restrooms	Lifeguard	Camping	Showers	Beach Access	Hiking	Trail	Handicapped	Boating	ORV Access	Fishing	Programs	Historic	Sand Beach	Dunes	Upland	Wetland
Cape Lookout National Seashore		•	•		•		•	•	•		•	•	•	•	•	•	•	•	•
Portsmouth Island			•		•			•	•		•	•	•	•	•	•	•	•	•
North Core Banks			•		•		•	•	•		•	•	•		•	•	•	•	•
Cedar Island	•	•								•									•
Public Boating Access: Lola	•										•		•						•
Cedar Island National Wildlife Refuge	•							•	•		•							•	•
Public Boating Access: Thorofare Bay	•										•		•						•
Atlantic	•		•								•		•					•	•

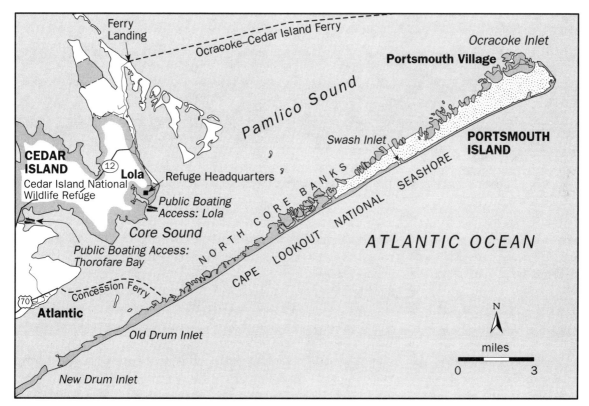

Map 15. Portsmouth Island to New Drum Inlet

Portsmouth Village. (Courtesy of N.C. Travel and Tourism Division)

to walk around the island, so take sunscreen lotion, drinking water, insect repellent, and comfortable walking shoes.

On your way to Portsmouth from Ocracoke, you'll pass by Beacon Island and Shell Castle Island in the waters west of the inlet. Approximately 400 yards long, Beacon Island was named for the presence of two beacons used by pilots to navigate Ocracoke Channel. The south end was fortified in 1794–95 by an act of Congress because of the importance of the shipping channel. Shell Castle Island was the site where John Gray Blount and John Wallace launched a speculative venture to expand the island in order to make a more favorable "lightering dock" for oceangoing vessels. In the 1800s, Shell Castle supported a lumberyard, tavern, dwelling house, and notary public's office. Hurricanes sweeping through the inlet sealed the fate of both islands, however.

Access

Trips to Portsmouth Village depart from Ocracoke. The Austin family charges $40 for two or fewer or $15 each for three or more for a round-trip passage, all year. You may call the Austins at 919-928-4361 or 919-928-4281. Portsmouth Island ATV Excursions, 919-928-4484, operates guided interpretive tours by all-terrain vehicles departing from Ocracoke. For additional operators, call the Ocracoke Island Visitors Center at 919-928-4531 or Cape Lookout National Seashore at 919-928-2250. For additional operators during the summer months, call the Ocracoke Island Visitors Center at 919-928-4531.

Information

For information, call the Ocracoke Island Visitors Center at 919-928-4531 or the Cape Lookout National Seashore Visitors Center on Harkers Island at 919-728-2250, 8 A.M. to 4:30 P.M. daily, or contact Superintendent, Cape Lookout National Seashore, 131 Charles Street, Harkers Island, NC 28531.

The Coastal Constant Is Change

Coastal geologists and oceanographers describe the relationship of natural forces such as the wind and sea level to barrier islands as a system having a "dynamic equilibrium." Loosely translated this means a "moving balance." A person riding a unicycle has dynamic equilibrium. The rider maintains balance as long as there are no restrictions on movement; if the rider stops, the system slips out of sync, with predictable results. The dynamic equilibrium of the coastal system is analogous in theory but much more complex. In order to survive as islands, barrier beaches must be able to shift and reshape freely in response to the effects of wind and waves. Since the island is part of a system including other islands, restrictions on its ability to respond naturally introduce a "wild card" that may play havoc elsewhere—an adjacent island perhaps—albeit in an unpredictable manner and sometimes at a much later date.

Unrestricted barrier islands, such as those of Cape Lookout National Seashore, constantly shift and reshape in response to the cycles of wind and wave action throughout the system. The whole system stays fairly constant; coastal geologists have established that the total amount of sand in the system changes little, but how and where the sand is piled changes constantly. While a severe storm may diminish the size of a headland at an inlet or flatten the profile of a beach, it doesn't destroy the sand that formed the headland or the beach, it just moves the sand elsewhere.

You could characterize the response of barrier islands to wind and waves as a form of coastal aikido— they literally roll and rearrange with the punches. They are malleable; they do not actively resist the forces, and in so doing they "survive" as a system.

The greatest force at work on North Carolina's barrier islands is the rising sea, changing elevation at the rate of one foot per century. The barrier islands respond to this chronic pressure (as opposed to the acute attack of storms) by deliberate, strategic retreat, moving landward before the steady urging of the ocean. The sequence of steps by which an island retreats is predictably sequential and readily observable. Sand fills the marsh behind the island, and vegetation secures this new sand; then the entire vegetation and land pattern of the island creeps landward, moving toward the mainland and shifting the stable ground of the island steadily away from the ocean.

This island migration may be seen in places such as "Wash Woods" in Currituck, where tree stumps, once well inland, protrude from the wet sand beach. On Bear Island in Hammocks Beach State Park, you may find ancient oyster shells in the beach sands. Since oysters live in brackish waters, the presence of these shells on the beach indicates that the island has migrated inland over ancient oyster beds.

The rate of march—how far an island will move each year—is determined by the slope of the offshore bottom (which is not constant along the coast) and can be calculated. The ballpark range is as follows: for every one inch in sea-level rise, the coastline retreats somewhere between 10 feet and 100 feet. The extreme southeastern part of the coastal plain is steeper, so the horizontal displacement is not as great there as it is further north.

As mentioned earlier, the islands sustain the same total mass of sand within the barrier island chain, taking a little sand from one location and distributing it elsewhere. At some locations, the beach is diminishing; at others, enlarging. Some inlets are stable; some, migrating. Some marshes are silting in, while others are developing. Each change depends on the forces acting directly on the area under study, but the sea is the primary architect with long-term help by wind.

The system is not unlike an unbreakable balloon filled with water—the force you exert on it will squeeze out in an unexpected place. Similarly, if we interfere and try to keep a part of an island (usually sand) from moving where nature directs it (by constructing a jetty to trap sand, for example), we rob the replenishment material from other beaches. Erosion is not really stopped, it's just directed elsewhere.

If the coastal system is moving (geologically speaking), then permanent structures are at an inherent risk. The operative question about artificial structures on nearly every barrier island is *when* they will be threatened, not *if* they will be threatened (although the time period could be quite lengthy—Ocracoke and Portsmouth Village have been around for more than 200 years).

It is difficult for us to think this way, but storms don't threaten the islands themselves—the island is not permanent but a movable part of a system that is permanent. Storms threaten humans and their "permanent" possessions. Put another way, you don't own land on the barrier islands, you rent. Some leases are longer than others depending primarily on their location and elevation above sea level.

The changes along our coast are severe enough to be noticed from season to season because there are many benchmarks—homes and businesses mostly—marking the advance of the sea. The Halloween Storm of 1991 opened up the horizons at the Kitty Hawk regional access site and severely chewed the artificial dune line of Pea Island National Wildlife Refuge. Today, there are roadside views of the ocean from NC 12 on Hatteras Island; tomorrow, there may not be a road, but there will always be an island.

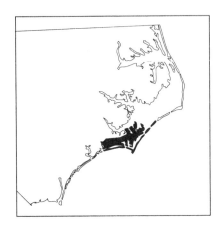

Carteret County

Carteret County claims 75 miles of barrier islands, almost as much beachfront as Dare County. The wave action in Carteret, however, is not nearly as dramatic or energized as it is to the north. Carteret waves laze, lap, and plop across the sands, running through swashes, mounting a more understated corrosive attack on the several lengthy islands. During some sensational storms, the sea has surged across the barrier islands to assault the mainland and completely destroy some communities, Beaufort among them, but the islands here do not feel as braced against the ocean as do those of Dare County.

Carteret offers distinctly varied beach experiences. Cape Lookout National Seashore is at one extreme—beach au naturel; Atlantic Beach, among other resort communities on Bogue Banks, is at the other—beach au boogie. If you want a wild beach in Carteret County, you can find one, no matter what your definition of wild might be.

This county of contrast is more comprehensible if you view it from an imaginary line through Beaufort Inlet. To the west are the vibrant, developed, tourist-haven beaches, and to the east, the equally vibrant experience of those whose livelihoods are tied to the ebb and flow of more natural coastal seasons, including the preservation of the unaltered coast in the Cedar Island National Wildlife Refuge and Cape Lookout National Seashore. The geography of the county is the primary reason for the division in character.

At Cape Lookout, the generally southwest string of barrier beaches begins an almost compass-perfect reach due west. The islands align to bend in a great concave arc that sweeps inland from Cape Lookout to a midpoint on Topsail Island before arcing out again to the promontory of Cape Fear. The waters embraced by the points of the horns, Capes Lookout and Fear, are known as Onslow Bay. Even though the same crescentic pattern exists between Capes Hatteras and Lookout to the north, which encompass the waters of Raleigh Bay, the similarity in pattern doesn't result in similarity in the character of the barriers. The orientation of the island chains leads to their differences.

The northeast-southwest orientation of Core Banks in the eastern part of Carteret County aligns the island chain with the prevailing winds. One result is that the islands of Portsmouth and Core Banks do not receive a steady landward breeze. Consequently the sand is not pushed up onto the beach but is streamed parallel to the islands and moves without interruption. There are days when you cannot recline on Core Banks beaches without eroding on one side and building your own nascent dune on the other. It never falls out of the current of wind or water and never has a chance to aggregate, a stinging reminder of how wild the beach can be.

Because of this alignment, the resulting island profile is low and flat, with very little foredune. The lack of dune buildup means that virtually the entire island is subject to flooding and salt-spray shearing of vegetation. There is no protection for forests to develop on the inland side of the island.

In contrast, the east-west oriented islands of Shackleford Banks and Bogue Banks in southern Carteret County are blessed with a steady supply of sand, driven by onshore winds and deposited by waves, which is not scoured away by the trend of the breezes. The result is the formation of a relatively stable dune advance guard, which in turn deflects salt spray up, allowing vegetation to take hold, topsoil to form, and the subsequent evolution of an island maritime forest. In fact, Shackleford Banks features one of the few remnant stands of maritime forest in this particular section of coastline. There are plenty of forested acres on Bogue Banks as well, which have attracted great numbers of two-legged migratory nesters and seasonal carpenters.

The stage was set very early for the parceling of the county's available oceanfront into two opposite opportunities: Core Banks for the pleasures belonging to the hardy souls that brave the waves, mosquitoes, and wind for the enjoyment of guaranteed solitude and Bogue Banks for the pleasures of summer serendipity.

In addition to the national seashore, Carteret County has one component of the National Estuarine Research Reserve program: Rachel Carson, comprised of Horse Island and Bird Shoal, south of Beaufort. In the northeast tip of the county are 12,000 acres of wildlife preserve, the Cedar Island National Wildlife Refuge. In Beaufort, a National Register Historic District guards the remnants of the state's third oldest town and one of the liveliest historic communities you'll ever visit.

Beaufort is the county seat, testimony to the habitability of the site and the fact that it is as centered as a city can be in Carteret County. Its picturesque charm contrasts with the enthusiastic commercial swing of nearby Morehead City, which is not only a state port but a very popular dining and tourist destination. Morehead is the working waterfront of Carteret County while Beaufort is a sailor's (yachtsman's) town, where you may grab a slice of history with your sandwich before going back to the water.

Whereas the resorts of Atlantic Beach and Emerald Isle lose their energy when summer ends, the eastern and inland parts of Carteret County stay fairly lively. Further east, as the influence of tourism fades, the rhythms of life are more even throughout the year.

The villages east of Beaufort are locally known as "downeast" and their inhabitants "downeasters." When you travel downeast to Harkers Island, Davis, Sealevel, or Atlantic, you leave convenience and services behind. Downeast communities are traditional fishing villages sheltered by the barrier of Core Banks, which limit the accessibility to the ocean. Such "inconvenience" kept settlement to a minimum in this area. Harkers Island, within easy reach of Beaufort Inlet and the trickier Barden Inlet, became a fishing center as did Atlantic, opposite Drum Inlet. In recent years, limitations on waste management have dramatically restricted development.

The National Park Service maintains its primary visitors center on Harkers Island, where you can learn the best means and locations to enjoy the seashore. The Cape Lookout National Seashore headquarters are in Morehead City and are open during regular business hours.

Access

The individual municipalities and management agencies in Carteret County provide beach access locations. It is a daunting task and considering the growing numbers of people that come to the region, primarily to Bogue Banks, a task that will be unending and perhaps never complete.

Generally speaking, access is a problem at the popular resort beaches on Bogue Banks only for those visitors who come for the day. Between Memorial Day and Labor Day, parking, particularly on weekends, is available only for early birds. Weekend parking can become difficult as soon as Easter vacation. The separate descriptions of the locations on Bogue Banks below detail specific access sites.

The most visited state park in North Carolina is Fort Macon on Bogue Banks. Part of the attraction is two very large parking lots, one at a regional access area and the other at the fort. These provide direct beach access to the eastern end of Bogue Banks. Atlantic Beach maintains several regional oceanfront access sites. There is a smaller neighborhood access site in Indian Beach. Carteret County maintains a major regional access site in Salter Path on 22 acres of land donated, in part, by the heirs of Theodore Roosevelt. This fully developed site stays full, and if you want one of the 65 parking spaces any time between Memorial and Labor Day, you must arrive early. Emerald Isle maintains one regional access site.

Other access on Bogue Banks is simply best maintained by renting a cottage or staying in a motel. During the busy time of the year, both parking and access are difficult and the closer you can sleep to the water, the more you will eliminate the stress of trying to find a location to park your car.

The county also maintains a soundside access on the Newport River at the north side of US 70 and a recreational fishing dock beside the bridge to Harkers Island.

The Cape Lookout National Seashore presents an altogether different access problem, which is addressed in the separate section on the seashore.

Handicapped Access

The regional access areas at Fort Macon and Salter Path are fully handicapped accessible. Both have designated parking places and dune crossover ramps to the oceanfront.

The regional access sites in Atlantic Beach and Emerald Isle are accessible to handicapped travelers.

Information

For information on accommodations, contact Carteret County Tourism Development Bureau, P.O. Box 1406, Morehead City, NC 28557, 1-800-SUNNYNC.

The National Park Service Visitors Center on Harkers Island handles questions on access to Cape Lookout National Seashore. You may call 919-728-2250 for a touch-tone listing of ferry operators. The center is open from 8 A.M. to 4:30 P.M. daily. For additional information or a list of ferry operators, contact Superintendent, Cape Lookout National Seashore, 131 Charles Street, Harkers Island, NC 28531.

Cedar Island

The western terminus of the Ocracoke ferry is the slice of land known as Cedar Island. Ferry riders approaching the dock see almost a miniature island—some small dunes, a layer of shrubs, and trees sheared by salt spray. Just inland from the ferry are several small houses, a church, and family graveyards. This is a remote, "end of the road" kind of place.

As you head southwest toward Beaufort on a winding, unhurried passage, there is quite a surprise awaiting you—the marshes of Cedar Island National Wildlife Refuge.

Access

There is a large parking lot at the ferry dock where you may leave your car while you take the ferry to Ocracoke. An improved private boat ramp is available for a fee. The Driftwood Campground has numerous camping sites; call 919-225-4861. There is also a motel and restaurant that do a fair business with travelers waiting for the ferry or hunters and fishermen who hire the local guides.

Reservations for the ferry are recommended year round and can be made by calling 252-225-3551 or 800-773-1094. You may reserve a space up to 30 days but at least 1 or 2 days before departure. Your name and the vehicle license number are required when making the reservation. Be at the ferry terminal at least 30 minutes prior to leaving to claim your reservation.

Handicapped Access

There is only limited handicapped access here.

Cedar Island National Wildlife Refuge

NC 12 knifes through the middle of the 12,525 acres of undeveloped habitat in Cedar Island National Wildlife Refuge, at the extreme eastern end of Carteret County. By its own accounting, the U.S. Fish and Wildlife Service describes the refuge as 10,000 acres of irregularly flooded salt marsh, 2,450 acres of woodland, and 75 acres of cleared land. This refuge is classic marsh, with magnificent stretches of shimmering needlerush and cordgrass. The passage through the Cedar Island Marsh rivals the exquisite winding of Princess Anne Road onto Knotts Island in Currituck County.

Established in 1964, Cedar Island is a rare traverse indeed, glowing in the warm light of the low-angled sun of a winter's dusk, when the grasses waver bleached against the horizon. High ground—hummocks supporting shrubs, live oaks, and several species of pines—punctuate the plains of pale threads, but it is the expanse of marsh, spreading endlessly to either side, that makes the lasting impression.

Nearly 270 species of birds can be seen here each year. December and January are the peak season for waterfowl, and the predominant species are redhead ducks, lesser scaup, and a few black ducks. During the summer season, even on a quick drive-through, you will likely see some of the permanent populations of wading shorebirds.

As an undeveloped wildlife refuge, Cedar Island offers little access to vehicles and there are few public facilities. Hunting and fishing are permitted. The road crosses a 40-foot-wide slough leading from Thorofare Bay on the east side of Cedar Island to West Thorofare Bay on the west side of NC 12. All lands west of NC 12 are in the refuge; the land on the southeast side of the slough is not. There is a boat-launching ramp at this location frequently used by fishermen and hunters.

The headquarters of the Cedar Island National Wildlife Refuge are at the south end of Cedar Island on SR 1388, known locally as Lola Road. Inside you may obtain information and maps of the refuge. Interested groups may arrange outdoor education or refuge tours by request.

Access

Cedar Island National Wildlife Refuge is open during daylight hours all year.

There is an improved boat-launching ramp at the refuge headquarters on Lewis Creek south of Lola and a boat-launching ramp on the southwest side of NC 12 at the Thorofare Bay bridge.

Information

For information, contact Cedar Island National Wildlife Refuge, Cedar Island, NC 28520, 919-225-2511. Office hours are 7:30 A.M. to 4:30 P.M.

Atlantic

Nearly 1,000 people call Atlantic home, and many more know it as the departure point for ferry service to Cape Lookout National Seashore. Atlantic is at the eastern end of US 70; SR 1387 leads to NC 12 north of the center of town. Atlantic is a traditional downeast fishing village, and the livelihood of many of its inhabitants is dependent on a passage to the ocean known as Drum Inlet.

The closing of the first Drum Inlet sometime during the eighteenth century made the passage to the ocean arduous. A new inlet was dynamited in the early 1970s nearly due east of Atlantic. Already the inlet shoals heavily, and from Core Banks, Drum Inlet almost seems to be a crossing that could be made on foot at low tide.

The lack of reliable access to the open ocean throttles commercial fishing from the small community. However, Atlantic is becoming a sailing and fishing center since the shallower drafts of smaller boats allow sportsmen to pass through Drum Inlet.

The Morris family, who once owned nearly 1,000 acres of land on Core Banks, operates the ferry concession, Morris Marina, Kabin Kamps, and Ferry Service. The ferry is equipped to carry four four-wheel-drive vehicles and disembarks passengers at a dock on North Core Banks, north of Drum Inlet.

Access

Ferry service and cabin rentals on North Core Banks are offered by Morris Marina, Kabin Kamps, and Ferry Service, 1000 Morris Marina Road, Atlantic, NC 28511, 919-225-4261.

There are several private marinas with launching ramps in Atlantic that provide access to Core Sound for a launch fee. The North Carolina Wildlife Resources Commission maintains a fishing and boating access area at Salters Creek, at the northeast end of the high-rise bridge crossing Nelson Bay, south of Atlantic on US 70. From Beaufort, follow US 70 east until you reach Nelson Bay, approximately 7 miles from Atlantic. Parking is available and there is no launch fee.

Information

For information on accommodations, contact Carteret County Tourism Development Bureau, P.O. Box 1406, Morehead City, NC 28557, 1-800-SUNNYNC.

For information about the Cape Lookout National Seashore, call the Cape Lookout National Seashore Visitors Center on Harkers Island at 919-728-2250, 8 A.M. to 4:30 P.M. daily.

Davis

Ferry access is provided to Core Banks from Davis, an even smaller village than Atlantic. A very sharp right turn on US 70, the prim white houses lining the roadway, and the shade trees sheltering the road signal the community. The rest of Davis strings along US 70 and sprawls down several small side roads.

Davis is a traditional launching point for fishermen and hunters crossing to Core Banks. There is a small campground here. Alger Willis Fishing Camps operates the ferry service to South Core Banks and rents cabins there. The ferry dock is due east of the right-angle turn in the highway.

Visitors using this ferry access, which docks on the barrier island less than 600 yards from the Atlantic Ocean, may see the structure known as the Core Banks Club, a private club that still retains a lease on their building and grounds and fishing and hunting privileges in the seashore. Substantial landholdings of the Core Banks Club were purchased by the state of North Carolina and turned over to the National Park Service in 1976.

Access

Ferry service and cabin rentals on South Core Banks are offered by Alger Willis Fishing Camps, P.O. Box 234, Davis, NC 28524, 919-729-2791.

Information

For information on accommodations, contact Carteret County Tourism Development Bureau, P.O. Box 1406, Morehead City, NC 28557, 1-800-SUNNYNC.

For information about the Cape Lookout National Seashore, call the Cape Lookout National Seashore Visitors Center on Harkers Island at 919-728-2250, 8 A.M. to 4:30 P.M. daily.

Harkers Island

Harkers Island stands alone, a village that is off the beaten track. You must aim to go there since it tucks into the inside of the elbow of Cape Lookout. It is likely that a fair number of people discover it by mistake since National Park Service rangers report being asked numerous times every year for the dock location of the Ocracoke ferry.

Harkers Island is decidedly "downeast." Literally and figuratively, it is out of the ordinary tourist loop, even though the park service maintains its main Cape Lookout National Seashore Visitors Center at Shell Point, the end of the road in Harkers Island. Those who go to Harkers Island like the out-of-the-mainstream offerings of the island as well as the national seashore.

There is much to do here—fishing, sailing, kayaking, canoeing, and glimpsing life in a traditional boat-building center. Within easy reach, by boat of course, are the Cape Lookout Lighthouse area of Core Banks and Shackleford Banks. Several ferry operators serve the seashore from Harkers, in addition to commercial charter fishing services. The island lives on the water in more ways than one.

Harkers Island is aligned on the same east-west arc as Shackleford Banks, visible to the south across the very shallow waters of Back Sound. The shelter of Core and Shackleford Banks exact a price in the form of sometimes precarious channels that web outward to reach the inlets. This clearly doesn't stop residents from traversing the waters, however, since there are four marinas on the island.

You cross to the island by a causeway and two bridges, one of which is a low-water, fixed-span bridge and the other a swing bridge over local waters known as "The Straits." The crossing connects the forested mainland to the wind-sheared low island, a difference you see almost immediately. A local dock lined with stout working boats beside the road as you reach the island signals that you are going to a waterman's island, not a playground.

Harkers blends into the shallow, greenish sound waters with ruffles of marsh and armies of pilings, legions of piers and docks, old boats, boats under construction, and salt-sheared cedar trees, modest homes, a school, and limited services. The main street is not lined but framed by the live oaks of adjoining yards. It feels like a neighborhood, not a thoroughfare.

It is a keep-to-yourself kind of place, opening up a little bit if you come here to go fishing—then islanders become outspoken and more outgoing. If you need a boat, you can hire one or you can order one custom-made.

The island has a tradition of building sturdy wooden working boats and is still peopled with artisans who can look at a stack of lumber and envision how to rearrange it to make a boat. It's a process well documented at the North Carolina Maritime Museum in Beaufort.

Today, because of the excellent docking facilities and the proximity of two popular portions of the Cape Lookout National Seashore, the island is a launching point for day-tripping and camping at the edge of the sea, on the islands of the horizon. But you can get away here as well. In a pleasant, languorous way, Harkers Island is a respite with a hardened, working edge. I once watched in near terror and complete awe as an electrical storm danced across the Shackleford and Core banks in a stroboscopic nightmare of charged exchanges, the kind of storm that melts sand. Every flash painted the wavering, uneven line of the islands on the horizon, and the ever-steady flash of the Cape Lookout Lighthouse seemed comic in comparison. It was a wild night, full of ozone and the silhouettes of the fishing fleet out of my window. Harkers Island became welded into my memory then.

But memory-fixing experiences are probably the exception rather than the rule here, possibly because

	Fee	Parking	Restrooms	Lifeguard	Camping	Showers	Beach Access	Hiking	Trail	Handicapped	Boating	ORV Access	Fishing	Programs	Historic	Sand Beach	Dunes	Upland	Wetland
Davis	•	•			•													•	•
South Core Banks					•		•	•	•		•	•	•		•	•	•	•	•
Cape Lookout Lighthouse			•				•	•	•		•	•	•	•	•	•	•	•	•
Cape Lookout N.S. Visitors Center		•	•							•	•	•			•				•

the island is one large neighborhood surrounded by water. When you drive to the end of the island, you have seen it all.

There are several places to stay, which is a boon to anglers and hunters since fishing trips depart very early and taking a room the night before is a big help. Two major marinas on the island offer rooms, boat rentals, and docking services.

At Shell Point, at the end of SR 1335, you might see at least one or two cars drive to the dead end and turn around. It's not people looking for the Ocracoke ferry, it's the locals. There is a tradition, noted in the island cookbook, that if you're a true islander you have to drive down to Shell Point at least once a day. They do it, too.

Access

The Cape Lookout National Seashore Visitors Center includes a large parking lot and picnic area at Shell Point, at the end of SR 1335. You may inquire about ferry schedules and operators to reach Cape Lookout National Seashore at this location.

There are four private marinas on Harkers that offer access for boaters for a fee.

On the east side of the fixed bridge to the island, Carteret County has constructed a small T-shaped wooden accessway for fishing or crabbing near the north bridge. There is ample parking.

Handicapped Access

The visitors center is accessible to handicapped travelers. Access at private enterprises on the remainder of the island varies by establishment.

Information

For information on accommodations, contact Carteret County Tourism Development Bureau, P.O. Box 1406, Morehead City, NC 28557, 1-800-SUNNYNC.

For information on the Cape Lookout National Seashore, call the Cape Lookout National Seashore Visitors Center at 919-728-2250, 8 A.M. to 4:30 P.M. daily.

Shackleford Banks

Shackleford Banks is currently under review as a possible wilderness area, a curious, ironic legacy of a late nineteenth-century hurricane season. By federal standards for inclusion in the wilderness system, this 7-mile-long, 2,500-acre barrier qualifies since there is no development, few artificial structures, and no roads; the island is unaltered and federally owned and managed. The irony of its possible designation as a wilderness area is that in the nineteenth century as many as 600 people lived and fished from here. The island once supported two thriving whaling communities, Diamond City at the east end and Wade's Shore on the west, but the series of hurricanes that pummelled the island beginning in the 1890s destroyed the maritime forest and many of the houses that were in it.

The livelihoods, houses, and communities were either beaten to pieces or lifted from their foundations. Several people were killed, and eventually the survivors abandoned what had been a village of

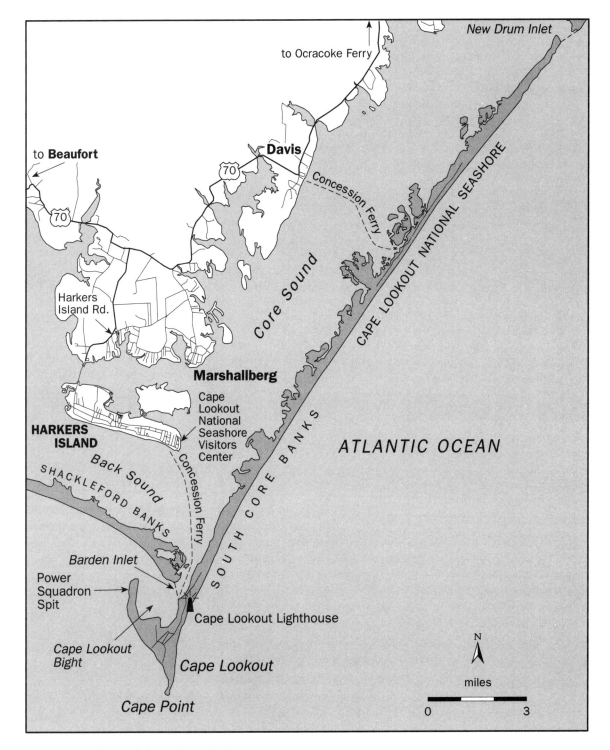

Map 16. New Drum Inlet to Cape Lookout

Shackleford Banks, soundside. (Courtesy of N.C. Travel and Tourism Division)

at least 500 people at Diamond City, leaving only grave markers and some livestock behind. Some moved to Harkers Island, others sailed to what is now Salter Path on Bogue Banks, and a third group settled in a section of Morehead City described by one resident as the "Promise Land." For many years, the only inhabitants of Shackleford Banks were a thriving feral animal population.

With no fences, all animals were free to roam the island. The National Park Service removed the sheep because their grazing method, which consumes roots of the pioneering grass plants, was harmful to the island's natural systems. Horses are not as damaging, however, and have been allowed to remain. Many horses run free on the island, and your chances of seeing them are excellent. However, they are wild and should not be approached.

Shackleford's maritime forest is still recovering from the damage of hurricanes and several generations of occupancy. Most of the rejuvenating forest is along the western third of the island, behind the extensive dune ridge that in some locations is more than 40 feet above sea level. The eastern end of the island, the closest to Cape Lookout, is low and flat, resembling neighboring Core Banks in its physical appearance. One can imagine the little protection these sands would have offered from the force of a hurricane surging over them.

Shackleford is perhaps the least known of the barrier islands, a function of its comparative inaccessibility. However, you can go there by ferry or private boat, and in recent years, it has become an increasingly popular spot for residents of Beaufort and Morehead who have boats. When you step off of the ferry onto the island, near the jetty

	Fee	Parking	Restrooms	Lifeguard	Camping	Showers	Beach Access	Hiking	Trail	Hardicapped	Boating	ORV Access	Fishing	Programs	Historic	Sand Beach	Dunes	Upland	Wetland
Shackleford Banks			•		•		•	•	•		•		•		•	•	•	•	•

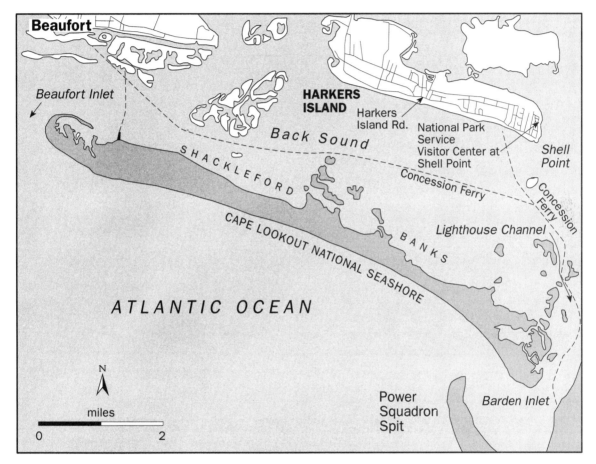

Map 17. Shackleford Banks

at the northwest end, you are entering a sanctuary of natural systems. You are very much a guest, and virtually everything on the island is protected. The restrictions may seem severe, but they protect an island in a dynamic balance with the sea and change. Following these rules is a small price to pay for what the island offers—7 miles of shelling or fishing and generally very little competition for either.

If you visit Shackleford, take plenty of water and food. As you make preparations for the visit, particularly if you're going fishing, remember that you will be carrying everything you bring. There is a water pump and restrooms near the jetty on the island's west end.

The park service places the following restrictions on your visit in order to protect the island's resources:

— All wildlife is protected. Since endangered species nest in the area, look out for posted areas.
— All vegetation is protected and should not be disturbed.
— Fires are allowed only below the high-water mark.
— Walk only at the lowest part of the dunes.
— Shelling is limited to two gallons of uninhabited shells per person per day.
— Metal detectors are prohibited.
— Carry your trash off the island.

Access

Access to Shackleford Banks is strictly by boat. The following firms offer ferry transport to Shackleford: From Beaufort: Outer Banks Ferry Service, 919-728-4129; Island Ferry and Tour Service, 919-728-5247 or 919-728-6888; Lookout Cruises, 919-504-SAIL; Good Fortune Sail Charters, 919-247-3860; Mystery Tours, 919-726-6783 or 919-728-7827 (boat). From Harkers Island: Barrier Island Transportation Co., Inc., 919-728-3907, 919-728-3908, or 1-800-423-8739 (North Carolina only); Cape Lookout Ferry Service, 919-728-3575; Sand Dollar Transportation, 919-728-6181, 919-504-3939, or 1-800-281-3978. From Morehead City: Anderson/Muns Maritime, Inc., 919-728-3988 or 919-240-2177.

You may also take your own boat. There are no restrictions on landing, save one—you cannot tie up at the jetty, although you may unload there.

Information

For information, call the Cape Lookout National Seashore Visitors Center on Harkers Island at 919-728-2250, 8 A.M. to 4:30 P.M. daily, or write Superintendent, Cape Lookout National Seashore, 131 Charles Street, Harkers Island, NC 28531.

Beaufort

If Beaufort has a secret, it may be how it has stayed Beaufort. I suspect this delightful port and county seat flourishes on the same persevering spirit that has made it the third oldest town in the state. Beaufort simply, collectively, doesn't want or need to be anything other than what it is—a nearly three-century-old waterfront community, once serving industry, now serving hospitality, history, good food, and a real easy attitude.

The community seems to have made a habit of saying no to things that don't fit in. Very early in the historical preservation game, Beaufort staked itself out as a place that needed renovation, not reconstruction. The job was made all the easier in that the town has weathered hard times with most of its buildings occupied. People stayed here, and by the time the town was taking on a new life as a tourist destination, the historical preservation

effort was more than a fashion, it became a belief. Fitting into the fabric and feeling of salt-swept history is what this charming soundside town is about.

Beaufort is such a nice surprise, a contrast to what you have been led to expect near salt water. Walking the town lets you absorb the wonderfully cockeyed architecture of the former fishing village. Everything seems slightly askew, and the cants and tilts of age are proudly worn badges merely supplemented by the shields on the door, which bear the date of construction.

The soul of the town is the National Register Historic District, which encompasses most of the town from Broad Street south to Taylor Creek (the waterfront) and Live Oak Street to the east to the water of Beaufort Channel. It gives the community a special status among coastal towns. While you can pitch for Ocracoke as the quintessential living-history village, where both the village appearance and way of life persevere in the face of tourism, you must agree that Beaufort is more the Mystic Seaport of North Carolina. It is a town more carefully set as a museum display than as a working village. People can live in Beaufort and work elsewhere, earning the funds necessary to afford the historical ambience. Prices of buildings in the historic district are stellar.

You arrive in the village through the eighteenth-century portals of the historic homes that occupy 15–20 blocks of the town. If you're arriving from Morehead City, turn

Public fishing pier adjacent to the Harkers Island Bridge. (Photograph by the author)

south at the light at the intersection of US 70 and Turner Street.

You'll pass the red-brick Carteret County Courthouse, occupying a square bounded by Cedar and Broad streets to the north and south and Turner and Craven streets to the west and east, respectively. Almost immediately after crossing Broad Street (note the railroad tracks that arc through town), you'll be greeted by the homes, columned porches, and full-width balustrades that seem to smile, grinning side by side with a colonial air of dominion over the water.

Turner Street passes several parking lots, and if you should find parking here, take it. Beaufort is a town to walk in, and you'll be quicker on foot in the seasonal crush than you will be on four wheels. If you wish to take the historical plunge full tilt, stop at the Beaufort Historical Association Welcome Center and arrange a guided tour of the eight-building complex known as Old Beaufort By the Sea, which is open all year. There are some fine sights within the buildings, and the tour sets the tone of the town. Four sites include the Car-

teret County Courthouse of 1796, an 1859 apothecary shop, and the 1829 Carteret County jail. The Beaufort Historical Association is responsible for the significant preservation of the sites.

All of this is the wrapping, the historic paper surrounding the bustling waterfront of the present. Today, Beaufort may, in fact, be busier as a port of call than ever before, with one major change—the boats that dock here unload people, not fish, according to the wishes of the community. You will notice as soon as you walk along Front Street that

The Shapes of Islands

Although all southeastern states have barrier islands, they differ in form and alignment. Obviously, different forces must influence the molding of sand into the barrier shapes we observe.

North Carolina's barrier islands are long and narrow, typical of barrier islands shaped by wind, wind-generated waves, and strong currents. Texas has similar islands, and Texas's Padre Island National Seashore is virtually a mirror image of North Carolina's barrier preserves.

Along coasts where the dominant force shaping barrier islands is tidal and the predominant source of new material is alluvial (coming from inland rivers), as along the South Carolina and Georgia coasts, barrier islands tend to be drumstick shaped, short and wide.

Even along the North Carolina coast, island configuration varies greatly. The differing barriers provide visible evidence of the way different forces affect the common building block of the island, which is sand.

Nowhere is the contrast in island-shaping effects so clearly juxtaposed as it is at Cape Lookout. The Cape Lookout Lighthouse is on South Core Banks, the southernmost lengthy northeast-to-southwest trending island of the Cape Lookout National Seashore. Adjacent lies Shackleford Banks, the first of the barrier islands that is oriented east and west.

What a contrast! Core is low with sparse vegetation and barely any dune formation; Shackleford has thickly forested lengths with extensive dune formation. The difference is the response of the islands to the wind that predominantly blows north or south. The wind carries sand particles deposited on Core Banks up and down the beach, parallel to the ocean, in stinging, wispy streaks that can make a windy day on the beach something to be endured. It makes dune formation very difficult indeed. The same wind moves sand perpendicular to the east-west orientation of Shackleford Banks in a steady process that results in the widening

of the island and increasing dune height.

The pattern of dune buildup is repeated periodically along the coast as the orientation of the barrier islands shifts between north-south and east-west. At three locations along the barrier chain (approximately every 100 miles), the orientation of the island formation alters: at Cape Hatteras, Cape Lookout, and Cape Fear. Each westward bend of the islands changes the effect of the prevailing winds. Although one might expect that the islands trending east-west would typically have higher dunes, sheltered forests, and higher elevations, it is not necessarily true. Other factors intervene, keeping geologists on their toes. Ironically, although each island responds individually to the forces of nature, the chain of islands adapts collectively to the same forces. The way wind and water affect one island changes the way it affects an adjacent island, proving that, really, no island stands alone, or stands still very long, either.

Beaufort took some steps to capitalize on its waterfront history. The town is, in fact, trading on its past as the means to build a future. In the late 1970s, it completed an ambitious, nearly audacious, waterfront restoration smack in the heart of this seafaring town. The heart of town is still the heart of town, and that is Front Street. It runs as it always has along Taylor Creek, but there is a new shine to it that is different from the glint of traditional tin-roof fish shacks—it's the gleam of brass fittings on cruising yachts and pleasure sailboats. Beaufort is one of the prime transient harbors for the sailing and power-cruising set.

What the waterfront restoration did was create a downtown that you want to approach from both directions, water and land. Some older buildings—one lifelong resi-

	Fee	Parking	Restrooms	Lifeguard	Camping	Showers	Beach Access	Hiking	Trail	Handicapped	Boating	ORV Access	Fishing	Programs	Historic	Sand Beach	Dunes	Upland	Wet and
Public Boating Access: Taylor Creek		•									•		•						•
Beaufort		•	•							•	•		•		•				
North Carolina Maritime Museum		•	•							•				•	•				
Public Boating Access: West Beaufort Road		•									•		•						•
Carrot Island and Bird Shoal								•	•		•		•	•		•			•
Radio Island		•											•						•
Regional Access: Newport River		•	•					•			•		•						•
Morehead City Municipal Park		•	•							•	•		•						•
Carteret County Museum of History		•	•							•				•	•				

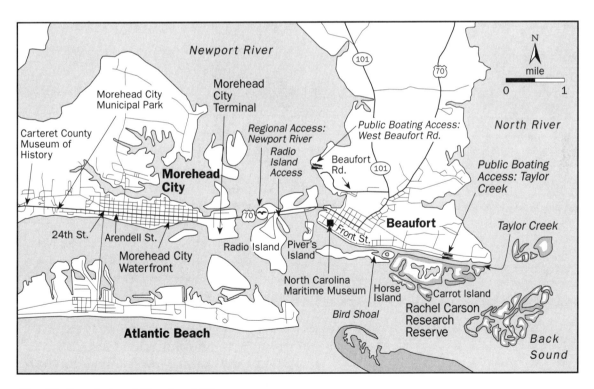

Map 18. Beaufort and Morehead City

Beaufort waterfront.
(Photograph by the author)

dent recalled them as "fish houses" serving local trade—blocking access to the water were removed, some were renovated, and the water was made the feature of the community. The dockmaster's office sits directly between two double-bayed parking lots overlooking the waterfront boardwalk that is beside the boat slips, which are formally called Beaufort Docks. The boat slips are available for $1 per foot per night on a first-come, first-served basis. The harbormaster knows how to pack the boats in, and they haven't turned anyone away yet. Taylor Creek, out of the channel, is open water. It is particularly delightful at dusk, when the setting sun casts a golden glow across the marsh grasses and myrtles on Carrot Island across Taylor Creek, part of the Rachel Carson component of the National Estuarine Research Reserve system and home to a small herd of feral horses. The boardwalk and streets are busy with folks walking. There is a restaurant in the middle of the waterfront development with a harbormaster office in the same building. If you were ever looking to prop your feet up and watch the world sail by, it might as well be here as any small harbor I've visited.

Beside Beaufort Docks is a small commercial cluster known as Somerset Square, almost directly at the end of Turner Street. Several restaurants line the 300 block of Front Street, and at the end of Orange Street, the beginning of the 200 block of Front Street, is the dock serving the Shackleford and Carrot Island ferry. This spot, where Orange Street "tees" into Front Street, provides one of the richest, all-encompassing views of the town and its surrounds. The remainder of Front Street is residential, and the homes look toward the waterfront. The five adjacent houses in the 100 block have both first- and second-story porches that appear as if built to a single chalk line. The porches frame the view of Piver's Island and the Duke University Marine Laboratories nicely as you look along the length of Front Street.

The remainder of the town is similar, with block-by-block variations. It's an open-air museum, filled with bed-and-breakfast establishments and wonderful walkable streets.

Access

There is off-street and on-street parking near the waterfront. Several large parking lots are available approximately one block from Front Street.

The city has two parks on Taylor Creek: Grayden Paul Park at the end of Pollack Street, two blocks east of the waterfront, and Jaycee Park at the east end of Front Street, which has parking for approximately 30 cars and two small boat ramps.

The North Carolina Wildlife Resources Commission maintains a boat-launching ramp near Beaufort that provides access to Taylor Creek. To reach it, follow US 70 east from Beaufort, turn south on SR 1310 (Lennoxville Road), follow 1.5 miles, turn right on SR 1312, and the ramp is 100 yards ahead on the left.

Beaufort is the departure point for several of the concession ferries carrying passengers to Cape Lookout National Seashore and the Rachel Carson preserve, directly across Taylor Creek from the waterfront. The park service can advise you on carriers and their schedules, and the Beaufort Docks harbormaster can give you additional docking information. The following ferry services dock along Front Street: Outer Banks Ferry Service, 328 Front Street, Beaufort, NC 28516, 919-728-4129; Island Ferry and Tour Service, 300 Front Street, 919-728-5247 or 919-728-6888; Lookout Cruises, Beaufort Docks, 919-504-SAIL; Good Fortune Sail Charters, 919-247-3860. For diving access, contact Discovery Dive, 919-728-2265.

Carteret County and local sportfishermen established a boating access site on the Newport River. Cross US 70 north on Turner Street and turn left after the railroad tracks on West Beaufort Road. The ramp and parking area are at the end of the road.

Handicapped Access

The waterfront is readily accessible for handicapped travelers, as are some of the shops and restaurants on Front Street.

Information

For information, contact Carteret County Tourism Development Bureau, P.O. Box 1406, Morehead City, NC 28557, 1-800-SUNNYNC, or Beaufort Historical Association, P.O. Box 1709, Beaufort, NC 28516, 919-728-5225.

North Carolina Maritime Museum

It doesn't seem possible that the nearly 18,000-square-foot North Carolina Maritime Museum could be tucked into residentially scaled Front Street, but it has been, and with parking no less. It is equally amazing that such an institution, so full of information and staffed by people ready to help you, could be so accessible and free. This institution is one of the finest educational resources you will visit, and if you want to plunge into the maritime history of the state, then step right through the doors and get your curiosity wet. It's also a great place to

Harvey W. Smith Watercraft Center, North Carolina Maritime Museum, Beaufort. (Courtesy of N.C. Travel and Tourism Division)

gawk. The building tips its architectural hat at the styling of the U.S. Life-Saving Service stations and the Beaufort vernacular as well. Inside, in the rich honeyed finishes of a wooden vessel, is a treasure ship for sea lovers.

The museum focuses on North Carolina nautical traditions and how the various seafaring livelihoods found their own indigenous forms and expression. The museum shows graphically what's in the sea and then what seafaring folk put on it and beside it.

Mounted game fish ornament the walls, and shells by the thousands are cataloged in cases in the auditorium. All this is a backdrop to the museum's central features—the stories of boats and those who sailed them.

There are several authentic wooden boats made by area boat builders, exquisite replicas of faithful ships and designs, and detailed scale models of famous vessels as well. The story of waterfowl hunting, decoy carving, and the hunting tradition is depicted in one corner. Perhaps the most moving of all the exhibits is the story of the lighthouses and the crews of the U.S. Life-Saving Service. One poignant vignette in this exhibit is the Gold Life-Saving Service Medal awarded to Rasmus S. Midgett for single-handedly saving 10 members of the barkentine *Priscilla* on 18 August 1899 from the Gulf Shoal station on Hatteras Island.

The museum contains an excellent bookstore and gift shop and is one of the largest dealers in nautical charts on the East Coast. The museum also sponsors a research library.

Across the street is the newly opened Harvey Smith Watercraft Center, where a variety of traditional boats are on display and others are being repaired or restored. The boat building and restoration exhibit is an outgrowth of one of the museum's important preservation efforts to find representative North Carolina sailing and working craft and preserve the skills that built them as well.

Throughout the year, the museum sponsors programs in-house and provides invaluable access to the cultural and ecological history of the coast through its field-trip programs. The museum publishes calendars of its programs three times a year. The trips are by reservation and the fee varies. In the past the museum has offered different workshops in the Cape Lookout Studies Program, which uses the former U.S. Coast Guard Station on Cape Lookout as an education center and overnight facility. Fees for these programs include ferry travel to the cape. Programs have also been held at the Rachel Carson component of the North Carolina National Estuarine Research Reserve, directly across Taylor Creek from Beaufort. With Duke University Marine Laboratories, the museum cosponsors trawl and dredge trips to collect research specimens for the laboratory. These are working trips, a behind-the-scenes look at marine biology, and should not be mistaken for pleasure cruises.

Access

The museum is open 9 A.M. to 5 P.M. Monday–Friday; 10 A.M. to 5 P.M. Saturday; 2 P.M. to 5 P.M. Sunday. There is no admission.

Handicapped Access

The museum is accessible for handicapped travelers.

Information

For information, contact North Carolina Maritime Museum, 315 Front Street, Beaufort, NC 28516, 919-728-7317.

Carrot Island and Bird Shoal

The narrow, protected channel serving Beaufort's waterfront is Taylor Creek, an ordinarily shallow passage that has been dredged to 13 feet by the U.S. Army Corps of Engineers. The spoil from the dredging has been deposited on Carrot Island and Bird Shoal, which, along with other acreage, compose the 2,625-acre Rachel Carson component of the North Carolina National Estuarine Research Reserve system.

The filled areas from the dredging notwithstanding, these islands and flats are relatively unspoiled sanctuaries supporting a diversity of wildlife in many varied habitats. Mostly they are islands for birds. Authorities have recorded twenty-three species of birds that are endangered, threatened, or decreasing in number as users of the site, and more than 100 total species have been recorded here.

Historically, residents have used these islands for recreation and for horse pasturage, although the horse herd will be monitored for their health and damage to the ecology of the islands. These isolated hammocks almost became condominiums. In 1977, however, the proposal was thwarted, and the North Carolina Nature Conservancy purchased 474 acres of Carrot Island. Since that time the remainder of the marsh, tidal flats, and barriers have been secured, protecting both the charm of the Beaufort waterfront and the integrity of the sites.

During the summer months, the North Carolina Maritime Museum occasionally conducts guided interpretive walks on Bird Shoal. Check with the museum for the schedule and fees.

Access

Check with the harbormaster at Beaufort Docks or call the National Park Service for information on ferry service to the sites. Outer Banks Ferry Service of Barrier Island Adventures, 328 Front Street, Beaufort, NC 28516, 919-728-4129, and Island Ferry and Tour Service, 300 Front Street, 919-728-5247 or 919-728-6888, offer transport.

Information

For information, contact North Carolina National Estuarine Research Reserve, 7205 Wrightsville

Avenue, Wilmington, NC 28403, 919-256-3721, or Division of Coastal Management, P.O. Box 27687, Raleigh, NC 27611, 919-733-2293.

Duke University Marine Laboratories

If you walk to the west end of Front Street in Beaufort and look across the water, you'll be looking at the close, villagelike campus of a major oceanographic research institution. Duke University in Durham, North Carolina, staffs a marine science laboratory for undergraduate and graduate degree programs in marine sciences and related subjects. The campus is on Piver's Island, which it shares with a National Marine Fisheries Station. A boat dock is reserved for the use of the two institutions. Although the campus is open to the public for selected programs and talks, it is a research and teaching facility that is not designed to accommodate visitation.

It was from the campus of Duke University Marine Laboratories that Rachel Carson wrote part of her superb seashore ecological book, *The Sea Around Us*. Carson drew heavily on her visits to nearby Bird Shoal and Carrot Island, which is now set aside as the Rachel Carson component of the North Carolina National Estuarine Research Reserve.

Information

For information, call the Office of the Director, Duke University Marine Laboratories, at 919-728-2111.

Radio Island

Radio Island is one of the best of the informal and undeveloped access sites in the area. The site is in the thick of the port action, within easy bait-casting distance of the channel and blessed with protected waters for swimming. It has traditionally been a local access area.

Recently, the North Carolina State Ports Authority acquired a significant portion of Radio Island and restricted access into the area. It subsequently leased a 12-acre site to Carteret County for use as public access. The county installed approximately 72 parking spaces and restricts access to daylight hours. The lease specifies that the State Ports Authority can terminate the lease for any infraction of the posted rules governing use and access, so obey the posted regulations.

There are no concessions, so carry what you will need to be comfortable.

Access

Radio Island is reached by turning south off of US 70 at the first median break east of the high-rise bridge over the Newport River, which is opposite the turn to the Newport River regional access area. Turn on the island, travel for several hundred feet, and turn left on the paved road.

Handicapped Access

There are designated handicapped spaces in the parking lot. The water, however, is a good distance over sandy terrain from the parking lot.

Newport River Regional Access Area

You can pull over to fish or sunbathe by the Newport River at the regional access site on the northeast side of the causeway, at the east end of the high-rise bridge over the river. This is a fully developed regional facility, with restrooms, a boardwalk, picnic tables, a dune crossover, and trails leading to riverfront fishing sites. The site provides excellent opportunity for fishing and crabbing along the Intracoastal Waterway, which follows the Newport River here.

The access area is built on a dredge-spoil site, which seems stable and is certainly serving good use now. The boardwalk overlooks the state port terminal at Morehead City. It is a surreal view, the many domed storage buildings interlocked with catwalks and conveyor-belt delivery tracks. A dune ridge trail leads among plantings of seaside goldenrod and other pioneering plants to views of the north side of the basin and the Newport Marsh.

Access

The access area closes at sunset.

Handicapped Access

The site is fully accessible for handicapped travelers.

Information

For information, contact Division of Coastal Management, P.O. Box 27687, Raleigh, NC 27611, 919-733-2293.

Morehead City

Morehead City is one of the state's main ports for people going to sun and for goods going to sea. If you arrive here on US 70, you drive parallel to the railroad tracks that continue through the center of the town. These tracks are reminders of the formative role of the railroad in Morehead City's history, and the tracks still carry freight, a sign that the port of Morehead and the dream of its founder remain vital.

Governor John Motley Morehead, who served from 1841 to 1845, literally made tracks in North Carolina as a rail baron. By the 1850s, rail lines to Carteret County terminated at Beaufort, the major shipping and shipbuilding community of the central coast.

Morehead foresaw the need to develop another deep-water port (Wilmington was the only one), so he purchased 600 acres in this area in 1853. Served by the railway, Morehead City quickly became a fashionable resort during the Victorian era, eventually becoming a major port much later. After substantial financial commitments by the state to improve docking facilities and the harbor channel, Morehead became the dependable deep-water port its founder envisioned.

Morehead City began growing as a vacation location first, when the railway came to town. In 1883, the famed Atlantic Hotel opened and became known on the East Coast as a major resort destination, a place of gala ballroom dancing. The lights by Bogue Sound in Morehead belonged to social luminaries. In this golden age of railroads, Morehead City attracted the barons of incredible industrial wealth steadily through the 1920s.

On April 15, 1933, the lights went up in a blaze when the Atlantic Hotel caught fire. (Photographs of the hotel and the fire may be seen at the Carteret County Museum of History next to the Morehead City Civic Center.) The fire and the Depression dramatically altered the role Morehead City would play in the social life of the East Coast.

The Jefferson Hotel now stands on the site of the Atlantic Hotel. If you look west from the entrance, you can see the 1918 railroad passenger terminal buildings known today as Waterfront Junction. In outward disrepair but still open as private shops, the classically designed buildings stand on either side of the original tracks and ties. Waterfront Junction is at the corner of Sixth Street and Arendell Street, or US 70, at the center of the action during the railroad era and near the center of Morehead City tourism today.

Morehead City is more an auxiliary destination than a prime vacation spot, making the most of its safe harbor and excellent channel to the sea. It is a sportfisherman's haven and a seafood lover's mecca. While vacationers prefer to spread their towels on the resort beaches of Bogue Banks, they still spill over the sound to eat, fish, and shop along the waterfront.

The hub of this activity is the east end of the community. US 70 enters from the west and routes by attractive tree-lined streets and residential neighborhoods along Bogue Sound. The traditional western end of town is at the junction of US 70 and Bridges Street, an area known as Camp Glen. During World War I, this was an army encampment, and the Carteret County Museum of History on Wallace Street, the road leading to the Civic Center, was the original school on the base.

Shortly past where the median of Arendell Street widens for the tracks of the railway, look for the Crystal Coast Information Center. This A-frame building on Arendell Street at the Morehead City Municipal Park should be your first stop for information on programs, facilities, and current events in the area.

The municipal park, with its live oak–shaded picnic areas and ample parking, has a free boat ramp serving Bogue Sound. Check out the memorial obelisk behind the visitors center. It honors Josiah Bogue, who deeded to his daughter land known as Shepherd's Point, which became the site of Morehead City.

If you're in a hurry to go to the beach, zip east to Twenty-fourth Street and turn right over the bridge. However, if you're curious about old Morehead City, turn into the municipal park and drive east on Evans Street. You'll be in a neighborhood of bungalow cottages and permanent homes, many of which are holdovers from the first wave of second-home construction and the continual resettling of Morehead City as a retirement community. These soundside homes are sheltered by the native live oaks and stand shoulder-to-shoulder, close enough to be cozy but not quite crowded. The homes on Sunset Drive, a bulge into the sound, are larger but have a weathered presence that evokes vacation places such as Martha's Vineyard. Evans Street is not a shortcut; it is a drive through a neighborhood, so be careful of your speed.

Morehead City's residential neighborhoods continue on the eastern side of the bridge/causeway leading to Bogue Banks. The mainland bulges two more blocks to the southeast of Twenty-third Street, where Shepard Street, which carries you to the commercial district, and Shackleford Street, the waterfront road, run parallel to Arendell Street.

The historical commercial center lines both sides of the train tracks. The park on Tenth Street marks just about the center of the main business district, which is compact with a small-town character, reminiscent of Scotland Neck and Nashville. It

doesn't look like what you would expect near salt water. The buildings sit close to the roadway with streetside parking.

Shepard Street angles north to join Evans at Seventh Street. There is a lot of activity from this point east. At the corner of Evans and Eighth is the Mediterranean villa–styled fire/police station; next door is the Quonset-hut headquarters of the U.S. Marine Corps Shore Patrol. Across Shepard Street a duck crossing sign signals the beginning of Morehead City's thriving waterfront and tourist service business, which runs along the sound to Fourth Street and slightly beyond. There's something here for everybody, particularly if you are interested in eating seafood, buying seafood, or catching seafood. You can park, if you're lucky, in the municipal lot at the city park at Sixth Street and Evans, where there are also public restrooms. You will compete for a parking space with fishermen and diners. Several of the restaurants along this stretch have their own parking lots.

Parking being as tight as it is, you might consider parking on Arendell Street and walking the short distance to the waterfront. South of Waterfront Junction, at the corner of Sixth and Arendell streets, is the entrance to the city park parking lot.

The waterfront boardwalk is brand new and amazingly squeaky clean for a working charter center, the home port of one of the largest fleets on the East Coast. You can choose from Gulf Stream outings or head-boat trips for bottom-fishing excursions. Several annual fishing tournaments use the waterfront as their headquarters. Morehead City is also a center for charter diving trips.

The waterfront hums: kiosks are covered with local information, diners stroll after their restaurant meals, charter crews tend to their boats.

The high ground of cedar-covered Sugarloaf Island is the backdrop to the moorings. It's visible between the facades of buildings and from some of the restaurants. There are also shops and restaurants on the north side of Evans Street.

Morehead City stays busy as a gateway, and you only pick up a little of the residential flavor of the town before going downeast or crossing Bogue Sound. The traffic you encounter, however, is much less than it used to be before the opening of the high-rise crossover to Bogue Banks in the early 1990s. Gone today is the rite-of-passage traffic stall of east-bound US 70, backed up and waiting for the swing bridge to pivot shut to allow the oceanfront migration to proceed. In the heat of summer, this was a fine test of the cooling system in your car, as well as your own ability to maintain your cool. While you steamed, literally and figuratively, recreational sailors in Bogue Sound opened the bridge on their vacation and closed the roadway on yours. The new bridge speeds the access for everyone, swimmers and fishermen alike, but

at the faster speeds, you miss the opportunity to soak in the sound-side bungalow view. Traffic still can be a little dicey at night, however, because the trains do much of their maneuvering back and forth, using the middle of town—the limits of the switching yard end at just about Sixth Street—to align cars onto the proper spur. They can block the intersection of US 70 and the bridge road. If you go west, you can usually move around them.

The Morehead City Terminal, which is open to the public for tours during weekdays, serves ocean-crossing vessels from all seafaring nations. It is also a major shipping port of call for the U.S. Marine Corps from nearby Camp Lejeune.

Heading east, you cross the tracks and vault over the Newport River bridge to Beaufort. Here you can sometimes see an immense pile of an indistinguishable material. The product is hardwood chips from the North Carolina coastal plain forest, destined for Asia to make fine papers. A tremendous covered building on the north side of US 70 is a shelter for phosphate, mined near Aurora.

Access

Morehead City has no beach access and only limited locations for public access to sound waters. Swimming is not recommended in these locations.

The North Carolina Wildlife Resources Commission maintains a boating access ramp to the waters of Bogue Sound at a city park

located at Thirty-fifth Street. There is another boating access location approximately 1.5 miles east on US 70 after the junction with NC 24. The access area is near the western city limits on the right-hand side as you travel east. You'll see a glimpse of water as you drive toward the city; slow down at that point and look for the diamond-shaped sign indicating the access location. Morehead City has become a center for wreck diving offshore. Contact Olympus Dive Center at 919-726-9432.

Handicapped Access

The Morehead City waterfront and docks are accessible for handicapped travelers. There are designated handicapped parking spaces in the municipal parking lot at Sixth Street.

Information

For information, contact Carteret County Tourism Development Bureau, P.O. Box 1406, Morehead City, NC 28557, 1-800-SUNNYNC.

Carteret County Museum of History

While you can't possibly collect everything that makes a county into a single building, you can certainly include enough to communicate the riches of life downeast. This is exactly what the Carteret County Museum of History in Morehead City accomplishes.

The nifty package of volunteer work has assembled a delightful cross-cultural portrait of Carteret County. The recipient of one of the state's highest awards for historic preservation, the museum is just east of the beginning of the divided highway in Morehead City; turn on Wallace Street at the signs for the Civic Center and look for the big anchor in the lawn. During World War I, this area was an army encampment known as Camp Glen, and the museum building was the original school on the base. Subsequently, it became a Methodist church. Now it is restored and a wonderful display of the past lives of Carteret County, from duck hunters to ballroom dancing.

Access

The museum is open 1 P.M.–4 P.M. Tuesday–Saturday.

Handicapped Access

The museum is accessible for the handicapped with some assistance.

Information

For information, contact Carteret County Museum of History, Civic Center Drive, P.O. Box 481, Morehead City, NC 28557, 919-247-7533.

Bogue Banks

Bogue Banks is approximately 28 miles long, the longest island south of Cape Lookout and one of the most popular destinations in the state. It is also, technically, the most

southern barrier island of the Outer Banks, although not commonly considered part of the Outer Banks.

You can find a variety of attractions here, cultural and natural. There's a pre–Civil War fort, an aquarium and state natural area, luxury condominiums, a community with "property owners only" restricted access, an amusement park, shopping centers, a go-cart track, jungle golf, beachfront hotels, fishing piers, and trailer parks. There are marinas, sailing schools, and wild places that will stay that way except for observation trails. In some locations, dunes soar 15 to 20 feet above the tide line; in others, the dunes are flat as biscuits. A lot happens in these 28 miles of gently sloping beaches.

There are four incorporated communities—Atlantic Beach, Pine Knoll Shores, Indian Beach, and Emerald Isle—and one stubbornly independent settlement—Salter Path. "Salter Pathers" adhere to traditional fishing and attitudes about fishing as a means of making a living.

The main attraction here is the wide, gentle, south-facing beaches of Bogue Banks, first named for settler Josiah Bogue. The history begins with the quiet story of small fishing communities on the soundside of the island and roars through a second-home explosion following the 1971 opening of the west-end bridge to Cape Carteret that is only now slowing. Looking at the island today, it is difficult to believe that recreation and second-home con-

struction did not become a force here until after World War II. A bridge between Morehead City and Bogue Banks led to the creation of the playground of Atlantic Beach in the late 1920s. However, most of the remainder of the island, from Atlantic Beach west, belonged to two people, Alice Green Hoffman and Henry Fort, who, followed by their respective heirs, controlled the island up until the 1950s.

Alice Hoffman became the most colorful, notorious, and ironically beneficent owner of land here. Her domain, and she treated it as such, extended from Atlantic Beach to Salter Path. She constructed a large estate with elaborate gardens on the soundside of the island in what is now Pine Knoll Shores. (The estate was razed long ago, but for some time the foundation was visible along Oakleaf Drive, near the intersection of Hawthorne Drive.) Her disagreements with local fishermen (she sued for trespass and lost) led to the legal establishment of Salter Path.

At her death, she willed the land to her niece, Mrs. Theodore Roosevelt, Jr. The Roosevelt heirs sold most of the land, which was subsequently developed, but they dedicated 290 acres to the state for the Theodore Roosevelt State Natural Area. Indirectly, Hoffman returned a portion of the property she had sued to protect to the people of North Carolina for their enjoyment.

Hoffman's next-door neighbor in an insular sort of way was Henry Fort, an entrepreneur from Penn-

	Fee	Parking	Restrooms	Lifeguard	Camping	Showers	Beach Access	Hiking	Trail	Handicapped	Boating	ORV Access	Fishing	Programs	Historic	Sand Beach	Dunes	Upland	Wetland
Fort Macon Museum and State Park		•	•				•	•	•	•			•	•	•	•	•	•	•
Regional Access: Fort Macon		•	•	•		•	•			•			•			•	•		
Regional Access: Les and Sally Moore		•	•			•	•			•	•	•	•			•	•		
Atlantic Beach ("The Circle")		•		•			•									•			
Regional Access: West Atlantic Blvd.		•	•	•		•	•			•		•	•			•	•		
Iron Steamer Pier	•	•	•				•						•		•	•			
Theodore Roosevelt State Natural Area		•						•	•					•	•			•	•
N.C. Aquarium, Pine Knoll Shores		•	•					•	•	•				•	•			•	•
Regional Access: Salter Path		•	•		•		•			•			•			•	•	•	
Indian Beach		•					•				•	•				•			
Indian Beach ORV Access		•			•		•					•	•			•			

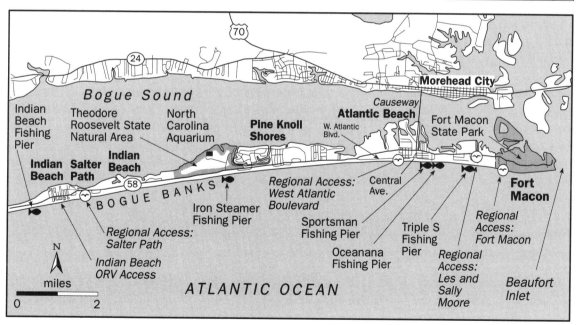

Map 19. Bogue Banks: Fort Macon to Indian Beach

sylvania who planned to build a tremendous resort on his property, which encompassed a great deal of the island west of Hoffman's estate. He needed a bridge to serve his development but was never able to get permission from the state for construction. His plans summarily died with the Great Depression.

The development of Atlantic Beach began with the economic boom following the Second World War. However, even though the island was accessible by bridge, very few people owned cars. The concept of extended vacations seems to have grown both as an idea and reality with the steady climb of the postwar industrial economy. The few folks who could drive to the island did not travel much farther than Atlantic Beach or the points east of there. The only road to the west, continuing to Salter Path, was not paved, and not many travelers wanted to go to Salter Path, anyway.

By the early 1950s, the demand for land was rising, but the island was essentially still not available. This changed in the mid-1950s when the heirs to the Fort property sold the western half of the island and Alice Hoffman died, leaving her property to the Roosevelt family, who began selling their lands also. In effect, all of Bogue Banks west of Atlantic Beach was placed on the market at a time when the economy cycled high.

Within thirty years, it was a done deal and access was becoming a problem because of the great numbers of people visiting each summer

and because providing access to the beaches was an afterthought. As one Emerald Isle town official commented, "A few simple things a long time ago would have made a difference. If we had extended the right-of-way of the north-south streets to the water, we would have had plenty of access." But they didn't; Bogue Banks construction surged forward, and more and more of the beach became hard to reach.

You can develop a feeling today for which areas of the island date from earlier times. Careful siting of structures within the existing dunes and maritime forest yielded quickly to more expedient lot-clearing attitudes that were harsher on the land. Much of the wetlands adjacent to the causeway at Atlantic Beach were filled in to increase the numbers of homesites. The island showcases every barrier environment from low, narrow, treeless lengths, windswept and unsheltered, to salt-pruned and sculpted forests of live oak and yaupon. There are tall, grassed dunes and expanses of low plains of American beach grass. The older settlements such as Salter Path are on comparatively high ground in the soundside forests; the newer developments are everywhere. The character of the development is as varied as the island environment. There are cushy second- and permanent-home estates and trailer parks, high-rise condominiums and mom and pop private campgrounds.

The two high-rise bridges—from Morehead City and Cape Carteret—

loop NC 58 over the sound, along the spine of the island, and back to the mainland. It is a very leisurely loop—the speed limit on NC 58 is 45 miles per hour and closely enforced, particularly in Indian Beach, where it drops to 35 miles per hour. During summer, speed limits can be reduced further. Since you can rarely see the ocean from the highway, it is often difficult to tell that you are on an island. Some of the more intriguing stretches of the drive occur when the road tunnels through the salt-sculpted trees. The twisted trunks flash by at eye level, and the sheared tops undulate like closely cropped topiaries.

Access

Access is difficult on Bogue Banks and becomes more difficult the farther west you go on the island. Although there are clearly reserved public ramps to the beach, places to park are few and far between.

The state and local governments provide access, but there is very little predictability about the location of sites. Pine Knoll Shores has no public access sites at all since it is a private, residential community, and there is no parking along the streets. There are several private parking lots but they are owned by the local homeowners' association. Access is only by rental or ownership.

Fort Macon State Park, the largest and one of the most popular access locations on the island, serves Beaufort Inlet and the beaches at the east end of the island. Atlantic

Fishing in Beaufort Inlet at Fort Macon State Park. (Courtesy of N.C. Travel and Tourism Division)

Beach maintains two regional access sites, the Les and Sally Moore Regional Access at New Bern Street and the new West Atlantic Boulevard Regional Access just west of the "circle."

Salter Path has a beautiful 22-acre regional access site featuring 65 parking spaces, a bathhouse, and an elegant, decked dune crossover. Another regional access site with ample parking is near the eastern town limits of Emerald Isle.

One bright note of this somewhat restricted access situation is the entrepreneurial spirit of some owners of fishing piers and, to a lesser extent, larger hotels. Nearly every pier owns a substantial parking lot that can easily serve its fishing needs. The pier owners reserve parking for fishermen first but will also allow varying amounts of parking for beachgoers. They do discourage parking for surfers, who by law cannot surf within 200 feet of a pier. (In Emerald Isle, this restriction is 500 feet.) Some piers issue parking permits or decals with the purchase of admission to the pier, a price of usually less than $5 per day. Remember that the piers and the parking lots are private property. Courtesy will go a long way here. You'll probably improve your chances immeasurably if you buy a couple of soft drinks and a pack of crackers before asking permission to park. It takes the edge off owners who must deal with more than their share of people demanding "something for nothing."

Handicapped Access

The regional access sites at Fort Macon, Atlantic Beach, and Salter Path are accessible to handicapped travelers and have restrooms. Both the Fort Macon and the Salter Path access sites have terrific views from elevated, ramped dune crossovers.

The West Atlantic Boulevard access location in Atlantic Beach has handicapped spaces adjacent to a boardwalk and restrooms and provides access to the Atlantic Beach boardwalk as well as the oceanfront.

Information

For information, contact Carteret County Tourism Development Bureau, P.O. Box 1406, Morehead City, NC 28557, 1-800-SUNNYNC.

Fort Macon State Park

There is something eerie and almost unnerving about Fort Macon, which at one time commanded the approach to Beaufort Inlet and dominated the east end of Bogue Banks. Part of this feeling comes from the approach to the fort. From the parking lot, you follow a path that passes through the maritime forest to gradually descend an old brick road with reinforced stone wheel tracks, constructed to bear the weight of caissons and cannon carriages. You enter the massive enclosure through the walls of the outer ramparts, crossing the moat on a wide wooden bridge, and then disappear into the heart of the fortification. Inside the citadel, you walk the geometrical parade ground walled by the bricked facades of vaulted casemates or underground

barracks. Three staircases lead to the top of the citadel.

Fort Macon imparts a medieval feeling that is nearly oppressive. The walls of the citadel loom above the parade ground, trapping the heat and the sunlight. It is a place that is desperately in need of a shadow. When the fort was garrisoned, the soldiers took refuge in the cool, cavelike casemates.

Perhaps the most impressive feature of the fort is the silence. Should you visit on a day when no children are playing tag along the ramparts—unlikely during the summer season—it is hauntingly quiet. From the inside, your view is of the sky; only when you ascend to the gun emplacements at the top of the citadel or on the covertway, the outer wall, can you see the ocean.

One of the most surprising views when you ascend the covertway is toward the entrance road. The fort is so skillfully sited and constructed that you don't notice it when you drive by it to the parking lot. From the gun emplacements, you can see the field of fire that the location controlled.

The army built the fort between 1826 and 1834, using nearly 15 million bricks for the construction. Although the fort secured the inlet militarily, the cannon were useless against the encroachment by the sea. Erosion and hurricanes had claimed earlier fortifications, and by the time the current fort was completed, it was determined that protection was needed for it as well. During the 1840s a young West Point

graduate by the name of Robert E. Lee designed and supervised the construction of the jetty that still protects the inlet and provides great recreation for visitors.

During the Civil War, Fort Macon was quickly seized by Confederate troops. On April 25, 1862, the Confederate soldiers surrendered the fort after an 11-hour siege by Union forces. Following the war, the fort served as a penitentiary. The jail cells are under the outer ramparts.

Fort Macon became North Carolina's second state park in 1924 by an act of Congress permitting the state to take over the officially abandoned federal facilities for the sum of one dollar. It languished until the Civilian Conservation Corps restored it during the mid-1930s and was officially opened in 1936. Although the fort is the centerpiece of the park, there are 389 acres in the entire preserve, much of which you drive through on the way to the parking lot adjacent to the fort.

Exhibits inside the fort detail typical Civil War artillery, most of which was found on the grounds. Watch your step as you walk through the casemates—the bricked floor is uneven. Exhibits include furnished officer's quarters, more stylishly comfortable than one would imagine considering the starkness of the vacated casemates. A new exhibit is a reconstructed barracks from the World War II era, when the fort garrisoned a coastal artillery defense troop that had gun emplacements seaward of the fort

Fishing at sunrise at the Fort Macon regional access. (Photograph by the author)

Dune crossover, Fort Macon regional access. (Photograph by the author)

walls. It takes a little more than an hour to wander the hallways and battlements.

The Elliot Coues Nature Trail, a self-guided walk through a maritime shrub thicket, leads up to higher ground that is the beginning of a maritime forest. Unusual, multi-branched eastern red cedars, which hold their branches very low to the ground, grow along the trail, as does a beautiful specimen of prickly ash or Hercules club, a spiny tree pioneering in sandy soil. After leading you through this emerging forest with varying ecological niches, the trail reaches the high dune ridge and beach overlooking the inlet and then returns to the parking lot at the fort. The stroll takes about 45 minutes.

Besides the fort itself, one obvious park attraction is the beachfront on the waters of Beaufort Inlet and a large regional access facility with a very lengthy stretch of beach. Fishing and bathing are permitted in the park. The inlet location provides both choice beach and angling. A very high dune system fortifies the seaward edge of the park; some individual dunes reach more than 40 feet high. Lee's jetty caps the east end, arresting erosion at the inlet and protecting the fort. The jetty also creates some shallower,

Cones, Coils, and Columns

I still have not realized a childhood seashore yearning: to look around the corner of a conch. How does the shell hold all that ocean I can plainly hear? I continued to try to bend my eyesight even after learning that I didn't hold a conch but a whelk. It is still a smoothly blind alley that only nimble hermit crabs seem destined to know.

What began as childhood curiosity has developed into appreciation and fascination with the exquisite beauty of the coiling class of Mollusca known as gastropods or snails. In a fantastic diversity of variation on a successful concept, nature took a simple form, the cone, and applied a simple formula, the coil, and then gave it a decorative twist. Snail quarters are some of the finest houses you'll ever find. The Greeks knew it—they transcribed the spiral of a snail to become the volute or curved decorative capital appearing on the Ionic column.

What the Greeks noticed about the coil of the whelk was that it enlarged in an elegant manner. It seems proportional, and, indeed, it is, as Descartes deftly discovered. The French mathematical genius analyzed the graceful curve of snail shells, naming the mathematical function that describes it the equiangular spiral. Each successive coil of a snail's shell enlarges from the previous coil by a fixed proportion. A baby channel whelk is mathematically similar to a mature channel whelk; the proportions of the shells are the same—one is merely smaller than the other.

If you have ever opened the egg case of a whelk—the canvas-colored strings of rounded "pocketbooks" looking something like vertebrae—and found juvenile snails inside, then you have observed this mathematical precision. The spiral growth of the shell is logarithmic and numerically graphical (as if snails appeared cut from a digitized pattern).

To this self-regulating, enlarging shape, nature added curious ornaments, such as the knobs of the whelk, the flared lip of the queen conch, or the irregular mouth of the helmet shell—embellishments on the theme of cone and coil. Color and pattern adorn the snail further, but the greatest variation comes from the experimentation with the basic formula—the twisting, tapered tube.

If you can imagine that a cone is stretched out before you (or try one with modeling clay) and that you are the molluscan artist, first coil the cone in one plane, flat on the table, like the fiddlehead of a fern. This is the shell of the nautilus, native to gift shops on our coast. Next coil the cone to the left. This is a sinistral shell (like that of the left-handed lightning whelk). Reverse the coil, and you have a dextral shell. Whichever hand's fingers cup behind the mouth of the shell when the thumb points in the same direction as the top of the shell determines its handedness. This is important if you are cooking left-handed whelk chowder, for example.

If the cone is fat and curls in a cushion, you have an example of the coil familiar as the moon shell. Stretch the coil out for a great length in few revolutions, and you have the horse conch. Coil the cone tightly in a narrow taper, and you have created the auger.

Each snail species has its own rules for coiling and color pattern. Among individuals of a given species, color and patterning vary sufficiently to strike a note of individuality, but the coiled shape remains constant and telltale, as does the basic patterning of coloration.

calmer waters for swimming, but as with any inlet, caution should be observed when swimming here. The parking lot at the fort is close to the jetty. You have a direct access to the inlet and can watch the port traffic using Beaufort Inlet. Shackleford Banks of Cape Lookout National Seashore is across the inlet.

There is also a U.S. Coast Guard Station on the grounds of the park, which you will see before you reach the fort. The station is not closed to the public, but no public services are offered.

Access

The park is open 8 A.M. to 9 P.M. during June, July, and August. During April, May, and September, the park is open 8 A.M. to 8 P.M., and during October–March, 8 A.M. to 6 P.M. The fort is open 9 A.M. to 5:30 P.M.

The regional access site at the park is the major access point on Bogue Banks. The entrance to the site is a right turn soon after entering the park, which winds through the maritime shrub thickets into a dune field and a splendid 300-car parking lot. The access area includes showers, restrooms, concessions, telephones, and a boardwalk dune crossover. Programs by park rangers are occasionally offered at the site. The guarded swimming areas are open 10 A.M. to 5:50 P.M. during June, July, and August.

There is also a smaller parking area at the fort, near the inlet waters. The breaking-wave beach is

south from the fort area. It is a hike to the beach from this lot.

Since Fort Macon is the most visited park in the state system, to be sure of a parking place, you need to be there before 10 A.M. on summer weekends.

Handicapped Access

Fort Macon is negotiable by handicapped travelers but not easily.

The regional access site is fully handicapped accessible.

Information

For information, contact Fort Macon State Park, P.O. Box 127, Atlantic Beach, NC 28512, 919-726-3775.

Atlantic Beach

Each turn of the coast has one place that pops and jumps with a higher-voltage vacation energy. Atlantic Beach fills that role for this length of North Carolina oceanfront. People convene here, collect here, figuratively wash up on shore here, and wish they could stay and play forever. Then Labor Day arrives and it's time to go home.

Appearances are now sprightly around the "circle"—the area directly south of the Morehead City causeway. The traditional center of the resort community sports a new civic landscape to go with its never-ending summer atmosphere. It's a fine makeover of this young and restless place that has the reputation of being *the* place to go.

Atlantic Beach became the "center" of dancing and band music when the original bridge opened in 1928 and the oceanfront was literally the end of the road. Once, the central feature of the compact, early resort was a pavilion and dance hall. Today, there is no central element that provides a similar social and visual focus. A younger crowd moths to the private clubs that align the circle's perimeter. Recent civic improvements seek to recapture the role of the causeway and the circle as the family gateway to the island.

Although in the 1950s NC 58 was opened along the length of Bogue Banks, old patterns persist, and even today commercial and entertainment activity clusters around the junction of the bridge/causeway road from Morehead City. The town reaches east to Fort Macon State Park and west to its residential neighbor, Pine Knoll Shores, with an intervening unincorporated parcel between the two communities. Previous expansion of the town limits was accomplished under protest. In an unsuccessful effort to thwart incorporation, the original developer of Money Island intentionally skewed Tryon, Dobs, and Caswell streets so they would not align with the corresponding streets in Atlantic Beach. As a result, not all the streets running parallel to the ocean align, which reduces through traffic in the neighborhood and confounds newcomers.

The greatest number of hotel rooms on Bogue Banks are in Atlantic Beach, the moderate climate keeping them busy with convention and business gatherings. However, by no means is there a wall of commercial buildings barricading the oceanfront. Hotels are interspersed with other property uses, which "soften" the beachfront appearance. While many major chains are represented west of the causeway, there is a lively apartment rental market and family-owned motel business in the direction of Fort Macon.

This is a town that is busy in all directions—oceanfront and soundside. In the last decades, while the beach was growing with higher-profile buildings, the soundside took off with a parallel boom of marinas and private communities. The causeway is inseparable from the remainder of the city in mood and function; it screams a commercial welcome. You can rent a sailboard, charter a fishing trip, dine on fresh seafood, or buy a T-shirt. There's a type of touristy congestion at Atlantic Beach that has its own appeal, and you almost have to be in motion to appreciate it.

The streets in the older central section, between Durham and Wilson avenues, form a grid. The causeway (named Morehead Avenue) becomes Central Avenue and runs to the water, ending in Atlantic Avenue, which is parallel to the ocean. East and West drives fork off to either side of Central Avenue and curve to intersect Atlantic also. The three streets form a "Y" with Central Avenue in between them. An amusement park once occupied the open area between these roads, now replaced by a go-cart track. The rigid street matrix extends three blocks in either direction from the "circle." The "circle" and the boardwalk are still a beachfront focus. The boardwalk is concrete and not elevated, and it overlooks beach volleyball courts—at least between Raleigh Street and East Drive.

Downtown Atlantic Beach is on an upswing. The older residential streets flanking the "circle" and honoring the natural dune line have been saluted by recent civic improvements. It's evident that civic pride is growing side by side with the new civic plantings.

In the summer, the beach itself is the central focus, and this popular coast-to-sound city is wall-to-wall people. What still works about Atlantic Beach is the wide, gently sloping sands of Bogue Banks. However, even this has been tricky to hold on to.

Although a sea wall had been constructed at Atlantic Beach following the invasion of Hurricane Hazel in 1954, there was no follow-up program to build up the beach. By the early 1980s, waves were slapping at some of the front-row cottages, particularly those east of the causeway.

Luckily, in 1986 the city received a windfall, or "dredgefall"—an entire island's worth of free sand. After the Environmental Protection Agency determined that a spoil island in Beaufort Inlet had too much sand and had to be moved, Atlantic Beach accepted the sand, which made nearly 200 yards of beach. The town carefully placed sand fences to retard sand movement, planted dune grasses, and posted the dunes. The result is a lot of beach. The sea wall is no longer visible, now buried beneath new dunes. Although the replenishment has been generally a success, by the winter of 1991, erosion had again shortened the beach a good bit. One pier owner rejoiced at the erosion—the original filling had effectively "shortened" his pier by building beach under it.

Second-home construction has prospered since the 1960s, and the city and island have benefited from more sensitive approaches to building at the beach. Many housing units have been added, but there's a great deal of open space because newer units are clustered. Some locations, such as the private property of the Dunes Club, visible from the Les and Sally Moore Regional Access Area, give you an idea of unaltered Bogue Banks.

A great deal of subdividing occurred before a beach access program mandated public accessways. In the older parts of Atlantic Beach, there are walkways serving the neighborhoods, but as in the other island communities, they are inadequate to serve day-trippers since they provide no parking. The picture improves each year, but access is still at a premium, particularly if you drive your car over for the day.

Access

If you're renting a room or cottage that's not on the oceanfront, there are many local trails or access areas for pedestrians. But remember, a "short walk" to the beach can be long since you must carry everything with you.

Public beach access with parking is rare at Atlantic Beach. There is also little parking on residential streets, so be careful where you leave your car.

The first area to check for a stopping place after crossing the bridge is around the "circle," which is directly ahead at the main intersection with NC 58 or Fort Macon/Salter Path Road. This is the major public beach in the town, and there are lifeguards here during the peak season. There is angled parking along West and East drive, with nearly 300 spaces plainly marked and available on a first-come, first-served basis. If you are creative, you might be able to invent a parking space out of some of the odd-shaped parcels of land remaining in the circle, but do so at your own risk.

One-half block west of West Drive is the West Atlantic Boulevard Regional Access, which puts you right in the heart of the old Atlantic Beach, and it is a beauty. There are about 75 parking spaces, restrooms, a bathhouse, and a deck that leads to the concrete boardwalk.

There is an off-road-vehicle ramp at the south end of Raleigh Avenue, the second road west of the causeway off Salter Path Road. The beach is closed to vehicular traffic between Good Friday and Labor Day. You must obtain a decal from the town and display it. Local restric-

tions on beach driving are explained when you purchase your sticker, and you are subject to all North Carolina driving and licensing laws.

Further west on Salter Path Road, shortly after passing the post office, the Sheraton provides parking for nonguests in a graveled oceanside lot either daily, weekly, or monthly at reasonable rates. The lot is attended and signed as a public access and includes more than 120 spaces.

Sportsman Pier at Money Island Road has a small private parking lot for pier users, with some overflow parking available for a fee. Fishermen receive a pass that allows them to park all day. The owners monitor the lot during the Good Friday–Labor Day season.

Oceanana Fishing Pier and Family Resort has a parking lot with more than 100 spaces. Fishermen get first preference, so it is advised that you check with the owners before parking.

Immediately west of the Dunes Club at New Bern Street is the Les and Sally Moore Regional Access Area. This is a heavily used access area with 51 parking spaces. There are restrooms and a boardwalk dune crossover leading to a children's play structure at the foot of the primary dunes.

The Triple S Pier at the end of Henderson Boulevard allows some overflow parking for nonfishermen. Signs are posted warning against parking in the neighboring motel lot, but the pier parking may be available by asking.

The causeway is a boating center.

There are a number of marinas running fishing trips to the Gulf Stream and closer waters. There are also several locations for sailboat and sailboard rentals as well as sailing lessons. Private boats may launch as well.

Handicapped Access

The following access locations in Atlantic Beach are fully handicapped accessible: Fort Macon Regional Access Area, the Les and Sally Moore Regional Access Area, and the downtown access area at West Atlantic Boulevard.

Information

For information, contact Carteret County Tourism Development Bureau, P.O. Box 1406, Morehead City, NC 28557, 1-800-SUNNYNC.

Pine Knoll Shores

Pine Knoll Shores is virtually an island on the island, exerting strong control over land use and beach access through zoning restrictions and limiting beach access to the members of local homeowners' associations that control the access locations. In this respect, it parallels Southern Shores in Dare County; both are incorporated, primarily residential communities that are essentially incorporated subdivisions. If it weren't for the city limit signs, you would think that you were driving through a subdivision of Atlantic Beach.

The visual transition is not remarkable as you drive into Pine Knoll Shores from the east, since there are several hotels and motels along the oceanfront. Not only are these about the only commercial ventures within the city limits (there's also at least one bank), but they comprise nearly the only means of reaching the beach without buying or renting a single-family home or condominium.

You will see a couple of beautifully sited and landscaped parking lots that look like access parking areas, but you must be a member of the appropriate homeowners' associations to use them. Don't park there; Pine Knoll Shores tickets and tows.

The town itself occupies some of the highest land and most developed maritime forest on the island. In some places, the trees crowd the highway right-of-way and the road seems to tunnel through the live oaks and yaupon hollys. The road looks like a gash through the woods and reveals a wild, natural beauty in the salt-groomed tops of the vegetation and the smooth, mottled trunks of the yaupons. Occasionally, driveways wander into the interior of the forests, seemingly burrowing into the island, but you see surprisingly few homes.

North of the highway, the woods become more diverse. Pine trees, youthful hardwoods, and understory trees form the forest cover. The town hall, off of Pine Knoll Boulevard, occupies a beautiful wooded setting. Nearby, nearly next

door, sprawls the similar woods of the Theodore Roosevelt State Natural Area, with the North Carolina Aquarium and hiking trails through the forest.

Pine Knoll Shores developed quickly but instituted controls to keep the appearance of the town intact. While it has a town hall and full municipal services, it doesn't have a visibly identifiable town center. It certainly has no center for public access.

Access

There is essentially no public beach access in Pine Knoll Shores. The parking areas that are visible belong to associations and you must be a member to use them. The parking lots are clearly posted with warnings against public parking. In addition, there is no parking along the streets within the community.

Driving on the beach is not permitted in Pine Knoll Shores at any time.

Information

For information, contact Carteret County Tourism Development Bureau, P.O. Box 1406, Morehead City, NC 28557, 1-800-SUNNYNC.

Iron Steamer Pier

The Iron Steamer Pier juts into the ocean nearly at the western limits of Pine Knoll Shores and is part of a commercial complex that includes a hotel and restaurant, the Iron Steamer Pier and Resort. The

name honors the wreck of the *M. V. Prevensy*, a side-wheel steamer and blockade-runner that ran aground and wrecked here on June 9, 1864. A spur from the pier overlooks two eroded metal shapes, visible at low tide. The largest piece is the axle that turned the side wheel, the smaller is part of the boiler.

Access

There are 130 parking spaces at the resort, and some may be available to nonguests by permission of the owner. Although it is not well marked, the state maintains an access walkway on the west side of the Iron Steamer Pier property.

Theodore Roosevelt State Natural Area

The Theodore Roosevelt State Natural Area is the only location where you can experience fully the natural richness of undeveloped Bogue Banks. The Roosevelt descendants inherited the 265-acre preserve from its litigious former owner, Alice Green Hoffman. Her lawsuit against the owners of cows that destroyed one of her gardens led to the legal establishment of Salter Path. When Hoffman died, she willed the land to her niece, Mrs. Teddy Roosevelt, Jr. The family, in turn, dedicated it to the state as a natural area in memory of President Theodore Roosevelt.

The preserve is a coastal ecological laboratory, under the adminis-

A busy day at the Iron Steamer Pier, Pine Knoll Shores. (Courtesy of N.C. Travel and Tourism Division)

tration of the staff of Fort Macon. As is the case with all state natural areas, part of the management scheme is to leave it alone; the public is given access, but only to a limit. It has become a refuge on the island by default and a destination that makes for a stimulating side trip.

The North Carolina Aquarium is within its borders, sited at the edge of a small tidal creek and marsh, with the woods of the preserve walling it off from the rest of the island. The natural area preserves the many varied ecological niches that establish on an undeveloped barrier island, from dominant maritime forest to freshwater bogs, salt marsh, and sound. Trails through the area provide visitors an opportunity to experience the full range of island vegetation and the chance to possibly glimpse one of the preserve's rare inhabitants—resident ospreys.

A self-guided nature trail, also used for interpretive walks, starts at the northeast corner of the parking lot, leading into the woods and eventually to the marsh. It's a good introductory hike to the thick forested regions of the banks. The birds you will hear and see are usually land species.

Either bring plenty of insect repellent or wear long-sleeved shirts and long pants. Mosquitoes, no-see-ums, and deer flies abound. You should also be alert for snakes in warmer months.

Access

The gate to the area at the entrance of Roosevelt Drive off of Pine Knoll Boulevard usually opens by 8 A.M. and closes at 5 P.M. Parking for the natural area is at the North Carolina Aquarium.

Information

For information, contact Theodore Roosevelt State Natural Area, P.O. Box 127, Atlantic Beach, NC 28512, 919-726-3775.

North Carolina Aquarium, Pine Knoll Shores

The North Carolina Aquarium brings you face-to-glass with the fishes and creatures that mingle in the local waters. The ocean off of Carteret County has both cold-water and warm-water creatures and plant life. The Gulf Stream cradles the warm-water species close to shore, while the cold-water fauna drift south past Cape Hatteras on the inland cold-water currents originating near Labrador. The currents and everything that rides them mix at Cape Lookout, creating a remarkable diversity of fishes, crustaceans, and other sea life.

Two exhibits have traditionally been a highlight at the aquarium. The first is the touch-and-see tank, with urchins, horseshoe crabs, channel whelks, knobbed whelks, and hermit crabs within arms reach of little fingers. The second, titled the "Living Shipwreck," is more contemplative and perhaps more relevant. This very large exhibit shows the colonization that occurs on the slowly corroding metallic remnants of shipwrecks that are common off of the Outer Banks. A ship provides both shelter and anchorage for the open-water food chain, or at least certain members of the chain. You can study the creatures that adhere to the metal, forming a living decoupage, and then filter feed from the water and can watch the smaller fish that take shelter in the niches of the wreck. Predators follow the smaller fish, completing a chain of life around the corroding hulk. Altogether, the exhibit presents a family portrait of an ecological corner that represents new life on the relics of a catastrophe.

The newest exhibit highlights one of the endangered periodic visitors to the North Carolina coast, the pelagic or sea turtles. The leatherback, loggerhead, green, and hawksbill turtles are known to nest on the islands that arc between Cape Lookout and the South Carolina border each year. The exhibit, which highlights the mystery of the turtles' migratory life, reinforces the staff's active efforts to boost public awareness of turtle nestings and to protect known nests from disturbance.

The aquarium features films, slide shows, and lectures in its auditorium in addition to the regular exhibits.

Access

Signs along NC 58 at the western end of Pine Knoll Shores mark the turn for the aquarium. The aquarium is open 9 A.M. to 5 P.M. on weekdays and Saturdays; 1 P.M. to 5 P.M. on Sundays. There is ample parking.

Handicapped Access

The aquarium is fully accessible for handicapped travelers.

Information

For information, contact North Carolina Aquarium, Pine Knoll Shores, P.O. Box 580, Atlantic Beach, NC 28512, 919-247-4003.

Indian Beach (East)

A portion of Indian Beach is adjacent to Pine Knoll Shores; the remainder is on the west side of Salter Path. Here, just west of Pine Knoll Shores, the island becomes narrower and the land is much more intensely developed. The several large condominium projects on the oceanfront are the most visible evidence of the change of communities. The town is split by the unincorporated community of Salter Path. If you are driving west, the first section of Indian Beach is just under a mile in length, then suddenly you are in Salter Path. There are no public access facilities in this portion of Indian Beach.

Information

For information, contact Carteret County Tourism Development Bureau, P.O. Box 1406, Morehead City, NC 28557, 1-800-SUNNYNC.

Salter Path

Indian Beach sandwiches unincorporated Salter Path, practically in the middle of Bogue Banks. The sturdy classic homes—obviously not vacation-home design—and a laissez-faire unfolding of land uses along a curving length of NC 58 signal Salter Path. You also see the accumulations of maritime items you normally find in old fishing villages. Salter Path is the oldest settlement on the island, the only genuine "old ways" village.

Most of Bogue Banks witnessed a spit-and-polish beach buildup after 1971, when the high-rise bridge opened from Cape Carteret, but Salter Path did not. It's not quite as "shiny" as the rest of the island, but it isn't rusty either. Salter Path's days in the sun have weathered it. It remains a fisherman's village, populated by folks who, in many respects, sail against a tide of change around them.

NC 58 curves through what was a live oak forest in a gradual arc from soundside to the oceanfront. Most of the village homes are on the soundside of the island. Several private campgrounds and private marinas provide access to Bogue Sound and, indirectly, to the beaches. What you will notice most about Salter Path

is the advertisements for fresh fish. These folks still set their nets in the ocean off of the beach, tying them off for a rise of the tide then pulling a seine net in beside the set net. The fish you buy in Salter Path is about as fresh as you'll find on Bogue Banks.

The settling of Salter Path rivals the history of any coastal community for intrigue and curiosity. When Riley Salter settled on Bogue Banks in 1880, he certainly didn't intend to start anything; he just wanted to fish and be left alone. Salter and his neighbors, who sailed their goods, their dismantled homes, and their families to this yaupon and live oak–sheltered cove nearly in the middle of Bogue Banks, stayed busy fishing and living, even though they didn't have a deed or permission. The pace of life picked up considerably in the fall when great schools of mullet migrated close to the beach. The villagers mobilized, set nets, and hauled in fabulous catches. The women of the village cleaned and gutted the fish, salting the catch in great barrels that they would leave on the beach until they could transport them to the soundside of the island. The path they wore through the island to the sound went by Riley Salter's house, hence it was called Salter Path.

This was the beginning of a small, stubborn enclave that would continue to hold on to older ways even as they became surrounded by vacation destinations. When these move-weary families, driven by hurricanes and shifting sand dunes elsewhere, illegally established residence on the property of Bostonian John A. Royall at the turn of the century, they started a controversy that set them apart from other island residents. They were squatters. The land passed from Royall to Alice Green Hoffman, who built an estate in present-day Pine Knoll Shores. Hoffman sued the residents of Salter Path in 1923 because their cows wandered onto her estate and destroyed a garden.

The court settlement, known locally as "The Judgment," decreed that the residents of Salter Path could remain but their cows could not graze on the Hoffman estate. The village was restricted to the 81 acres the squatters occupied at the time, and direct ownership of the beachfront was not granted to any single person but to the village to use collectively, since they fished it that way. The ruling further maintained that only the current residents and their descendants could occupy the property. It did not give them title, however.

The villagers lived in a legal nether world until 1979 when Carteret County conducted a tax assessment. The court again stepped in and sorted through the entangled ownership web, which included the residents of Salter Path and the heirs of President Theodore Roosevelt who had inherited the land from Alice Hoffman. The upshot was that Salter Pathers could now hold title to their property—and be taxed for it—which, believe it or not, was something new. Salter Path, which

had been on the map for so long, was now on the books as well.

Access

Carteret County maintains a 22-acre access area in Salter Path beside NC 58, possibly the most beautiful access area along the coast. The area is clearly marked from the highway by the familiar access logo. The parking area is fronted by a picket fence, and the lot looks as though it belonged to a large residence. The access area includes 65 parking spaces, restrooms, a bathhouse, a deck, and a dune crossover walkway. The walkway is simply wonderful; you gradually, deliberately ascend above the trees of the property, emerging from the foliage to overlook a beautiful dune field. The undeveloped ocean frontage that you see from the boardwalk is the communal beach of Salter Path.

Not surprisingly, the area stays full from dawn to dusk during the summer season since it carries the burden of access demands for the central part of Bogue Banks, so arrive early.

Handicapped Access

The parking lot has designated handicapped parking spaces, and the access area is fully accessible by handicapped travelers.

Information

For information, contact Carteret County Tourism Development Bureau, P.O. Box 1406, Morehead City, NC 28557, 1-800-SUNNYNC.

Indian Beach (West)

The largest portion of Indian Beach is west of Salter Path. At Joseph Drive, you will see the town hall on the north side of the highway, a small building almost in the woods behind a tree-shaded parking lot at the edge of Paradise Bay. When the finger canals of Paradise Bay were excavated, the contractor uncovered a Native American burial ground, confirmation of very early occupancy of Bogue Banks, perhaps as a summer fishing village.

Indian Beach is laid-back and easy, a solid blue-collar beach with probably the highest density of trailers and campsites on the island. A small cluster of businesses seems tuned to serving year-round needs more than summer traffic. The town is holding out against the second-home crush, although not completely. There is a wonderful visual juxtaposition here, one of the most vivid on any of the barrier islands. Near the western town limits of Indian Beach is a beautifully crafted, massive oceanfront retreat named Summer Winds, one of the few rental locations here. It communicates exclusivity and dwarfs the Ocean Front Trailer Court, its immediate neighbor. The transition is so abrupt that it looks like the island was grafted together with the seam between them.

The landscape changes as you drive west past Summer Winds. The natural tree line recedes inland as the island narrows, until you begin to move into the dune field

Salter Path boardwalk. (Photograph by the author)

of this very narrow part of Bogue Banks. The vegetation is mostly grasses, and the landscape looks like rumpled plains. At the Indian Beach Fishing Pier, close to the edge of the town limits, you have already visually moved into a different part of Bogue Banks. Before you know it, you're through the town; it's only a mile long.

Access

Indian Beach has the only off-road-vehicle access location in the middle of the island, with limited parking as well. The access ramp is at the end of SR 1192, the only paved road heading south. Look for the sign for Squatters Seafood. There are 25–30 parking spaces along the east side of the road at the ramp. The water is right at the foot of the access-way at high tide, and the sand is soft. You must have a permit from the town before taking your vehicle on the beach, and you best have a four-wheel-drive.

At the west end of town, Indian Beach Fishing Pier allows the use of some parking spaces in addition to those allocated to trailers. Check inside before you park.

Information

For information, contact Carteret County Tourism Development Bureau, P.O. Box 1406, Morehead City, NC 28557, 1-800-SUNNYNC.

Emerald Isle

The western third of Bogue Banks is the town of Emerald Isle, a municipality that is more an assemblage of distinct neighborhoods and beaches than one unified community. The island itself varies naturally enough within the 11-mile length of the town

How to Behave on a Pier

Maybe this should be how *not* to behave on a pier.

Several years ago, a genuinely grizzled, red-eyed, end-of-the-pier, foul-weather-loving, mackerel-slaying veteran of the fabled Kure Beach Fishing Pier groused about the lack of consideration shown by other anglers. To paraphrase his complaint (he was more descriptive and colorful), he could get no respect and less room to land a fish. When he hooked something large, other anglers, instead of clearing room for him to play the fish, rushed beside him to cast their lines in the same vicinity. It was Keystone Cops time with all the lines crossing.

While it is a humorous image, such conduct violates the code of pier behavior. It's the equivalent of a stranger spreading a blanket beside you when there are miles of open beach in either direction. A little courtesy goes a long way in the short confines of a pier. Among the fraternity of pier anglers, there exists an informal etiquette, or perhaps it is better called pier protocol. It's a self-policing way of keeping order.

Regular pier fishermen know the essential truth about this type of angling: some days you catch them, some days you don't. It takes time either way (have you noticed how many people carry folding chairs to the pier?), and it's nothing personal if you're skunked. The angler 30 feet away from you who is catching everything is probably not fishing any differently than you are. If you persist, your time will come as well. Meanwhile, keep these things in mind:

— Buy something from the pier owner (soda, cheese crackers, bait); it lubricates conversation and you might land a good tip.
— Some piers will rent fishing equipment if you just want to try pier fishing and don't own equipment.
— The first angler to arrive at a given length of pier has seniority. Ask this angler for permission before setting up shop immediately adjacent.
— Unoccupied coolers, rods, and chairs stake claims for anglers who are temporarily absent. Honor the claim.
— When you set up shop, allow plenty of elbowroom between you and your neighbor.
— Don't intentionally cast across another angler's line.
— After you *accidentally* cast across another line, apologize and then *you* move around the victim to retrieve your lure.
— If you do this again, you need to move.
— If someone hooks a fish that really runs, provide the angler room to play the fish.
— If you have questions, ask. If people don't want to talk, be quiet. A crowded pier is where some people go to be alone.
— Mind your children. Pier fishing is boring to small children, and small children can become boring to pier fishermen.
— Watch where you, and your children, walk. You don't want to walk behind someone casting. Similarly, always look behind you before you cast.
— Don't litter.
— Don't stand behind anglers casting.
— After you backlash or throw your rig off, just turn red and get on with it. You're not the first (but everybody is laughing anyway).
— When you catch a big fish, don't crow. Everybody will share your joy and stifle their envy. Why make it hard for them to swallow your success? Instead, you'll make the pier real chilly.

	Fee	Parking	Restrooms	Lifeguard	Camping	Showers	Beach Access	Hiking	Trail	Handicapped	Boating	ORV Access	Fishing	Programs	Historic	Sand Beach	Dunes	Upland	Wetland
Emerald Isle		•	•				•			•		•	•			•	•	•	•
Regional Access: Emerald Isle		•	•				•			•			•			•	•		
Cedar Street Park		•								•									•

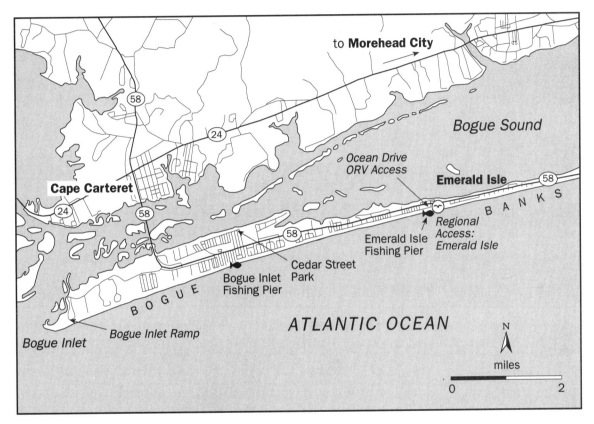

Map 20. Bogue Banks: Emerald Isle to Cape Carteret

to give you the impression of many different places—small residential communities but nonetheless distinguishable.

Emerald Isle is pleasant in a low-key, nonassertive manner. It doesn't grab you, grab at you, or push you away. There's some showiness, but it doesn't stray beyond residential grandiosity at the beach. The actual oceanfront doesn't seem to be any nicer or desirable in one part of town than in another, but the real estate sure does. The oceanfront and undeveloped property remaining in Emerald Isle—most of it toward the west end of town—is pricey.

Off-road-vehicle access ramp at Bogue Point in Emerald Isle. (Courtesy of N.C. Coastal Management Commission)

If you arrive here from Cape Carteret, there are few cues from the highway that this is an island. NC 58 enters through a heavily wooded section of the island. Don't look for a dominating focus or center of activity and recreation—there doesn't seem to be one. Accordingly, Emerald Isle may strike you as an everyone-entertain-themselves kind of beach, more individual recreation than communal beaching. In this sense, it is the polar and insular opposite of Atlantic Beach.

There are nearly 2 miles worth of island west of the bridge, and it still looks like woods, even as you drive past golf fairways. If you turn south at the intersection of Coast Guard Road and NC 58, after an easy drive, you wind out of the forest close to the beachfront. But unless you have an off-road vehicle and the appropriate permit to drive to the inlet, this is strictly a tourist drive. You can wear yourself out looking for a spot to leave your car and hit the beach—there simply aren't any. The off-road-vehicle access ramp

to the inlet is your only outlet on this end of the island.

If you arrive from Indian Beach, you are driving along the narrowest part of Bogue Banks at the east end of Emerald Isle. The first paved road after the town sign is First Street, and the streets continue to be numbered, rhythmically spaced, through Nineteenth Street. Along these streets you see houses in a dune field. One block south, Ocean Drive runs parallel to NC 58 in the trough between houses on the parallel peaks of the dune field, a passage that ends as you approach the wooded section of the island. You can see the ocean at the end of nearly every numbered street. In the still-forested sections of town, the glimpses of ocean blink as a bright flash at the end of a wooded tunnel.

The town incorporated in 1957, and a small commercial interlude along NC 58 at the intersection of Bogue Inlet Drive still seems to be the figurative center of the community. It has seniority at least. Here you have a commercial nexus. If you turn south on Bogue Inlet Drive, you reach the Bogue Inlet Pier and several small motels. If you turn north, you reach the sound.

Given the summer influx of people and considering other resorts, you might anticipate more commercial enterprises. In fact, stores and services are few, modest, and practical places such as groceries, hardware stores, and gas stations. Although newer shopping areas have been added one mile west of Bogue Inlet Drive, "beach boutique" doesn't thrive in Emerald Isle. Given the size and age of the community, this sets it apart from the rest of the Bogue Banks towns. It feels permanent here.

West of the curve in NC 58 and the light at Coast Guard Road are the newer subdivisions and houses, upscale living isolated in the higher, more forested parts of the island that were forests twenty years ago. Once you're out of the tall woods and into the dunes, the remainder of the community is unabashedly summer second homes and rental property.

Emerald Isle keeps to itself. It is certainly not closed off but not necessarily vividly memorable. You will see many houses with screened porches that are a short walk from the oceanfront, and the composite community picture is stable, beautiful-beach ordinary. You could rent for a week, know the neighbors by day two, and suddenly be packing to leave wondering where the week went. It's a nice beach for decompression.

Ironically, while it's the first place you come to from the western bridge, it does not easily accommodate day travelers or overnight guests. Motel/hotel space is limited, as is beach access.

Access

Emerald Isle has an overwhelming number of pedestrian access locations but a horrible parking shortfall. Nearly every street that is perpendicular to NC 58 terminates in an access location that is designed to serve the residents of the street and nearby neighborhoods, but there is no place to park your car. The city did not require that the right-of-way of perpendicular streets extend across Ocean Drive to the tide line. Although this would have cost a beachfront lot or two, it would have left great land resources in the public domain.

Emerald Isle is evaluating the access program to see what kind of improvements can be made. Where possible, the town may improve local access paths by providing a parking space or two. The town is considering providing spaces at the end of some streets primarily for handicapped travelers. The following access locations offer parking and beach or soundside access.

At the east end of the city, Third Street Park, which is closer to Fourth Street, has 10 parking spaces and is open 7:30 A.M. to 9 P.M.

A grant from the Coastal Area Management Act enabled Emerald Isle to develop a handsome regional access site near the east end of the city limits after purchasing a former trailer park. The site was once referenced by the Emerald Isle Fishing Pier, which came under long-term jeopardy following its foreshortening by the 1996 hurricanes. The storms swiped beach from the access area as well, but this is still the largest available parking and access area on the west end of Bogue Banks. The site has 125 parking spaces, restrooms, showers, a dune crossing, and picnic tables.

West of the Emerald Isle Fishing Pier 400 yards is an off-road-vehicle access ramp.

The Cedar Street Park is a soundside park with a pier with comfortable benches and a magnificent view of the sound. Turn north on Cedar Street, which is four blocks east of Bogue Inlet Drive. There are 7 parking places and a small garden lining the path leading to the pier. There's another treat as well. Directly across the sound is an auxiliary navy landing field. You may be sitting quietly at this park when a navy or marine jet rises silently above the northern horizon, the sound following afterward. The jets sometimes turn east directly above the park, looping their flight pattern back to Morehead City to align for another touch and go.

On Black Skimmer Drive opposite City Hall is an off-road-vehicle ramp.

There is parking for a fee at Boardwalk by the Sea Arcade. To reach this amusement center, turn south off of NC 58 onto Islander Drive, turn east onto Reed Drive, then turn south on Boardwalk Drive. In addition to parking, there are showers and concessions.

There is parking for a fee available at Bogue Inlet Pier. Check with the owner about where to park. There is some vacant land nearby, and you may leave your car there to use the beach.

The Inlet Drive off-road-vehicle ramp leads to Bogue Inlet, but there is no parking. Turn west on Coast Guard Road and follow it until it dead-ends. Turn right onto Inlet Drive, and the access is at the end of the street.

You must obtain a permit from the town to drive on the beach, and driving on the beach is not permitted between Memorial Day and Labor Day. The town recently de-feated a proposal that would have banned all oceanfront driving.

Handicapped Access

The town plans to improve three or four existing dune crossovers to make them accessible to handicapped travelers and designate handicapped parking spaces at the same locations.

The regional access area adjacent to the Emerald Isle Fishing Pier site has fully handicapped-accessible restrooms. Although the 1996 hurricane season altered the beach profile, the site will be restored to full handicapped accessibility.

Cedar Street Park is negotiable by handicapped travelers. There is a gentle gradient from the parking area to the dock.

Information

For information, contact Carteret County Tourism Development Bureau, P.O. Box 1406, Morehead City, NC 28557, 1-800-SUNNYNC.

Cape Carteret to Cedar Point

NC 24 intersects with NC 58 at Cape Carteret, a commercial center for many Bogue Banks visitors and residents. The road east heads back to Morehead City, a trip that looks fairly long but is much quicker than the island route during the summer. This road is named the Freedom Way, in honor of the marines in Camp Lejeune who served in operation Desert Storm.

Driving west (and south) on NC 24 takes you to Swansboro through the hamlet known as Cedar Point. A sign claims that Cedar Point was established in the early 1700s, but there is not much visible from the roadway that evokes that era.

One of the most elegant portions of this drive is a length close to the White Oak River where the road is lined with mature red cedar trees. The windswept, sculptured evergreens create a memorable passage along an otherwise ordinary roadway. These plantings may be threatened if the state widens NC 24 to four lanes from the White Oak River Bridge to Cape Carteret.

Access

There is a boat-launching ramp along the causeway on NC 24 crossing the White Oak River further south.

Hook, Line, and Rulebook

Coastal fishing, particularly surf fishing, is one of the last free forms of recreation left. So are crabbing or "chicken-necking" off of a pier and clamming (and oystering when permitted), rating close seconds in popularity.

If you are a recreational fisherman, you do not need a license for surf fishing, crabbing, clamming, or oystering, but you do need to be knowledgeable about state and federal regulations that affect these activities. The purpose of the regulations is to protect the fishery resource. Even as a vacationing player, you are accountable for what's in the creel or cooler. Simply put, there are some fish you don't want to be caught with, for the sake of the fish and yourself.

Three different agencies govern fishing on North Carolina's coast: the North Carolina Wildlife Resources Commission governs inland creeks, bays, and rivers; the Division of Marine Fisheries governs coastal creeks, bays, rivers, sounds, and the ocean out to 3 miles; both of these agencies govern joint creeks, bays, and rivers; and finally the National Marine Fisheries Service governs ocean fishing beyond the 3-mile limit.

Although there is a book full of regulations, compliance is simple as long as you stay out of a boat and don't plan to sell anything you catch. Generally speaking, if your feet are on the sand, staying abreast of regulations is easy. Boaters may stray into some waters (such as Currituck Sound, Kitty Hawk Bay, and others) where you must have a North Carolina fishing license or waters that are closed to certain types of fishing. If you plan to sell anything, either you or your boat will need a license of some sort.

Although the entrance to restricted waters will be posted, it's prudent to know where you're going and what you're going after before you start out. Check with local marinas or tackle shops to find out about restrictions you are likely to encounter. The following is a sketch of regulations that may affect you as a vacationing, part-time family fisher person. These will change, so take the time to ask before you cast.

Crabs

You and your children may go "chicken-necking" for crabs off of a dock or pier without worry. You may even use a crab pot as long as it is tied to the dock or pier. When you start using a boat to drop crab pots, you cross into regulated territory. There is a 5-inch minimum (tip-to-tip across the shell) for males and immature females. There is no restriction for mature female crabs.

Oysters

The oyster season is usually in the fall. Because of pollution-decimated populations, some waters may be closed. It is advised that you check with the North Carolina Division of Marine Fisheries to determine the areas in which oystering is permitted.

Clams

Clam season is open year-round. You may collect 100 per day per person or 200 per day per vessel without a license. The clams must have a minimum thickness of one inch.

Shrimp

You may use a cast net to shrimp. There are no restrictions on the net mesh size, but you cannot collect more than 100 shrimp per person per day for any purpose.

Fish

Two popular game fish, striped bass and red drum, could hook you if you don't know the regulations. They are closely regulated because of declining numbers.

Striped bass, which usually have spawning runs into fresh water in spring, must be a minimum of 18 inches long from nose to tail. How many you can catch depends on where you are fishing. Check with the Division of Marine Fisheries for exact information.

Red drum migrate through the surf zone in fall and spring. The minimum size is 18 inches, and up to 5 a day may be in possession. However, no more than one fish greater than 32 inches in length may be kept each day.

Both of these fish are illegal to possess beyond the 3-mile limit (in federally regulated waters) regardless of where they are caught. Do not transport either of these fish into federal waters. If you catch one in federal waters, you must release it.

Flounder, another popular summer fish, must be a minimum of 13 inches. There are no creel restrictions, nor are there any restrictions on night-time gigging as long as the fish meets the minimum length.

Bluefish must be a minimum of 10 inches, and you may keep no more than 5 longer than 24 inches per day, something that could happen quickly in a bluefish "blitz."

It's a good idea to know what you're catching. If you have any doubts about the legality or the identity of the fish you've caught, then either ask someone or release it.

Piers, tackle shops, and marinas can advise you of these restrictions, but the only sure way to comply is to have a copy of the regulations. *The Recreational Guide for Sportsfishermen* explains the regulations and may be obtained by contacting the North Carolina Division of Marine Fisheries, P.O. Box 769, Morehead City, NC 28557. A 24-hour toll-free line is available for specific questions; call 1-800-682-2632 (North Carolina only).

Onslow County

Topsail Island, 22 miles long, is the second-largest island of the southern banks after Bógue Banks and the primary barrier island of Onslow and Pender Counties. The boundary between counties is close to the midline of the island, with the slightly lengthier segment being in Onslow County.

The island has always had a kind of sleepy magic, existing into the early 1990s in a wonderful halcyon time warp. While the remainder of the coast thundered with second-home construction, Topsail Island and its three communities, North Topsail Beach in Onslow County and Surf City and Topsail Beach in Pender County, remained out of the building storm. Early in the decade, the lack of pressure to construct on the island resulted in a steady growth that didn't overwhelm the island or the means to provide beach access. Fishing in the sound waters and the easy access to the open ocean buttressed the appeal of the beachfront, resulting in a clustering of marinas near inlets such as New River and Topsail.

Topsail Island remained sparsely populated until the mid-1990s, when a slow influx of construction gained momentum. The island's inherent appeal became irresistible, and in spite of prohibitions on the availability of federal flood insurance, Topsail Island, particularly North Topsail Beach, began a residential construction boom. This happy-days era ended in the late summer and early fall of 1996, when Hurricanes Bertha and Fran made direct hits on this narrow, low-profile barrier island.

Bertha, an 85-miles-per-hour Category I storm, served as a setup, crossing Cape Fear to the south on July 12, 1996. The storm piled water up and over Topsail, eroding an already stressed dune line, threatening NC 50 and NC 210, and overwashing SR 1568. Fran, a Category III behemoth with winds in excess of 135 miles per hour, made landfall in Brunswick County on September 6, 1996. The powerful northeast quadrant of the storm took dead aim and slammed a tremendous storm surge and splintering winds onto Topsail Island, crushing it. The force destroyed at least 80 percent of the buildings and nearly permanently severed the island in two locations. In addition to the overwhelming damage to structures, those returning to the island found most vegetation uprooted or salt-browned, as well as an absence of all wildlife, even birds.

Fishermen unloading the day's catch of oysters. (Photograph by the author)

Onslow County worked frantically to restore basic services to the island and to repair the public access areas, since the hurricane had destroyed the bathhouses and crossovers at these locations. By the summer of 1997, the parking areas were open, the dune crossovers rebuilt, and portable restrooms made available at the access sites. County officials will decide later whether or not to reconstruct the bathhouses.

The northernmost island in the county, Bear Island, is the site of Hammocks Beach State Park, which may be the gem of the entire state park system. Accessible only by ferry, it is the one island in the state, in the view of some marine biologists and coastal ecologists, that most closely approximates an unaltered, natural condition. Unlike many islands along the southern length of the Outer Banks, Bear Island has an ample sand supply. Though subject to the typical "nibblings" of inlet migration, the beach is consistently increasing in width. The beaches in the center of Onslow County are included in Camp Lejeune. Some lengths of beach are reserved for base recreation; others serve as landing sites and bombing ranges for the Marine Corps amphibious mission.

Coastal geography isolated Onslow County from the west-to-east intrastate commerce in the nineteenth century. The deep-water ports of Wilmington and Morehead City became the destinations of railroads from the Piedmont, directing attention away from the sparsely populated and forested county more or less between them.

Even the dredging of the Intracoastal Waterway in the 1930s failed to stimulate growth on the islands. If anything, the new "moat" made access to the islands more difficult, discouraging growth. Onslow remained sleepily rural until the 1940s, when World War II brought a tremendous military presence to the county, ending its isolation and altering traditional use of some of its beachfront.

The construction of the Camp Lejeune Marine Corps Base on the banks of the New River as the headquarters for the Second Marine Division and a primary amphibious training base absorbed the barrier island, Onslow Beach. Holly Ridge, southwest of Jacksonville, became the focal community for Camp Davis, an artillery and antiaircraft training base with nearly 200,000 personnel. On deserted Topsail Island, Operation Bumblebee, a military rocket-testing program, launched its early research efforts.

After building Camp Lejeune, the military widened US 17 to Wilmington to facilitate troop movement. In the late 1940s, when Operation Bumblebee was completed, the military left their bunkhouses, a launching pad, concrete observation towers, and a rocket assembly building on a comparatively untouched Topsail Island, which was linked to the mainland by a pontoon bridge over the Intracoastal Waterway. Except for the pontoon bridge, which has been replaced by a swing bridge carrying NC 210 and NC 50 into Surf City, some of the military structures remain.

The military still occupies substantial acreage in the county. With more than 110,000 acres and nearly one-half of the county oceanfront, Camp Lejeune functions as a city of 30,000. It is not a walled city by any means, but the citizens dress alike. To cap it off, Camp Lejeune will be expanding its borders to reach Holly Ridge, purchasing 42,000 acres of a pocosin area known as Great Sandy Run between Verona and Holly Ridge. The expansion has not been particularly welcomed locally since some of the acreage will be used for a firing range.

The beachfront communities and Camp Lejeune are not the only locations in the county to experience changes. Small mainland communities such as Sneads Ferry, south of Camp Lejeune, are being transformed from traditional fishing and agricultural centers to the locations for self-contained resorts. One of the lures of this area is the access to open ocean through New River Inlet.

The beaches of Onslow County once held simple pleasures: abundant sand, sun, and fishing. Those pleasures were dearly paid for in 1996.

Certainly Topsail Island itself will readjust, but the island's innocence has been blown away. It is likely that much of Topsail Island will remain open and undeveloped. The losses were too substantial to be rebuilt in kind, and public sentiment seems to be gradually rising against unconditionally supporting construction in such potentially perilous locations.

Soon enough, though, the sound and ocean waters will offer excellent sportfishing again. The piers will likely be fewer, but the mackerel will come and the boats will leave their inland docks again to make their catches. Sleepy as before, but with one eye slightly open.

What will remain is the gentle apron of sand that gradually eases into the ocean, the slight slope that is the heart of the appeal of Onslow County. If walking the beach and searching for seashells is a pleasurable notion, you will find the storm-tempered communities of Onslow County satisfying.

If you wish to fish, there are several piers, charter boats, and a competitive tournament or two. The sound and ocean waters offer excellent extended sportfishing seasons, mostly from offshore craft. Pier fishermen, and to a lesser extent surf-fishermen, make excellent catches when the water warms to temperatures preferred by mackerel.

Access

Hurricane Fran changed the access equation on Topsail Island. Beach-front property was wrecked and so too was all official and unofficial access. "Access is everywhere," noted one official in the fall of 1996, referring to the fact that little remained of what was once considered private beachfront property. The area north of the NC 210 bridge, a part of North Topsail Shores, was wiped clean. Although the state highway department quickly returned SR 1568 to service again (Hurricane Bertha also damaged it), for the first time the wisdom of perpetual maintenance came into question.

By the early summer of 1997, the four regional access areas in North Topsail Beach that Hurricane Fran leveled were again available for use. The Onslow County Parks and Recreation Department reconstructed the dune crossovers and provided temporary restrooms. Rebuilding of permanent structures is under consideration. A description of the pre-Fran sites follows.

After crossing over to Topsail Island on the high-rise bridge on NC 210, turn left on SR 1568 and continue north about 4 miles. Onslow Beach Access Site number 1 is slightly south of the Topsail Dunes development, on the north side of the road. There are 70 parking spaces, pay telephones, and restrooms. A dune crossover across the roadway leads to a much flattened beach. Hours are April 1–September 30, 9 A.M. to 8 P.M.; October 1–March 31, 9 A.M. to 5 P.M.

Access site number 3 is farther north at the end of the private road that winds through the high-rise towers near the New River Inlet. This area offers parking for 135 cars and fishing access to the inlet.

Access site number 2, the county's largest, is 4 miles south of the NC 210 bridge, approximately ½ mile east of the site of McKee's Fishing Pier. Originally, the site had a 300-space parking lot, restrooms, showers, telephones, and a dune crossover. Additional sound-side parking is across the highway.

The second-largest Onslow County access location, Onslow Beach Access Site number 4, stood one mile north of NC 210 on SR 1568, where the road swerved inland away from the beach. The 175 parking spaces, restrooms, showers, gazebo, and dune crossovers will be obvious.

The North Carolina Wildlife Resources Commission maintains several fishing and boating access sites in the county. Access to the Intra-coastal Waterway is on the north side of the NC 210 high-rise bridge that crosses the waterway. To reach the Turkey Creek access area, which also serves the Intracoastal Waterway, from the junction of US 17 and NC 50 in Holly Ridge, go north on US 17 for 4 miles to Folkstone, turn east on SR 1518, travel 1.5 miles, turn south on SR 1529, go nearly 2 miles, and turn south on SR 1530. The area is almost a mile from the turn.

Handicapped Access

Access sites 1, 2, and 4 have designated handicapped parking places, restrooms with facilities for handicapped travelers, and ramped access over the dunes.

Information

For information, contact Onslow County Tourism, 614 College Street, P.O. Box 1226, Jacksonville, NC 28541, 910-455-1113, or Greater Topsail Area Chamber of Commerce, NC 210, New River Drive, Surf City, NC 28445, 910-328-0666.

Swansboro

Swansboro has the bundled-up coziness of a New England seafaring settlement. It began as a fishing

	Fee	Parking	Restrooms	Lifeguard	Camping	Showers	Beach Access	Hiking	Trail	Handicapped	Boating	ORV Access	Fishing	Programs	Historic	Sand Beach	Dunes	Upland	Wet and
Swansboro		•	•								•		•		•			•	•
Hammocks Beach State Park	•	•	•	•	•	•	•	•	•		•		•	•		•	•	•	•

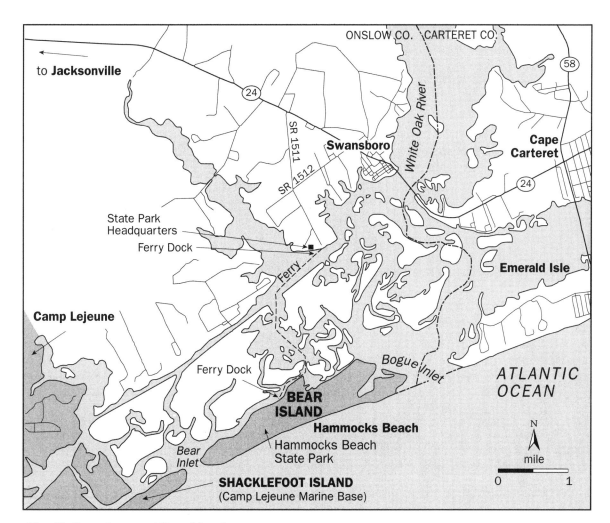

Map 21. Swansboro and Bear Island

community, and surprisingly it still retains much of that flavor. You can easily amble through its narrow streets in a morning stroll.

Small clapboard houses march down the hill to the banks of the White Oak River, which opens to the sea through Bogue Inlet. The open water begins at the end of a wandering passage through channels threading salt marsh islands. The inlet has been open and navigable since the first settlers arrived in the mid-eighteenth century. The community grew around a local plantation known as the Wharf and thrived in its early years as a port for the trading of naval stores, cotton, and timber. By the Revolutionary War it was the only town on the coast between Beaufort and Wilmington.

The General Assembly passed articles of incorporation for the community in 1783 and formally named the town Swannsborough (shortened in 1877), honoring Samuel Swann, a former Speaker of the House from Onslow County. Shipping and shipbuilding dominated the economy following incorporation. In Bicentennial Park, on the north side of NC 24, a statue honors Captain Otway Burns, a daring privateer during the War of 1812 who was born nearby. In 1818, Burns built the *Prometheus*, one of the first steam-powered vessels constructed in the state, in Swansboro. Burns is better known in Beaufort, where he is buried in the historic cemetery, the Old Burying Ground, and is also honored in the naming of Burnsville in Yancey County.

Many of the older buildings in Swansboro are marching into their third century, renovated for reuse. Several older mercantile buildings on Front Street now house craft and antique retailers. The town itself unfolds with richer and richer discoveries as you stroll outward from the center. At the town library located on NC 24 you may make a copy of a local history booklet that will direct you on a walking tour of the individual homes. There is a small copy fee. The library opens at 9 A.M. on Monday–Saturday and closes at 8 P.M. on Monday, Tuesday, and Thursday, 6 P.M. on Wednesday and Friday, and 1 P.M. on Saturday.

Access

Swansboro has no beach access, but charter fishing and head-boat fishing trips depart from the village docks to both sound and open water. There are several marinas and boat ramps that provide access to the White Oak River.

There is a town dock extending into the White Oak River at the end of West Main Street, with 8 parking places. A floating dinghy dock serves the Intracoastal Waterway boaters.

At Cedar Point on the Intracoastal Waterway, one mile north of Swansboro on NC 24, the North Carolina Wildlife Resources Commission maintains a boating access area with a launching ramp.

Handicapped Access

Bicentennial Park is accessible for handicapped travelers.

Information

For information, contact Onslow County Tourism, 614 College Street, P.O. Box 1226, Jacksonville, NC 28541, 910-455-1113.

Hammocks Beach State Park

The most natural of all the barrier islands in the state may be Bear Island, now set aside as part of Hammocks Beach State Park. Lying 2 miles off of the mainland across a bewildering salt marsh maze, it is accessible only by private boat or toll ferry. The crossing is pleasant but slightly disorienting if you are not accustomed to navigating in a salt marsh.

During the first half of the century, William Sharpe, a New York neurosurgeon, owned Bear Island, its marshes, and considerable acreage on the mainland as a recreational hunting and fishing area. John Hurst, a black hunting guide who lived in Onslow County, originally directed Sharpe to the property and became his preferred guide. Sharpe wanted to will the property to Hurst and his wife, Gertrude, in 1949, but at her request, he left Bear Island and marsh holdings to the North Carolina Black Schoolteachers' Association. In 1961, the association gave the land to the state for a park. Today, Hurst's grandson, Jessie Hinds, is a ranger at the park, symbolizing the constancy of the park lands during the nearly forty years he has visited Bear Island.

Hammocks Beach State Park. (Courtesy of N.C. Travel and Tourism Division)

Your trip begins at the ferry dock overlooking the extensive marsh and labyrinth of channels. There is a picnic shelter here and some concessions. In the distance you may hear the thump of the impact of artillery rounds fired within Camp Lejeune.

Bear Island is nearly 3 miles long, with approximately 900 acres of varied habitat, including salt-tolerant trees and shrubs along the marsh side. The most imposing feature is the sand dunes, which vary between 30 and 60 feet in height and form possibly the largest intact natural dune field along the North Carolina coast. There are no restrictions on walking among the dunes, and they offer more than enough quiet places for sunning. The dune area is extremely hot, however. Park rangers have observed that not too many visitors linger amid the dunes during the busy season, which is fine with the rangers since they want visitors to explore the entire island.

The island is moving inland and has migrated over ancient sound and lagoon sites, which are now seaward of the island. Many of the shells found here are between 7,000 and 9,000 years old, having been uncovered by wave action, which rips the shells free from the beds and deposits them on the beach.

Park visitation stays at capacity during the summer season, but this is not to say that the island stays full. The capacity of the park is determined by the numbers of people that the ferry can return to the mainland before the park closes, and the ferry capacity fills long before the island does. You can virtually disappear into the surf and sand on the island, but be back at the ferry dock before the last departure, unless you have a camping permit.

There are 14 designated family campsites on the island, all of which are also available for individual campers, and 3 group campsites. Four of the family sites are located at the north and south points of the island, primarily to serve campers arriving in private boats. The other 10 are scattered along the length of the island just behind the primary dunes. The campsites are available on a first-come, first-served basis by securing a permit at the park headquarters before going to the island. The permitting process prevents quarrels over campsites. Because of the popularity of camping here, almost every weekend campsite is taken by the end of the day on Friday. Weekday camping is not nearly as competitive. The park is a favored nesting site for the loggerhead sea turtle. During the three-day full moon period of the nesting season in the months of June, July, and August, the park restricts camping.

There is a central bathhouse and restrooms approximately ½ mile from the ferry landing. Bring plenty of insect repellent and suntan lotion. When planning your visit, remember that camping is primitive and you must carry in what you will use.

Access
The 1996 hurricanes took their measure of Bear Island, shoveling the primary dune line, destroying the campsites, and wrenching the bathhouse from its foundation. Inland, the storm surge also smacked the mainland dock, arresting ferry service to the park's major attraction. Immediately, park officials began working to reopen the park. Although altered, it's still the best little island around.

To reach the park headquarters, west of Swansboro turn south off of NC 24 onto SR 1511, which goes directly to the headquarters. You may also turn south at Hardee's outside Swansboro, follow this road even after the pavement ends, turn left at the stop sign onto SR 1511. The park office opens at 8 A.M. for permitting. The ferry service runs weekends only during May and September; Memorial Day through Labor Day the ferry operates every hour Monday–Tuesday, every half hour Wednesday–Sunday. There is a nominal fee for the crossing. Usually by 1:30 P.M. the ferry stops taking visitors to the island because it cannot get them off before closing. Arrive early in the morning to be assured of a campsite or a full day on the island.

Note: Campsite reconstruction may be slow and may not return to the original numbers listed above. Camping fees are sure to be nominal, regardless. Check with park personnel to determine availability.

Handicapped Access
The large shelter on the mainland with restrooms is accessible once the three steps at the entrance are negotiated.

There are steep steps down to the ferry, but once these are negotiated mobility-impaired passengers may ride the ferry to the island.

The island itself should be considered inaccessible for mobility-impaired travelers.

Information
For information, contact the park office at Route 2 Box 295, Swansboro, NC 28584, 910-326-4881.

Camp Lejeune

A city of more than 30,000 covering more than 110,000 acres, Camp Lejeune is the training base for the U.S. Marine Corps Second Marine Expeditionary Force and the Second Marine Division. It is an amphibious training ground that surrounds the New River nearly from the historic river crossing town and port of Jacksonville to the New River Inlet, which opens to the Atlantic. It is also growing. In 1991, the secretary of the navy authorized funds for the purchase of nearly 42,000 acres of land southeast of the current boundary, US 17, from Jacksonville to Holly Ridge.

Within the borders of Camp Lejeune are the islands and beachfront that comprise the middle third of Onslow County's oceanfront, Brown's Island and Onslow Beach. These beaches are not accessible to the general public, but if you could go there you would be visiting a remarkable transition area for the coast. Bear Inlet separates Hammocks Beach State Park from

A newly hatched loggerhead turtle at Hammocks Beach State Park. (Courtesy of N.C. Travel and Tourism Division.)

Brown's Island, also referenced as Bear Island or, an older designation, Shacklefoot Island. Very similar in topography and landscape to the park, Brown's Island is also backed by extensive salt marsh along the Intracoastal Waterway. Brown's Inlet separates this island from the landform known as Onslow Beach, which is an island in that the Intracoastal Waterway separates it from the mainland. If you look at a map of the entire coast, Onslow Beach is a bulge in the otherwise smooth arc from Cape Lookout to Cape Fear. This is the location where it appears most likely that the barrier islands have completely migrated back to the mainland.

The Beirut Memorial stands along the Jacksonville-Lejeune Boulevard (NC 24), paying tribute to the 268 marines and sailors from Camp Lejeune who died in the 1983 barracks bombing in Beirut, Lebanon. The granite memorial wall, set in a grove of oak trees and dogwoods, lists the names of the casualties of the bombing along with three servicemen who died on Grenada. The memorial is never closed.

NC 172 routes through the southern portion of the base. You don't see much as you approach the entry checkpoint except exquisite coastal plain woods and a few houses outside the base perimeter. After the guard waves you through, pay attention to the highway and warning signs. Camp Lejeune posts one of the state's most memorable cautionary signs. It is a yellow diamond, just like a deer-crossing sign, only this shows the silhouette of a tank. "Tank Crossing" is painted on the road across a massive crossing area as if to caution you not to hurt one. Obey the restrictions imposed by the sentries and any temporary signs that are posted. It's not the sort of place to wander aimlessly or to get out of the car and go for a hike in the woods. Camp Lejeune conducts live-fire drills, sometimes across highways, and you could wander into an impact area, that is, the area where live ammunition hits the ground and explodes. Although the marines are extremely conscientious and thorough about posting warnings and restricting access to dangerous parts of the base, if you disregard the warnings, you could end up somewhere you don't want to be.

Access

Tours of the base for groups may be arranged in advance through the Joint Public Affairs Office, Camp Lejeune, Jacksonville, NC 28543, 910-451-5782. Civilians may visit the base as long as they produce a valid driver's license, proof of automobile insurance, and their automobile registration. The main gate is on NC 24 in Jacksonville.

Sneads Ferry

Sneads Ferry is one of the oldest settlements in the county. Although it is uncomplicated, it is slightly difficult to draw a boundary around. When you turn off of NC 172 to go to Sneads Ferry, do not expect to find a community as tightly defined as Swansboro. Instead, you will find an aggregation of small places. The older part of Sneads Ferry is a modest-sized fishing village off of NC 172 with a cluster of small stores and a few churches well away from the water of New River.

The first licensed ferry operator here, Edmund Ennett, started the passenger business in 1725. Robert W. Snead arrived in 1760, took over the ferry, and opened a tavern. His name stuck to the vicinity, even after the bridge over the New River was built in 1939 upriver from the ferry landing.

The town sprawls freely amid fields and coastal forests. You don't feel a sense of place, which is compounded by the absence of road signs. The numbered secondary roads do not relate easily to any readily available map. Despite the sprawl, however, the town does have a central post office. For all practical purposes, everything south of NC 172 and north of NC 210 claims a Sneads Ferry address. There are several expansive and expensive developments under way here, at least one offering golf-course living and others, waterside homes. These new developments skew the perception of Sneads Ferry, which is very small, very quiet, and very local.

The nearest marinas are southeast of Sneads Ferry. Nearby Fulcher Landing and Hatch Point on the New River are the principal commercial fishing docks in the area with several seafood companies and a restaurant. Swan Point is a commercial and recreational boating center downriver from Fulcher Landing, taking advantage of the Intracoastal Waterway leading to the New River Inlet.

Access

There is no direct access to the oceanfront, but there are several private marinas that offer charter head-boat fishing. There are also boat ramp locations on the Intracoastal Waterway at Swan Point and a private boat ramp at Fulcher Landing.

Information

For information, contact Onslow County Tourism, 614 College Street, P.O. Box 1226, Jacksonville, NC 28541, 910-455-1113, or Greater Topsail Area Chamber of Commerce, NC 210, New River Drive, Surf City, NC 28445, 910-328-0666.

Topsail Island

Topsail Island is the beach for Onslow and Pender counties. If you are arriving from the northeast, NC 210 arcs over a high-rise crossing of the Intracoastal Waterway. The marsh of the Intracoastal Waterway is curiously channeled in a geometric pattern creating a series of fingers of water. NC 50 also crosses onto Topsail Island from the mainland directly into the heart of Surf City. The passage over the Intracoastal Waterway here is on one of the few remaining swing bridges left in North Carolina.

So much water makes for plentiful crabs, shrimp, water-skiers, and marinas. Most marinas, as you would expect with such a lengthy island, are at the east and west ends, reducing the cruising time necessary to reach open ocean, where the mackerel, bonito, and other popular game fish swim.

This 22-mile-long barrier is second in length only to Bogue Banks of the islands between Cape Lookout and the South Carolina state line. It features a south-facing oceanfront as do its neighbors to the east, Onslow Beach within Camp Lejeune and Hammocks Beach State Park.

	Fee	Parking	Restrooms	Lifeguard	Camping	Showers	Beach Access	Hiking	Trail	Handicapped	Boating	ORV Access	Fishing	Programs	Historic	Sanc Beach	Dunes	Upland	Wetland
North Topsail Beach		•	•			•	•			•	•		•			•	•		•
Public Boating Access: North Topsail Beach		•									•		•						•
Regional Access: Onslow No. 1		•	•				•			•			•			•	•		
Regional Access: Onslow No. 2		•	•			•	•			•			•			•	•		•
Regional Access: Onslow No. 3		•						•					•			•			
Regional Access: Onslow No. 4		•	•			•	•			•			•			•	•		
Permuda Island Coastal Reserve								•			•		•					•	•

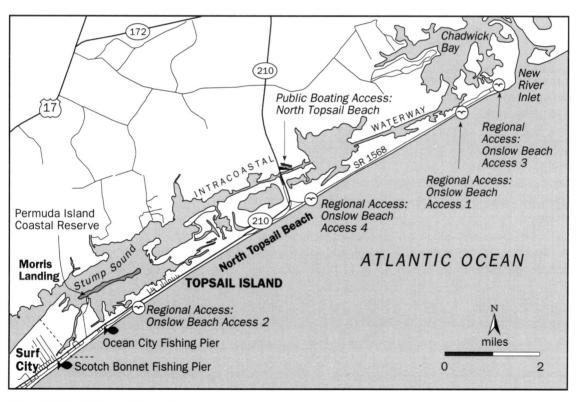

Map 22. North Topsail Island

The island actually aligns more northeast-southwest, making compass directions confusing. North Topsail Shores is at the north end of the island; Topsail Beach is at the south end. Topsail is the midpoint of the westward crescent that begins at Cape Lookout. The deepest part of the Onslow Bay arc seems to be in the vicinity of Topsail Beach.

Geologically, Topsail Island is nearly welded to the mainland; the sound waters to the north are narrow and filled with marsh. In fact, north of the New River, only the channel of the Intracoastal Waterway maintains Onslow Beach as an island. The marsh indicates that the sound is beginning to silt in, and peat deposits on the beach reveal that the island has indeed migrated inland over ancient sounds.

Long subject to steady erosion, the single dune line that ran the length of the island was flattened by the 1996 hurricanes. The storms extended the wide, flat, and gentle beach so far landward that the normal high tide could rush to the foundations of cottages once sheltered by dunes.

There are three communities on the island: North Topsail Beach, formerly West Onslow Beach, in Onslow County and Surf City and Topsail Beach, both in Pender County. Except for the extreme north end, Topsail Island is lightly populated. Compared to other resort beaches along the coast, it has a very low density of permanent residents. The permanent population of the island is estimated at just over 2,500; the largest community is Surf

City, with more than 1,400 of the island's residents. By the time you disperse these numbers over its entire length, the island seems roomy, particularly during the off-season.

Loggerhead turtles frequently lumber ashore; in recent years as many as 100 nests were confirmed on the island. Because of the low-density oceanfront housing and wide, gentle beaches, these giants crawl to dig nests in the sand between April and May. The lack of houses provides a darkened skyline for the turtles, a key they use to judge the safety of a potential nesting site. The nesting is monitored by local volunteers and is one of the celebrated natural summer rituals of the island. Eggs usually hatch in August.

One curiosity on the island are the obviously abandoned reinforced concrete towers along the length of the island, beginning at the first tower in Topsail Beach. The U.S. Navy built these monumental structures in the 1940s as observation platforms for the nascent rocket-testing program, Operation Bumblebee, headquartered at Topsail Beach. Seven towers still stand and probably will forever. The first tower at Topsail Beach is a private residence, and another has been incorporated into the structure of the Ocean City Fishing Pier.

Because they were used to document the flight of early rockets, the towers were precisely located in relation to each other and the longitude and latitude of their location was exactly recorded. In fact, the U.S. Coast and Geodetic Survey

used the first tower as a sea-level monitoring station.

Visiting Topsail Island is like returning to a beach thirty years ago. The island has predominantly modest single-family cottages, and the focus of activity is the beach. Some resort-style construction is finding its way to Topsail Island, particularly at North Topsail Beach, but for the most part, east to west, sound to sea, Topsail is folksy and casual. It's bound to be discovered, but then it really hasn't been hiding.

Access

Four regional access sites in North Topsail Beach provide public access. These top-of-the-line facilities may be only partially restored to their pre–1996 storm season condition.

There is a boating ramp and access location on the Intracoastal Waterway on the north side of NC 210 at the mainland.

Handicapped Access

Reconstructed regional access sites in North Topsail Beach are fully accessible to handicapped travelers.

Information

For information, contact Greater Topsail Area Chamber of Commerce, NC 210, New River Drive, Surf City, NC 28445, 910-328-0666.

North Topsail Beach

On January 1, 1990, West Onslow Beach officially became North Topsail Beach, the lengthiest community on Topsail Island, extending from the New River Inlet to the city limits of Surf City. The incorporation seems to have been a response to recent building trends at North Topsail Shores, the portion of the island north of the NC 210 bridge, which at that time was one of the most dangerous and endangered locations on the entire coast.

On September 6, 1996, Hurricane Fran changed the outlook at North Topsail Beach from endangered to nearly extinct. High winds and a mammoth storm surge swept the beach like a massive eraser, splintering all illusions of the newly incorporated town as a sleepy, sun-drenched, undiscovered retreat. Nearly every item in the community, from fishing pier to campground, from trees to road signs and the road itself, sustained debilitating damage. Complete destruction was the rule; severe damage was to have gotten off lightly, indeed.

Ironically, this very small new town with a permanent population of just about 750 incorporated in order to come to grips with development that occurred in the extreme north end of Topsail Island when it was an unincorporated part of Onslow County. Many tall buildings crowd the north end near the inlet, looming over a leveled and duneless beach. Previously platted lots to the northwest were obliterated years ago; showcased as riverfront sites, they are still on the books even though they are under water.

Except for this concentration of development at the extreme north

and around Ocean City on the south end, North Topsail Beach is a thread of island and road linking individual summer homes and trailers. There's just a smattering of residents scattered throughout the more than 11-mile length of island.

There never has been much of a commercial center or downtown to the young community. Instead of shopping on the island, residents and summer guests would drive north to the intersection of NC 172 and NC 210 (nicknamed "four corners") for everyday needs.

The beach has always been low and flat and, until the storms, the wave energy has always been low. The dune line itself was never impressive and in recent years has been nibbled at successfully by winter storms. New River Inlet Road, or SR 1568, has been under assault since the winter of 1991 when the ocean broke through the dunes here and undermined the roadway.

Hurricane Bertha trashed the road again; no sooner had repairs been completed when along came the big wash, Hurricane Fran. It so happens that the island has enjoyed a nearly 50-year hiatus from a severe storm, but that last storm, Hurricane Hazel in 1954, was a doozy. It, too, wiped the beach clean.

Certainly North Topsail Beach can now claim some of the cleanest, least-commercial beaches on the coast. The problem facing the community may be how to keep it that way. A sad byproduct of the storm was the realization of some property owners that insurers

had, for whatever reasons, sold federal flood-insurance policies covering properties previously redlined as uninsurable by the program. However this occurred, it meant the homeowners could not file claims for storm damage. Some of the insurance companies did, however, refund previously paid premiums.

Access

All the streets perpendicular to NC 210 provided pedestrian access to the beach prior to the storm. Some of these streets may have parking spaces available. The shoreline configuration is so altered that dune crossovers will be rebuilt as needed.

Onslow County quickly reopened the access sites in North Topsail Beach that were destroyed by Hurricane Fran. The possibility exists that the sites may be completely reconstructed, but at the very least parking, dune crossovers, and interim restrooms are available. A description of the pre-Fran sites, listed from the north end of the community south, follows.

After crossing over to Topsail Island on the high-rise bridge on NC 210, turn left on SR 1568 and continue north about 4 miles. Onslow Beach Access Site number 1 is slightly south of the Topsail Dunes development, on the north side of the road. There are 70 parking spaces, pay telephones, and restrooms. A dune crossover across the roadway leads to a much flattened beach. Hours are April 1– September 30, 9 A.M. to 8 P.M.; October 1–March 31, 9 A.M. to 5 P.M.

Access site number 3 is further north at the end of the private road that winds through the high-rise towers near the New River inlet. This area provides parking for 135 cars and fishing access to the inlet.

Access site number 2, the county's largest, is 4 miles south of the NC 210 bridge, approximately ½ mile east of the site of McKee's Fishing Pier. Originally, the site had a 300-space parking lot, restrooms, showers, telephones, and a dune crossover. Additional sound-side parking is across the highway.

The second largest Onslow County access location, Onslow Beach Access Site number 4, stood one mile north of NC 210 on SR 1568, where the road swerved inland away from the beach. The 175 parking spaces, restrooms, showers, a gazebo, and dune crossovers will be obvious.

Handicapped Access

If completely reconstructed, Onslow Beach Regional Access Sites 1, 2, and 4 will be handicapped-accessible.

Information

For information, contact Greater Topsail Area Chamber of Commerce, NC 210, New River Drive, Surf City, NC 28445, 910-328-0666.

Permuda Island Coastal Reserve

Permuda Island is a marshy island that rises slightly above sea level in Stump Sound west of North Topsail Beach. The island is about 1.5 miles long, with its center nearly due west of the Onslow Beach Access Site number 2. The state owns the 50 acres of upland on Permuda Island, and it is included in the North Carolina Coastal Reserve program.

The island narrowly escaped modernization in 1983, when a proposal to develop it met tremendous, prolonged opposition. Development, opponents argued, would irreparably damage the shellfish harvest in Stump Sound. In January 1985, the North Carolina Coastal Resources Commission officially designated Permuda Island as an Area

of Environmental Concern because of the significant archaeological features on the island, including a centuries-old Native American living site.

The Nature Conservancy eventually purchased the island for $1.7 million. In January 1987 the state purchased half of the island from the Nature Conservancy, completing the purchase the following September. There are no plans to change the traditional use of Permuda Island for fishing or hiking.

Access

The closest marina is at Morris Landing in Bethea, at the end of SR 1538. You could also probably slip a canoe into Stump Sound from Onslow Beach Access Site number 2, but there is no boat-launching ramp.

Information

For information, contact North Carolina National Estuarine Research Reserve, 7205 Wrightsville Avenue, Wilmington, NC 28403, 910-256-3721.

Plane Speaking

You'll probably hear them before you see them. Military jets outrun their sound, and by the time the engine roar crashes over the ocean's song, the planes are a memory. There's no stealth involved in this bird-watching. Fortunately for us big kids, the skies of our coast and coastal plain stay busy with the flights of military aviation. Here are some field guide keys for plane-watchers.

Activity is highest around major nesting sites, such as Cherry Point Marine Air Station near Havelock or Seymour Johnson Air Force Base in Goldsboro. Oceana Naval Air Station in Virginia Beach has wide-ranging fliers that are frequently seen along the northern banks. Your chances increase if you are near these bases or near Stumpy Point in Dare County, which is used by several services as a target range.

The two most important keys to identifying these birds are tail configuration and wing shape.

Twin-Tail Planes

There are three twin-tailed fliers: the F-15 Eagle (air force), the F-14 Tomcat (navy), and the F-18 (navy and marines). The F-15 and F-14 are large species frequently confused with each other by novice watchers. They may be distinguished by the following characteristics.

F-15: Twin tails (rudders) extremely tall in proportion to body, one with light or sensor in tip. Profile sleek and flat with high-domed canopy. May have one or two fliers. Wings rigid and small ailerons at rear extend past tail to form noticeable "notch." General aspect: Even though this is a large plane, it is very agile with a streamlined wedge shape that is unmistakable because of the high tail. Location: Coastal plain near Goldsboro.

F-14: Twin tails lower and more in proportion to body. Slight outward cant. Profile thick, heavyset yet streamlined. Similar domed canopy with two fliers. Wings variable and may be swept back. Outer half of wings appear to emerge from sleeves and seem stiff when fully extended. Wings fold back to form delta (triangular) configuration with rear ailerons. Two exhausts, tail profile even. General aspect: A brooding, powerful flier that seems compact and very explosive, more brutal in appearance than the F-15. Location: Northern banks; occasionally spotted over Emerald Isle practicing landings at Bogue Field.

F-18: Twin tails set forward of rear wings and ailerons an immediate giveaway. A much smaller craft than the other two as well. Tails canted at an angle much as if holding up two fingers. The twin engines' exhaust extends far past the vertical tails. The wings are fixed, and the plane has a long nose extending in front of the single-seat cockpit. General aspect: More waspish and lithe than the F-15 and F-14. Location: Northern banks (navy) rare; Havelock/Jacksonville some.

Single-Tail Planes

The most frequently spotted single-tail planes are the F-4 (marines), F-5 (navy), A-6 (navy), A-7 (navy), AV-8 (marines), and A-10 (air force; detached to marines).

F-4: Two seats. Recognized by its big, thick beak, upward canted wingtips, and downward canted ailerons. Nicknamed the Phantom, it's a loud, smoky plane. The bulging cockpit is set forward on the body with the enormous engine intakes just aft of the seats. General aspect: Brutal, raw power. Location: Jacksonville/Havelock.

F-5: One seat. Recognized by its stiletto profile and short wings extending straight from the middle of the plane. Looks like a dart. There are twin intakes and twin exhausts. This is a small, lithe flier. The navy uses it as a trainer (two seats) and to simulate enemy tactics. General aspect: Darting, swift flier. Location: Northern Banks.

A-6: Two-seater, side by side. This twin-engine plane has a bulging front end that tapers rapidly to thin fuselage. The engine intakes are under the wings, which are long for the body. The A-6 is a navy attack jet. General aspect: Deliberate, steady flier. Location: Stumpy Point.

A-7: Single seat. You don't see many, but the single huge intake in the front, angled wings high on the body, and the single high tail make recognition instantaneous. These are also attack jets. General aspect: Deceptively quick but still awkward. Location: Northern banks.

AV-8: Single seat. This is the Harrier, a vertical-takeoff jet with single tail. It is heavy through the middle with variable-angle thrust deflectors under the wings. The wings have distinctive ribbing. Although "chunky," it is still streamlined, with some speed in the lines of the plane. Camouflage coloring is a good tip-off. The jets practice takeoffs at the auxiliary field at Bogue. General aspect: Efficient, deliberate flier; not really remarkable. Location: Havelock, Stumpy Point.

A-10: Single seat. This is the Warthog and it's ugly. Engines are mounted in the rear above the fuselage. The nose is blunt, the speed is slow, and it is as aerodynamic as a roller skate. It is a ground-attack plane, unequaled in fulfilling its mission, which is destroying tanks, or at least scaring them to death. General aspect: Like a deadly crop duster. Location: Havelock, Goldsboro.

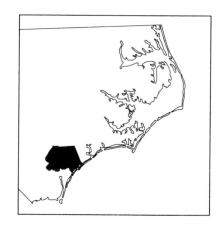

Pender County

Area code 910

Even from the racetrack of I-40 you get a limited impression of what you might find on the slower secondary roads through Pender County. The interstate, paralleling the Seaboard Coastline tracks to Wilmington, divides Pender County; to the west are well-tended fields, to the east, tangled, impenetrable woods. A highway map confirms this pattern, showing immense areas without roads, which is where the wild things are. Pender County is for growing things, tamed or otherwise.

The fresh water of rivers and rainfall has left its mark within the borders of the county. The Northeast Cape Fear River bisects the county north and south, east of I-40. The highway and the rail line ride the gently sloping ridges above the river floodplain. On the western border of the county is the Black River, where during the last decade scientists discovered bald cypress trees more than 1,500 years old. Between these two waterways and their rich swampy floodplains stretch the agricultural fields of Pender County, some of the finest farmland in the state, known for the blueberries it produces.

East of the interstate—the big empty spots on the map—are the huge evergreen shrub bogs managed as game lands by the North Carolina Wildlife Resources Commission. These are fascinating ecosystems, recognized as unique by pioneering botanists two centuries ago but even now not fully appreciated or understood. Characterized by boggy conditions but not necessarily peat forming, these great expanses have been called variously evergreen shrub bogs, pocosins, or bays for the bay-shaped leaves of the characteristic evergreen shrubs and the elliptical ponds within them. The predominance of broad-leaved evergreen plants is one of the most noteworthy characteristics of these regions.

These two game lands—Angola Bay and Holly Shelter—present different management challenges. Angola Bay, in the northeast part of the county, is the wilder of the two, occupying 21,000 acres with no roads and few fire lanes. In contrast, Holly Shelter, in the east-central part of the county, has 48,000 acres actively managed for hunting of all kinds—big game and waterfowl. There is better access to the interior here, but it is a wild, generally poorly drained area. Both are rich in fragrant flowering shrubbery and rare herbaceous plants.

These wild, forbidding lands shaped the settlement of the county by thwarting commerce and easy transportation. US 17 and another rail line parallel the coast southeast of the Holly Shelter Game Land. Both of these transportation corridors ride a high ridge between drainageways. Southeast of US 17, the land drains into the sounds, behind the barrier beaches of Topsail, Lea, and No Name islands.

Pender County mirrors neighboring Onslow County in that it has been relatively overlooked compared to other county coastlines. The only resort beach is on Topsail Island. NC 50 crosses the Intracoastal Waterway with NC 210 at Surf City on one of the last remaining swing bridges in the state, and NC 50 turns southwest. Slightly less than half of Topsail Island, including the largest island communities, Surf City and Topsail Beach, is in Pender County.

The isolation of Topsail Island—though people have summered here since before the 1930s—has made the island beaches economically more "accessible" than many other locations for summer "second homes." There are several mobile home and camper parks on the island. The last decade, though, has seen a slow but steady increase in construction, both in numbers of homes built and in height above the beach. As a result, there are far more houses than existed before Hurricane Hazel wiped the island clean in 1954. Surf City and Topsail Beach are steadily growing. In recent years, more folks have moved here permanently, choosing to work in Burgaw or Wilmington, just 30 miles down the road.

The widest portion of Topsail Island is in the Surf City area. While there is a substantial width of island behind the high-tide line here, the barrier profile is quite low. Hurricane Fran flattened the island's meager and solitary dune line. Today, high tide, which previously left a swash mark just a hop and skip beyond once well-nibbled dunes, races farther inland. There are some parts of the island that lack any natural protection now and are especially vulnerable.

Until the summer of 1996, Topsail Island enjoyed 42 catastrophe-free years in the sun. While the ocean had sheared the dune, leaving a drop-off as sharp as a shovel cut, it only marginally inconvenienced those headed for one of the gentlest profiles along the entire coast. The beach slope made it very popular with families.

There are 6 miles between Surf City and Topsail Beach. It is an area that experienced much building in the years before 1996. The objective from this point forward will be rebuilding. Topsail Beach, with far fewer houses than Surf City, seemed to be the less for wear and tear—the beachfront, of course, where nearly all of the houses and the island beneath them vanished, is the exception.

Also like Onslow County, Pender includes two islands that don't seem likely to be developed, at least not safely anyway—Lea Island and No Name Island, both southwest of Topsail Island. Both of these barrier spits are extremely low-profile islands, highly erodible, and generally not very stable or accessible except by boat. Nonetheless, some folks have been trying to stake out their place in the sun on Lea Island, although there is no electricity, no sewer, and no telephone. The first futile efforts to build have been rebuked by erosion.

The inlets between the three islands—New Topsail Inlet between Topsail and Lea islands and Old Topsail Inlet separating Lea and No Name islands—provide rich fishing, even though the depths of the channels shifts around enough to make boating a challenge. Each of the inlets is migrating south, though at different rates, which means that each of the islands is gaining ground by accretion on its southern end. However, such added landmass has been shown to be unstable over time for any use other than as a delightful beach.

All three islands have wide marshes to the west. Finger canals poke into the marsh on Topsail Island in several locations. Once the marsh and sound waters supported a rich fishery because the small, rural, mostly wooded watershed filtered rainwater runoff, maintaining a clean, healthy estuary. However, the sound waters are now showing deterioration from construction pollutants, the destruction of the woods, and the increasing numbers of people and boats using the sound. Certain portions of the sound may soon be closed to shellfishing.

Back on the mainland, the land between Holly Ridge and Hampstead east of US 17 has gone to golf. The resort real estate market in Pender County is becoming an increasingly important player in the local economy, which will no doubt result in changes along the coastline.

Access

There is a regional access site at New Bern Avenue, approximately three blocks northeast of the center of Surf City, where NC 210/50 becomes Roland Avenue and intersects Topsail Drive. This site offers 25 parking places, restrooms, showers, and a dune crossover at the site.

Additional access may be found at the south end of streets perpendicular to North Shore Drive.

Handicapped Access

The regional access site at New Bern Avenue is fully handicapped-accessible.

Information

For information about Angola Bay and Holly Shelter game lands, contact North Carolina Wildlife Resources Commission, 512 North Salisbury Street, Raleigh, NC 27611, 919-733-3391.

For information on Topsail Island, contact Greater Topsail Area Chamber of Commerce, NC 210, New River Drive, Surf City, NC 28445, 910-328-0666.

Surf City

I don't think this is the Surf City Jan and Dean had in mind when they recorded their chart-topping single in the early 1960s, but if ever a song painted a mood and attitude about the generic summer at the beach, it could have been that song and this beach. The waves aren't nearly as big, but the small-town, summer of '62 feeling lingers at Surf City. You almost feel as though you should set your watch back a decade or two.

This community of some 1,400 people could have been the movie set for the boy-meets-girl-at-beach summer movie of twenty years ago. There are just enough amusements and hangouts and not quite enough parking to keep things moving on summer nights, stirring up the evening the way the under-twenty-one beach crowd wants it to be—or at least the way us older folks remember wanting it stirred.

Surf City is the largest of the permanent communities on Topsail Island and is compressed around the junction of NC 210 and NC 50, which continues southwest through the wide and most heavily developed portion of Topsail Island to Topsail Beach. The city limits of Surf City actually extend over the Pender County line at Broadway Avenue into Onslow County and include portions of Old Settlers Beach; to the southwest, Surf City borders Topsail Beach. The swing bridge over the sound provides one of the highest vantage points at this end of the island, offering a quick glimpse of the modest center strip of this beachfront community. Commercial enterprises fan out from this junction—there's even a waterslide—creating other commercial nodes of services and shops along the strand. Low-rise commercial services provide the island wel-

	Fee	Parking	Restrooms	Lifeguard	Camping	Showers	Beach Access	Hiking	Trail	Handicapped	Boating	ORV Access	Fishing	Programs	Historic	Sand Beach	Dunes	Upland	Wetland
Regional Access: Surf City	•	•				•	•			•			•		•	•	•		
Topsail Beach	•	•					•				•		•		•	•	•		•

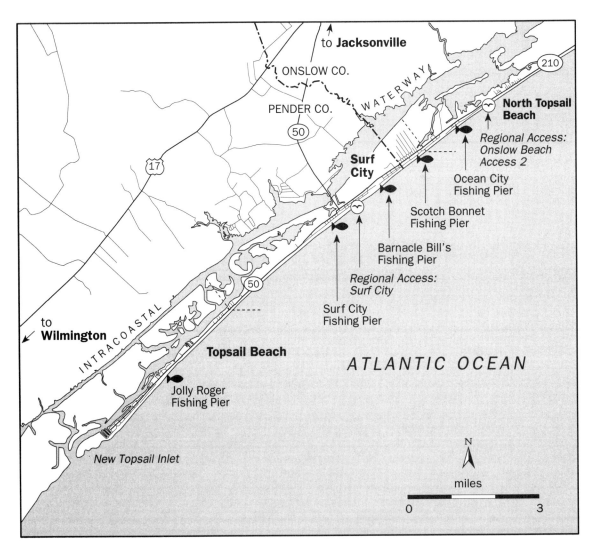

Map 23. South Topsail Island

come, and the town hall is two blocks north on NC 210. A fishing pier and a few smaller motels fan out from the small commercial junction and that's the town.

On September 5, 1996, the strongest winds and highest storm surge of Hurricane Fran piled into Surf City, destroying most oceanfront buildings including the fishing piers, which were also recreational centers in this sleepy beach community.

Undoubtedly, rebuilding will bring a different look to Surf City but probably not much change in the easy attitude and laid-back atmosphere. Expect a great beach for a blanket, book, or boat—pier fishing, however, may never be restored.

Access

There is a regional access site at New Bern Avenue northeast of the center of Surf City, where you cross the bridge into town. This site offers 25 parking places, restrooms, showers, and a dune crossover at the site. Next door is one of the seven observation platforms used during Operation Bumblebee. The tower, which weathered Fran, is plainly posted no trespassing.

There are also signed neighborhood access points with a number of parking places available at many of the streets that dead-end into

Shore Drive, the road directly behind the dune line. Several parking lots on Shore Drive south of the central fishing pier, within easy view, have more spaces. You may have a better chance finding parking at Wilmington and Kingston avenues southwest of the pier than at the smaller areas in the more populated portions of town toward the Onslow County line.

Informal access is also available. Surf City Pier has been known to open its parking lot for beachgoers; check with the owner. There is also some parking spillover into the grocery store lot on the next block inland. You may also be able to park at two piers north of Surf City center, Barnacle Bill's in Surf City and the Scotch Bonnet at the city limits; check with the owners. Be mindful that destruction of the piers may have altered this parking option. In addition, the island is much more crowded at this end, and parking may not be available.

Handicapped Access

The regional access site, when restored, will be accessible to handicapped travelers.

Information

For information, contact Greater Topsail Area Chamber of Commerce, NC 210, New River Drive, Surf City, NC 28445, 910-328-0666.

Topsail Beach

The Topsail Beach town limits begin after a 3-mile drive southwest from Surf City. This easy drive along NC 50 is a ride through a long residential street, though there are far fewer houses along the oceanfront. Hurricane Fran not only shattered the dwellings on both sides of NC 50, but in many locations it consumed the oceanfront, rendering the once-prime locations unbuildable. The houses that were closer to the sound fared far better.

In a few locations, these residential streets seem to tunnel into the maritime forest, boring a path to the sound. The illusion from NC 50 is that you are traveling at a much higher elevation than the water. Sometimes this is true. At the town limits of Topsail Beach, the road crests along the back ridge of the frontal dunes and the seaward houses perch on the precipice above the beach. When you reach downtown Topsail Beach, the road is no longer at the oceanfront but instead parallels Ocean Boulevard, directly behind the dunes.

Topsail Beach is a tight and tidy little town, a collection of homesteads and vacation outposts built for the love of the beach. The once-protective dune line is gone, as are many of the homes that occupied oceanfront lots in early summer 1996. Ocean Boulevard is less threatened than the remaining restored and repaired beachfront houses, which have little natural buffer from the nibbling sea.

NC 50 becomes North Anderson until approximately the intersection with Banks Channel Court, where it becomes South Anderson. There is a bike path along the soundside of Anderson leading into the central business portion of Topsail Beach. The Jolly Roger Motel and Pier mark the approximate central district and certainly the historic part of the island. The patio of the motel is on the site of the launching pad of rocket tests conducted here by the navy in the 1940s, named Operation Bumblebee. The original building of the motel dates from that era. The rocket assembly was in the soundside building now known as the Arsenal Centre. The rockets moved from this assembly station to the launching pad underground. The reinforced concrete observation towers were used to track the flight of the missiles. Other buildings still standing here served in support of the effort, identifiable by the vintage architecture and the lean square chimneys in the middle of the buildings. When the military abandoned Topsail, it returned the island and sold the buildings to the former owners, and the resort era began.

Hurricane Fran inflicted $400,000 in damage to the Jolly Roger Fishing Pier, effectively closing the business. The storm also destroyed many of the oceanfront properties and businesses along Ocean Boulevard from the pier southwest. These had suffered from accelerating erosion in recent years. In a hard smack, Hurricane Fran shut off a heated debate about attempting to arrest the insidious erosion that had been carving sand away from the beach southwest of the pier, carrying it along shore, and depositing much of it in the inlet, increasing the flats at the end of the island.

At New Topsail Inlet, the beach is building, which is extending the island. Serenity Point, a new development on land that in 1938 was the location of the inlet, faces nearly 100 yards of new, wide, flat beach. It's the best beach in the town now and the place to head, particularly for fishing and shelling. Swimming is not advised because of the currents of New Topsail Inlet.

Access

There are no regional access locations in Topsail Beach. Each street that is perpendicular to the oceanfront terminates in a dune crossover, and there are a few parking spaces available near each. There is a parking area at Serenity Point that leads by boardwalk and stairs up over the dune line, providing access to the inlet and the newly accreted beach at the southwest end of the island. You must get there early to squeeze into one of the parking spaces.

According to law enforcement officers in Topsail Beach, parking is permitted pretty much anywhere as long as you observe the following commonsense rules:

— Don't park where signs indicate no parking.
— Pull your car completely off of the pavement.
— Park at least 15 feet from a water hydrant.
— Don't block anyone's

driveway, sidewalk, or service area.
— Don't park on anyone's property without permission.

Several marinas offer boating access to Topsail Sound. There are four fishing piers that offer angling, including one soundside pier.

An unimproved off-road-vehicle access is at the ocean terminus of Drum Avenue.

Information

For information, contact Greater Topsail Area Chamber of Commerce, NC 210, New River Drive, Surf City, NC 28445, 910-328-0666.

New Topsail Inlet and Lea Island

New Topsail Inlet is beyond the beach west of the Serenity Point development in Topsail Beach. From the inlet, you see the low profile of Lea Island. An attempt to build a house there in recent years failed due to a natural southerly migration of the channel of New Topsail Inlet. The vanished house, named "Glump's Folly" for its owner, was claimed by the inlet.

Lea Island, the next island in the sequence along the Pender coast, is generally small and low, but it does have some higher elevations. Although the island is inaccessible except by boat, usually from the Hampstead marina, lots have been sold there and it does seem as though some people will try to

build on Lea. Nearly forty lots were platted on the island as recently as ten years ago. Since then, at least five have gone under the shifting inlet waters. Although some lots will accommodate septic tanks, there is no electricity or telephone service on the island.

Note: South of Lea Island, separated by Old Topsail Inlet, is No Name Island, which is a name of local reference. Accessible only by boat, this 2.5-mile-long island is unoccupied but privately owned.

Hampstead

While the traffic slows very little as it passes through Hampstead, the undeniable impression is that life slows and beats to a rhythm indifferent to the drumming of tires on US 17. The speed limit dips to 45 miles per hour, and your curiosity heightens as the highway narrows.

There are several churches, a school, and some shops clustered along the highway on the west side of a historic railroad right-of-way lining US 17 or the King's Highway, which served as the colonial post road. The community's oldest commercial structure, the Weir Building, still stands, although it is now empty. Until the opening of Hampstead Crossing shopping center, it housed a barber shop and video store. George Washington stopped at Hampstead during his southern tour in 1791, and south of town, beside the right-of-way, the Daughters of the American Revolution have designated a live oak tree as the site of his encampment. NC 210 turns to the west at Hampstead, leaving behind seafood packers and wholesalers and a small Mormon graveyard.

In all, Hampstead is a pleasing interlude along US 17, but it will not remain so for long. In 1994, work was to begin on widening 23 miles along US 17 to five lanes, including the stretch through Hampstead. This will alter present-day Hampstead beyond recognition, claiming several businesses and nearly all of the trees shading the present road. It should take two years to complete the entire segment.

Access

There is no direct access from Hampstead to the waters of Stump Sound, but there are private marinas at the ends of the secondary roads that lead east from US 17.

Poplar Grove Plantation

James Foy established Poplar Grove Plantation in 1795, which is now in the small town of Scott's Hill. Following a fire that destroyed the original home, his son Joseph M. Foy built the present plantation manor in 1850. A pioneer in peanut cultivation, Foy rebuilt the family fortunes of the 685-acre landholding through the economic sways of the Reconstruction era. The manor house, long central in the affairs of the plantation, exemplifies antebellum plantation architecture and lifestyle in the area. The building, which is on the National Register of Historic Places, has been open to the public for tours for eleven years.

The grounds are open to the public without charge, but there is a fee for the guided tour of the manor. The elevated first-floor living quarters of the manor house are an example of architectural adaptation to the humid climate of the coastal plain; the high floor level caught the prevailing winds and channeled them through the house for cooling.

For many years, the manor house was also a restaurant, but a new restaurant has been constructed on the grounds, freeing the interior of the manor house for exhibits. In addition to the house, there are several outbuildings open to the public, including a tenant house, kitchen, blacksmith shop, salt works, and turpentine display. Children will enjoy the farm animals (petting is permitted).

Access

Poplar Grove is alongside US 17 in Scott's Hill. The plantation is open February–December, 9 A.M. to 5 P.M. Monday–Saturday; 12 P.M. to 5 P.M. Sunday.

Handicapped Access

Because of its age and architectural styling, the manor house is not very accessible. The barn and craft center have accessible restrooms for handicapped travelers.

Information

For information, call the plantation at 910-686-9518.

What's behind the Breakers?

Telling a child that a great machine sends waves crumpling over their feet is closer to the truth than you might think. You can feel the soft touch of the wave generator on your face or watch it skitter a cap across the sand. Most of the waves you see are products of the wind.

However, the wave-building wind may not be the same zephyr tousling your hair. Imagine a becalmed sea, hundreds, perhaps thousands of miles away from you. A breeze gusts the ocean's surface, pushing the water into ripples and creating an effect similar to when you blow on the surface of a bowl of soup. The breeze continues, and the ripples, gathering energy from the wind, pile together to build into waves that travel across the sea to froth at your feet. The friction of air moving over water is sufficient to begin an ocean wave, but the effectiveness of the wind to forge waves depends on the average velocity of the wind, the duration of the wind, and the fetch—the reach of open water—that the wind traverses. The stronger the wind, the longer it blows, and the greater the distance of open ocean across which it pushes the water, the greater the waves that reach the shore.

Wind is neither predictable nor simple, nor are waves, although all waves have some characteristics in common. Short gusty winds—local winds—generate mature waves of all sizes in a fragmented pattern. Some merge and some are overtaken by larger waves already on a transoceanic course. The large waves absorb and store the energy of their captured cousins.

Each ripple spawned by wind has a steep windward side that acts as a sail, a surface against which the wind drives it forward. Should the wind gust too sharply, the top of the youthful wave shatters, spilling over its leading surface or exploding in spray. A stormy coastal day reveals a frothing sea, in part because the wind shears the crests of waves and spits them about.

There is enough visible difference in the appearance of waves to enable you to play a guessing game about their origin from your beachside vantage point. Sharp, peaked waves, spilling whitecaps as they channel landward before breaking with a "groan," are probably young waves created by a nearby offshore storm. A wave that rolls into a crest that uniformly pipe-curls over, thunders into its trough, and breaks with a roar before pummeling the surf zone is ending a journey from far away by thrashing at your beach.

Have you ever seen a diamondlike pattern in the arriving waves? This occurs when different intersecting groups of waves, with different compass points of origin, do not march straight into land. These groups are called wave trains. Each marches to its own rhythm and has its own wavelength, period of repetition, and height—the vertical distance between a trough and a succeeding crest. When wave trains intersect and continue their separate tracks, the eye sees a diamond pattern.

When several wave trains cross, the separate crests of the two trains may combine to form a large single wave, or the crest of one train may combine with the trough of the other, reducing the effect. Should you notice that every fourth or fifth wave (or some other count) is larger than average (surfers do this all the time), the larger wave likely represents the coincidence of crests of two different wave trains.

I don't mean to imply that the initial wind-generated waves originating far offshore actually survive to run up on the sand. The wave train or series of waves does continue as long as the wind blows, but by the time it reaches shore, the initial wave has long been absorbed by the hundreds, even thousands, of new waves created at the back of the original chain. In a manner of speaking, the wave that eventually reaches the shore is a descendant of the initial ripple.

Offshore, in a boat, you experience surface waves as swells, which travel at an average rate of 3.5 times their period—distance between successive crests—in seconds. Thus a wave with a 20-second period travels at about 70 miles per hour. (The longest period of swell ever reported was 22.5 seconds, corresponding to a wavelength of 2,600 feet and a speed of 78 miles per hour—a serious wave.)

The wind can blow in any direction and waves can begin from any direction. Why, then, do they usually arrive at the beach, breaking parallel to shore? Waves refract or begin to "bend" as soon as the depth of the water is about one-half their wavelength. In addition, the wave responds to shallows by shortening its length, increasing its height, and reducing its speed, just like a man running uphill, who chops his steps, lifts his knees higher, and slows down.

The most dramatic evidence of this phenomena is at Cape Point, the spit of land extending southeast into the ocean at Cape Hatteras. The fishermen lining the two sides of the spit witness the spectacular clash of waves, which originate far out at sea. As the leading edge of these waves reaches the first shallows of Cape Point, the faster-traveling edges, which are in deeper water to either side of the spit, refract around the shallows, bending until you witness a spectacular head-to-head explosion of water.

The movement of water at the edge of land will always be one of the most enthralling and restful images on earth. The mystery of waves, their possible origin, the transoceanic crossings, the shapes and patterns that never repeat, will always be the attraction of the beach—a product of the great wave machine that gently tousles your hair.

New Hanover County

Area code 910

Wilmington makes New Hanover the most urban of the North Carolina coastal counties. If you're not familiar with the coast, Wilmington holds a romantic allure, but it is often wrongly assumed to be a beachfront city. The urban center of the North Carolina coast perches on the banks of the Cape Fear River, some 10 miles west of the nearest beach. Wilmington is a coastal destination of a different sort—a city, rich in history and architectural character.

Although New Hanover County is the smallest coastal county, it has approximately 27 miles of oceanfront, most of which is on barrier islands. There are three islands north to south: Figure Eight, Wrightsville Beach/Shell Island, and Masonboro Island. Each is very different, from exclusively re- stricted to densely developed to completely natural. Extensive marsh and the Intracoastal Waterway separate the islands from the mainland. Heading south from Wilmington on US 421, you will cross Snows Cut, the channel of the Intracoastal Waterway cut by the U.S. Army Corps of Engineers in the 1930s connecting Myrtle Grove Sound with the Cape Fear River. The channel sliced off the end of the county from the mainland, making a fourth island, Pleasure Island, which includes the communities of Carolina Beach, Wilmington Beach, and Kure Beach and the Fort Fisher State Recreation Area.

Pleasure Island is one location where the mainland of North Carolina comes down to the sea. This break in the coastal barrier island pattern begins east of the town hall building in Carolina Beach, extending south through unincorporated Wilmington Beach to Kure Beach and Fort Fisher. Prior to the opening of Snows Cut, this was part of the mainland, a narrowing neck of land that separated the Cape Fear River from the Atlantic Ocean.

When you include the Pleasure Island beaches among the beachfront experiences available in New Hanover County, you have a grand concentration of many different vacation opportunities. Couple this with the completion of I-40 from Raleigh to Wilmington, and you have a run on the beach. The ocean is now 2¼ hours from Raleigh.

New Hanover's coastal array includes Masonboro Island and Zeke's Island, two components of the North Carolina National Estuarine Research Reserve. Masonboro Island is a 9-mile-long, low barrier south of Wrightsville Beach, accessible by boat. Zeke's Island is at the end of US 421, beyond the Fort Fisher/Southport ferry dock, and contains a 4-mile-long barrier spit that extends south from the Federal Point access area. Because of these "free" beaches, New Hanover County has an extraordinarily balanced diversity of beach offerings.

Since the late nineteenth century, New Hanover County islands and beaches have been popular resort and vacation getaways. Close enough to be "bedroom communities" for Wilmington, there's more of a permanent character in appearance and attitude in some of these locations. Wilmington has the jobs and the resort beaches have the atmosphere. It's hard to resist being able to be in the ocean or sailing at 5:45 P.M. every day.

The towns of Wrightsville Beach, Carolina Beach, and Kure Beach are well established, self-sufficient communities with a varying degree of dependency on tourism that increases with the distance from Wilmington. Wrightsville Beach, the closest, has practically a suburban feeling, with a relationship to Wilmington that is similar to the relationship of Virginia Beach to Norfolk. Further south, Carolina Beach is definitely "beachy." There are fewer year-round residents and streets are quiet between Labor Day and Memorial Day. Kure Beach, more distant still, is a grand place to find surf and solitude and is extraordinarily quiet after the summer season.

There is a kind of cultural split in New Hanover County—Wilmington residents versus beach residents. Many who work in Wilmington live, vacation, or own homes on the barrier islands or along the Intracoastal Waterway in the county, and they have opinions about land use and accessibility there. So do those who live on the barrier islands all year and make a living from tourism or real estate. What is good for tourism or real estate may not always be sympathetic to the visual character of a community. This is not quite a Mercedes–dune buggy divide, but there is a schism in attitude that spills over into the access debate and the issues of land use and zoning controls.

Hurricanes Fran and Bertha piled catastrophic damage on top of the chronic beach erosion that already threatened portions of the coast. The storms swiped away most of the once-protective dunes, flooded low-lying inland locations, and leveled every fishing pier. Individual properties on Figure Eight Island and in parts of Carolina and Kure Beaches suffered randomly. While it didn't receive the widespread, total destruction wrought on Topsail Island, the beach was abbreviated, and the sense of serenity and peace of mind here was left unsettled.

Access

The individual municipalities maintain access sites in New Hanover County. There are four regional access locations at Wrightsville Beach, one at Carolina Beach, and a very large regional access area at Federal Point, south of Fort Fisher.

The New Hanover County Parks and Recreation Department has provided numerous access locations in the county in Wilmington Beach.

The county also maintains a 24-acre park, Snows Cut Park, off of River Road on the northwest side of US 421 (before you cross the Intracoastal Waterway to Pleasure Island). There are four boat-launching ramps, restrooms, picnic shelters, tables, grills, and a gazebo.

New Hanover County jointly maintains the regional beach access area at Fort Fisher with the state.

The county maintains a regional

river access on the west side of River Road north of Cathay Road.

The approach to Zeke's Island is accessible by car. Park at either the Federal Point regional access area or at the North Carolina Wildlife Resources Commission boat ramp south of the Fort Fisher/Southport ferry dock.

Handicapped Access

All of the regional access sites are accessible to handicapped travelers. The Federal Point access area has the shortest distance to the water from the end of the dune crossover ramp.

Information

For information, contact Cape Fear Coast Convention and Visitors Bureau, 24 North Third Street, Wilmington, NC 28401, 910-341-4030 or 1-800-222-4757, or Pleasure Island Chamber of Commerce, 201 Lumberton Avenue, Carolina Beach, NC 28428, 910-458-8434 or 1-800-228-8434.

Wilmington

Wilmington is capitalizing on its past mercantile prominence, digging into the stored wares and gutted trade houses of dusty decades to develop a refreshing, entertaining presence. It feels vital, beating with the pulse of a city building a commercial future around and within its heritage.

It certainly isn't hampered by its environment. Shaded by moss-draped trees, surrounded by floral gardens, and saturated with historic buildings and sites, Wilmington draws visitors both as a city and as a center of history. The fact that some of the finest beaches, swimming, and fishing are barely a half hour to the southeast doesn't hurt its attractiveness in the least.

Approaching from the north, US 17 deposits you directly into the heart of Wilmington, where it becomes Market Street. This uncommonly serene entry to a downtown area follows a planted median and carries you past one of your first stops, the New Hanover County Museum of the Lower Cape Fear at 814 Market Street. This free introduction to area history sets the stage for walking the town later and firmly fixes Wilmington's prominence.

Wilmington's place in North Carolina's history is secure. There are more historic markers here than in any other city in the state, including one noting the birthplace of Whistler's mother. Commerce has grown on these riverbanks since the early 1730s, and for several years in the eighteenth century it served as the state capital. Until 1910, it was the state's largest city.

Historically, the economy of the city was based on mercantile trade such as the production and shipping of naval stores from nearby pine forests. The secure harbor made Wilmington the only reliable natural deep-water port in the state. During the Civil War, the Confederacy tried to keep the port open and con-structed Fort Fisher to defend the entrance. Blockade-runners—privateers who knew the local waters and could press into the port at night—kept Wilmington a productive, though limited, port of call nearly throughout the war in spite of Union efforts to thwart shipments.

Let serendipity guide your discovery of Wilmington. First discover a parking place—perhaps near the visitors center in the restored 1892 courthouse at Princess and Third streets across from Thalian Hall, the city hall building. Inside the courthouse are the headquarters of the Cape Fear Coast Convention and Visitors Bureau. Collect the several self-directing fliers, spend fifteen minutes in the courthouse to absorb an introductory video on the Wilmington area, then head to the water, via Market or Princess Street.

Wilmington's commercial heart lies along the river, of course, and the street to walk is Front Street. The Cotton Exchange, between Grace and Walnut streets, is a boutique crafted out of old cotton warehouses. It provides a multileveled descent to public parking along cobbled Water Street and the promenade along the Cape Fear River. The backdrop to the setting is the magnificent *USS North Carolina* at berth across the river.

At Water and Market streets are public restrooms and a visitors center. You may also take a 1½-hour sightseeing cruise of the waterfront on the *Henrietta II* (adults $6; children $4). There is also a small launch that will cross the river to the battleship *North Carolina*.

Wilmington's historic district extends south from the downtown until it gradually becomes almost completely residential. At Water and Ann streets is Chandler's Wharf, a shopping exchange in historic structures. The cobblestones end, and a boardwalk sidles along the river. Head uphill and you ascend into the midst of the historic residential area beside the Governor Edward B. Dudley mansion. Dudley won the first statewide gubernatorial election in 1836 and was the president of the Wilmington and Weldon Railroad, which, at 161 miles long, was the longest continuous track in the world in 1840. The Dudley mansion is one of several fine houses along Front Street. Because of the number of historic markers in this area, it is a route better explored on foot than by car. On Third Street, you can also stroll through the magnificent Greenfield Gardens, an extraordinary landscape of trails and plantings crafted around a lake. You may even rent a paddleboat there.

Access

There is ample parking downtown, but you have to attend to the parking meters. There is a public boat ramp at the west end of Castle Street, two blocks north of the US 17, US 76 bridge.

Handicapped Access

Wilmington is a surprisingly hilly city and handicapped accessibility varies. There are handicapped restrooms at the visitor information center at Water and Market streets in Riverfront Park. The following are some of the more noted attractions in Wilmington that are accessible to handicapped travelers.

At Chandler's Wharf, 2 Ann Street, the streets are cobblestone, but some restaurants in the complex have ramped entrances. There are handicapped accessible restrooms in the Wharf Building.

The Cotton Exchange, North Front Street, is moderately accessible, but assistance would be best. Shops on the upper level are accessible from Front Street. Parking is on Water Street.

Greenfield Gardens, South Third Street, 910-341-7855, are very accessible, and wheelchairs are available with advance notice.

The *Henrietta II*, docked at the foot of Market Street at Riverfront Park, 910-343-1611, is accessible with staff assistance.

The New Hanover County Museum of the Lower Cape Fear, 814 Market Street, 910-341-4350, is fully accessible.

The Thalian Hall Center for the Performing Arts, Third and Princess streets, 910-763-3398, is accessible.

At the USS *North Carolina* Battleship Memorial on the Cape Fear River, 910-762-1829, the main deck, museum, and memorial area are accessible.

Information

For information, contact Cape Fear Coast Convention and Visitors Bureau, 24 North Third Street, Wilmington, NC 28401, 910-341-4030.

Figure Eight Island

Figure Eight Island is a privately held, exclusively developed island. Only homeowners and their guests may drive over the Intracoastal Waterway on the private causeway and drawbridge, after first stopping at a guardhouse on the mainland. Viewed from the mainland, the houses of the island seem to rise out of the salt marsh that buttresses the west side of the barrier. The tree and shrub cover of the island provide the only natural interruption in the island's low profile, which is visually dominated by the scale and size of the homes.

Figure Eight is an assembly of expensive private homes, with some extraordinarily fine construction along the winding roads. The roads thread atop the sparsely vegetated spine of the island, permitting building sites with oceanfront locations. The sensitivity shown in the planning of the island maintains much of the original natural features. The northeast end of the island is the most wooded area and care was taken to preserve the natural tree cover.

The extreme north end, adjacent to Rich Inlet, has been set aside as a preserve for island residents. Although this area has the highest dune line, it is erratic and not very well developed. Elsewhere, erosion carves the beachfront and is

The waterfront at Wilmington. (Courtesy of N.C. Travel and Tourism Division)

sufficiently close to threaten some homes. The south end of the island, which looks to neighboring Wrightsville Beach beyond Mason Inlet, is accreting sand in a low, wide fan. The nearest homes on Figure Eight are nearly ½ mile from the channel of Mason Inlet. Hurricane Fran hit many homes on Figure Eight hard but did not alter the steady southern migration of Mason Inlet that now threatens Shell Island Resort across the channel.

Access

Only homeowners and their guests can drive on the island. Boaters or swimmers may use the wet sand beach.

Wrightsville Beach and Shell Island

US 74 and US 76 share a drawbridge crossing the Intracoastal Waterway to carry you to the resorts of Wrightsville Beach and Shell Island. Wrightsville Beach is a venerable resort that has long been a popular getaway. In 1965, Moore's Inlet, which separated Shell Island from the north end of Wrightsville Beach, was filled in. The combined geography is today the town of Wrightsville Beach. "Shell Island" is still used in local conversation. The proximity to Wilmington is certainly a component of its viability. The community capitalizes on the commutable distance by encouraging year-round visitation, astutely providing easy access to the oceanfront. The beach here is wide and low-angled and has long been favored by families

Feeding the Beach

One of the few relief measures available to beachfront communities threatened by erosion is beach nourishment, pumping sand instead of iron. There is not much else you can do in North Carolina, since the state stands firm in its avowal to deny applications for beach-hardening structures such as groins, jetties, or other reinforcing measures to hold an edge against the ocean.

The process is straightforward. Sand dredged from inlets and sounds is pumped and deposited on the ocean berm, expanding the sand barrier to provide an additional buffer for developed property behind the dune line. However, it is an expensive and short-term solution. Beach nourishment can cost between $2 million and $10 million per mile of beachfront. Also, because the size of the particles of the dredged and deposited sand differs from that naturally deposited on the beach, the new beach is not really suited for the job and frequently disappears within two to five years, carried away by the very erosion it was supposed to help forestall. Wrightsville Beach and Carolina Beach have received several nourishments, conducted by the U.S. Army Corps of Engineers, the agency responsible for the supervision of this type of shoreline maintenance project. In fact, Wrightsville Beach has a history of nourishment that, while not as famous as that of Virginia Beach, which is replaced each winter, is gaining notoriety. It is a question of dollars and priorities.

Because of the high cost, the federal government subsidizes most of the expense. In recent years, this has prompted protest that beach nourishment is a futile expenditure of taxpayer money that benefits only a few property owners. It is a government subsidy—there is no other way to define it—but without it, there would not be Wrightsville Beach, which between 1965 and 1990 was nourished six times at a cost of $9 million, about $1.5 million of which came from state and local funds. Carolina Beach also received sand during this period.

In order to qualify for the corps' nourishment project, the value of the resources lost must exceed the cost of nourishment, a condition easily met in multistory beachfront locations. However, the pool of funds for replenishment is diminishing, but the ocean is not—it is rising. With more communities losing ground against the sea, the selection process will become tougher indeed as the cost of providing the service increases.

Feeding the beach is usually done in fall, during the off-season and just before the steady northeastern storms that cause the greatest erosion. Some sand is gone before it even settles, and therein lies the rub. Since sea level is rising, we're only renting beachfront at an increasingly expensive rate. Building sand castles is one thing, but building the beach so you can build sand castles is a measure of desperation.

with small children because of its gentleness.

The roads fork shortly after crossing the Intracoastal Waterway, and US 74 continues north closer to the Shell Island portion of Wrightsville Beach. After the road skirts extensive salt marsh and crosses a small tidal creek, it meets Salisbury Street. Directly ahead is a fishing pier, public parking, and a wooden sign that reads: "Our berm and dune system was created for your enjoyment and the protection it gives the town. Help us protect fragile vegetation by using designated access points only. Please use and enjoy the strand but do keep off the beach grass." This genteel request to protect the native vegetation is supported by very clearly marked beach access areas and a thorough municipal effort to accommodate parking needs.

There are four beach access areas with parking and public restrooms and several municipal parking lots with access to the beach that have dune crossovers. Additionally, each public street perpendicular to the ocean provides access at the eastern end. Please note that there are private streets at the north end of the island where public access is legally restricted. Courtesy and common sense are advised at these locations.

Wrightsville Beach accommodates large numbers of daily visitors through metered parking. Bring lots of quarters. Parking at access-area meters limits you to 4 hours at $.50 an hour; other metered locations have a 6-hour limit at $.50 an hour. If you park in a designated parking area or attend to a parking meter, you're okay anywhere in Wrightsville Beach. Stray out of unmarked spaces, leave your car blocking a drive or on the pavement of the main roads, or allow a meter to expire, and you run the risk of a ticket or towing.

Once you are parked, you will enjoy one of the gentler beaches in the state in surroundings that have a comfortable patina to them. Wrightsville Beach is "cottagey" in feeling, regardless of the height of the buildings. Even at the high-rise zoned lands of the Shell Island portion, the prevailing perception is "low," perhaps because the dune system is wide enough to balance visually the mass of the larger buildings.

A Holiday Inn (locally known as the "Holiday Inlet") now stands at the approximate location of the old Moore's Inlet channel, commemorated by Moore's Inlet Street. Be-

fore the inlet was filled in, only boaters and loggerhead turtles had access to what was known as Shell Island. The island narrows near the site of the old inlet, which restricts development to the east side of Lumina Drive. Extensive salt marsh is visible to the west. The only beachfront high-rise construction within the corporate limits of the island is on what was once Shell Island. The view of the ocean is obscured by these taller buildings, and revised zoning laws adopted in 1974 confine high-rise and mid-rise construction to those buildings you see today. At this point, there seems to be a strong resistance to further urbanization of the beachfront. What you see today is, for the most part, a resort rebuilding as best it can after the 1996 storms.

Lumina Avenue terminates at the north end of Shell Island in a modest-sized metered parking lot with restrooms and showers. This is where all the action, natural and legal, is on the island. In 1993, there was a ¼-mile walk to the inlet; today, the channel chews within 150 feet of the parking lot. Mason Inlet is shifting relentlessly southward, making the property owners of Shell Island Resort, the condominium tower, nervous. This circumstance has become a test case for the resolve of the North Carolina Coastal Commission which, thus far, has steadfastly refused to permit the construction of any permanent measures to "harden" the shoreline in order to protect private property. The case will be in court as surely as Mason Inlet will continue south.

Access

There are four regional access sites on Wrightsville Beach/Shell Island. The first is south of the Lumina Club Townhouses near the Oceanic Pier (aka Crystal Pier), sandwiched between Lumina Avenue and Waynick Boulevard. The area has 86 parking spaces, restrooms, showers, a gazebo, and a dune crossover. At Salisbury Street, almost directly at the end of US 74, there is a regional access site with 105 parking spaces, restrooms, showers, and a gazebo. There are 30 metered spaces with a 4-hour limit at the north end of Shell Island where Lumina Avenue loops to a close. This regional site, which has restrooms, showers, and a dune crossover, fills quickly during the season. There are 58 parking spaces, showers, and a dune crossover at Moore's Inlet Street next to the Holiday Inn at the fourth regional access site of this resort beach.

Several neighborhood access points offer parking and dune crossovers with lifeguarded beaches during the summer season. They are located at the eastern end of the following streets: Jack Parker Boulevard (20 spaces), with a dune crossover to the south end of the island and Masonboro Inlet, near the U.S. Coast Guard Station; and South Sea Oats Street (39), with a dune crossover.

There are also unimproved access areas with lifeguarded beaches located at Heron Street and Stone Street and many signed pedestrian paths throughout Wrightsville Beach.

	Fee	Parking	Restrooms	Lifeguard	Camping	Showers	Beach Access	Hiking	Trail	Handicapped	Boating	ORV Access	Fishing	Programs	Historic	Sand Beach	Dunes	Upland	Wetland
Wilmington		•	•							•	•			•	•			•	
Wrightsville Beach and Shell Island		•				•	•			•			•			•	•		
Public Boating Access: Wrightsville Beach		•									•		•						•
Regional Access: Shell Island		•	•			•	•			•			•			•			
Regional Access: Moore's Inlet		•	•			•	•			•			•			•	•		
Regional Access: Salisbury St.		•	•			•	•			•			•			•	•		
Regional Access: Lumina Ave.		•	•			•	•			•			•			•	•		
Masonboro Island Research Reserve							•	•		•			•			•	•	•	•

The Johnnie Mercer Fishing Pier at Salisbury Street and the Oceanic Fishing Pier at South Lumina provide fishing and limited parking access to the oceanfront. Check with the pier owner before parking.

The North Carolina Wildlife Resources Commission maintains a fishing and boating access area on the Intracoastal Waterway at Wrightsville Beach, adjacent to the US 74/76 drawbridge. Parking is available, and there is no launch fee.

Handicapped Access

The regional access sites south of the Lumina Club Townhouses near the Oceanic Pier, at Salisbury Street, at Jack Parker Boulevard, and at South Sea Oats Street are accessible for handicapped travelers. The first two have accessible showers and restrooms.

Information

For information, contact Cape Fear Coast Convention and Visitors Bureau, 24 North Third Street, Wilmington, NC 28401, 910-341-4030 or 1-800-222-4757.

Masonboro Island National Estuarine Research Reserve

In 1952, present-day Masonboro Island was isolated from Carolina Beach by the artificial opening of Carolina Beach Inlet for easier open-water access. This proved to be a blessing for Masonboro Island because it cut off direct access from the mainland, precluding construction. The island has remained pristine, frequented only by fishermen and beach lovers who enjoy the comparative solitude along the nearly 9 miles of beachfront.

Masonboro Island is one of the four components of the National Estuarine Research Reserve system in North Carolina. Acquisition of the 5,097 acres of island and mainland began in 1985 and is still under way. The few outparcels that have not yet been purchased do not restrict use or enjoyment of the island.

The island remains an astonishing sight in the rapidly developing coast. Except for a jetty created by the Corps of Engineers to stabilize Masonboro Inlet at the north end, there are no artificial structures. The largest undisturbed barrier along the southern portion of the North Carolina coast, Masonboro is markedly different physically from both Shackleford Banks in Carteret County and Bear Island (Hammocks Beach State Park) in Onslow County, its unaltered companions.

Approximately 453 acres of the

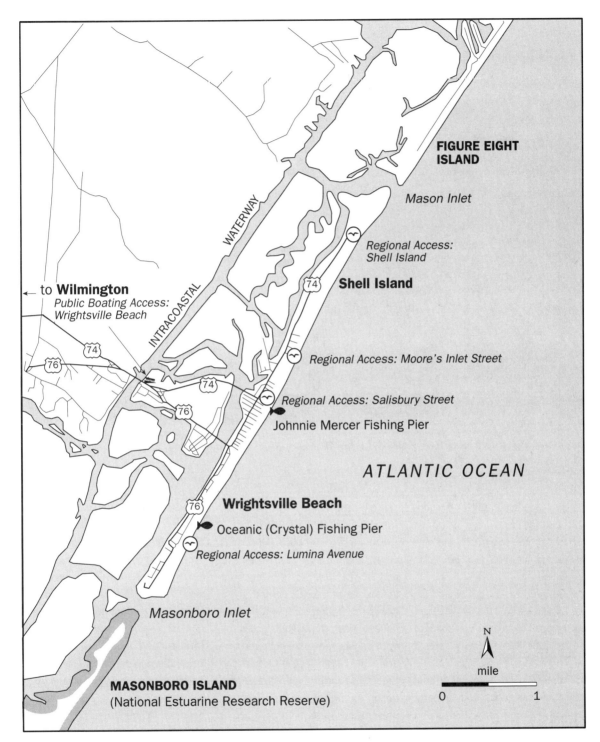

FIGURE EIGHT
ISLAND

Mason Inlet

Regional Access:
Shell Island

74 Shell Island

to Wilmington
Public Boating Access:
Wrightsville Beach

74

76

Regional Access: Moore's Inlet Street

74

76

Regional Access: Salisbury Street

Johnnie Mercer Fishing Pier

ATLANTIC OCEAN

76 Wrightsville Beach

Oceanic (Crystal) Fishing Pier

Regional Access: Lumina Avenue

Masonboro Inlet

INTRACOASTAL WATERWAY

N

mile

0   1

MASONBORO ISLAND
(National Estuarine Research Reserve)

Map 24. Wrightsville Beach and Shell Island

Neighborhood access facility, Wrightsville Beach. (Courtesy of N.C. Coastal Management Commission)

preserve is natural dune and woodlands and 166 acres are spoil islands next to the Intracoastal Waterway. The remainder of the island is marsh and tidal flats.

Masonboro is an "overwash" island, with a low, essentially duneless profile. The wide beaches and the solitude they provide are a haven for loggerhead turtles and piping plovers, two endangered species that can nest in comparative safety along the undeveloped shores. Gray foxes, river otters, raccoons, and opossums live in the upland portion of the island, safe enough from storm overwash to sustain a maritime forest habitat.

Although Masonboro Island has never supported a settlement, it may be that this was the first land in the New World sighted by a European explorer. Some historians believe that the island noted by explorer Giovanni da Verrazano several miles north of the mouth of the Cape Fear River in a 1524 report to his sponsor, Francis I, included present-day Masonboro Island.

Access

Access to Masonboro Island is by boat only. You will have to bring everything you need with you; there are no concessions of any kind and very little shade. No vehicles are allowed on the island.

Information

For information, contact North Carolina National Estuarine Research Reserve, 7205 Wrightsville Avenue, Wilmington, NC 28403, 919-256-3721, or Division of Coastal Management, P.O. Box 27687, Raleigh, NC 27611, 910-733-2293.

Snows Cut Park

Snows Cut Park is a 24-acre park maintained by New Hanover County on the water on the north side of Snows Cut, which links the Cape Fear River and Myrtle Grove Sound. To reach the park, turn right on River Road immediately before the Intracoastal Waterway bridge. The park has restrooms, picnic shelters, tables, grills, and a gazebo.

Information

For information, contact New Hanover Parks and Recreation Department, 414 Chestnut Street, Room 101, County Administration Annex, Wilmington, NC 28401, 910-341-7198.

Pleasure Island

Snows Cut is a passage for the Intracoastal Waterway created in the 1930s by the U.S. Army Corps of Engineers to link the Cape Fear River and Myrtle Grove Sound. Technically, the peninsula south of Snows Cut is an island. Recently, the citizens in Carolina Beach, Kure Beach, Fort Fisher, and the unincorporated beaches of New Hanover County have capitalized on this altered geography and have begun promoting this portion of the coast as Pleasure Island.

US 421 is the major access road and is locally renamed as Lake Park Boulevard shortly after the crossing of the Intracoastal Waterway. When you drive into Carolina Beach, the Chamber of Commerce is plainly

signed, a small house on the right side of the road. If you want to avoid the heavier summer traffic, turn right on Dow Road at the first intersection shortly after crossing Snows Cut. Dow is a two-lane soundside road bordering Carolina Beach State Park and will probably be less congested than US 421. Turn left on Harper Avenue to reach downtown Carolina Beach or continue to Ocean Boulevard for Wilmington Beach or Avenue K for Kure Beach.

Access

The individual municipalities manage access locations on Pleasure Island, and New Hanover County maintains several locations between Carolina Beach and Kure Beach. Specific access locations are noted following the municipal listings below. For a rule of thumb, sleep north and swim south; the farther south on US 421, the more convenient the access.

The North Carolina Wildlife Resources Commission maintains a fishing and boating access area on the Intracoastal Waterway at Carolina Beach, one mile east of US 421 at the south end of the bridge over the waterway. Parking is available and there is no launch fee.

Information

For information, contact Carolina Beach Chamber of Commerce, 201 Lumberton Avenue, Carolina Beach, NC 28428, 910-458-8434

Carolina Beach State Park

The 713 acres of Carolina Beach State Park are on the north end of Pleasure Island, approximately one mile northeast of Carolina Beach and 10 miles south of Wilmington. Heading south, shortly after US 421 crosses the Intracoastal Waterway at Snows Cut, turn right onto Dow Road. At the water tower, turn right onto SR 1628, which leads to the park.

Carolina Beach State Park is bounded by the Cape Fear River to the west, Snows Cut to the north, and Dow Road, which bisects the peninsula. The park provides boating access and camping and, most importantly, functions as a preserve and interpretive facility, exploring the natural history of the coastal plain.

One of the most biologically diverse parks in the entire state system, it includes an extensive interpretive trail system that winds through the preserve. Two of the most notable trails are Sugarloaf Trail and Fly Trap Loop.

Sugarloaf Trail skirts south from the park marina along the east bank of the Cape Fear. Quiet hikers can see egrets, herons, and kingfishers, among other water birds, along the salt marshes and sandy riverbank. After a mile-long walk, the trail reaches Sugarloaf, a large relic sand dune of Pleistocene age that is stabilized by live oak trees nearly 55 feet above sea level. Sugarloaf has long been a navigational landmark for Cape Fear sailors. Farther along

	Fee	Parking	Restrooms	Lifeguard	Camping	Showers	Beach Access	Hiking	Trail	Handicapped	Boating	ORV Access	Fishing	Programs	Historic	Sand Beach	Dunes	Upland	Wetland
Snows Cut Park	•	•								•	•		•					•	•
Pleasure Island	•	•	•	•	•	•	•	•	•	•	•	•	•	•		•	•	•	•
Carolina Beach State Park	•	•			•	•		•	•	•	•		•	•			•	•	•
Public Boating Access: Carolina Beach	•										•		•						•
Carolina Beach, North End	•						•						•	•		•	•		•
Regional Access: Carolina Beach	•	•	•	•			•			•			•			•	•		
Wilmington Beach	•						•			•			•			•		•	
Kure Beach	•	•					•						•			•			

the trail, there are several limestone sink ponds, formed when the underlying coquina rock collapsed after being dissolved by groundwater percolation and the new surface depression filled with water. The trail then loops back to the marina, and spur trails return to the camping area.

Fly Trap Loop leads through boggy ground populated by the carnivorous Venus's-fly-trap, sundew, and pitcher plants, which prefer the high moisture and spongy organic soil in limited areas of the coastal plain. The Venus's-fly-trap is found only within a 75-mile radius of Wilmington and nowhere else in the world. If you call the park in May, the rangers will be glad to tell you when the fly-traps will flower, a point in their life cycle that makes these diminutive predators more visible.

The remainder of the park is generally a combination of evergreen shrub savanna and sandy ridge vegetation. The juxtaposition of these strikingly varied environments is readily seen in the short Fly Trap Loop. In mid-to-early spring, the flowers of the sweetbay magnolia, which prefer the dark soil of the wetter areas of the park, perfume the trails. In mid-to-late summer the fragrant flowers of loblolly bay, an upright broadleaf evergreen tree, are in full bloom. In the drier sandy ridge habitats, wire grass and long-needle pine join blackjack oak to form the familiar sandhills associations.

Carolina Beach State Park provides one of the few public places to see these particular ecosystems and glimpse North Carolina plant communities that are reduced to vestigial locations even though they once covered the coastal plain.

Access

The park is open 8 A.M. to 5 P.M. November–February, closing at 7 P.M. in March and October; 8 P.M. in April, May, and September; and 9 P.M. June–August.

The park provides camping and boating access to the Cape Fear River and Intracoastal Waterway. The 83 tent/trailer campsites are first-come, first-served; groups may reserve sites. There is a central bathhouse and restrooms but no utility hookups.

The marina has 44 slips available for daily, weekly, or monthly rental. A full-service store and snack bar at the marina stocks such items as insect repellent, sunscreen, sunglasses, flares, and fishing tackle. The marina also has restrooms.

There is also a boat-launching ramp and parking for vehicles with trailers.

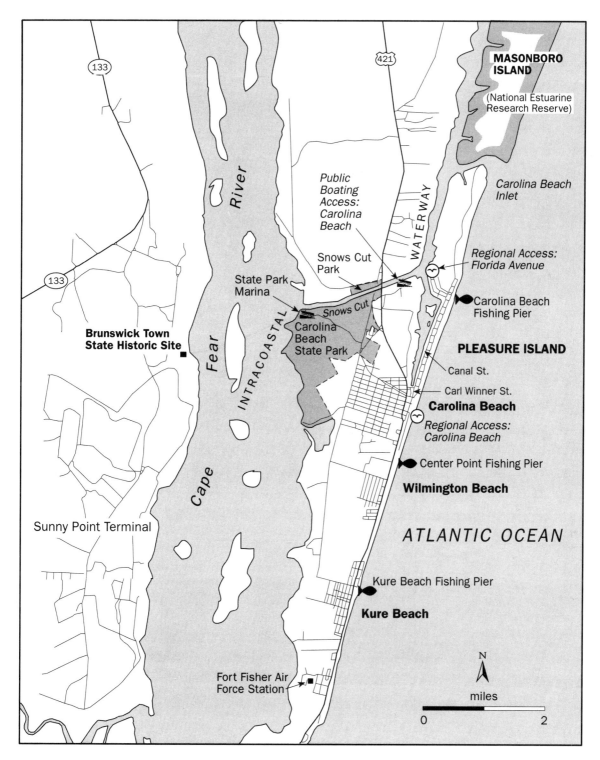

133

421

MASONBORO ISLAND

(National Estuarine Research Reserve)

River

Carolina Beach Inlet

Public Boating Access: Carolina Beach

WATERWAY

Snows Cut Park

Regional Access: Florida Avenue

State Park Marina

133

Snows Cut

Carolina Beach State Park

Carolina Beach Fishing Pier

PLEASURE ISLAND

INTRACOASTAL

Brunswick Town State Historic Site

Canal St.

Carl Winner St.

Fear

Carolina Beach

Regional Access: Carolina Beach

Center Point Fishing Pier

Wilmington Beach

Cape

ATLANTIC OCEAN

Sunny Point Terminal

Kure Beach Fishing Pier

Kure Beach

N

Fort Fisher Air Force Station

miles

0   2

Map 25. Pleasure Island

The Fly Trap Loop at Carolina Beach State Park. (Courtesy of N.C. Travel and Tourism Division)

Handicapped Access

The marina is fully accessible to handicapped travelers, including ramped access to the restrooms and the store. The campground restrooms are not readily accessible, and the trails are compacted sand, not easily negotiable in a wheelchair.

Information

For information, contact Carolina Beach State Park, P.O. Box 475, Carolina Beach, NC 28428, 910-458-8206.

Carolina Beach

Vacation rhythms accelerate at Carolina Beach, which buzzes, jumps, and pops with energy. This invigorating feeling of high recreational intensity establishes a very definite persona for the first city you come to after crossing the Intracoastal Waterway at Snows Cut. The place invites you to play hard. It is neon and beach music, with a distinctly collegiate feeling about it.

Carolina Beach has been a resort/entertainment destination since the late nineteenth century. The town incorporated in 1925, and there are still vague reminders of those early years. The median of Harper Avenue carried trolley lines once, and you could ride the rails directly to the center of downtown, where today there is a gazebo surrounded by six parking spaces and framed by six cabbage palmettos.

The northern portion of the incorporated city is actually a barrier island with the waters of Myrtle Grove Sound separating it from the peninsula. The barrier extends north from Carl Winner Street, one block north of Harper Avenue. The basin of Myrtle Grove Sound serves as the center of boating and fishing activity in Carolina Beach. Nearly all of the land between Myrtle Grove Sound and the Atlantic is residential.

Hurricane Fran pummeled Carolina Beach hardest at this end, whisking away the dunes and exposing the beach's rock armor, installed years ago. The remaining beach is wide and flat; the houses are intact, but with a heightened sense of exposure and vulnerability. It increases the huddled, urban feeling of this end of the community.

Because of the elevated construction, there is very little perception of beach. On busy weekends, the drive to the north end of Carolina Beach Avenue and the return by Canal Street is crowded, and you have very little hope of finding a parking space unless you are renting one of the units. This part of the community is mid-rise residential in character (although it seems high-rise at the flat beach), with narrow streets that do not accommodate on-street parking.

Where Canal Street and Carolina Beach Avenue North end, the sandy spit of the north end begins. This undeveloped barrier stretches to Carolina Beach Inlet. It is passable only by foot and four-wheel-drive vehicle and is a wonderful walk.

The artificial opening of the inlet in 1952 provided easier open-water access for the pleasure craft berthed in Myrtle Grove Sound or following the Intracoastal Waterway from the Cape Fear River. However, it interrupted the replenishing natural flow of sand from north of the inlet. Although beach erosion at the north end of the community is acute and accelerating, there still exists a very wide, low, dune line and a fairly gentle beach. At its intersection with Starfish Street, Carolina Beach Avenue angles east, and because of erosion, the beach decreases in width the closer you get to the Carolina Beach Fishing Pier. This angling of the road and the erosion have led to beach armoring at the extreme north end of the residential area, and some houses have experienced water damage.

There is both a visual and a psychological difference between the northern half of the town and the southern beach, City Hall at Carl Winner Street and Canal Street being the logical midpoint. The traditional cottage homes and the presence of motels, roominghouses, and rental apartments differentiate the southern part of town from the northern end. (There are a few long-established motels and hotels north of Carl Winner Street well before reaching the condominium boom.)

The combination makes the southern half of the city more relaxed and inviting. This part of town is on higher ground and has more vegetation than the barrier island northern extension. The open feel-

Blue Skies for the Brown Pelican

I remember seeing brown pelicans in the early 1960s, and then I saw none. Now they are back, steadily increasing in numbers, pushing their home range north along the coast as their surging population places pressure on available nesting sites in their traditional range further south. There are now permanent roosts (the brown pelican does not migrate) on spoil islands in Oregon Inlet, a historic first, especially for a species that hovered on the brink of extinction in the 1970s. The saga of the brown pelican is another happy ending resulting from the banning of DDT in the early 1970s.

And *how* they are back—gracefully, elegantly, wondrously lazing and dipping, gliding by the beach. To see a squadron pass, wing-to-wing or in an echelon grouping, feather-to-froth above the waves, is to witness the deliberate passage of great, dignified kites. So effortless is their habit of flight that pelicans appear to be magically suspended, pulled past the beach by invisible strings. They rule the skies above our coastal waters.

If you aren't sure you have ever seen a pelican, what you think may be a pelican probably is. They are huge—the largest birds you will see at the coast. When flying, the pelican pulls its head back on its shoulders and seems to tuck its nearly one-foot-long beak into its chest, a position that adds to the overall "what, me worry?" aspect of the bird's appearance.

The pelican's grace in the air may be nature's compensation for its awkward, virtually prehistoric appearance. The overlarge bill may be a pelican's meal ticket, but it sharply diminishes its aesthetic appeal. A pelican cannot be "cute" or "cuddly," but it can be adroit, nimble, and beak-bashingly brave when hungry.

Pelicans feed nearly exclusively on mullet, menhaden, and silversides and do so with the elegance of a dropped rock. They crash into the water from heights of 30 feet or more, the impact (bird bones are hollow) cushioned by air sacs under their skin that also permit them, beaks full, to bob to the surface like a cork. Stashed in the sac beneath the beak

---

ing is reinforced by Carolina Beach Lake Park, a freshwater lake set aside and developed as a city recreation area and a reminder that this part of the town was once mainland.

Carolina Beach is one of the few oceanfront communities that still presents a definite city center. There is a lively urban density to the central area with its hovering awnings and narrow passageways. The many entertainment possibilities include a small amusement park, bingo by the boardwalk, and live-music nightspots. The boardwalk comes alive at night, especially in the annual Beach Music Festival, when shaggers shuffle into town in a dance-loving mass. The center of town strikes you much like a carnival midway; in the off-season, it is an empty stage. It needs the smell of coconut oil and the roar of the waves and the crowds to be alive.

Access

Carolina Beach has a regional access site along the oceanfront, behind city center, with 36 parking spaces one block south of Harper Avenue, restrooms, and a boardwalk with several dune crossover ramps. The access is open year-round. There is also a regional access south of downtown at the corner of Woody Hewett and Hamlet avenues.

Eight large parking lots with over 500 spaces are within walking distance of the police and fire departments and permit all-day parking for $1. Of the total, nearly 400 spaces are within two blocks of the oceanfront. A handout available at City Hall shows the locations, nearly all of which are off of Canal Street.

Only a few access locations on the northern extension have park-is dinner. The water is squeezed out, the fish swallowed whole, and the pelican is on its way. If still hungry, it dives again.

This is quite a show. Brown pelicans are large birds—their wings may span nearly 7 feet—and their flying habit is so low-key as to be hypnotic to watch. However, when the dinner bell rings, it's flight of a different order—a sudden climb, a precipitous plunge, and a satisfied departure from the table, resuming its languid demeanor. If you didn't see it happen, you might not expect such aggression.

The brown pelican's recovery has been unexpectedly rapid as well. The Atlantic population is no longer on the endangered species list. The banning of DDT was the key. DDT persisted in the food chain, increasing in concentration the higher up it went. When pelicans retained high levels by eating contaminated fish, it resulted in nesting failure by reducing the calcium in the eggshells. Today, the threat removed, the bird flourishes in North Carolina because of suitable nesting habitat.

In the early 1980s, brown pelicans began nesting on spoil islands, artificial islands created by piling sand dredged from shipping channels and inlets, in Pamlico Sound. The islands have to be fairly old to have sufficient vegetation to be a rookery since adults construct nests about one foot high made of grass. Usually they lay two or three eggs in spring, and the eggs hatch in a month. The parents feed the chicks regurgitated fish. Volunteers who help biologists band the new chicks report that the rookery islands are aromatic and that reminders of their participation can linger for nearly two wash cycles.

Happily, the recent pelican colonies seem permanent. A census in 1990 counted 2,912 nests in seven separate colonies in the state. It seems certain that once again this commanding flyer is a player in the food chain along the barrier islands and doing much better than just sliding by this time around.

ing spaces, and they fill quickly since they have minimal designated spaces. These neighborhood access points are at the east ends of the following streets that run perpendicular to the beachfront: Sea Oats Lane (2 spaces), Sand Fiddler Lane (4), Periwinkle Lane (4), Pelican Lane (2), and Driftwood Avenue (3). There is a neighborhood estuarine access at the north end of Florida Avenue.

Handicapped Access

The regional access site at the center of town is handicapped accessible, in addition to five dune crossovers off of the boardwalk.

The east end of the following streets have handicapped access locations: Sand Dollar Lane (7 spaces), Sand Piper Lane (5), Sea Gull Lane (3), Scallop Lane (4), and Spartanburg Avenue (2).

Information

For information, contact Carolina Beach Chamber of Commerce, 201 Lumberton Avenue, Carolina Beach, NC 28428, 910-458-8434.

Wilmington Beach

Wilmington Beach is an unincorporated community in New Hanover County's Federal Point Township, immediately south of Carolina Beach. As you drive south on US 421, you are barely aware that you have left the corporate limits of Carolina Beach. Tennessee Street, which runs perpendicular to the beachfront, and Center Pier across the street approximately mark the northern edge of the Wilmington Beach community.

Wilmington Beach and the southern portion of Carolina Beach blend together with the same low-key feeling. A few high-rise buildings sprout here, but they are far enough apart to allow a glimpse of the ocean. The streets perpendicular to the ocean are named for states, except for Ocean Boulevard near the middle of the community. The streets parallel to the oceanfront are named for game fish that local anglers here frequently catch—or dream of catching.

A steep dune profile once blocked the view of the water from US 421, but Hurricane Fran removed it, putting surviving oceanfront structures on notice. Wilmington Beach has a steeper profile than Carolina Beach, indicating steady erosion at this mainland portion of the coast. The ocean here seems more active, with more energy and bolder wave action.

Access

The New Hanover County Parks and Recreation Department is in charge of the beach access in Wilmington Beach. Parking and dune crossovers are available at the east end of every street perpendicular to the oceanfront. The spaces are not paved but are clearly designated by means of wheelstops.

At present the access areas with parking are as follows: Tennessee Avenue (20 spaces), North Carolina Avenue (10), Ocean Boulevard (20), South Carolina Avenue (20), Texas Avenue (20), and Alabama Avenue (15). There are also parking spaces available at the Center Pier.

Information

For information, contact New Hanover Parks and Recreation Department, 414 Chestnut Street, Room 101, County Administration Annex, Wilmington, NC 28401.

Kure Beach

The city limits of Kure Beach are $^6/_{10}$ mile south of Dow Avenue, the southernmost street in Hanby Beach, which is the local name for a small community adjacent to Wilmington Beach. To the east along this stretch of US 421, secured by fencing, is LaQue Test Center, a beachfront field of metal with everything from paint samples to automobile bumpers and hubcaps, exposed to the direct sun and sea spray of the marine environment to test for corrosive effects. While it looks like a *Far Side* junkyard, this facility is operated by a subsidiary of Inco of Toronto and was founded in 1935 by scientist Francis LaQue. Warning signs against trespassing are posted by the Department of Defense. At another location in Wrightsville Beach, the center tests materials submerged in salt water. Among items under scrutiny are metal braces of varying composition that have been used in the refurbishing of the Statue of Liberty.

After this surreal welcome, the town of Kure Beach, established in 1947, seems to sit back and watch vacationers cruise through on US 421, stopping only for a red light at Avenue K. Downtown Kure Beach

and the Kure Beach Fishing Pier, the oldest pier in the state, are here at Avenue K. In 1923 L. C. Kure constructed the pier then promptly rebuilt it the following year after it collapsed. The pier has been rebuilt several times since then because of hurricane damage, but it continues to serve the many anglers who want to fish amid a sense of history and perseverance. A wonderful grizzled group hangs out on the pier for hours in the worst of weather waiting for the king mackerel to strike. By listening in, you can learn a lot about fishing and a lot about what's wrong with the town, state, world, etc.

Hurricanes Bertha and Fran thrashed Kure Beach, claiming the pier and several houses. Undaunted, the owners of Kure Beach Fishing Pier promptly rebuilt even higher than before, keeping their "oldest pier" accolade intact. Obviously, in spite of its natural elevation, Kure Beach has not escaped catastrophic erosion. In forty years, its oceanfront has retreated two blocks.

Its stormy history contrasts with the day-to-day ambience of the community as a relaxed place with a low vacation pulse. There are a number of motels and rental accommodations available, and its location between Carolina Beach and Fort Fisher makes it a convenient base for more intensive side trips north or south. It seems as if you could go to bed early and sleep late here without much interference. If you don't need much more than proximity to the ocean to enjoy a beach getaway, then Kure Beach is the place for you.

The city limits of Kure Beach extend to the Cape Fear River through the maritime woodland west of Ninth Avenue and Dow Road, the edge of the developed resort. Most of this area will stay undeveloped because it is a required buffer zone between the town and Sunny Point Army Terminal, a military fuel/ammunition depot across the Cape Fear River. South of Kure Beach, west of the highway, the U.S. Air Force maintains an electronic surveillance station, part of a nationwide network to provide early detection and warning of attack.

Access

Beach access sites are not clearly designated but are plentiful. Parking is available at the oceanfront ends of Avenues E through N. The access points at Avenues L and M have steps leading to the beach, which has been fortified with a bulkhead in an effort to arrest erosion.

Information

For information, contact Carolina Beach Chamber of Commerce, 201 Lumberton Avenue, Carolina Beach, NC 28428, 910-458-8434.

Fort Fisher State Historic Site

Three miles south of Kure Beach, Fort Fisher greets you with a surprising sight on this segment of the coast—a live oak forest. The wandering limbs support foliage that is salt sculpted, sheared, and molded by sea winds into topiaries that seem to hover in a canopy over US 421. The visitors center parking lot is to the west, as are the remaining earthworks and reconstructions of the fort, but your eye is drawn east to the sea, visible through the coiling, rough bark of the live oaks.

Fort Fisher served as the Confederate counterpart to the brick Fort Macon. Southern forces constructed the earthwork fortification in 1861 to protect the Cape Fear River's valuable port of entry. The fort and its Confederate forces succumbed to a merciless assault here on January 15, 1865, in one of the largest land-sea battles ever fought on U.S. soil.

Should you walk to the oceanfront, you will see that the devastation suffered by the Confederate troops pales when compared to the assault on the site by the ocean. Nearly two-thirds of the original earthworks of the fort has fallen into the sea. The rubble-armored coast protecting the Daughters of the Confederacy monument gives evidence of the desperate struggle against the natural forces.

In response, the state amended its administrative rules on erosion-control structures to permit the construction of a revetment that will serve to protect the remnants of Fort Fisher. While this is an exception to the flat prohibition of such structures embraced by the state, the amendment is so narrowly worded as to preclude any other locations except for vital bridges.

Ironically, it may be a Natural Heritage Site nearby that is forcing the chiseling away of the landmark earthwork fort. Around a quarter of a mile north of the monument, you can see a rocky outcrop, the only natural outcrop of its kind on the North Carolina coast. The outcrop is made of coquina rock (a hard limestone composed of the fossilized shells of a small bivalve), which originated during the Pleistocene era, somewhere between 10,000 and 2 million years ago. The exposed rock disrupts the normal north-south flow of sand, thereby creating mild erosion to the north and very pronounced erosion to the south, toward the fort.

There is no admission fee to visit the fort and view an interpretive slide show and exhibits that depict the fort's history. The state also maintains an underwater archaeological research laboratory on the grounds that studies preservation and restoration techniques for artifacts recovered from underwater sites across the state.

Access

The fort is open April 1–October 1, 9 A.M. to 5 P.M. Monday–Saturday, 1 P.M. to 5 P.M. Sunday; November 1–March 31, 10 A.M. to 4 P.M. Tuesday–Saturday, 1 P.M. to 4 P.M. Sunday.

There are 75 parking spaces at the visitors center. From the visitors center, you may walk along the beach to reach the coquina outcrop.

Name That Wave

Have you noticed the different shapes of waves? There are four identifiable types, and each one not only looks different but also has a different effect on the beach.

Spilling waves are identified by bubbles and turbulent water spilling down over the front face of the wave. Such a wave seems to break continuously over a long distance, a result of a shallow, sloping bottom.

Collapsing waves are usually low and very close to the beach; the lower half of the wave plunges abruptly and the wave plays out up the beach. This type of wave usually occurs where there is a short, steep beach profile.

A surging wave peaks noticeably but then the bottom moves rapidly forward to push the water up the beach. The wave seems to pulse forward.

A plunging wave is a surfer's wave, where the crest curls over creating an air pocket and then plunges into a trough. Plunging waves are the most spectacular and in our mind's eye the true beach wave. They occur when a swell reaches a water depth 1.3 times the height of the wave. At this point, the wave has shortened and its height has increased, but there is insufficient water (because of the shallow depth) for the swell to continue. The water particles at the top curl over and crash from lack of support.

You can estimate the height of breakers by walking toward the ocean until you reach a spot where the top of the breaking waves is aligned with the horizon. The height measured between your eye level and the lowest point on the beach where the water recedes after a breaking wave is equal to the height of the breaker, measured from its peak to its trough.

Waves are not the same throughout the year because they alter shape as the shape of the bottom changes. For example, offshore sandbars created by the stormy winter cause early spring and summer waves to collapse early. The bars may vanish as summer progresses, allowing the waves to approach closer to shore before they break.

You can estimate the height of breakers by walking toward the ocean until you reach a spot where the top of the breaking waves is aligned with the horizon. The height measured between your eye level and the lowest point on the beach where the water recedes after a breaking wave is equal to the height of the breaker, measured from its peak to its trough.

Much of the outcrop is in front of a private development that has some parking spaces on the west side of US 421.

Handicapped Access

The visitors center is accessible to handicapped travelers, but the restrooms are not modified.

Information

For information, contact Fort Fisher State Historic Site, P.O. Box 68, Kure Beach, NC 28449, 910-458-5538.

Fort Fisher State Recreation Area

The Fort Fisher State Recreation Area includes the Fort Fisher State Historic Site. The remainder of this 287-acre preserve provides access to more than 4 miles of beautiful and comparatively unused beach immediately south of the fort. Approximately $\frac{1}{10}$ mile from the fort on SR 1713, there is a major regional access facility with nearly 200 parking spaces, restrooms, showers, refreshments, and a dune crossover that leads first to a sun shelter/ gazebo and then to a splendid beach. During the summer months, the beach has lifeguards from 10 A.M. to 6 P.M. daily. There is excellent surf fishing here and a vehicular dune crossover ramp, frequently

	Fee	Parking	Restrooms	Lifeguard	Camping	Showers	Beach Access	Hiking	Trail	Handicapped	Boating	ORV Access	Fishing	Programs	Historic	Sand Beach	Dunes	Upland	Wetland
Fort Fisher State Historic Site		•	•				•	•	•	•			•	•	•	•	•	•	
Fort Fisher State Recreation Area		•	•	•		•	•	•	•	•		•	•			•	•	•	•
North Carolina Aquarium, Fort Fisher		•	•				•	•	•	•			•	•	•	•	•	•	•
Federal Point		•					•	•			•	•		•	•	•	•		•
Zeke's Island Research Reserve							•	•	•				•	•	•	•			•
Fort Fisher Ferry	•	•	•	•															•

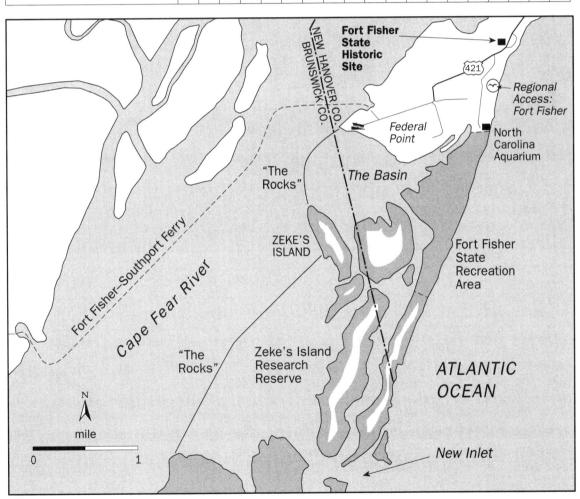

Map 26. Fort Fisher to Zeke's Island

A Civil War reenactment at Fort Fisher State Historic Site. (Courtesy of N.C. Travel and Tourism Division)

used by surf fishermen to travel south to the sandy barrier spit of the Zeke's Island preserve, which is the northern headland of New Inlet.

South of the access area, the beachfront becomes a barrier island (technically a barrier spit) backed by the waters of the Zeke's Island preserve. The mainland peninsula, known as Federal Point, arcs west. US 421 follows the general bowing of the mainland to the terminus of the highway at the Fort Fisher/Southport ferry dock and the North Carolina Wildlife Re-

sources Commission boat ramp at "the Basin" of Zeke's Island preserve.

Since Hurricane Fran in 1996, Fort Fisher Recreation Area has been recast as a high-visibility laboratory for the cycle of forces affecting a barrier island. The storm leveled the protective dune lines, changing the appearance of the access area. It also destroyed all existing ramps used by off-road vehicles. While the dunes began rebuilding shortly after the storm, the reconfiguration of the beach has modified

the appearance of the recreation area and altered vehicle access locations.

Access

Park personnel from Carolina Beach State Park staff the contact station seasonally and maintain the regional access location. The entrance is just north of the aquarium. The access area opens at 8 A.M. and closes November–February at 6 P.M.; March and October at 7 P.M.; April, May, and September at 8 P.M.; and June–August at 9 P.M.

Handicapped Access

This access area is designed to be accessible for handicapped travelers.

Information

For information, contact Carolina Beach State Park, P.O. Box 475, Carolina Beach, NC 28428, 910-458-8206.

North Carolina Aquarium, Fort Fisher

Could you stand eye-to-eye with a shark and not blink? Could you pick a safe shark from a dangerous one? The North Carolina Aquarium allows you the opportunity to pick the wrong shark in a safe place. The 20,000-gallon shark tank that exhibits these sleek, machine-eyed predators and additional tanks with other large game fishes are among the educational highlights at the aquarium.

The aquarium is carefully tucked into the upland region of the Fort Fisher Recreational Area. As do its counterparts in Manteo and Pine Knoll Shores, the aquarium explores the mysteries and wonders of the ocean. Exhibits concentrate on the marine and terrestrial life of the southern coast of North Carolina. Multiple programs are offered throughout the year, and the 200-seat auditorium stays busy with daily lectures and films.

The Hermit Trail leads to an abandoned bunker where a well-known hermit lived for a number of years. Excursions vary widely and include bird-watching in the salt marsh and a look at the other side of the aquariums. Some of the more popular programs require advance reservations.

Access

The center is open 9 A.M. to 5 P.M. Monday–Friday; 10 A.M. to 5 P.M. Saturday; and 1 P.M. to 5 P.M. Sunday.

Handicapped Access

The aquarium is fully accessible to handicapped travelers, including the restrooms. A wheelchair is available at the aquarium. Some of the exterior pathways are accessible to persons using wheelchairs.

Information

For information, contact North Carolina Aquarium, Fort Fisher, P.O. Box 130, Kure Beach, NC 28449, 910-458-8257. Ask for the printed calendar of programs.

Federal Point

There is no "point" at Federal Point anymore. The name has lost its precision since erosion, construction, and the many different agencies owning land here not only altered the terrain but renamed and resurveyed portions of it as well.

It is generally conceded that Federal Point is the terminus for US 421, but it is not specified whether the point is at the Fort Fisher/Southport ferry dock, at the turnaround at the nearby boat ramp, or perhaps within some of the wild acreage south of the road and bordered by the waters of "the Basin" in Zeke's Island preserve. It does seem fairly clear that the barrier spit of Fort Fisher Recreation Area is not included as a part of Federal Point. It seems that Federal Point historically was the most southeastern part of the mainland, which, because of Snows Cut, is now an island.

Access

It's accessible if you can find it. Park at the boat ramp past the Fort Fisher ferry dock or at the ferry dock. At this point, Federal Point is all around you.

Zeke's Island National Estuarine Research Reserve

The northern border of Zeke's Island National Estuarine Research Reserve begins at the traffic turnaround or the boat ramp at the end of US 421. Looking southwest from the ramp at low tide, you will see a breakwater known as "the Rocks" at the westernmost boundary of the preserve. The large bay of water inside the rocks is called "the Basin." If you follow the breakwater, you will reach a small, sandy spit, high enough to support some shrubby growth, which is Zeke's Island. Be

North Carolina Aquarium, Fort Fisher. (Courtesy of N.C. Travel and Tourism Division)

sure to set out for the island only at ebbing tide; "the Rocks" are not passable at high tide. Also, wear old clothes, carry water and bug spray, and walk very carefully—the wet, algae-covered rocks are treacherously slippery.

Zeke's Island is probably the most accessible component of the preserve system. It is approximately 1,165 acres of islands, marsh, tidal flats, shallow estuarine waters, and a barrier spit. The varied environment features extensive tidal flats that are extremely important to both the loggerhead turtle and many shorebird species. Because of its relative isolation, bird life is abundant in the tidal flats, and many species of herons, along with brown pelicans, are regulars. It is an extensive and important preserve, not only because of its wealth of habitat features but also because it is so close to other proven habitats such as Ferry Slip Island and Battery Island, which are important rookeries.

Zeke's Island supported a gun emplacement during the Civil War. "The Rocks," extending from the mainland near the Fort Fisher/Southport ferry dock to Zeke's Island and then south to just north of Smith Island, comprise a breakwater or jetty constructed by the Army Corps of Engineers between 1875 and 1881. Designed to reduce shoaling in the Cape Fear River from the old New Inlet, which was just south of the present North Carolina Aquarium connecting the Cape Fear River and the Atlantic, and Corncake Inlet, the jetty also

effectively closed New Inlet and resulted in the slow silting of the Basin. Zeke's Island grew following the construction of the jetty and became a fishing center and the site of a turpentine factory. The great hurricane of 1899 destroyed the wharf and fishing operations.

The depth of water in the basin has grown increasingly shallow during this century. The migration of New Inlet since the construction of the jetty left a growing spit of sand south of Federal Point. The preserve also includes North Island, once a barrier island south of New Inlet now parallel to the spit, and No Name Island, which has also formed as sand has slowly accreted in the preserve. This changing ecology is one of the great assets of the site, in addition to its pristine state.

Ironically, the jetty has proven to be an ecological bonus, creating a rocky shore that would not otherwise be found in these waters. Indeed, if you don't mind hopping on rocks, you can enjoy a lengthy excursion alongside the Cape Fear River.

Access

US 421 provides access to the major departure points for Zeke's Island. The highway ends at the North Carolina Department of Transportation parking for the Fort Fisher/Southport ferry. The North Carolina Wildlife Resources Commission maintains a boat ramp at the northern shore of the Basin near the ferry dock. Zeke's Island may be reached by walking "the Rocks" or by boat.

From the regional access at Fort

Fisher State Recreation Area, you may walk or drive to the barrier spit portion of the preserve and, if intrepid, venture south to New Inlet in its present location nearly 3.5 miles south of the aquarium.

Information

For information, contact North Carolina National Estuarine Research Reserve, 7205 Wrightsville Avenue, Wilmington, NC 28403, 910-256-3721, or Division of Coastal Management, P.O. Box 27687, Raleigh, NC 27611, 919-733-2293.

Fort Fisher Toll Ferry

The Fort Fisher/Southport toll ferry at the end of US 421 provides one of those marvelous interludes in the routine of a trip that only ferry rides seem capable of providing. But don't expect this one to be a quick hop in either direction for a night out on the other side of the river. The last departures are 6 P.M. from Southport and 6:50 P.M. from Fort Fisher. This is a daytime connector that runs every 50 minutes between April 1 and October 31 and every 1 hour and 40 minutes the remainder of the year. You may walk around while the ferry is crossing. The passage will be more enjoyable and informative with a bird guidebook, a bag of soda crackers for the gulls, and binoculars.

The ferry replaces about 40 miles of driving. It is definitely the rapid transit of north/south travel if you choose to hug the beachfront. The route crosses the Cape Fear River,

North Carolina's major river channel, and the ferry sometimes shares the channel with impressive freighters and other open-ocean vessels entering or leaving the port of Wilmington. The passage takes about 30 minutes and offers excellent views of Zeke's Island, Bald Head Island, and Oak Island. Like a mariner, you can mark the transit with two familiar landmarks, Old Baldy, the lighthouse on Bald Head Island, and the newer Oak Island light that replaced it. Between and beyond them is the open ocean and the hazardous navigation of Frying Pan Shoals.

The ferry also passes Bird Island. The crew member who told me I would "know it" when we got there wasn't being flip. The locally known sandbar has enough feathers to give it lift. It is covered in gulls and makes for animated viewing when great numbers of gulls ascend obligingly to follow the ferry for aerial handouts.

One particularly intriguing site on the west bank of the Cape Fear is the abandoned brick cone of Price's Creek Lighthouse, visible slightly downriver from the large commercial docks of Pfizer Chemical. Shortly after passing the Price's

Creek Lighthouse, which was once used to help navigate the channel to Wilmington, the ferry docks in a sheltered slip just a few miles north of Southport. You've ridden a ferry, crossed a river, and landed in Brunswick County, the southeasternmost county in the state.

Information

To contact the ferry docks, call 910-457-6942 (Southport) or 910-458-3329 (Fort Fisher).

Intracoastal Interstate

Somewhere along your travels to the beaches of North Carolina, you will cross the Atlantic Intracoastal Waterway. There's no way to avoid it and surprisingly little reason to note it since your crossing will likely be over one of the many modern high-rise bridges serving the barrier islands from the mainland.

Yet this remarkable ditch is one of the more ambitious and successful civil-engineering projects ever conducted by the U.S. government. It provides a safe, protected waterway route for light boats and barges not suited for the open ocean. If you're a boater and like lengthy, varied cruises, the Intracoastal Waterway, particularly in North Carolina, must be a magical trip. If you're going to the beach, however, it's a hurdle.

The waterway is an old idea. George Washington surveyed a canal route through the Dismal Swamp in the mid-1750s, and a completed canal in 1803 led to boom-town years for Elizabeth City. Other early barge/canal projects connected the Neuse and Newport rivers north of Beaufort in the early nineteenth century, to shorten the commercial route between New Bern and Beaufort.

The German U-boat attacks during World War I brought the necessity of a sheltered sea-lane home, and the project was pressed to completion by 1936. The construction had an immediate impact. In some locations,

such as present-day Oak Island, the waterway actually impeded access to the coast, in effect making an island. It also lopped off the tip of the mainland south of Wilmington at Snows Cut, linking Myrtle Grove Sound and the Cape Fear River. This technically made an island, Pleasure Island, of the previous mainland resorts of Carolina Beach, Wilmington Beach, Kure Beach, and Fort Fisher.

The waterway reaches from Massachusetts to Brownsville, Texas, using both natural waterways and artificial canals to provide a continuous navigable passage around 3,000 miles long. Approximately 330 miles of that route are in North Carolina, using the same combination of open natural waters and canals. Along the northern two-thirds of the coast, from the Virginia line to Morehead City, the route is considerably inland from the barrier beaches. From Morehead City south, however, the Intracoastal Waterway routes directly landward of the islands, and it is along this length of coast that you are most likely to be aware of crossing it.

In the last two decades, most of the swing bridges serving the islands have been replaced with faster four-lane crossings intended as a part of designated hurricane evacuation routes (since these routes are the only way off the islands), and crossing the waterway is uneventful. But as few as fifteen years ago, there

were memorable waits—agonizing crossings as, on the last stretch of the journey to the beach, you waited in line as the bridges lifted to permit a pleasure craft to continue its journey uninterrupted.

At most crossings, the waterway is less than 90 feet wide, but it could become a very effective moat, barring admittance to the coast. Some crossings became legendary, if not notorious. At Coinjock in Currituck County, it seemed the entire eastern seaboard backed up on the north side of the waterway, waiting for the bridge to drop back in place and the crossing warning arms to lift on holiday weekends. When the bridge opened, it was like waving the green flag at a NASCAR race, and it sent fuming tourists roaring to the beach. In the early 1980s, a barge rammed the bridge, jamming it, causing traffic of all kinds to grind to a halt until repairs were made.

Perhaps the most intractable bottleneck was between Morehead City and Atlantic Beach. In the summer, the waterway traffic was nearly as heavy as the traffic on the causeway to Bogue Banks, and the bridge flipped open and shut like it was part of a pinball machine. Traffic would back up US 70 west to the Morehead City limits on weekends. More than one dinner reservation fell victim to a recreational sailor asserting his right to continue on the high seas.

Waiting to cross Bogue Sound had the same inevitability as April 15 and was thought about in like fashion.

You can still snag a drawbridge today on busy routes. The waterway routes the length of the Alligator River in Dare and Tyrrell counties, and the long bridge over the river on US 64 still must lift for boating traffic, which, thankfully, is comparatively light there. Perhaps the most famous bridge remaining is the narrow Pontoon Bridge serving Sunset Beach. Although proclaimed a hazard in the event of hurricane evacuation, the bridge is a cause célèbre with residents and visitors. It literally and figuratively cuts the tie with the mainland and makes Sunset Beach slightly isolated, inconvenient, and old-timey.

This, of course, is a landlubber's point of view. If you look at the waterway through the eyes of a boater it's a different experience indeed. In North Carolina, it provides many of the public boating access sites serving the sounds and open ocean. Many of the North Carolina Wildlife Resources Commission boat ramps are located along its length, usually within easy access to coastal highways. Communities on the waterway close to inlets frequently have private marinas that take advantage of the access of the waterway to offer bustling charter-boat fishing and commercial fishing. Calabash, for example, is a fishing community on Calabash Creek with access to Little River Inlet by means of the waterway. Throughout its length, the waterway offers excellent crabbing from piers or banks. Fishing can be good as well, depending on where you are along the waterway's course.

Towns along the waterway, such as Belhaven, Beaufort, and Southport, have their own tourist traffic that comes to call by boat. These places pick up a decided cosmopolitan air during the fall and spring migrations of yachts traveling between northern and southern coastal ports.

It's hard to think of the Intracoastal Waterway as a "working road," but that is its primary purpose. You may cross it and never think a thing about it since to vacation-bound cars it is a 100-foot or so hurdle. To a barge loaded with containers, it's a 3,000-mile-long scenic highway.

Brunswick County

North Carolina's coast makes another abrupt geographical adjustment at the Smith Island Complex, a portion of which is known as Bald Head Island. This wooded salient is the most eastern of the Brunswick County islands, and west of it the once bypassed barrier beaches arc on a true western compass alignment. Visitors to the five islands—Smith Island, Oak Island, Holden Beach, Ocean Isle Beach, and Sunset Beach—can enjoy a full day's tanning without moving their blankets since these barriers face nearly due south. The early sun slants along the beach from the east end of the islands and settles beneath the horizon at the opposite end at day's end.

There are more than 50 miles of shoreline in Brunswick County and only slightly more than 200 available motel and hotel rooms. Brunswick County and its five island havens are among the quietest resort areas in the state, in spite of being sandwiched between the boisterous locales of Pleasure Island to the north and nearby North Myrtle Beach, South Carolina. The beaches have great family appeal because the local officials have worked hard to preserve the ecology of the beach and dunes. Their efforts to protect the elements of solitude and open sands have attracted permanent residents as well as visitors to the islands.

Community identification and association divide according to the county's geography. Southport and Oak Island, with the three communities of Caswell Beach, Yaupon Beach, and Long Beach, work closely together, supporting a mutual chamber of commerce. Bald Head Island, even though it is private, shares some resources with these two communities since Indigo Plantation in Southport is the ferry dock for transport to Bald Head.

The communities of Holden Beach, Ocean Isle Beach, Shallotte, Sunset Beach, and Calabash are far enough from the Brunswick County center and have sufficiently strong recreational appeal to foster a separate identity as the South Brunswick islands. Shallotte and Calabash participate in the marketing efforts of the South Brunswick Islands Chamber of Commerce, headquartered in Shallotte. Although this may seem confusing, the soundness of this division is quite apparent from an automobile—you do not traverse easily or quickly from Shallotte and points south to either Southport or Oak Island.

The beaches of Brunswick County are served by two major routes, the toll ferry crossing the Cape Fear River between Fort Fisher and Southport or US 17 from either Wilmington or the South Carolina/North Carolina border. US 17 runs sufficiently inland on its route from Wilmington to North Myrtle Beach to make visiting the barrier beaches a side trip—you must specifically decide to go to the islands. All roads leading directly to the beaches are North Carolina secondary roads. When you arrive, in most instances, you will find houses, but you won't find crowds.

The three most western (and southern) islands—Holden Beach, Ocean Isle Beach, and Sunset Beach—exist in their own island worlds, apart from the mainland and each other. It's almost as if they were in a different era, some thirty years ago. These beaches are developed, but the tempo of life, the mood of the islands, is more in step with earlier, less frenetic times. Oak Island is relatively more animated than its sister isles. Oak Island's three communities are villagelike in feeling, a characteristic of the entire county, which specializes in quiet ocean getaways and not high-energy entertainment.

Every community in the county with some sort of open water or beach access has the same type of sleepy charm. Southport, the oldest established community in the county and perhaps the largest, retains a salty, weather-beaten patina. NC 133, which links Wilmington and Southport, is a lazy, winding passage. It is the aged and venerable shore route and passes by Orton Plantation and Gardens and Brunswick Town State Historic Site. Orton Plantation is an eighteenth-century rice plantation well known for its extensive gardens. The gardens are at the peak of seasonal show in mid-spring, when an almost unsurpassed azalea planting erupts in bloom. Lesser-known Brunswick Town State Historic Site is the historical heart of Brunswick County. In 1725, the town was laid out as one of the new colony's premier cities. By 1760, more than 250 citizens and 60 structures formed the nucleus of the town, a wealthy community by the standards of the time. The British army razed it in 1776 as punishment for the residents' resistance to British rule. Brunswick Town was never resettled, and slowly the woodlands have reclaimed it. Now visitors can walk the sand beds of streets long gone, view the foundations of the houses overlooking the Cape Fear River, and learn the story of the community in a visitors center that houses archaeological relics of the site.

On the wild side, Brunswick County is something of a botanical wonderland, possibly hosting more species of restricted distribution than any other county in the state. The diversity of habitats covers the range from the Smith Island Complex, with extensive maritime forests, to the sinkhole ponds on the Sunny Point Terminal fuel and ammunition depot. The largest breeding colony of egrets, herons, and ibises in the state is on Battery Island, off of Southport, and the marshes of Brunswick host a goodly portion of the state's limited alligator population. Green Swamp, a 15,700-acre Nature Conservancy property, features one of the best, and last, longleaf pine savannas in the state. Within its borders northeast of Shallotte and east of NC 133 are fourteen species of insectivorous plants.

Access

The municipalities on the islands provide beach access locations, which are listed after the separate descriptions that follow.

Orton Plantation is off of NC 133 south of Wilmington. It is open daily 8 A.M. to 6 P.M. This is a private residence but the gardens and grounds are open to the public. There is an admission fee. For information, call 910-371-6851.

Brunswick Town State Historic Site is off of NC 133, south of Orton Plantation. Hours are April 1– October 31, 9 A.M. to 5 P.M. Monday–Saturday, 1 P.M. to 5 P.M. Sunday; November 1–March 31, 10 A.M. to 4 P.M. Tuesday–Saturday, 1 P.M. to 4 P.M. Sunday. For information, call 910-371-6613.

Handicapped Access

Orton Plantation is handicapped accessible, but some of the paths are gravel or packed sand and are not easily negotiable by handicapped travelers.

The auditorium in the museum at Brunswick Town State Historic Site is handicapped accessible; the grounds have paved paths near the ruins of St. Philips Anglican Church.

Information

For information about the Southport/Oak Island attractions, contact Southport/Oak Island Welcome Center, 4841 Long Beach Road Southeast, Southport, NC 28461, 910-457-6964 or 1-800-457-6964. Computer users may peek at the website, http://www.southport.net.

For information about the South

Brunswick islands of Holden Beach, Ocean Isle Beach, and Sunset Beach, contact South Brunswick Islands Chamber of Commerce, P.O. Box 1380, Shallotte, NC 28549, 910-754-6644.

Southport

Since 1748, when soldiers established Fort Johnston, folks have lived by the Cape Fear River in what is present-day Southport. From its sheltered basin, they sailed the Cape Fear River channel and followed the river to open water. It is a waterfront town in the weathered, salt-slapped, sun-bleached way of Knotts Island, Harkers Island, Ocracoke, and Swansboro.

All the "quaint little fishing village" clichés apply. Two-story, classically proportioned wooden houses line live oak–shaded streets. Moore Street, the road into town from the Fort Fisher/Southport ferry dock, passes by a wondrously serene town cemetery where live oaks shade the headstones. Southport sings of screened porches and cicadas, adapted in this electronic era with ceiling fans and foghorns. If the streets weren't paved, you could imagine a driving rain pelting the sandy soil, puddling and melting away. You smell river and marsh and fish, which are a part of the place. If there is something about Southport that seems ideal, romantic, and Tom Sawyeresque, read *The Old Man and the Boy* by Robert Ruark. This thoroughly charming book draws heavily on the author's boyhood ex-

periences with his grandfather, J. B. Ruark, a Southport resident.

Southport perches high on the mainland, a safe 26 feet above sea level. Bay Street follows the riverfront, along the natural bench or shoulder that is below the higher elevations of town center, where Moore Street (NC 211) and Howe Street intersect. Bay Street is the heart of the sea-based economy of Southport, where marinas, seafood markets, and restaurants line the riverfront. The pilot service that provides navigation assistance for the Cape Fear River channel is headquartered here. The pert little pilot boats that ferry the pilots to the oceangoing vessels requiring their assistance are docked at East Bay Street.

Looking north from Bay Street, you'll notice a large white Georgian building dominating an expanse of lawn. This is the officers' quarters, and the only remaining building, of Fort Johnston, established in 1748 as a protection against privateering from French and Spanish vessels. The original fortification also provided protection for the swelling numbers of settlers at Smithville, as it was called until 1899, honoring General Benjamin Smith. Whigs burned the original fort in 1775, chasing out royal governor Josiah Martin who fled by British vessel. The federal government rebuilt the fort in 1794–1809, and the town incorporated in 1805. As you might suspect, the fort was seized by Confederate forces in 1861. The strategic importance of the fortification and the town lay in their proximity

	Fee	Parking	Restrooms	Lifeguard	Camping	Showers	Beach Access	Hiking	Trail	Handicapped	Boating	ORV Access	Fishing	Programs	Historic	Sand Beach	Dunes	Upland	Wetland
Brunswick County		•	•				•			•	•		•		•	•	•	•	•
Southport		•									•		•		•			•	
Bald Head Island (private)	•	•	•				•								•	•	•	•	•
Bald Head Island State Natural Area							•	•			•		•			•	•	•	•

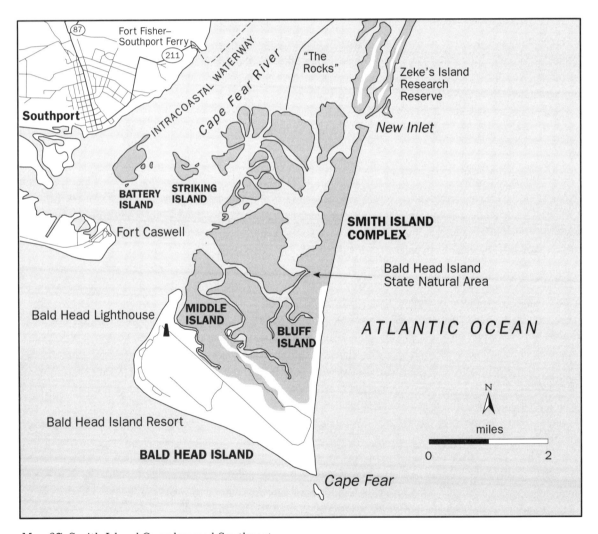

Map 27. Smith Island Complex and Southport

Trawlers docked at Southport. (Courtesy of N.C. Travel and Tourism Division)

to the river channel. Fort Caswell on Oak Island, Fort Fisher across the river, Fort Johnston, and other smaller gun emplacements kept the port of Wilmington open by creating a formidable gauntlet for Union forces entering the Cape Fear River.

The Whig forces that gave Josiah Martin a fiery send-off began a revolutionary tradition here. The officers' quarters building is a centerpiece for the official North Carolina Fourth of July celebration, which attracts more than 40,000 visitors to Southport each year.

Visit Southport another time of year and you may very well wonder where such numbers of guests could congregate. The antique and curio stores of the town center invite exploration in less pressing throngs. Southport is a bed-and-breakfast town, and that's the pace that suits it best.

Access

There is a wonderful public pier extending from Front Street into the Cape Fear River. There are two gazebos on the pier and, weather permitting, a lot of youthful fishermen. The pier is easily manageable by wheelchair, as is the town and many of the stores, although there are no public restrooms for handicapped travelers.

Information

For information about the Southport/Oak Island attractions, contact Southport/Oak Island Welcome Center, 4841 Long Beach Road Southeast, Southport, NC 28461, 910-457-6964 or 1-800-457-6964. Computer users may peek at the website, http://www.southport.net.

Smith Island Complex

The southeastern promontory of what is today known as Bald Head Island put the fear in sailors that led to the naming of the Cape Fear River. Giovanni da Verrazano discovered it in 1524, and it appeared on a 1590 map as "Promontorium tremendum," which has a much nicer ring to it than the official name Smith Island Complex, of which Bald Head Island is part.

Bald Head is as far south in the state as you can go and close enough to the coast-hugging flow of the Gulf Stream to be nearly a world unto itself. On a coast that is extraordinary for its astonishing number and variety of islands, Bald Head is itself extraordinary. It is accessible only by the ferry that runs round-trip from Indigo Plantation in Southport or by private boat.

It is certainly one of a kind within the state for its inventory of natural richness, and it may rival some of the islands of South Carolina and Georgia for the private development that simultaneously protects and makes available the island experience. It has been as prominent in the maritime history of the state as it is now in the evolution of a constructive blend of conservation and development.

The oldest state maps note the name of the island as Smith Island for Landgrave Thomas Smith, who acquired it in 1690. By the time the state wished to construct a lighthouse here to serve the Cape Fear River, Benjamin Smith (the name-sake of Smithville, later Southport, and perhaps an heir of Thomas) grazed sheep and cattle here. The civic-minded Smith offered 10 acres to the state as a site for the lighthouse in 1789, provided there were suitable protections for his chattel. By 1794, the grazing privileges had been protected by the General Assembly, and the light was completed and already deemed as inadequate. By 1817, another lighthouse, the present-day "Old Baldy," had been constructed and continued to illuminate the Cape Fear River entrance until it was decommissioned in 1903 for a taller lighthouse at the eastern end of the island. Old Baldy is the oldest standing lighthouse in the state, predating the Ocracoke light by six years. The name Bald Head originated from mariners' observations of the white sandy prominences at the southwest corner, adjacent to the oldest channel of the Cape Fear River and hence visible from the sea.

Although the lighthouse is the most storied feature, the remainder of the island is the featured story. There are more than 12,000 acres in the complex of marsh, tidal creeks, relic dune ridge lines, maritime forests, and beachfront within the accepted boundaries of Smith Island, which extend north from Cape Fear to Corncake Inlet, separating Smith Island from the barrier spit of Zeke's Island North Carolina National Estuarine Research Reserve in New Hanover County. Smith Island is the most northern habitat for the semitropical vegetation that characterizes the Sea Islands of South Carolina and Georgia. The tidal waters and salt marsh north of the semitropical maritime forests are immense, and a diverse population of resident and migratory wildlife populates the many habitats, including alligators. Nearly all of the acreage except for the 2,000 acres developed as part of the Bald Head Island Resort is protected by the state or under the auspices of the Nature Conservancy.

In the early 1970s there was much controversy over the proposal to develop Bald Head Island. It nevertheless has become a self-sustaining resort, with the natural features of the island—the marsh and mix of forests—a focal element of the resort experience. The island offers single-family homes, condominiums, a community center, a golf course, swimming pools, and a small store. The limited numbers of rental rooms available, the care taken to preserve the island's natural features, and the restriction of access to only boats make the island exclusive but not excluding. You are as welcome as a day guest as you would be if you rented a villa or private home for an overnight or weekend stay.

The 14 miles of beach attract visitors from both the land and the sea. The island has long been a prime nesting location for pelagic turtles, primarily the loggerhead turtle. The three-month summer nesting season, from June through August, is carefully monitored by federal and state naturalists. Helping these different groups live together has been a primary function of the Bald Head Conservancy, a private, nonprofit organization, which, in conjunction with the University of North Carolina at Wilmington, provides a full-time naturalist on the island who is responsible for assisting with the annual turtle watch. The Conservancy is one of the few private organizations authorized to participate in the federal tagging program for pelagic turtles. The naturalists note the location and type of nest, count the number of eggs, and place protective screening over the nest to thwart predators such as raccoons. If possible, they tag the mother turtle. The hatchlings emerge in approximately sixty days from nesting, enter the open ocean, and begin their lives at sea. In 1990, 187 nests were recorded on the island, 20 of which were lost to predation. Two nests were green turtle nests, a much rarer species than the more well-known loggerhead.

Access

Although Bald Head is promoted as a private resort, anyone can rent a villa or cottage on the island and you may visit the island for a day-trip. You may reach the island and the lighthouse by ferry from Southport at the Indigo Plantation. The fee for the ferry crossing is around $14 round-trip. Ferry departures are on the hour year-round, 8 A.M.–6 P.M.

Handicapped Access

The island is not designed to accommodate mobility-impaired travelers,

but it is negotiable with assistance. Contact the resort to see about access assistance and available rentals on Bald Head that may be suitable for handicapped visitors.

Information

For information on visiting or vacationing, contact Bald Head Island Information Center, 5079 Southport-Supply Road, Southport, NC 28461, 1-800-234-1666.

Bald Head Island State Natural Area

The North Carolina Division of Parks and Recreation manages a more than 10,000-acre state natural area of labyrinthine tidal creeks, marsh, bays, and uplands between Bald Head Island and Fort Fisher. The land was deeded to the Nature Conservancy in the 1970s by several owners, and the conservancy in turn gave it to North Carolina. The tract includes Bluff Island, one of three upland ridges (the other two are Middle Island and Bald Head Island) that, along with marshes, comprise the Smith Island Complex.

In 1991, North Carolina agreed to purchase 435 acres of uplands in Bald Head Island adjacent to the resort for $5.3 million. A 75 percent federal grant, plus a $1 million donation by the owner, Bald Head Limited, has reduced North Carolina's cash outlay to $325,000 over two years. Of the purchase, 174 of the evergreen oak/cabbage pal-

metto forest acres became a part of the North Carolina Coastal Reserve.

Access

Access is by boat or Bald Head Island Ferry. The North Carolina Wildlife Resources Commission boat ramp at Federal Point provides direct free access. Private marinas in Southport offer launching for a fee.

Information

For information, contact Coastal Reserve Coordinator, 7205 Wrightsville Avenue, Wilmington, NC 28403, 910-256-3721, or Carolina Beach State Park, P.O. Box 475, Carolina Beach, NC 28428, 910-428-8206.

Oak Island

Oak Island, the first of the Brunswick County barrier islands that you reach driving south from Wilmington or Southport, incorporates the three communities of Caswell Beach, Yaupon Beach, and Long Beach along its 13-mile beachfront. At the east end, on the Cape Fear River, are the North Carolina Baptist Assembly Grounds, which include the remains of Fort Caswell. Also at this end is a U.S. Coast Guard Station and the Oak Island Lighthouse, the most recently constructed light to aid navigation in the Cape Fear River. The Oak Island light is plainly visible from Southport, as are some of the buildings at the Baptist Assembly Grounds, but

Lighthouses

For more than two centuries, a network of lighthouses has guided mariners navigating the treacherous offshore waters of North Carolina's coast. These are true landmarks, structures visible and identifiable by day from their color or pattern and by night from their characteristic signal. Even in the era of electronic navigation, North Carolina's lighthouses are working reminders of the state's maritime history.

At present, six lighthouses serve the coast, marking, north to south, Currituck Banks, Oregon Inlet, Cape Hatteras, Ocracoke Inlet, Cape Lookout, and the Cape Fear River.

The first great light is the red-brick tower at Corolla, known as the Currituck Beach light. Once isolated because no road went to Corolla, the 150-foot-tall tower is one light where you may climb to the focal-plane catwalk. The tower itself is leased to a private conservation agency that uses the proceeds from a small admission fee to fund restoration of the lightkeeper's quarters and the grounds.

South of the Currituck light is the horizontally striped frustum of Bodie Island Lighthouse. Its beacon shines from 150 feet above the sandy base, signaling the entrance to Oregon Inlet, one of the more troubled inlets on the coast. The restored lightkeeper's quarters now serve as a visitors center for Cape Hatteras National Seashore.

The Cape Hatteras Lighthouse, at 208 feet tall, may be the tallest brick lighthouse in the world and is a cause célèbre among lighthouse aficionados. Built in 1873, the black-and-white barber-pole-striped light replaced an 1802 tower. The once-visible remnants of that tower, slightly southeast of the present lighthouse, were destroyed by a 1980 storm. The light still operates, maintained by the Coast Guard, but the tower belongs to the National Park Service.

There are plans to move the lighthouse inland. After emotional debate and multiple public meetings, it has been decided that moving the lighthouse is the only way to protect it from erosion. Although it was 1,500 feet from the ocean when it was

the Southport vantage embraces only the eastern part of Oak Island and views it across a great swatch of salt marsh at that.

NC 133 is the only road to the island, heading south from its intersection with NC 211 approximately 2.5 miles west of Southport. On the west side of NC 133, just south of the junction, is a welcome center maintained by the Southport/Oak Island Chamber of Commerce. This is an excellent source of information about the communities on the island and surrounding attractions as well.

NC 133, also known as Beach Road, crosses the Intracoastal Waterway over a high-rise bridge. Below the bridge on the mainland are the rusting ruins of a menhaden-processing plant, whose pungent odor used to signal the arrival to Oak Island. The bridge provides an elevated glimpse of the island. You see mostly green, with the peaks of some roofs jutting through the treetops in the distance. The bridge ends in a tree-covered section of the community of Yaupon Beach.

The road then changes to Caswell Beach Drive and curves east toward the residential community of Caswell Beach and the Baptist Assembly Grounds beyond. Yaupon Drive, the main road through Yaupon Beach, heads west and becomes Oak Island Road at the city limits of Long Beach.

Access

The individual communities maintain the access locations on the island. Specific sites are noted following the descriptions of the communities below. Generally speaking, access is better the further west you drive; the eastern communities placed in service, the ocean is now little more than 300 feet from its base. The lightkeeper's quarters serve as a visitors center.

The Ocracoke Lighthouse, dating from 1823, is the oldest continually operating lighthouse in the state. The squat, stuccoed tower is 65 feet tall, and the beacon is visible 12 miles out to sea. At one time, it served the busiest inlet, Ocracoke, and port, Portsmouth, in the state.

The Cape Lookout Lighthouse, south of Ocracoke on South Core Banks in Cape Lookout National Seashore, guards the entrance to Morehead City, warning mariners of the treacherous waters to the southeast known as Cape Lookout Shoals. Placed into service in 1859, this lighthouse became the model for the other majestic beacons along the coast. Its diamond-patterned black-and-white markings are incorrectly thought to be a mistake. Although its pattern seems to be more suited to Cape Hatteras because of its offshore Diamond Shoals, the lighthouse board did specify that the Cape Lookout Lighthouse be "checkered" in 1873.

The oldest lighthouse standing in the state is the Bald Head light on Smith Island, constructed in 1795. Although it is no longer illuminated, the tower once signaled the entrance to the Cape Fear River, North Carolina's only natural deep-water channel, ominously guarded by the shifting sands of an offshore sandbar known as Frying Pan Shoals.

Shortly after construction, the Bald Head light became obsolete because of a shift in the Cape Fear channel much farther north to a new inlet south of present-day Smith Island. A new lighthouse was authorized by Congress and placed in service in 1816, and the Bald Head light was retired. Eventually, the inlet shoaled and the channel shifted again to the southwest of Smith Island. By 1848, a new pair of lights (no longer evident) on Oak Island became the primary navigation aid to the mouth of the Cape Fear. In 1959, the current Oak Island Lighthouse was placed into service.

of Caswell Beach and Yaupon Beach are small, and access is very limited, serving primarily homeowners, rental visitors, and guests.

The Baptist Assembly restricts visitation to its grounds, but travelers may drive through to view the remnants of the fort.

The North Carolina Wildlife Resources Commission maintains a fishing and boating access area on the Intracoastal Waterway before Oak Island. From Southport, follow NC 211 west to NC 133. Turn south on NC 133, turn left on SR 1101, and the area is down the road on the left. Parking is available and there is no launch fee.

Information

For information, contact Southport/Oak Island Chamber of Commerce, 4841 Long Beach Road Southeast, Southport, NC 28461, 910-457-6964 or 1-800-457-6964.

Caswell Beach

After crossing the Intracoastal Waterway onto Oak Island, NC 133 becomes SR 1100, locally known as Caswell Beach Drive, and begins a gradual curve east into the community of Caswell Beach. The town hall stands just inside the city limits sign. The salt sculpting of the vegetation visible from the road provides the earliest clue that the road will soon travel parallel to the oceanfront, behind the south-facing berm of Caswell Beach.

Caswell Beach is quiet, restful, and neutral about tourism, neither inviting nor uninviting. It makes few overtures to visitors. Probably more salt marsh than either upland or beachfront, Caswell Beach has no

	Fee	Parking	Restrooms	Lifeguard	Camping	Showers	Beach Access	Hiking	Trail	Handicapped	Boating	ORV Access	Fishing	Programs	Historic	Sand Beach	Dunes	Upland	Wetland
Caswell Beach		•					•						•			•	•		
Oak Island Lighthouse		•													•				
Fort Caswell	•	•													•	•	•		•
Yaupon Beach		•					•						•			•	•	•	
Public Boating Access: Oak Island		•									•		•						•
19th Place East Walkway		•						•	•	•									•
Tidal Way Trails Park		•									•		•						•
Regional Access: 46th St.		•	•			•	•			•			•			•			
Robin Schuster Park		•	•								•		•						•

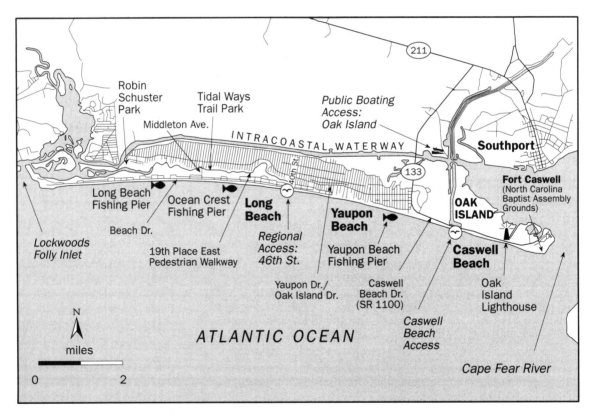

Map 28. Oak Island

commercial district. The only concessions available are those at the Country Club on the north side of Caswell Beach Drive. Caswell Dunes, a private golf course on the north side of Caswell Beach Drive, and Oak Island Villas, on the beachfront shortly after the town hall, are the most visible developments within the corporate limits. With a year-round population of around 200, the community almost seems to be a confederation of cottages rather than an incorporated entity with municipal boundaries.

Caswell Beach Drive, running very close to the narrow 2.5 miles of beach, is the primary access for both the oceanfront and second-row homes in this municipality. En route, it passes a large channel cut through the salt marsh to the north, which is a cooling channel used by Carolina Power and Light's Brunswick Plant, north of Southport. A pipe carrying cooling water from the plant passes under the road and continues 2 or 3 miles out to sea, where it discharges. Shortly past the channel, in the 700 block of Caswell Beach Drive, is a neighborhood access site on the oceanfront with parking.

Do not violate the no-parking signs in Caswell Beach. Some protect the town's underground drinking water lines, and you will get a ticket for ignoring the no-parking signs. Also, according to the town clerk, a few cars that parked errantly have sunk in the soft sands.

The beach is narrow, with evidence of erosion. Caution should be taken when swimming at Caswell Beach. Oceanfront currents here can be dangerous because of the discharge effects of the Cape Fear River, especially if you choose to swim closer to the inlet.

Caswell Beach Drive passes the Oak Island Lighthouse and the U.S. Coast Guard Station at the east end of the island outside the corporate limits of Caswell Beach. The road loops to an end before the gate of the North Carolina Baptist Assembly Grounds, which include the brick and earthen revetments of Fort Caswell, which protected the Cape Fear River entrance from 1826 to 1865.

Access

There is a neighborhood beach access site in the 700 block of Caswell Beach Drive with parking for around 40 cars, marked by the sunspots logo. Caswell Beach also has several neighborhood access locations in the west end of town.

Information

For information, contact Southport/ Oak Island Chamber of Commerce, 4841 Long Beach Road Southeast, Southport, NC 28461, 910-457-6964 or 1-800-457-6964.

Oak Island Lighthouse and U.S. Coast Guard Station

Constructed in 1958, the Oak Island Lighthouse is the primary light for the Cape Fear River, replacing the old Cape Fear light on the eastern beach of Bald Head Island which, when lighted in 1903, replaced "Old Baldy."

The Oak Island light is a statement of efficiency—tall enough to hold up the light, wide enough to accommodate enclosed stairs. The paint scheme is a curious banding, dark at the top to show against the daytime sky, white at the middle, and reddish-brown at the base. The light is 169 feet above ground, which is reached by ascending 132 steps within the tower. What the light doesn't do, at least as romantically as its older counterparts elsewhere on the coast, is serve as a landmark. The very ornate gothic gingerbread building across SR 1100 from the lighthouse is the old lightkeeper's quarters from an earlier era, which was auctioned, moved, and restored as a private residence.

There is a small parking area just downhill from the earthen berm supporting the lighthouse. A sign states that all visitors are to report to the officer of the day at the nearby U.S. Coast Guard Station, which has a two-fold mission of search and rescue and navigation-aid maintenance to the South Carolina border. Although the base is not generally open to the public, group tours of the facility may be arranged in advance.

Behind the building is the dock serving the station's vessels, including a boat that tends the navigation equipment, a small boat for emergency calls, and a 44-foot motor lifeboat for rescue in severe seas.

Lifesaving crews such as this one on Oak Island, ca. 1915, remained alert for emergency missions along the coast. (Courtesy of N.C. Department of Archives and History)

Information

For information about scheduling a group tour of the Coast Guard Station, contact U.S. Coast Guard, Oak Island Station, P.O. Box 1030, Long Beach, NC 28465.

North Carolina Baptist Assembly Grounds/Fort Caswell

Caswell Beach Drive ends at the gates to the grounds of the North Carolina Baptist Assembly, a coastal retreat that serves primarily as a summer camp for Baptist youths. The assembly includes the remnant earthworks of Fort Caswell, constructed in 1826 to guard the entrance to the Cape Fear River. The fort was seized in 1861 by Confederate forces and remained in their hands until taken in 1865 by conquering Union troops.

During the Spanish-American War and both world wars, this point of land was again garrisoned and fortified against coastal invasion. The fortifications visible on the island are a mishmash of additions and improvements added to the brick portions of the works, which date from the Civil War. The concrete bunkers that dot the seaward side of the headland are vestiges of the twentieth-century fortifications.

Many of the structures in current use at the assembly grounds are refurbished U.S. Army barracks and outbuildings. The architecture is unmistakable and the orderly layout of the buildings and grounds leeward of the revetments confirms the longtime importance of this piece of ground to military planners. From a deep-water channel overlook on the assembly grounds, you can see the maritime trade of the Cape Fear River that passes along the eastern-

most tip of the island to and from port in Wilmington.

Access

During the summer, the assembly grounds are reserved strictly for the youths attending camp and are closed to visitors. However, from Labor Day to Memorial Day, you may drive through the assembly grounds to visit the fort for a $2 fee, which covers the cost of insurance that the assembly must carry because of the extensive and possibly dangerous fortifications on the grounds. All visitors must report to the office, a clearly signed refurbished barracks. The assembly reserves the right to restrict visitation and requests that visitors be considerate and respectful of the property.

Sea Oats

Sand dunes are a movable story, a single frame in the cinema of wind, water, and sand. Geologically, sand dunes last only an instant, yet, in our human frame of reference, they seem formidable—certainly insurmountable to the short legs of a three-year-old. As a component of the barrier islands, sand dunes are the first line of defense against the assault of storms, a malleable response line that forces a storm to deplete a great deal of its energy before pushing inland. Nature builds sand dunes with wind, time, and available sand. People use sand fences or heavy equipment to create dunes faster. Both nature and people, however, rely on sea oats, the rugged pioneer grass that endures the worst conditions of salt, wind, and drought, to secure the dunes as an edge against angry seas.

Sea oats are coarse, pale green plants that form tough clumps that die back to the surface of the dune each year. They may grow at the very edge of the wet sand beach, staking a claim to a normally sun-bleached, grainy, and restless piece of real estate, which is the harshest, most demanding environment on the barrier islands. The fact that it is virtually the only plant to grow this close to the ocean is evidence of the inhospitable nature of this microenvironment.

The value of sea oats is not what you see above ground but what goes on beneath the surface. Spreading by underground stems, sea oats can colonize over the top of a dune, while beneath the surface of sand, they anchor the core of the dune with a vigorous root system that threads its fibrous tendrils throughout the dune. It is an extraordinarily effective anchor, capable of withstanding all but the most vicious storms.

In mid-to-late summer, sea oats produce tall stems, over 3 feet tall, bearing clusters of oatlike seed spikelets, hence the common name. These featherlike plumes ripen to a golden color in September—in glorious contrast to the polarized cobalt skies of early autumn. The plant stakes its claim against the sea, even in the face of the traditional tropical storm season.

Ironically, the same storms that may destroy the sea oats may also give them life. Studies reveal that germination of the seeds is best achieved after a period of soaking in salt water; waves harvest the seeds and then plant them again in a curiously macabre recycling of the plant and, in some instances, the very island itself.

Because of their important ecological role, sea oats are protected by law; you may not harvest the strands when they are in full flaring array and most attractive—in fact, you may not pick them at any time. If left undisturbed, they will form thick protective coverings on the dunes. As the dune builds, sea oats push through from beneath, anchoring the new sand blown on top of their previous points of emergence. As sea oats go, so go the dunes. As dunes go, so go the islands. As you go, leave the sea oats behind.

Information

For information, contact North Carolina Baptist Assembly, Oak Island, NC 28465, 910-278-9501.

Yaupon Beach

Yaupon Beach, the smallest of the three Oak Island communities, has less than a mile of beach within its town limits. The beach here is sequestered; you cannot directly reach Ocean Drive, the beachfront road, from NC 133. To see the sands of Yaupon Beach, you must sidestep through residential neighborhoods to reach one of the north-south streets that run to the oceanfront. The roads seem to encourage you to move through Yaupon Beach rather than stopping here. To quote a local police officer, "If you're looking for a Myrtle Beach type of vacation, you won't find it here." Without being offish, Yaupon Beach seems quite content not being a primary destination. It seems quiet, even in July.

After NC 133 crosses the Intracoastal Waterway onto Oak Island, Yaupon Drive continues west from the island's major intersection, splitting the community of Yaupon Beach into two residential sectors. After about ten blocks, the street changes its name to Oak Island Drive at its intersection with Seventy-ninth Street East, the western city limits of Yaupon Beach and the beginning of Long Beach.

Heading west, any left turn off of Yaupon Drive will lead you to the water. Parking is available at the beachfront at the end of each named north-south street as well as selected signed locations. If you turn left on Womble Street, you will reach the parking area serving the Yaupon Beach Pier and the pavilion area, the center of the low-energy beach.

Most of Yaupon Beach is in the woods. The first impression of the town, formed primarily as you drive through the residential areas to reach the beach access locations, is one of an inland, wooded subdivision with sandy soil and even, unpaved roads. The tree cover of the upland portion of the island extends quite nearly to the oceanfront.

The houses settle amid live oak trees mixed with loblolly pines and the town's namesake tree, the yaupon holly. In the areas close to the beach, the landward island-woods yield to lower salt-sheared shrubs that in turn roll down into shrubby, grassy plains in a natural line that if unaltered would almost melt into the wet sand beach. The sandy berm of Yaupon Beach has a very low profile, giving the impression that the ocean could just slide smoothly up and into the center of the forest with little resistance. The gradient of the beachfront is appealing for its gentleness.

Access

Yaupon Beach is a primarily residential resort beach. Except for three motels or so, you are more apt to secure beach access through cottage ownership or rental. The parking spaces and walkways provided by the town mostly serve the needs of the inland residents lacking direct beach access.

The largest parking area is at the pavilion at Womble Street and Ocean Drive.

The following north-south streets have access points: McGlamery Street, Sellers Street, Mercer Street, Norton Street, Trott Street, Keziah Street, Barbee Boulevard, Sherril Street, and Crowell Street.

Some parking for beach visitors may be available at the Yaupon Beach Pier on Womble Street. Check with the owner before you park there.

Information

For information, contact Southport/ Oak Island Chamber of Commerce, 4841 Long Beach Road Southeast, Southport, NC 28461, 910-457-6964 or 1-800-457-6964.

Long Beach

After crossing the bridge over the Intracoastal Waterway on NC 133, continuing west on Yaupon Drive, and passing through Yaupon Beach, you enter the corporate limits of Long Beach, Oak Island's largest community, at Seventy-ninth Street East. At this point, Yaupon Drive changes its name to Oak Island Drive. It is nearly 9 miles from the eastern city limits of Long Beach to the loop at the western extreme of Oak Island.

Generally speaking, ample beach access parking is provided for visitors, and most visitors secure access by weekly rental within walking distance of the wet sand beach. Just as in neighboring Yaupon Beach, you must travel south on one of the intersecting streets to reach the water. From Seventy-ninth to Fifty-eighth streets, this maneuver is not recommended, since these streets dead-end close to the water. Although there is parking there, if you can't find a spot, you must return to Oak Island Drive to continue further west. Fifty-eighth Street Southeast will carry you directly to the water and the eastern end of Beach Drive, which continues to the west end of the town to Seventy-third Place West.

Regional access site at Long Beach. (Courtesy of N.C. Coastal Management Commission)

When you reach the water at Fifty-eighth Street, you will find the heart of this single-family residential beach community. There are few hotels and motels in Long Beach and few commercial diversions from the experience of salt water and sand. Even the surf seems lazy. The oceanfront is a long beach strand of private cottages, with few "collecting spots," interrupted only by two fishing piers, the Ocean Crest Pier and the Long Beach Pier.

Approximately 2,500 people call Long Beach their primary community. Second and retirement homes are abundant. Between Memorial Day and Labor Day, the rental business is predominant; thereafter, the retirement-home market sets the tone of the community. The wooded half of the island, north of the Big Jim Davis Canal, is the preferred location for retirement homes.

Much of the community's commercial services are along East Oak Island Drive in the several blocks before and after the intersection with Fifty-eighth Street. Gas up if you are headed west. It's a very long way to the western edge of the island and services become fewer.

Every third street from Fifty-eighth to Fortieth Street connects Oak Island Drive and Beach Drive. The intervening streets stop at East Pelican Drive parallel to the beach inland. The town hall is on East Oak Island Drive, at the Forty-sixth Street intersection, the town's only stoplight. There's a large recreational-vehicle parking area nearby and a major regional beach access parking area at the oceanfront terminus of Forty-sixth Street Southeast.

Fortieth Street is at the east end of the headwaters of the Big Jim Davis Canal, which divides the remainder of the island into a sandy barrier beach to the south and a wooded landmass to the north, separated from the mainland by the Intracoastal Waterway. You cannot cross the canal by automobile for another 40 blocks, until Middleton Avenue, where East Oak Island Drive changes to West Oak Island Drive before continuing for another 30 blocks.

Long Beach does provide a delightful walkway over the canal, accessible from Nineteenth Place East on the south shore of the canal and south Twentieth Street East on the north shore. There are several parking places along the residential streets, and a gazebo provides shade. The scenic walkway over the salt marsh and tidal creek displays a range of vegetation, beginning with a live oak and pine forest with a wax myrtle understory and grading through vegetation with increasing salt and water tolerance to the spartina marsh. Redwing blackbirds flit through the marsh grasses and shrubs, while ghost crabs scurry across the mud flats of the marsh. At low tide, oyster reefs are exposed, and mullet fingerlings swirl beneath the shadows cast by the walkway.

Additionally, at 31st Street Southeast, next to the Long Beach Recreation Center, which faces Oak Island Drive East, there is the Tidal Way Trails Park. The park has a small boardwalk and a canoe-launching site on the canal with a gazebo and picnic tables. This is one of the few designated canoe-launching sites on the entire coast and allows easy launching for canoes and kayaks only.

The last convenient route to the beach is Middleton Avenue, which crosses to Beach Drive. Both east and west of Middleton Avenue, the streets perpendicular to the oceanfront are numbered erratically in increasing value, beginning with Second Place West to Sixtieth Place West toward Lockwoods Folly Inlet and Third Place East toward Yaupon Beach. You can continue along Oak Island Drive until reaching Robin Schuster Park, a recreational facility at the western end of the island on the Intracoastal Waterway.

Generally speaking, the beachfront at Long Beach seems vulnerable. The dune line is low to nonexistent, and the gradient of the beach is very flat, which makes it a very gentle beach in terms of wave action. At the west end of the island, extensive sand flats reach more than 600 yards beyond the end of the road, before inlet waters.

Access

Long Beach has a major regional access area at the end of Forty-sixth Street, with 43 parking spaces, restrooms, a gazebo, and two dune crossovers.

There are many neighborhood access points as well. The following streets have dune crossovers and parking: Seventy-ninth, Seventy-eighth, Seventy-sixth, Seventy-fourth, Seventy-second, Seventy-first, Seventieth, Sixty-ninth, Sixty-fourth, Fifty-eighth, Fifty-fifth, Fifty-second, Forty-ninth, Forty-third, Twenty-fifth Place East, Fifty-ninth Place East, Sixteenth

Place East, Fourteenth Place East, Third Place East, South Middleton Avenue, Fifth Place West, Seventh Place West, Tenth Place West, Thirteenth Place West, Twentieth Place West, Twenty-third Place West, Twenty-seventh Place West, Thirtieth Place West, and Thirty-third Place West.

Paved bikeways along Oak Island Drive and Beach Drive have eased conflicts between cars, pedestrians, and bicycles.

Handicapped Access

The regional access site at Forty-sixth Street is fully accessible for the handicapped, with accessible restrooms as well.

Information

For information, contact Southport/ Oak Island Chamber of Commerce, 4841 Long Beach Road Southeast, Southport, NC 28461, 910-457-6964 or 1-800-457-6964.

Green Swamp

North from Supply off of NC 211, Green Swamp is a 25,000-acre expanse of pine savanna and upland evergreen shrub bog, designated a National Natural Landmark by the U.S. Department of the Interior.

Once more than 200,000 acres, Green Swamp has been timbered, drained, and put to the plow, but in the 1970s a major landowner, the Federal Paperboard Company of New York, donated nearly 14,000 acres to the Nature Conservancy, which has expanded its holdings to the current number of acres. What looks barren and unpromising to the eye is actually one of the richest plant habitats in the state, and it harbors the greatest number of carnivorous plants found in the country. The density and diversity of plant species within the swamp rank it as one of the finest unaltered habitats in the state. Ecologists have mapped at least two distinct types of pocosin here, differentiated by their various understory and tree species mix and by the amount of sphagnum moss in the surface.

This is a virtually roadless tract of land and just plain difficult to move around in. A topographic map shows the natural crown in the land, nearly like a ridge, that is north of Supply. The natural drainage moves away from the crowning earth. The permeated nature of the surface made road building and farming difficult.

Access

The North Carolina Nature Conservancy controls access to Green Swamp but can arrange permission for visitation and tours of some of the acreage.

Information

To arrange a field trip, contact North Carolina Nature Conservancy, Suite D-12, Carr Mill Mall, Carrboro, NC 27510, 919-967-7007.

Lockwoods Folly Inlet

Lockwoods Folly Inlet, the outlet of the Lockwoods Folly River, separates Holden Beach and Oak Island. The dark tannic river is considered by boating enthusiasts to be one of the most scenic tidewater rivers in the state. The slowly flowing waters thread through a maze of cypress and live oak trees draped by Spanish moss.

The river originates west of Spring Lakes in Brunswick County and flows northwest before looping underneath NC 211 a few miles east of Supply. The river you cross at this point does not draw much attention.

Access

Access to the river and the inlet is at Sunset Harbor, on the east bank of the river on the mainland.

Shallotte

Once little more than a wide spot in a road through a rural county, Shallotte is now the commercial hub of southern Brunswick County, with the largest concentration of stores and services centrally accessible to the three island communities of Holden Beach, Ocean Isle Beach, and Sunset Beach. Stop here and stock up at the grocery, dry goods, and service shops. Shallotte also has national chain restaurants, scarce indeed on the quieter beaches that

are the prime destinations of vacation travelers.

Some items available here, such as alcoholic beverages, you cannot buy in the island communities. Also, stop at the roadside markets for some of the finest produce in the state or some fresh shrimp.

Information

For information, contact South Brunswick Islands Chamber of Commerce, P.O. Box 1380, Shallotte, NC 28549, 910-754-6644 or 1-800-426-6644.

Holden Beach

Holden Beach is the most easterly island of the necklace of South Brunswick islands made up of Holden Beach, Ocean Isle Beach, and Sunset Beach. If you miss your turn off of US 17 onto NC 130 or SR 1115 from Supply or can't seem to find Holden, you have discovered the secret of the South Brunswick islands—they're slightly out of the way. About thirty years, actually. Like its South Brunswick sisters, Holden Beach puts few temptations between you and "getting away from it all."

While Holden's eastern neighbor, Oak Island, barely beyond shouting distance across Lockwoods Folly Inlet, bustles with a seasonal population of 25,000, Holden Beach brims full but never seems packed with visitors. The largest community of the trio, Holden is 11 miles long. The overwhelming perception

Lockwoods Folly Inlet at Long Beach. (Courtesy of N.C. Coastal Management Commission)

of Holden Beach is spacious, with plenty of beach to go around and plenty of island to enjoy.

Holden Beach became an island in the 1930s when the Intracoastal Waterway severed it and the remainder of the South Brunswick islands from the mainland. Most of the island belonged to members of the Holden family, who acquired it in the eighteenth century. Since the 1950s, family members have slowly developed their real estate holdings into a successful summer resort. Holden is truly a "family" beach.

There is a touch of neon here, but it is mostly a very quiet place. Promotional literature boldly claims, "You won't find much to do except swim, fish, and sunbathe." There's the Surfside Pavilion, a video game amusement center with a county fair midway flavor, and there's also a pier. You walk the pier, you fish, you sunbathe—that's Holden Beach.

Before 1984, when a new high-rise bridge spanning the Intracoastal Waterway replaced the old drawbridge, which had replaced a ferry, it was quieter still, with fewer comings and goings. The new bridge assured both easy access and evacuation and brought a building boom of sorts. Still, there are no high-rise buildings or hotels or motels on the island, but mostly single-family cottages for rent or sale.

Most of the services are along the mainland causeway leading to the bridge. There are tackle shops, gift shops, dry goods merchants, restaurants, sundry stores, and service stations. Along the Intracoastal Waterway are several seafood-packing houses open to the public. A number of shrimpers have home port in Holden Beach, and shrimp

	Fee	Parking	Restrooms	Lifeguard	Camping	Showers	Beach Access	Hiking	Trail	Handicapped	Boating	ORV Access	Fishing	Programs	Historic	Sand Beach	Dunes	Upland	Wetland
Regional Access: Holden Beach		•	•			•	•			•			•			•			
Ocean Isle Beach		•					•						•			•	•		
Sunset Beach		•					•				•		•			•	•		

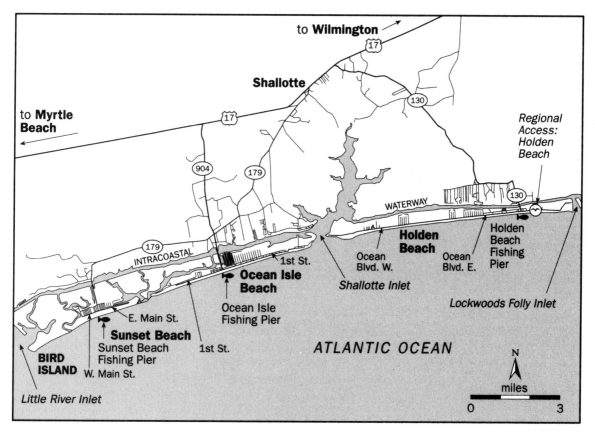

Map 29. Holden Beach, Ocean Isle, and Sunset Beach

is almost always a good buy in the summer season.

From the island terminus of the bridge, it is a short drive to the east end, where there are several parking places and ample access to the beach. Beach erosion at this end of the island threatens several homes, and efforts have been made to armor the headland of the island against the migration of Lockwoods Folly Inlet by constructing a bulkhead. If you are fortunate enough to secure one of the parking spots, you can take advantage of the solitude of the point, popular for bathers and surf fishermen who work the tidal changes for flounder and other fish. The inlet current is modest; strong swimmers need not fear the water here. Plentiful shoaling of the inlet and the gentle beach gradient creates tidal pools that are excellent for younger children. At low tide, sand dollars and hermit crabs abound. There are no public restrooms at this end of the island.

There is a regional access area with substantial parking, restrooms, and cold showers underneath the high-rise bridge. The parking is a short walk from designated dune crossover locations. There are also additional parking places at the Holden Beach Fishing Pier, west of the bridge.

Because of beach erosion, Holden Beach has constructed a berm at the oceanfront, and there is a $50 fine for walking on the sand dunes. Dogs are prohibited on the beach from 9 A.M. to 5 P.M. and at other times must be leashed or restrained. In summer the community has a beach patrol that enforces these regulations.

The west end of Holden Beach was closed to the public for some time and currently has only limited access. In 1986, a lower-court ruling allowed a private development, Holden Beach Enterprises, to restrict the use of the only road leading to Shallotte Inlet to property owners in the development and their guests. A guardhouse just after Strawflower Drive cut off the last mile of the island and overland access to Shallotte Inlet. The

North Carolina Supreme Court reversed this ruling in 1991, on the basis that the public had established a "prescriptive easement" through the development since people had traditionally traveled to the inlet for more than twenty years. Even though the specific route to the inlet may have shifted over the years due to natural forces that have changed the formation of the island, access to the inlet is guaranteed by the principle of prescriptive easement. The results of the judgment have yet to reach the beach.

Access

There is no parking on Ocean Boulevard, the main street parallel to the ocean. You may park on side streets, but your vehicle must be completely off of the pavement. Permission of the adjacent property owner is advised.

There is a regional access area under the high-rise bridge, with 90 parking spaces, restrooms, cold showers, and dune crossovers a short walk away.

There are smaller parking locations and dune crossover sites at the south end of Heritage Harbor, Dream Harbor, and Colonial Beach. Other designated access locations are at Avenue D, Avenue C, Avenue B, Avenue A, Holden Street, and Ferry Road.

Handicapped Access

The regional access facility under the bridge is accessible to handicapped travelers, including the restrooms.

Information

For information, contact South Brunswick Islands Chamber of Commerce, P.O. Box 1380, Shallotte, NC 28549, 910-754-6644 or 1-800-426-6644.

Ocean Isle Beach

While Ocean Isle Beach is between Holden Beach and Sunset Beach in the South Brunswick islands in position and in length, it's very different in mood and atmosphere. At first glance, as you cross the Odell Williamson high-rise bridge that carries NC 904 over the Intracoastal Waterway, two impressions come to mind: there are too few trees to soften the abruptness of the view of rooftops from the crest of the bridge, and there are a lot of houses on Ocean Isle Beach. This is a booming retirement and second-home community, particularly on the soundside, where finger canals offer boat access to the Intracoastal Waterway.

There is a lot of desirable beach here. The island has the same east-west orientation as its neighbors and the same broad expanse of sand, with its natural, south-facing sauna. For most of its length, the beachfront has a gentle gradient and a very low dune line that has been scalloped by the sea.

The central commercial district features a water slide, a nature museum, and a liquor store. As you drive the island, the initial impression fades. Ocean Isle Beach is neat and less packed than you might ex-

Water in Orbit

Why, if waves keep marching to you at the beach, does the water not slosh up into the dunes? This is a simple question with a charmingly simple answer. While waves move through water horizontally, the actual water molecules move very little. Passing waves move floating objects back and forth, up and down, but never really transport them very far. If you could see seaweed swaying with passing wave action, you could readily observe this.

Waves are motion—energy—passing through a medium—the ocean. The actual particles of water in a wave move in a circular orbit, as shown in the diagram. This circular pattern of water particle movement was first observed by 1802 by German Franz Gerstner.

As a wave approaches a droplet, it carries the droplet in the direction of transport along with the crest of the wave. Then the trough of the wave follows, and the droplet moves against the direction of the wave for almost the same horizontal distance. During the swell, of course, the droplet is elevated and subsequently "dropped" as the swell passes and the trough approaches. In fact, the water particle returns to almost its original position.

The diameter of the circle is, of course, equal to the height of the wave. When a wave approaches shore, there is insufficient room for particles to make their circular path. The orbit flattens, the droplets tarry at the top of the swell, pushed higher and ever forward with no support beneath them. The circle is broken, and the wave breaks on the sand.

---

pect given the bridge-top glimpse. It also has sidewalks parallel to the beachfront along East Front Street, an unusual urban element in a small vacation island. The sidewalk provides a safe location for bicycles, strollers, and people going for a walk.

Ocean Isle Beach approaches parking with the same up-front, practical approach. There are marked places to park about every six blocks at the ends of streets running toward the ocean. And, like elsewhere, the ones closest to the center of town fill up first. Police officials at the town hall point out that even on the most crowded days a few spaces are usually open at the lots farther east.

The east end is the major playground for Ocean Isle Beach. There are numerous places to park, many not officially marked but obvious locations to pull completely off the road. The eastern tip of the island at Shallotte Inlet is fighting a losing battle with erosion as the inlet migrates toward the island. At least four distinct rows of pilings in the inlet are the remnants of failed headwalls or groins. Beyond these, there are wide flats extending between ¼ to ½ mile to the inlet. The beach gradient makes it a reasonably safe place to take small children, and they cover the place up. Not surprisingly, the parking spaces at this end of the island are taken quickly.

The west end of the island is owned privately by Ocean Isle West, which prohibits land access to the inlet, a circumstance that may change following the 1991 ruling by the North Carolina Supreme Court in a case at Holden Beach. The court ruled that the public had the right to access to the inlet on the basis of the principle of prescriptive easement, which guarantees traditional access. This end of the beach has marked erosion.

A series of artificial canals

Public access ramp, Ocean Isle. (Courtesy of N.C. Coastal Management Commission)

dredged into the soundside of the island provides harbor for a large number of charter and head-boat fishing operations. The easy access to open water through Tubbs or Shallotte Inlet makes the charter and head-boat fishing fleets of Ocean Isle Beach a major vacation attraction.

Access

Your first opportunity to park is just as you arrive on NC 904 across the causeway at a central parking location directly ahead.

The following streets have neighborhood access sites: Monroe Street, Concord Street, Newport Street, Raeford Street, Leland Street, Goldsboro Street, Chadbourn Street, Winnabow Street, Greensboro Street, and Beaufort Street.

Use common sense about parking in unmarked locations: don't block drives, sidewalks, flower beds, or side streets and pull completely off of the pavement. Dune crossovers are located at the south ends of High Point Street, Shelby Street, and Driftwood Drive.

Information

For information, contact South Brunswick Islands Chamber of Commerce, P.O. Box 1380, Shallotte, NC 28549, 910-754-6644 or 1-800-426-6644.

Sunset Beach

How about this for disorienting geographic trivia: Sunset Beach, the westernmost barrier island in North Carolina, is nearly due south of Raleigh. It floats in its own little world tied to the mainland by one of the last small-scale drawbridges in the state. The mainland of Brunswick County has gone to golf in a big, big way, and this makes for wonderful juxtapositions. West of the drawbridge on the mainland, just a few miles along NC 179, is the entrance to Oyster Bay, a golf resort/development. There is a wonderful visual contrast along this part of roadway—manicured hybrid-grass fairways on one side, a sea of marsh on the other.

The drawbridge causeway is one of the most intimate and truly delightful crossings along the coast, ranking with the ferry rides on the Outer Banks in how firmly it marks transition. When you cross to Sunset, you leave a lot behind. Carry binoculars; the causeway is busy with bird life, and there are plainly marked parking pullouts where you can stop and view the marsh.

Sunset Beach is small, merely 3 miles in length, yet it fields one of the widest dune zones in all of North Carolina. When you park your car at Sunset Beach, the trip to the beach has just begun. Between the beachfront homes and the Atlantic Ocean is a long walk—around 200 yards from an access area at Fortieth Street and West Main.

Looking west from this access point, you see Mad Inlet and, beyond, a small island known variously as Price Island, Bird Island, or Bird Shoal. It is not far and is wadeable during low tide. Mad Inlet and the tidal waters of Blaine Creek, between the island and the mainland, are excellent locations for canoeing or kayaking.

At the west end, the town has constructed a boardwalk, which makes a steep ascent over the primary dune line. The beach has a gentle gradient, and the quality of the beach experience is paralleled in the state only by the most remote lengths of Outer Banks beachfront and the jewel of Hammocks Beach State Park in Onslow County. There is not quite as much isolation on Sunset, but there is plenty of peace and quiet. The oceanfront streets are so distant from the beach that there are no traffic sounds—no sounds at all really except those of the edge of the sea.

The homeowners of Sunset Beach displayed an extraordinary sensitivity to the dunes when building. In addition, for more than thirty years, the beach has been advancing out to sea. The fact that the island is growing, along with the fact that there are only 300 residents who live here full-time, makes Sunset Beach one of the least crowded of the Brunswick islands.

Access

There is all-day parking at the Walt and Doris, Inc., Sunset Pier for $4. The pier is just west of the south end of Sunset Boulevard.

The Fortieth Street access location has a dune crossover.

There are 25 unimproved access points at First through Eleventh and Twenty-seventh through Fortieth streets. Parking is permitted at all access locations even though no parking spaces are specifically provided.

The North Carolina Wildlife Resources Commission maintains a fishing and boating access area on the Intracoastal Waterway near Sunset Beach, at the end of Park Road, ½ mile west from the junction of NC 904 and NC 179, in the Sea Trail development. Parking is available and there is no launch fee.

Information

For information, contact South Brunswick Islands Chamber of Commerce, P.O. Box 1380, Shallotte, NC 28549, 910-754-6644 or 1-800-426-6644.

Bird Island

Bird Island, with its tangled forest and extensive sand flats and dunes, is one of the last privately owned barrier beaches in North Carolina. New River Inlet borders it to the southwest, Mad River Inlet, wadeable at low tide, separates it from neighboring Sunset Beach.

"The idea of owning my own island appealed to me," Greensboro resident Ralph Clay Price explained long ago about his purchase of Bird Island. Price, son of Julian Price, the driving force behind the Jefferson-Pilot Corporation, had the money and the dream, and so, in the late 1950s, sight unseen, he purchased a 1,150-acre island, the most southern of all North Carolina barriers. He then built a bridge to the island from Sunset Beach, crossing the shallow creek forming Mad Inlet. The island has been without access since the 1960s when arsonists burned the bridge that Price built. The arsonists also spread tacks in the road to slow fire trucks rushing to the conflagration. The

Price family never reconstructed the bridge. When Ralph Price died in 1987, he left the island to his wife.

What will happen to the island is unknown. In the late 1960s, the 153 buildable acres were platted with fifteen 4-acre lots. In early 1992, Mrs. Price applied for a permit to the Division of Coastal Management to rebuild the bridge to the island. The application for a bridge is likely to be vigorously contested since although the island is privately owned, it is publicly loved. It has become a local resource that is treasured by Brunswick County residents, many of whom boat to the island or wade across Mad Inlet at low tide.

Calabash

Calabash is synonymous with seafood dining, indulgence, or maybe overindulgence. You go to Calabash to eat seafood, along with nearly everybody else from Wilmington to Myrtle Beach.

Calabash is a town and an event. In the 1940s it was little more than a small fishing community where two local families, the Becks and the Colemans, held outdoor oyster roasts for folks. The logical extension of the outdoor feast was an indoor restaurant, and the two families eventually opened rival restaurants. Today, it really doesn't matter which family started the restaurant challenge; more than thirty restaurants here are trying to capitalize on the national reputation Calabash developed in late 1960s and 1970s.

The restaurants' popularity is based on the cooking style—the seafood is lightly breaded and fried, and you can still identify what you're eating through the breading. Accompanied by hushpuppies, sweet iced tea, coleslaw, and a potato, the style of cooking caught on, and Calabash exploded as a dining center. Some of the restaurants serve such "traditional" items as lobster. There are also souvenir shops and T-shirt shops.

At the immense white oak tree in the center of town, look for a turn to go down to the banks of the Calabash Creek. There the glitzier restaurant facades of NC 179 give way to the dockside make-do of the older part of the community. The closer you get to the water, the closer you get to a taste of old Calabash and the more the signs proclaim words such as "old" or "original."

You can walk out on the docks or wander into a seafood market and load up a cooler for the ride home. There are even harbor cruises, and the place looks, feels, and smells like a fishing community. It feels like a tidewater fishing community, where everybody is a captain. You hardly even notice that you can see golf carts across the creek.

Handicapped Access

Handicapped access varies with the individual enterprise, but in nearly half of the restaurants the entire dining area is on one floor with fully accessible entrances. Restroom accessibility is limited.

Information

For information, contact South Brunswick Islands Chamber of Commerce, P.O. Box 1380, Shallotte, NC 28549, 910-754-6644 or 1-800-426-6644.

With Mollusk Aforethought

That glimmer of color in the sand, the rounded form emerging from the foam of a wave, the calcareous rainbow shimmer at the edge of a pool is an abandoned home. For every shell that plays a tune of the sea in our ears, there is another that composes a song of wonder in our hearts. I have stopped collecting and started admiring shells as part of nature's artwork. Some of the best architects I know are mollusks.

A mollusk is a soft-bodied creature that comes in six basic body styles, three of which are responsible for producing the shells that we might reasonably expect to find on North Carolina beaches. Two mollusk classes, the Gastropoda, or snails, and the Pelecypoda, or bivalves, by far have more species, so you are most likely to find shells from these classes. The snails have one-piece shells with one opening; the bivalves are hinged shells such as oysters, clams, coquinas, and scallops. The tusk shells, members of another class, are infrequently found.

The mix of shells that you discover on a particular beach is determined by the ocean environment—the nature of the seafloor, the water temperature, and the other creatures that share the benthic (ocean bottom) habitat. Sandy or muddy ocean bottoms favor bivalves; harder bottoms, resistant to burying, usually support larger numbers of snails, which are mobile.

The evolutionary change that turned a two-piece fortress into a one-piece armored personnel carrier set some mollusks in motion. Snails inch across the ocean floor on their "foot," either grazing or hunting less-agile bivalves. Bivalves "hide" through burrowing or coloration. Bivalves are considered more general feeders; snails are specialty diners, and some, such as the Atlantic oyster drill, are efficient enough at feeding on their prey that they compete with commercial oystermen.

The Molluscan lifestyle produces extraordinary architecture, from humble bungalow to exuberant gingerbread Gothic, each of which, although resembling the neighbors, has a "personal" touch. Although the creature re-creates certain characteristics of the species such as the color, the pattern of coloration, and the shape of the shell, custom-tailored differences always exist. These are, after all, individuals, and their houses have a purpose.

A shell is first and foremost armor, developed in response to the creature's necessity to protect its soft body parts. (Other Mollusca such as squids and slugs have other survival strategies since they wear no shell.) But why such differences in design and pattern? Probably in response to the environment in which the creature lives and perhaps whimsy—why should there not be variety for its own sake?

Each shell-producing mollusk has an important organ known as a mantle, a fleshy, capelike covering lining the inside of the shell and wrapping around the remainder of the mollusk. From its food, and to a limited extent the surrounding water, mollusks extract calcium and magnesium carbonate, the minerals in solution that will crystallize to form the shell. The mantle is the paintbrush of the mollusk, spreading the liquid carbonates and other minerals on the inside of the shell, where it rapidly crystallizes into the complex and rigid lattices that comprise the hard protective covering.

Mollusks do not grow constantly but experience periods of growth followed by rest. This shows in the shell in the form of ridges of enlarging dimension emanating from the hinge of the bivalve or the axis of the coil in snails. While the ridges of a shell reflect periods of growth, they are not annual measurements such as the concentric rings in a tree. The periods of shell growth may correspond to seasonal change but do not correlate on a calendar basis. You can't determine a mollusk's age from its shell.

Most important, each shell is a

different creature—the shell is the visual cue and defining taxonomy for creatures infrequently seen and morphologically very similar when caught outside their homes. You must judge a snail by its cover.

Clues about a mollusk's benthic habitat may be inferred from the shape, color, and pattern of shell ornamentation. Ornately structured shells, such as the murex, are found in calmer, lower-energy waters, generally south of Cape Fear, where the protuberances on the shells are not jeopardized by waves. In contrast, shells such the channel whelk, aptly named for the high-energy environs they inhabit, have a streamlined shape that offers slight resistance to wave action. Offshore from the churning barrier islands, below the effective level of daily wave action at the seafloor, more ornamentally inclined shell builders find water-motion levels compatible with their shell construction and are likely to flourish undamaged.

The ocean is tough on shells exposed to its tumbling action and the lapidary effect of the sand, which in North Carolina is composed of continental shelf sand and shell debris. A shell cannot resist the grinding effect, and, especially with no creature inside to replenish the worn surfaces and keep the shell anchored or moving upright, it weathers rapidly. Even the durable, thick-walled helmet shell and whelks can be tumbled to pieces in as few as three weeks. Bright shells, vibrant with color and comparatively unscathed, are probably very recently abandoned. A lingering fetid odor provides the ripest clue of recent abandonment.

However, in the complex ocean environment, nothing is simple; shells of great age—fossil finds—survive because they were buried under sediment and were recently unearthed by storm action. Some shells recovered on North Carolina beaches have been judged to be more than 18,000 years old.

Appendixes

Appendix A: Information

The following agencies and organizations offer useful information for planning a trip to the North Carolina coast. Allow at least three weeks for a response to your inquiries.

National Parks

Cape Hatteras National Seashore
Route 1 Box 675
Manteo, NC 27954
252-473-2111

Cape Lookout National Seashore
131 Charles Street
Harkers Island, NC 28531
252-728-2250

Fort Raleigh National Historic Site
c/o Superintendent, Cape Hatteras
   Group
Route 1 Box 675
Manteo, NC 27954
252-473-2111

Wright Brothers National Memorial
c/o Superintendent, Cape Hatteras
   Group
Route 1 Box 675
Manteo, NC 27954
252-441-7430

National Wildlife Refuges

Alligator River National Wildlife
   Refuge
P.O. Box 1969
Manteo, NC 27954
252-473-1131

Cedar Island National Wildlife
   Refuge
Cedar Island, NC 28520
252-225-2511

Currituck National Wildlife Refuge
P.O. Box 39
Knotts Island, NC 27950
252-429-3100

Lake Mattamuskeet National
   Wildlife Refuge
Route 1 Box N-2
Swan Quarter, NC 27855
252-926-4021

Mackay Island National Wildlife
   Refuge
P.O. Box 39
Knotts Island, NC 27950
252-429-3100

Pea Island National Wildlife Refuge
P.O. Box 150
Rodanthe, NC 27968
252-987-2394

State Parks and Recreation Areas

North Carolina Division of Parks
   and Recreation
512 North Salisbury Street
Raleigh, NC 27611
919-733-4181

Carolina Beach State Park
P.O. Box 475
Carolina Beach, NC 28428
910-428-8206

Fort Fisher State Recreation Area
c/o Carolina Beach State Park
P.O. Box 475
Carolina Beach, NC 28428
910-458-8206

Fort Macon State Park
P.O. Box 127
Atlantic Beach, NC 28512
252-726-3775

Hammocks Beach State Park
Route 2 Box 295
Swansboro, NC 28584
910-326-4881

Jockey's Ridge State Park
P.O. Box 592
Nags Head, NC 27959
252-441-7132

State Natural Areas

Bald Head Island State Natural
  Area
c/o Carolina Beach State Park
P.O. Box 475
Carolina Beach, NC 28428
910-458-8206

Theodore Roosevelt State Natural
  Area
P.O. Box 127
Atlantic Beach, NC 28512
252-726-3775

North Carolina
Coastal Reserve

Coastal Reserve Coordinator
North Carolina National Estuarine
  Research Reserve
7205 Wrightsville Avenue
Wilmington, NC 28403
910-256-3721

Division of Coastal Management
North Carolina Department
  of Natural Resources and
  Community Development
P.O. Box 27687
Raleigh, NC 27611
919-733-2293

State Historic Sites

North Carolina Division of Archives
  and History
109 East Jones Street
Raleigh, NC 27611
919-733-7862

Brunswick Town State Historic
  Site
Route 1, P.O. Box 55
Winnabow, NC 28479
910-371-6613

Currituck Beach Lighthouse and
  Lightkeeper's Quarters
Outer Banks Conservationists, Inc.
P.O. Box 361
Corolla, NC 27927
252-453-4939

Elizabeth II State Historic Site
P.O. Box 155
Manteo, NC 27954
252-473-1144

Fort Fisher State Historic Site
P.O. Box 68
Kure Beach, NC 28449
910-458-5538

Aquariums

Office of Marine Affairs
417 North Blount Street
Raleigh, NC 27605
919-733-2290

Fort Fisher
P.O. Box 130
Kure Beach, NC 28449
910-458-8257

Pine Knoll Shores
P.O. Box 580
Atlantic Beach, NC 28512
252-247-4003

Roanoke Island
P.O. Box 967
Manteo, NC 27954
252-473-3493

North Carolina
Maritime Museum

North Carolina Maritime Museum
315 Front Street
Beaufort, NC 28516
252-728-7317

Ferries

Cedar Island, 252-225-3551,
  800-856-0343
Cherry Branch, 800-339-9156
Fort Fisher/Southport,
  800-368-8969
Hatteras, 252-928-3841,
  800-368-8949
Knotts Island, 252-232-2683
Ocracoke, 252-928-3841,
  800-345-1665
Pamlico River, 252-964-4521
Swan Quarter, 252-926-1111,
  800-773-1094

Boating and Fishing Access

North Carolina Wildlife Resources
  Commission
Archdale Building
512 North Salisbury Street
Raleigh, NC 27611
919-733-3393, 800-662-7350

Saltwater Sportfishing
Restrictions

North Carolina Division of Marine
  Fisheries
P.O. Box 769
Morehead City, NC 28557
800-682-2632 (North Carolina
  only)

General Tourism

North Carolina Bed & Breakfast
  and Inns
P. O. Box 1077
Asheville, NC 28802
800-849-5392

North Carolina Campground
  Owners Association
1002 Vandora Springs Road
Garner, NC 27529
919-779-5709

North Carolina Division of Travel
  and Tourism
430 North Salisbury Street
Raleigh, NC 27611
919-733-4171, 800-VISITNC

National Seashore
Campground Reservations

DESTINET, 800-365-2267

Mainland Attractions

Belhaven Memorial Museum
P.O. Box 220
Belhaven, NC 27810
252-943-3055, 252-943-2242

Historic Albemarle Tour, Inc.
P.O. Box 759
Edenton, NC 27932
252-482-7325

Historic Bath State Historic Site
P.O. Box 148
Bath, NC 27808
252-923-3971

Historic Halifax State Historic Site
P.O. Box 406
Halifax, NC 27839
252-583-7191

Port o' Plymouth Roanoke River
  Museum
Historical Society of Washington
  County
P.O. Box 296
Plymouth, NC 27962
252-793-1377

Somerset Place State Historic Site
P.O. Box 215
Creswell, NC 27928
252-797-4560

Tryon Palace Restoration and
  Gardens Complex
P.O. Box 1007
New Bern, NC 28560
252-638-1560

Northern Coast

Currituck Chamber of Commerce
  and Tourism Bureau
P.O. Box 1160
Grandy, NC 27939
252-453-9497, 877-287-7488

Dare County Tourist Bureau
P.O. Box 399
Manteo, NC 27954
252-473-2138

Greater Hyde County Chamber of
  Commerce
P.O. Box 178
Swan Quarter, NC 27885
252-926-9171, 888-HYDEVAN

Ocracoke Civic Club
Ocracoke Island, NC 27960
252-928-6711

Outer Banks Chamber of
  Commerce
P.O. Box 1757
Kill Devil Hills, NC 27948
252-441-8144

Central Coast

Beaufort Historical Association
P.O. Box 1709
Beaufort, NC 28516
252-728-5255

Carteret County Tourism
  Development Bureau/North
  Carolina Coast Host
P.O. Box 1198
Morehead City, NC 28557
252-726-6831, 252-726-8148,
  800-NCCOAST

Greater Topsail Area Chamber of
  Commerce
P.O. Box 2486
Surf City, NC 28445
910-328-0666

New Bern/Craven County Chamber
  of Commerce
Drawer C
New Bern, NC 28560
252-726-6831

South Coast

Cape Fear Coast Convention and
  Visitors Bureau
P.O. Box 266
Wilmington, NC 28402
910-341-4030

South Brunswick Islands Chamber
  of Commerce
P.O. Box 1380
Shallotte, NC 28459
910-754-6644

Southport/Oak Island Chamber of
  Commerce
P.O. Box 52
Southport, NC 28461
910-457-6964

Appendix B:
Festivals and Events

The following is a brief listing of festivals and events in North Carolina coastal communities. Most of the numerous local Fourth of July celebrations are not listed. Check with the local chamber of commerce or visitors bureau for exact dates or other events. The North Carolina Division of Travel and Tourism also provides a listing by calling 800-VISITNC.

April

Battle of Plymouth Living History
   Weekend
Plymouth
Historical Society of Washington
   County
252-793-1377

Hatteras Island Blues Festival
Rodanthe
252-987-2201

North Carolina Azalea Festival
Wilmington
910-763-0905

Onslow County Museum Kite
   Festival
Topsail Beach
910-324-5008

Spring Jubilee
Topsail Island Chamber of
   Commerce
910-328-4722

Gardeners' Weekend
New Bern
Tryon Palace
252-638-1560, 252-633-6448,
   252-638-8558

Victorian Day
Elizabeth City
252-338-4104

May

Hang Gliding Spectacular
Nags Head
Kitty Hawk Kites
252-441-4124

Pepsi New River Heritage Festival
Jacksonville
Onslow County/Jacksonville
   Chamber of Commerce
910-347-3141

Pleasure Island Spring Festival
Carolina Beach
Pleasure Island Chamber of
   Commerce
910-458-8434, 800-228-8434

Riverspree
Elizabeth City
Elizabeth City Chamber of
   Commerce
252-335-4365

Traditional Wooden Boat Show
Beaufort
North Carolina Maritime Museum
252-728-7317

Colonial Living Day
New Bern
Tryon Palace
252-638-1560, 252-633-6448,
   252-638-8558

June

Arts by the Sea
Swansboro
Jacksonville Arts Council
910-455-9840

Dare Day Festival
Manteo
Dare County
252-473-1101

Rogallo Kite Festival
Nags Head
Kitty Hawk Kites
252-441-4124

Wanchese Seafood Festival
Wanchese
473-2138

July

Croaker Festival
Oriental
Pamlico Chamber of Commerce
252-249-1787

Fourth of July Celebration
Swansboro
910-326-1145

North Carolina Fourth of July
   Festival
Southport
Southport/Oak Island Chamber of
   Commerce
910-457-6964

Summer Festival
Washington
Greater Washington Chamber of
   Commerce
252-249-1787

Surf, Sun, and Sand Celebration
Wrightsville Beach
Wrightsville Beach Parks and
   Recreation
910-256-4744

August

Michelob Cup Regatta
New Bern
New Bern Rotary Club
252-636-BOAT

National Aviation Day
Kill Devil Hills
252-441-7430

New World Festival of the Arts
Kitty Hawk
252-473-2838

Sneads Ferry Shrimp Festival
Sneads Ferry
910-327-4911

Strange Seafood Exhibition
Beaufort
North Carolina Maritime Museum
252-728-7317

September

Autumn with Topsail Beach
Topsail Beach
Topsail Island Chamber of
   Commerce
910-328-4722

Perquimans County "Indian
   Summer Festival"
Hertford
Hertford Chamber of Commerce
252-426-5657

Spot Festival
Hampstead
Hampstead Volunteer Fire
   Department
910-270-4719

October

Chrysanthemum Festival
New Bern
Swiss Bear, Inc.
252-638-5781

Harvest Time
Beaufort
Beaufort Historical Association
252-728-5225

Marsh and Sea Fest
Manteo
North Carolina Aquarium, Roanoke
   Island
252-473-3494

Mullet Festival
Swansboro
910-326-4996, 910-326-7101

North Carolina Dive Weekend
Atlantic Beach
North Carolina Aquarium, Pine
   Knoll Shores
252-247-4004

North Carolina Festival by the Sea
Holden Beach
Holden Beach Merchants
   Association
910-842-3828

North Carolina Oyster Festival
Shallotte
South Brunswick Islands Chamber
   of Commerce
910-754-6644

North Carolina Seafood Festival
Morehead City
252-726-6273

Peanut Festival
Edenton
Edenton Chamber of Commerce
252-482-3400

Riverfest
Wilmington
910-452-6862

November

Christmas Flotilla
Swansboro
910-326-3128

Holiday Flotilla
Wrightsville Beach
910-256-9650

Surf-Fishing Weekend
Atlantic Beach
North Carolina Aquarium, Pine
   Knoll Shores
252-247-4004

December

Christmas by the Sea Festival
Southport/Oak Island Chamber of
   Commerce
910-457-6964

Christmas Candlelight Tours
Edenton
Historic Edenton
252-482-3663

Christmas Celebration/Candlelight
   Tours
New Bern
Tryon Palace
252-638-1560

Old Wilmington by Candlelight
Wilmington
Lower Cape Fear Historical Society
910-762-0492

February

Southern Lights, Canadian Days
Cape Fear Coast
Cape Fear Convention and Visitors
   Bureau
800-222-4757 (U.S.A.),
   800-457-8912 (Canada)

Appendix C:
Saltwater Fishing
Tournaments

You may wish to try your hand at competitive saltwater fishing and with good reason—the prizes can be lucrative and the competition is intense but good-natured. Entry rules vary and some tournaments, the invitationals, for example, may require some persistence to enter. Entry fees can be stiff as well, but the larger the entry fees, the greater the prize money.

Tournaments are becoming an important part of local tourism, and new events emerge each year. The following list is a starting point. For up-to-date information about tournaments at the destination of your choice, contact the local chamber of commerce or visitors bureau.

April

Hatteras Island Blues Festival
  Fishing Tournament
Rodanthe
252-987-2911

Ocracoke Surf-Fishing Invitational
Ocracoke Village
252-928-4351

Small-Boat Fishing Classic
Manns Harbor
252-473-5150

May

Cape Fear Open Marlin
  Tournament
Wrightsville Beach
910-256-6550

Spearfishing Contest
Beaufort
252-728-2265

Swansboro Rotary Memorial Day
  Blue Water Fishing Tournament
Swansboro
910-354-2787

June

Big Rock Blue Marlin Tournament
Morehead City
252-247-3575

Fisherman's Inn Marina Cobia
  Tournament
Harkers Island
252-728-2265

Hatteras Harbor Blue Water Open
  Billfish Tournament
Hatteras
252-986-2166

Hatteras Invitational Marlin
  Tournament
Hatteras
252-986-2454

Outer Banks Celebrity Tournament
Manteo
252-473-3906, 800-367-4728

Pirate's Cove Inshore/Offshore
  Shootout
Manteo
252-473-3906, 800-367-4728

Raleigh Saltwater Fishing Club
  King Mackerel Tournament
Atlantic Beach
P.O. Box 3374, Raleigh NC 27606

Scotts Hill King Mackerel
  Tournament
Scotts Hill
910-686-0896

Shallotte Point Flounder
  Tournament
Shallotte
910-754-6985

July

Captain Fanny's Billfish
  Tournament
Atlantic Beach
252-726-4423

East Coast Got-Em-On King
  Mackerel Classic
Carolina Beach
910-458-9576

Morehead City Rotary Club King
  Mackerel Tournament
Morehead City
252-726-8033

Sea Mark/Oscar Mayer Children's
  Tournament
Manteo
252-473-3906, 800-367-4728

August

Captain Stacy Masters King
    Mackerel Tournament
Atlantic Beach
252-247-7501

Carteret Sportfishing Association
    Ladies Mackerel Tournament
Atlantic Beach
252-726-4548

Ducks Unlimited Billfish Release
    Tournament
Manteo
252-473-3906, 800-367-4728

Long Bay Lady Anglers King
    Mackerel Tournament
Southport
910-278-5327, 910-457-6510

Pirate's Cove Billfish Tournament
Manteo
252-473-3906, 800-367-4728

Poor Boy Shark Tournament
Shallotte
910-754-6233

Topsail Offshore Fishing Club King
    Mackerel Tournament
Topsail Beach
910-328-5681

Virginia Ducks Unlimited Billfish
    Tag and Release Tournament
Atlantic Beach
252-787-0522, 252-726-1441

September

Bailey's Marina V.I.P. King
    Mackerel Tournament
Atlantic Beach
252-247-4148

Carolina Croaker and Marlin Club
    King Mackerel Tournament
Atlantic Beach
252-752-4220

Carolina Pirate's Cove Big Game
    Tournament, Small-Boat Classic
Manteo
252-473-3906, 800-367-4728

Hardee's Atlantic Beach King
    Mackerel Tournament
Atlantic Beach
252-247-2334

Hatteras Village Invitational
    Surf-Fishing Tournament
Hatteras
252-986-2131

Oregon Inlet Billfish Release
    Tournament
Nags Head
252-441-6301

Pirate's Cove White Marlin Release
    Tournament
Manteo
252-473-3906, 800-367-4728

South Brunswick Islands King
    Classic
Shallotte
910-754-6644

Wrightsville Beach King Mackerel
    Tournament
Wrightsville Beach
910-256-3661

October

Carteret County Bottom-Fishing
    Tournament
Atlantic Beach
252-726-4548

Carteret Sportfishing Association
    King Mackerel Tournament
Atlantic Beach
252-726-4548

Nags Head Surf-Fishing Club
    Invitation Tournament
Kill Devil Hills
252-441-7251

Outer Banks King Mackerel
    Festival
Manteo
252-473-3906, 800-367-4728

Pleasure Island Surf-Fishing
    Tournament
Carolina Beach
910-458-8434

U.S. Open King Mackerel
    Tournament
Southport
910-457-6964

World Championship Red Drum
    Tournament
Avon
252-995-6026, 302-328-5854

November

Cape Hatteras Anglers Club
    Surf-Fishing Tournament
Buxton
252-995-4253

December

North Carolina Saltwater Fishing
    Tournament
Morehead City
800-682-2632

Taft's Poem

for Taft Lee Morris

February 2, 1979–February 4, 1989

Once,
The silver sea slip foamed around your ankles
And high above your sun-towed head the man-birds roared,
And rolling split the sky.
We built castles and the sea pulled them in
And laughingly, we built them again
In brash defiance.
We hallowed pools for your splashing and small fish
Caught to stock your private puddle-sea.
To this mooring, you brought ropes,
Tangled, tentacled frondlings, and with sticks and boat bones
Secured your palace of sand.
You came to this at three
And I, at thirty-three,
Had not grown enough to know you.
A thousand questions flowed
And I of answers stood silent for one.

Your gentle mother told you
Your spirit will live forever.

You knew and smiled.
I know now and cry still.

For once,
The silver sea slip foamed around your ankles
Slid past your toes and ebbed,
Leaving forever your palace of sand
Grain by grain
Behind.

Glenn Morris
February 7, 1989

Index